*The Hour and the Woman*

Harriet Martineau in 1849, by George Richmond.

# The Hour and the Woman

## Harriet Martineau's
## "Somewhat Remarkable" Life

DEBORAH ANNA LOGAN

NORTHERN ILLINOIS UNIVERSITY PRESS / DEKALB

Published by the Northern Illinois University Press, DeKalb, Illinois   60115
Manufactured in the United States using acid-free paper
All Rights Reserved
Design by Julia Fauci

Library of Congress Cataloging-in-Publication Data
Logan, Deborah Anna, 1951–
The hour and the woman: Harriet Martineau's "somewhat remarkable" life /
Deborah Anna Logan.
     p.     cm.
Includes bibliographical references and index.
ISBN 0-87580-297-4 (alk. paper)
   1. Martineau, Harriet, 1802–1876. 2. Women and literature—Great Britain—
History—19th century. 3. Authors, English—19th century—Biography. 4. Social
reformers—Great Britain—Biography. 5. Feminists—Great Britain—Biography. I. Title.
PR4984.M5 Z68 2002
823'.8—dc21
[B]   2002022608

*For my mother, Edna R. Logan—*

*a first-rate needlewoman—*

*with love and thanks*

# CONTENTS

ACKNOWLEGMENTS

• I am greatly indebted to Western Kentucky University for supporting the research and travel necessary to complete this book. Funding includes the Junior Faculty Research Grant, two Faculty Fellowships, and travel grants from the Faculty Development Program. In addition, both the Potter College and English Department Travel Committees provided generous support that enabled me to gather a significant amount of Martineau's far-flung correspondence. The Willson Wood Professorship, awarded to me by the English Department for 2000–2001, funded a research trip to Boston and enabled me to secure photographs and permissions for the reproductions included in this book. I am deeply grateful to each of these sources for facilitating important and timely research on this pivotal Victorian figure.

Special thanks are due to Dr. Ted Hovet (Western Kentucky University), who not only read parts of this manuscript and offered extensive comments and suggestions but who also, through many long conversations while en route to Nashville, helped me to formulate and to clarify my ideas on the significance of Martineau's needleworking and letter writing. In addition, Ted's expertise in nineteenth-century American studies and Civil War history proved invaluable to my study of Martineau's relationship with the American abolitionists.

Professor Beverly Taylor (University of North Carolina at Chapel Hill) also read the manuscript with her usual scrupulous care and attention to detail. This book has been improved in every way by her generosity in taking time from her very busy schedule to do this for me and by her incomparable expertise in crafting the most subtle turn of phrase and in helping me to clarify the complex ideologies relevant to Martineau and to feminist studies.

At Northern Illinois University Press I thank editor Martin Johnson for his initial and continued support of my work on Martineau. I thank also editor Susan Bean and both readers whose initial endorsements resulted in this book. The thoughtful comments and suggestions by these readers have improved my arguments and presentation throughout the work.

I thank Dr. Linda Calendrillo, department head of Western's English Department, for her continued enthusiastic support of my research and writing.

And to Dean David Lee of Potter College (Western Kentucky University), a very special thanks for additional funding for the color reproductions of Martineau's needlework. I am indeed blessed by a wealth of support and encouragement from my colleagues at Western.

For a wide variety of research assistance and support I thank Debra Day of Western's Interlibrary Borrowing Office and the staff of Vanderbilt University's Heard Library.

*Symbiosis Journal* printed an earlier version of chapter 3, "Harriet Martineau and America's Martyr Age," and I thank editors Chris Gair and Richard Gravil for permission to use that material in this book.

For permission to quote from Harriet Martineau papers and letters I thank the University of Birmingham (U.K.), with special thanks to Christine Penney for her generosity and enthusiasm for my work on Martineau. I thank also the Boston Public Library, in particular, curators Bill Faucon and Roberta Zonghi; the Houghton Library of Harvard University and curator Leslie A. Morris; curator Susan E. Snyder of the Bancroft Library, University of California at Berkeley; the curator of manuscripts, National Library of Scotland; and Anne Summers, curator of modern historical manuscripts, British Library.

For permission to reprint photographs and drawings of Martineau I thank the National Portrait Gallery, London. For permission to print photographs of Martineau's needlework I thank Lynda Powell, curator of the Armitt Museum and Library in Ambleside (the Martineau sofa) and also the Wordsworth Trust in Grasmere (the Martineau chair). I am also pleased to acknowledge photographer Alex Black for his fine original photographs of these two pieces.

I thank my friends who support me in other ways: Jeff Logan—my best friend and brother—Bob Ramirez, Ted Hovet, Bonnie Wehrle, and Bev Taylor. Finally, but not least, I thank my family—Jake, Lauren, and Zack—for the parts they play in my life and work and for their direct contributions to the creative impulse.

# A NOTE ON THE LETTERS

• Martineau frequently abbreviated common words, like "wd" (with the d superscripted) for "would," true also of "should" and "could"; "and" is generally "&." In my transcripts of and quotations from the letters, I have spelled these words out for ease of reading. Also, citations of letters include whatever classification system is used by the holding library, including folio numbers where available, since classification methods vary from archive to archive.

*The Hour and the Woman*

# Literary Grandmothers and the Spirit of the Victorian Age

creeping in and out
Among the giant fossils of my past,
Like some small nimble mouse between the ribs
Of a mastodon, I nibbled here and there.

—**Elizabeth Barrett Browning,** *Aurora Leigh*

• Elizabeth Barrett regretted the absence of "literary grandmothers" who could have served as role models for Victorian women writers like herself seeking to participate in a male-dominated realm.[1] Like Aurora Leigh nibbling "between the ribs / Of a mastodon," present-day scholars are resurrecting women's contributions to literature, effectually reconstructing the history Barrett sought in vain during her poetic apprenticeship. Barrett would surely appreciate the irony implicit in the fact that much of her own work has been the subject of contemporary scholarly "digs" in our attempts to unearth the literary grandmothers who seem to have disappeared almost as soon as they arose. Both Elizabeth Barrett and Harriet Martineau, who never met but who corresponded and admired each other's work, based their careers on an informal education and haphazard training in Milton, Wordsworth, and Shakespeare, a background offering little guidance for constructing literary identities as women writers. Lacking predecessors, both writers made their own history, as did others—Charlotte Brontë, George Eliot, Elizabeth Gaskell—whose inherent intelligence triumphed over the social obstacles and limitations confronting even the most privileged Victorian women. Barrett may not have had literary grandmothers—at least, writers whose work was accessible to her—but she did have the example of history in the making in the person of her contemporary, Harriet Martineau.

By viewing Martineau as one of the Victorian era's primary cultural influences, my design is to shed light on the life and work of a writer oddly neglected by literary and social history. The "Hour" of Victorian history is defined by social reform, and its premier woman reformist writer is Harriet Martineau. Martineau's work reads like a *Who's Who* of Victorian people and issues, yet most of her books remain out of print. Although a contemporary of regularly anthologized nonfiction prose writers like Matthew

Arnold, John Stuart Mill, Thomas Carlyle, and John Ruskin, she is today regarded as a comparatively obscure figure despite her commanding presence among Victorian people of letters during her life. This book seeks to contribute to recent scholarly interest in a writer who modestly dubbed herself more of a "popularizer" than an inventive genius but who, from the 1832 through the 1867 Reform Bills, was at the forefront of the period's social and political debates.[2]

Martineau's work offers essential insights into the late industrial, early modern period, an era that gave rise to the fullest development of women writers in the West. In terms of her career's duration (about half a century), its scope and its prodigious volume, her work deserves not only to be made available to present-day readers but also to be analyzed critically in the context of the period that is itself the grandmother of our own. By analyzing some of the primary themes of Martineau's writing, my aim is to show how one woman negotiated the often treacherous critical terrain of nineteenth-century literature, a milieu notorious for its antipathy toward women writers. Such an approach reveals that, distinct from many of her better-connected contemporaries and as a woman writer without social class, economic standing, formal education, or marital status to recommend her, Martineau had more than just literary prejudices to overcome.

My study begins by exploring Martineau's identity as a Victorian woman of letters. "Popularizer and Prophet: A Victorian Literary Identity" (chapter 1) traces her evolution from a docile middle-class girl (whose rebellion was never far from the surface, despite outward appearances) to a young woman whose overnight success as a writer established her as a political and social authority of international significance. Having made the phenomenal leap from provincial obscurity to worldwide fame, with all the notoriety inevitable with such prominence, Martineau proved herself sufficiently sophisticated to hold her own among carping critics throughout a career spanning nearly fifty years: no small feat, given the acerbity of some Victorian literary circles. A measure of her professional authority is seen in her decision, at the height of her fame, to retire to remote Ambleside in the Lake District, where she conducted her literary affairs far from London's cultural center. In Ambleside, she enjoyed the best of both worlds, maintaining a high profile in the press while surrounded by the natural beauty and rural solitude she found essential to her well-being. Distinguishing between professional and personal realms and cultivating both are ideas central to Martineau's identity as a woman writer.

An unusual sequence of events conspired to provide Martineau with a window of opportunity to become a professional writer rather than "vegetate," as she says, in poverty and obscurity. Her first major success, *Illustrations of Political Economy* (1832–1834), early indicated that her true forte was nonfiction writing, involving genres and styles conventionally associated with male writers. This inclination leads to a consideration of the various claims critics and scholars have made on Martineau's behalf, including her feminism (she champions education reform for women and girls), her antifeminism (she questions the timeliness of the women's franchise), her masculinity (she is unmarried and strong-minded), her femininity (she valorizes domesticity), and her identification with and resistance to the male literary hegemony. That analyses of her writing have been driven by speculations about her gender and sexuality throughout nearly two centuries of Martineau criticism offers remarkable commentary on critics' curious inclination to focus on her sexual and psychological states rather than to assess her work itself. I will be looking at that discourse and at the ways it has held Martineau in literary obscurity even when aimed at bringing her back to the forefront of literary studies. The question of gender identity complicates Martineau's modest claim that she was no genius, only a popularizer. The evidence, in fact, points to the contrary: her sense of timing and subtlety of insights often cast her as a social visionary, a sort of prophet. In being both popularizer and prophet, Harriet Martineau aptly represented the spirit of the Victorian age; she was truly the woman of the hour.

Using chapter 1's biographical overview of key points in Martineau's life as a basis, the remainder of this book examines issues central to her achievements as a feminist literary grandmother. Chapter 2, "Fancywork and Bluestockingism; or, Needles and Pens," explores the predominance of the needle-and-pen metaphor, which represents the two primary interests of Martineau's life, the domestic and the literary. Throughout her life, Martineau took pride in the fact that her ability to sew cast her as more than "just" a literary woman, just as her writing ability propelled her beyond the limitations ordinarily binding Victorian women's lives. Exchanges between needle and pen are frequent throughout her busy life, from memorizing poetry while sewing during girlhood to periods of invalidism when, too incapacitated to continue writing in support of social reforms, she produced needlework to raise money for those causes. The interplays between needle and pen, fabric and paper, thread and ink provide revealing insights into the gender politics of a writer whose readers continue, to this day, to be as anxious to claim her support for their individual ideologies as her contemporaries were.

"America's Martyr Age" (chapter 3) investigates the social reform issue that interested Martineau more than any other: the abolition of slavery. From her early anti-slavery publication, "Demerara" (1832), to her various travel writings published as a result of her American tour, and from her hundreds of *Daily News* leaders to her more in-depth occasional journal articles on American affairs, Martineau's commitment to eliminating slavery shaped her public career as well as her private character. As her various writings on the issue illustrate, aside from overt slavery on American and West Indian plantations, she perceived a more covert slavery masquerading as "legitimate" gender relations: in the "quadroon connexions" of New Orleans; in Egyptian harems (to which she compares American plantations); in poor Irish women bound to relentless childbearing by religious custom; in working-class English women caught in cycles of abuse, alcoholism, and ignorance; and in women of color doomed to sexual exploitation at the hands of white masters. Her subtle understanding that race, gender, class, and cultural and ethnic oppressions are all expressions of the same institution—patriarchy—anticipates postmodern analyses of the political and domestic ramifications of the dyad of imperialism and capitalism. Her admission that "I had a devouring passion for justice;—justice, first to my own precious self, and then to other oppressed people" (Martineau 1983, 1:18) encapsulates the motivation underpinning her writing: to expose tyranny and promote liberation on every level, and to empower individuals through knowledge and ideological insights.

Chapter 4, "I Would Fain Treat of Woman," considers Martineau's fiction and nonfiction as expressions of her idiosyncratic brand of feminism. Although literary history has not been kind to certain aspects of Martineau's works, her gift for characterization is one of the most affecting aspects of her writing, offering a primary site through which to assess her gender politics. That her unusual degree of empathy is what permits her to characterize so convincingly is proved by her renderings of fictional women characters as well as by her nonfictional "types" such as maids and factory workers. My focus on her women characters and her nonfiction treatment of such women's issues as education, employment, health, economics, and protective legislation aims to uncover a feminism expressed through example rather than public grandstanding. True of all her undertakings, practice wedded to theory is key to her gender politics.

Continuing with this theme on a nonliterary level, "Not Fine Ladies, but True-Hearted Englishwomen" (chapter 5) analyzes Martineau's relationships with some of the foremost women of the era: the Englishwomen Mary Wollstonecraft, Charlotte Brontë, Elizabeth Gaskell, Elizabeth Barrett Browning, George Eliot, Florence Nightingale, Queen Victoria, and Josephine Butler and the Americans Maria Weston Chapman, Harriet Beecher Stowe, and Margaret Fuller. Martineau's candid portrayals of these women sometimes aroused criticism of her unblinking utilitarian pragmatism, although her critique of those who contributed to or detracted from "Woman's Cause" doubled when she scrutinized herself. Having early in life put aside her own "special trial," Martineau had little sympathy for women whose passions or sentimentality compromised their "coolness of mind" and their ability to perform their chosen work. Her respect for marital relationships based on genuine partnership is not the issue: Martineau's concern is with women whose identities, abilities, and energies become permanently submerged in and stymied by the marriage contract or, worse, by superficial romanticism. The standard by which she measures women worth emulating relies on their personal fidelity to truth and propriety and on the corresponding example of political and social commitment they present to the public world. This standard is for her the prerequisite for any woman presuming, through her words and actions, to represent other women.

"(*Entre Nous,* Please)": "Letters Are the Thing" (chapter 6) studies Martineau's character through her epistolary writing, including private letters and published nonfiction prose. Since, as she claimed, "Epistolary correspondence is written speech and . . . best illustrates character," and since by her own admission her style of writing in all genres "went off like a letter" (1983, 1:3–4, 195), Martineau's epistolary writing offers the best evidence that her public persona dovetailed with that of her personal relationships. By posing this public-private dichotomy, I in no way suggest that Martineau endorses two separate standards of behavior, since she in fact strives to bring the two into alignment and expects (perhaps unrealistically) others to do the same. My analysis will show, however, that while an interplay between the two characterizes much of her work, this exceptionally forthright woman displays a greater degree of candor in her private correspondence than in her public documents, including the *Autobiography*. Although Martineau has been criticized for what Dickens termed her "grim determination" to reform the world, the letters reveal other qualities, like her sense of humor and appreciation for the absurd, her simple delight at receiving gifts and her warm generosity in giving them, her loyalty to controversial beliefs, and her distress over conflicted family relationships. Her use of the form for nonfiction writing stemmed from her aim to personalize certain topics and issues for a mass audience. The overlap between the two offers a relevant avenue through which further to explore Martineau's identity as a strong-minded, opinionated, compassionate woman.

Finally, my epilogue, "The One Thing Needful," concludes this analysis of primary themes in Martineau's life and work by reconsidering assessments of her appearance by various contemporaries, her droll sense of humor, and her historical legacy and its continued influence. Writing in a period when a woman's face was her fortune (or misfortune), Martineau was judged by some to be a writer by default because of her plain appearance and consequent failure to find a suitable mate; another popular target was her disability—deafness—which some claimed inhibited her ability to think critically. Victorians' excessive interest in Martineau's appearance demonstrates an emphasis on the woman writer's physical characteristics and biological functions that precludes serious critical analyses of writing style and content. Critics hostile to a woman writer of nonfiction used Martineau's unmarried status and the physical plainness it implied to denounce her work. This in turn segued into innuendoes that there was something vaguely immoral about a single woman writing about such women's topics as birth control and excessive child-bearing with the authority of a man.[3] Even benevolent critics like friends Maria Weston Chapman, Catharine Sedgwick, and James Payn sought to offset such impressions by shifting the focus to discussions of Martineau's graceful hands or to her maternal appearance in her mature years. Finally, examples of her droll, unconventional sense of humor and a survey of memoirs, obituaries, and reviews of her posthumously published *Autobiography* concludes this analysis of the primary themes shaping her life and career.

Although she admired some women writers who preceded her, Harriet Martineau had few literary grandmothers to guide her in fashioning her career; she was herself a literary grandmother. "The pains of the lonely course of such a lady would be most acute at the outset," writes Shelagh Hunter, "when she would be, as Martineau described herself, 'a solitary young authoress who has had no pioneer in her literary path but steadfastness of purpose'" (1995, 43). The prospect seemed dizzying to a young woman envisioning a career of intellectual pursuits committed to the service of public instruction:

> I have determined that my chief subordinate object in life shall henceforth be the cultivation of my intellectual powers, with a view to the instruction of others by my writings. . . . [A]s various circumstances have led me to think more accurately than some women, I believe that I may so write on subjects of universal concern as to inform some minds and stir up others. (Pichanick 1980, 31)

Her assertion, "of posthumous fame I have not the slightest expectation or desire. To be useful in my day and generation is enough for me" anticipates critics who have dismissed her work as anachronistic but also signals the importance of our study of one who so profoundly influenced her own generation. The history and current status of Martineau scholarship proves that the relevance of her example to Victorian studies continues to provide a rich field for present and future exploration and to offer essential insights into the era closest in spirit to our own.

# 1
## Popularizer and Prophet

### A Victorian Literary Identity

Authorship has never been with me a matter of choice. . . .
Things were pressing to be said; and there was more or less evidence that I was the person to say them.
—**Harriet Martineau**

I am a radical, and am known to be so, wherever I go.
—**Harriet Martineau**

I *must* keep my mission in view, and not my worldly dignity.
—**Harriet Martineau**

Her stimulus in all she wrote, from first to last, was simply the need of utterance.
—**"Harriet Martineau's Obituary"**

## Women Writers, Gender, and Genre

• During the Victorian era, female identity was so narrowly defined as to admit few anomalous behaviors from women seeking to maintain social respectability. According to reigning stereotypes, women's options, bound as they were by the madonna or harlot dichotomy, permitted little more than marriage and motherhood and, perhaps, charity or philanthropic work through religious and social reform organizations.[1] The period's domestic ideology associated women's respectability with the economic prosperity and leisured lifestyles provided by the men in their lives, men by whom they were protected from the degradation of wage earning and from whom they were expected to derive their sense of identity. Accordingly, women so unfortunate as to lack a man on whom to depend economically, women forced to earn their own livings, found themselves branded as unrespectable, even "fallen": or, at least, falling. Because women's work was often criticized on the basis of their sexuality rather than on their professional ability, the opposite extreme to domestic decorum—notoriety—constitutes the other primary identity offered to women, rendering sexually suspect and potentially promiscuous any woman making her way through life alone and unchaperoned.

According to popular culture, at least, these were the polarized options available to Victorian women. But the range of experiences between these two extremes reveals a more realistic picture of women's lives during the nineteenth century. In rejecting either option, Harriet Martineau (1802–1876), whose life spans both the Romantic and Victorian eras, sculpted for herself one of the most idiosyncratic identities—male or female—of the nineteenth century. Early in her writing career, Martineau virtually abandoned the popular trend of fiction writing thought to be especially suitable for women writers, favoring instead nonfiction genres with their more masculine (factual, empirical) connotations of authorship. The traditions of literary convention were predicated on the notion that men wrote "serious" literature while women, if they wrote at all, were capable of producing only "lightweight" texts. Martineau broke all the rules, not only by writing in a variety of genres but also by publishing under her real name and, in her nonfiction periodicals writing, by discussing topics typically reserved for male writers. The Victorian fondness for separate spheres ideology extended to writing style, content, and genre: short poems, stories, and novels focusing on domestic issues and romance belonged to the feminine sphere, while epic poetry and "serious" prose writing on political issues and social reform were masculine. Highlighting critical prejudices against women nonfiction writers, biographer Florence Fenwick Miller observes that "in their unconscious insolence," some male critics praised Martineau's work as impressive *for a woman*, others praised her "masculine intellect," while others refused to believe that writing of such quality could have been produced by a woman at all (1884, 84). Martineau, who objected to Charlotte Brontë's essentializing romanticism, would have been amazed that Lord Russell denounced her autobiography for the same quality: it does not exhibit "a manly reticence. The woman who has got rid of the customary mental sterility of her sex" should have been able to avoid the "unhealthy, foolish brooding—acrid dribblings of her private pen" (Myers 1980b, 73). Perhaps it was not her "foolish brooding" but her free-thinking political ideology to which he objected, since the *Autobiography* was and still is widely regarded as charming, lively, and engaging, a virtual *Who's Who* of the nineteenth century filled with sharp, insightful analyses of the era's prominent issues and people.

Like his Victorian predecessors, twentieth-century Martineau biographer R. K. Webb argues that Martineau's is a masculine intellect—this he presents as appropriate and desirable—and accordingly he discounts the relevancy of Maria Weston Chapman's biographical *Memorials* because she lacks "the essentially masculine nature of Miss Martineau" (1877, 26). In contrast, Mitzi Myers argues that Martineau "makes it quite plain that her unorthodox achievements were not the result of an essentially masculine nature" but of her domestic and familial influences (1980b, 76), an idea illustrated by my analysis of the centrality of needlework to her life and work (chapter 2). Whether the analogy is intended as condemnation or praise, assigning gender to genre or language or intellect is problematic at best and, at worst, avoids confronting texts and writers on the basis of their cultural impact, to be assessed according to literary merit rather than sexuality or gender. Of course, *who* decides what constitutes literary merit is the primary issue underpinning the entire enterprise of literary criticism, until recently an enterprise notoriously male-biased and Eurocentric. After first outlining Martineau's literary apprenticeship, I will return to this genre/gender question—its impact on the reception history of her writing and its influence over her development as a writer—later in this chapter.

An examination of the factors directing Martineau away from fiction writing reveals how her identity as a woman and as a writer constructed and was constructed by the nonfiction medium she naturally gravitated toward. Martineau's example proves viable the notion that neither literary nor female identity was *naturally* dependent on sex and gender roles; instead, in her words,

> There can be but one true method in the treatment of each human being of either sex, of any color, and under any outward circumstances—to ascertain what are the powers of that being, to cultivate them to the utmost, and then to see what action they will find for themselves. This has probably never been done for men. . . . It has certainly never been done for women. (Quoted in Yates 1985, 51)

That women might choose to develop alternative identities—not out of economic necessity or, more radically, in reaction against accepted "norms" but simply to realize their creative capacity as humans—was a novel idea indeed. Martineau's growth as a woman writer, her role in world politics, and her contributions to resolving the period's social problems cast her as a quintessential Victorian with pervasive cultural influence. Key events in Martineau's life reveal that her resistance—initially tentative, later emphatic—to women's narrow options in itself reflects the evolution of not only her own private and public identities but also of the broader status of women in Victorian society.

## The Early Years: From Provincial to Popularizer

As the daughter of a Norwich factory owner, Martineau was trained in the accomplishments considered appropriate for a respectable middle-class girl whose purpose in life was to become a respectable middle-class wife. But she was more fortunate than most girls in that her parents believed both daughters and sons should be educated. Although university was not an option for her, she did have several years of formal schooling and she benefited from the tutoring her college-bound brothers received. Combined with Unitarianism, a dissenting theology rooted in questioning accepted dogma and in the promotion of social welfare, her early training in intellectual inquiry established the foundation for one of the most prolific literary careers of the nineteenth century.[2] Little did her liberal-minded parents dream that their permissiveness in allowing Harriet access to books would enable her to become a genuine Victorian oddity: a self-supporting yet respectable single woman, an internationally influential professional writer, and a strong-minded free-thinker unafraid to challenge such entrenched cultural institutions as aristocratic privilege, parliamentary law, organized religion, and the medical establishment.

Several factors, regarded by Martineau as fortuitous rather than tragic, contributed to the identity she established by the age of thirty, an identity in which the personal and professional realms define each other. First, the early onset of deafness led to her being excused from attending chapel and other mandatory social rituals; in an era when women must perpetually be available to serve the needs of others, this rare gift of time and privacy allowed her to transform herself into a "walking Concordance" of Milton, Shakespeare, and Wordsworth (1983, 1:72). Then, as a nineteen-year-old girl inconsolable when her brother James, "my idolized companion" (1983, 1:117), left for college, Martineau acted on his suggestion that she find comfort for her "widowhood" in writing.[3] The result of her first effort, "Female Writers on Practical Divinity," published under a pseudonym in the *Monthly Repository* (1822), provided an early indication of her impending literary career. When brother Thomas discovered that the article was written by his sister, he urged her to abandon needleworking for writing (1983, 1:120). Martineau's poignant response, in which she marveled at his calling her "dear" for the first time, hints at the dynamics of a family reared according to the "taking-down" system of strict, no-nonsense discipline. The verbal endearment nearly overshadowed the writing success, encouraging Martineau to choose authorship as a primary medium for personal and professional gratification.

Martineau next confronted two crucial components of her mature literary identity: spinsterhood and poverty. Chapman records Martineau's perspectives on marriage at age eighteen, when she expressed regret upon learning of a friend's engagement "because it would deprive her of larger opportunities of usefulness to the world" (Chapman 1877, 22). The observation proved to be prophetic when, plagued by ill health and a series of family deaths, Martineau also faced "my own special trial" (1983, 1:130) in the form of John Worthington, the suitor whose marriage proposal promised to remove her from the infamy of having to work for her living. Still the pliable Victorian daughter, Martineau agonized over the decision to marry; she was unwilling to defy either communal or familial expectations, yet she chafed under the compulsion to perform the "duty" she dreaded (her account of this episode is markedly devoid of romantic sentiment). Delivered from a conventional fate by Worthington's sudden death, Martineau's relief was immediate; years later she wrote, "There has never been any doubt in my mind that . . . it was happiest for us both that our union was prevented. . . . I am, in truth, very thankful for not having married at all" (1983, 1:131). She notes that, as public figures, literary ladies often receive marriage offers, but such "annoyances" can be eliminated by cultivating "coolness of mind." During the early period of her literary fame, the thirty-year-old Martineau discouraged potential suitors, observing that she had reached "an age at which, if ever, a woman is certainly qualified to take care of herself" (1983, 1:132). Although she embraced domestic values despite her rejection of marriage—domesticity was not, for her, contingent upon one's marital status—she was determined that the emotional lack of her early years would not find compensation through another's identity but through the development of her own: "The veneration in which I hold domestic life has always shown me that that life was not for those whose self-respect had been early broken down, or had never grown." Demonstrating the degree to which her self-respect grew, the middle-aged Martineau rejected "Miss" as too youthful as well as ludicrous in its insistent reference to one's (lack of) marital status and adopted, interestingly, "Mrs. Martineau"—according to tradition, an address of respect denoting mature womanly wisdom not limited to wives. Pointing out precedents as well as convenience, Martineau wrote to Chapman, "Wasn't there Mrs. Hannah More and Mrs. Edgeworth? I see there were reasons for it: I will be Mrs. Harriet Martineau, which will, besides, obviate mistakes in the delivery of letters, there are so many Misses Martineau!" (Chapman 1877, 273).[4]

Clear, at least, about the direction her life would *not* be going in, Martineau weathered the next challenge of her formative years with enviable style and grace. With the collapse of the family business in 1826, Martineau took up her sewing needle—which she had formerly used primarily for ritualized fancywork—and her pen—till now used only in rare moments of spare time—in earnest. She actually welcomed the prospect of socially "losing face" because "there was scope for action," whereas previously "there was nothing possible but endurance" (1983, 1:141–42). While it is true that she enjoyed a rare degree of education for a girl of her class, she was also compelled to keep her scholarly and intellectual inclinations subsidiary to such visible signs of respectability as perpetual needleworking. Now blessed by "a wholly new freedom," concealing her writing was no longer necessary, "for we had lost our gentility." Employing the editorial "we" when writing of matters that in fact refer primarily to herself, she observed,

> but for that loss of money, we might have lived on in the ordinary provincial method of ladies with small means, sewing, and economizing, and growing narrower every year; whereas, by being thrown . . . on our own resources, we

have worked hard and usefully, won friends, reputation and independence, seen the world abundantly, abroad and at home, and, in short, have truly lived instead of vegetated.

That this quotation in fact refers to *she* rather than *we* elides the issue of Martineau's gradual estrangement from her family as her fame grew, a separation fueled by her radicalism and prompted, some argue, by familial jealousy of her public prominence.[5] Martineau's habit of employing the editorial "we" leads some critics to perpetuate, rather than deconstruct, the Victorians' association between genre and gender. The claim that "we" is a "universally" recognized *male* referent prompts some to conclude that Martineau's linguistic "cross-dressing" compromised her contributions to Woman's Cause (see chapter 6). Alternatively, Martineau may be said to break down conventional, male-determined boundaries and rebuild them to suit her own purpose. Far from betraying a feminist agenda, her example demonstrates most compellingly the cultivation of a literary identity that itself enacts Woman's Cause at its most uncompromising.

## The Spirit of the Age: Illustrations of Political Economy

Sewing for hire by day, grueling work with small remuneration, Martineau never lost sight of her plans to write a series of instructive tales illustrating the principles of political economy. Aimed at edifying those most adversely effected by economic principles, the working class, and at clarifying the economic and social responsibilities of the rising middle class, she planned to publish the tales in affordable "little books" that would fit in a pocket or in the "workies'" lunch boxes. Martineau's account of this period, during which she sewed by day and wrote at night, punctuated by the difficulties of marketing such an unusual work by an unknown author, reads like someone giving birth to herself. Worn out with ill health and overwork, discouraged by publishers resistant to a deaf, provincial spinster, Martineau labored away trying to sell her idea. Transition, when the laboring mother is most discouraged and the temptation to give up is strongest, prompted the despairing Martineau to write the preface for a project that promised to be stillborn. But because the willingness to give up or relinquish control often, paradoxically, heralds the shift necessary in order to progress to the delivery stage, Martineau in quick succession signed a publishing contract and witnessed the remarkable success of her first number.[6] Long before the series was completed, her fame was international, her finances solid, her literary reputation established, and her identity as a writer in place: "I had now, by thirty years of age, ascertained my career, found occupation, and achieved independence; and thus the rest of my life was provided with its duties and its interests. Any one to whom that happens by thirty years of age may be satisfied; and I was so" (1983, 1:181).

Martineau's desire to instruct "my great pupil, the public" made her, in Shelagh Hunter's term, "governess to the nation."[7] Hunter credits the *Illustrations'* phenomenal success to its unique synthesis of author and public, gender and political economy, fiction and didacticism so peculiarly suited to the needs and temper of the era: Martineau's "moment of personal self-identification is also historically significant as a well-documented example of society's adaptation . . . to its own newly identified needs" (1995, 38, 41). Those needs, some acknowledged for the first time in history by the passage of the 1832 Reform Bill, found apt expression in the *Illustrations*. Although initially publishers used the Reform Bill controversy as an excuse to reject Martineau's proposal, the series' success instead proved its perfect timeliness and the accuracy of its author's insights.[8]

Martineau's emerging identity is best seen in the persistence with which she pursued publication of the *Illustrations*. Frustrated by publishers' rejections, she observed, "You know what a *man* of business would do in my case. . . . Go up to town by the next mail, and see what is to be done" (1983, 1:164; emphasis added). Go she did—not as a man but as a woman of business—and, face-to-face with a reluctant publisher, announced, "I tell you this:—the people want this book, and they *shall* have it" (1983, 1:170). In another act of surprising assertiveness, she accepted her mother's suggestion to send copies of her prospectus to every member of both Houses of Parliament: "There was nothing of puffery in this. . . . It was merely informing our legislators that a book was coming out on their particular class of subjects" (1983, 1:175). Even before realizing literary success, then, and despite prejudices against a deaf, unknown spinster from a provincial town, Martineau exhibited the qualities that would ensure her lifelong fame and prosperity. Her transformation from a dutiful, pliable daughter to an assertive professional woman dramatized Victorian women's potential once they were freed from the trappings of social propriety.

The *Illustrations'* innovation is its synthesis of fiction and instruction to illustrate contemporary theories of political economy. Typically, each tale takes as its framing device a principle of political economy, for instance, supply and demand or Malthusian population theory. Martineau's characters and episodic plots present various perspectives on the issues, peppered by somewhat self-conscious expository conversations and punctuated with a "Summary of Principles Illustrated by this Volume." Through this unusual combination of fiction and nonfiction, she aimed to reach educated (through theory) as well as uneducated (through example) audiences, although her utilitarian compulsion to employ entertainment (fiction) only insofar as it would provide instruction (nonfiction) is, some claim, a primary weakness of the series. Her method of composition, in which she first numbered the pages, then filled them with writing, seems more mechanical than creative, although her refusal to edit or revise indicates a mind that thrives on a spontaneous model of composition perhaps more typical of creative and journalistic writing. "There can be few examples,"

notes Louis Cazamian, "of such logical and deliberately-willed artistic creation" (1973, 52): terms that some might argue are mutually exclusive.

In the critical temper of the time, some reviewers regarded literary new-
comers as prime targets for ridicule. The infamous review of the *Illustrations* in the *Quarterly Review* offers the most notorious example of this
trend and demonstrates the extreme degree of sexism and classism confronting any woman attempting to write in genres and on topics traditionally reserved for men. Dismissing the series' more serious qualities as "absurd trash" couched in "dull didactic dialogues," reviewer John Wilson
Croker—who had brazenly announced his intention to "tomahawk Miss
Martineau"—declares the author "unfeminine and mischievous" and proceeds to attack not her intellect, but her sexuality. Targeting her mild suggestion in "Weal and Woe in Garveloch" that overpopulation might easily
be managed by exercising a "preventive check" (sexual abstinence), Croker
begins by belittling the unmarried Martineau's lack of sexual experience
even as he implies that she is not quite respectable:

> A little ignorance on these ticklish topics is perhaps not unbecoming a young
> unmarried lady. But before such a person undertook to write books in favour
> of "the preventive check," she should have informed herself somewhat more
> accurately upon the laws of human propagation. Poor innocent! She has been
> puzzling over Mr. Malthus's arithmetical and geometrical ratios, for knowl-
> edge which she should have obtained by a simple question or two of her
> mamma. (1833, 141)

While this part of Croker's argument depends on ridiculing her spinsterhood and casting aspersions on her sexual respectability, what follows is designed to discredit her as a woman whose lack of maternal "instinct" and
social compassion render her monstrous in Victorian eyes: "This maiden
sage . . . [is a] *female Malthusian. A woman* who thinks child-bearing a *crime
against society! An unmarried woman* who declaims against *marriage!! A young
woman* who deprecates charity and a provision for the *poor!!!*" (1833, 151).
Conceivably, Croker's hyperbolic rhetoric, designed—complete with italics
and ever-increasing exclamation points—to fan the flames of outrage
aroused by the unconventionalities Martineau represents, may have done
her some good: even bad publicity is still publicity, as the *Illustrations'* sales
numbers demonstrate.

Quoting a different perspective on the series, Maria Weston Chapman
asserts that Martineau's work also enjoyed strong support: "In this new literature of the people Miss Martineau takes a high rank. Inspired with the
finest affections of a woman, and taking her stand on all in human nature
and the counsels of God which her affections reveal, her clear understanding gives her a wide and true view of social relations and duties" (1877,
179). Chapman's perspective, too, relied on conventional notions of femininity, but turned to a typically Garrisonian purpose: to co-opt the stereo-

types employed to suppress women by presenting them as the very qualities justifying women's place outside the limitations of home.[9] In this configuration, the passive angel-in-the-house compares unfavorably with the
avenging angels of social reform who take the feminine moral imperative
to the streets, to the lecture halls, and to the popular press.

Although Martineau's literary identity continued to develop throughout
her life, the *Illustrations* provides early proof that her strongest gifts lay in
nonfiction writing. While the popular success of the series is legendary, critics have commented on this experimental genre's inability to stand the test
of time, arguing that its subject matter and didactic style are anachronistic.[10] Writing in 1884, Martineau biographer Florence Fenwick Miller
claimed the tales are "inevitably damaged, as works of art, by the fact that
they were written to convey definite lessons" and are thus "fettered" as
"novels with a purpose" or social problem fiction (1884, 81). Others, like
Victorian writer Mary Russell Mitford, predicted that the tales would not be
read by subsequent generations: "The only things of hers I ever liked were
her political economy stories, which I used to read, skipping the political
economy. Fifty years hence she will be heard of as one of the curiousities of
our age, but she will not be read" (Courtney 1920, 236). Apparently forget-
ting about the prolific forty-year writing career that followed the *Illustrations,* Janet Courtney agrees: "No, she will not be read; but she will be remembered for all time as one of the women—perhaps the first amongst
them—who made the nineteenth century the dawn of freedom for half the
human race." Today, however, "curiousities" of an age are themselves often
the subject of scholarly endeavor since, for an example, anyone credited
with liberating "half the human race" must surely be worth recuperating.

Recent scholarly interest in literary history beyond mainstream texts, a
critical conversation in which this study takes part, reinforces the con-
tention that literature is best understood in its fullest historical context.
Martineau's writing is integral to a comprehensive view of Victorian society,
an idea to which both her contemporary and our contemporary critics attest. Of the *Illustrations,* Victorian Daniel Maclise observed: "As felicitous illustrations of important truths they are of great and enduring value; and
they will doubtless continue to be read for their interest as works of fiction
and admired for the ingenuity which the writer has shown" (1883, 207).
And Victorian publisher Charles Knight asserted that the *Illustrations* "led
the way in the growing tendency of all novel-writing to extend the area of
its search for materials upon which to build a story, and to keep in view the
characteristic relations of rich and poor, of educated and uneducated, of
virtuous and vicious, in our complicated state of society" (Cazamian 1973,
59). It may be that Martineau's reach exceeded her grasp aesthetically, yet
the *Illustrations'* great innovation lay in bridging two crucial genre gaps:
first, by joining "silver fork" with working-class concerns and clarifying
their economic interdependence and second, by demonstrating that theory
(principles) and practice (fictional narrative) are similarly interdependent.

Contemporary scholars credit the series with the inception of the social problem genre popular throughout the century. These critics argue that the series' originality played a central role in the development of the Victorian novel, a genre that raised enduring concerns not only about the relations between fictional narratives, imagination, and realism but also about shifts in social relations resulting from industrialization. Louis Cazamian, for example, claims the *Illustrations'* challenge to conventional genres sparked the development of social problem fiction-writing during the 1840s, best seen in the work of Charles Dickens, Benjamin Disraeli, Elizabeth Gaskell, and Charles Kingsley. Similarly, Monica Fryckstedt recognizes the *Illustrations* as a primary forerunner of the developing industrial novel (such as Gaskell's *Mary Barton* and *North and South,* and Dickens's *Hard Times*), while Valerie Sanders cites its influence on such quintessential Victorian novelists as Brontë and Eliot. Of the *Illustrations'* impact on the development of the Victorian novel, Sanders writes:

> Her tales discussed all the most topical questions that were agitating the country in the 1830s, at least ten years before the major Victorian novelists began to consider them. . . . Her lasting significance rests on her advancement of new ideas, her exploration of new areas for the novel to claim as its legitimate territory, and her embodiment of the leading doubts and convictions of the age. (1986b, 195)

The *Illustrations* also influenced American literature. Clare Taylor credits Martineau's "view of labour as a measure of value, and her trick of expounding classic economic doctrine through a didactic tale" with shaping Harriet Beecher Stowe's approach to social reform in *Uncle Tom's Cabin* (1995, 97), an opinion shared by Gillian Thomas. Taylor further claims that Stowe's second anti-slavery novel, *Dred* (1856), "seems derived from Harriet Martineau's 'Demerara.'" Martineau's unique blend of fictional narrative with didactic principles and reform-era concerns may now be unfashionable, yet it also comprises the series' particular strength and innovation. Relevant to literary, social, and economic history, the *Illustrations* raises issues about inequities still unresolved in postindustrial, postmodern society.

In view of the series' phenomenal popular success, the *Illustrations'* lapse into obscurity raises questions about literary history, particularly what it chooses and does not choose to record as significant contributions to the field. As these criticisms show, Martineau is both praised for her artistry and condemned for lacking it; she is lauded for her innovative influence on the history of the novel and dismissed for the series' lack of staying power; she is admired for her class-transcending humanism and condemned for the logical—because not always comforting—extremes of her political economy; she is praised for her ability to "write like a man" and condemned for addressing topics considered outside women's narrow sphere of influence: such as, ironically, birth control and excessive child-

bearing. While some of these criticisms reflect outdated Victorian attitudes, they do not explain either her immense popularity during her life
or her relative obscurity since her death.

Notoriety seems inevitable to the *Illustrations,* which effectually propelled Martineau to instant fame. She became known internationally,
prompting the courts of several European countries to buy the series; it is
another measure of her influence that her sometimes unflattering portrayals of some European governments—she never shrank from exposing corruption—later led to their banning Martineau and her books. Noting that
the *Illustrations* was translated into French for use in the national schools,
Florence Fenwick Miller observes: "she afforded the first instance on record
of a woman who was not born to sovereign station affecting practical legislation otherwise than through a man" (1884, 88). At home, British parliamentarians, both Whigs and Tories, regularly solicited her support in popu-
larizing pending bills and reform issues through her writing. But again, she
was not afraid to risk political disfavor by implicating the government in
systematic oppression of the unrepresented classes. In her preface to *Poor
Laws and Paupers* (1833), she boldly asserts that "vice and misery can be in-
disputably referred to the errors of a system rather than to the depravity of
individuals. . . . The more clearly evils can be referred to an institution, the
more cheering are the expectations of what may be effected by its amendment." Such a perspective is remarkable in that it goes against the grain of
popular beliefs about the lower classes, whose miseries stemmed, it was assumed, from their own inadequacies rather than from hegemonic sources.

Martineau's move to London in the early months of the *Illustrations'* success reflects her clear purpose and mission: "It is not merely the pleasure I
have in being in London which has determined me to make it my resi-
dence, but the facilities which it affords to the prosecution of my work,
and, yet more, the claims of the Government work which I have undertaken make it my *duty* to stay where I can work best."[11] Her commitment to
herself and to her "duty" found a welcoming home in London's political
and literary circles. But independence was short-lived, as her mother, wishing to be a part of the excitement, moved into Harriet's London home.

Mrs. Martineau's support of her daughter's career represents only part of
the complex relationship between the two women. The early conflict between the sensitive, ailing child and the strict mother committed to the
"taking-down" system of child-rearing—a recurring theme throughout
Martineau's writings (*Household Education* and the *Autobiography,* for instance) was never fully resolved. There are indications that Mrs. Martineau,
an intelligent woman who perhaps herself struggled with frustrated intellectual inclinations, was jealous of her daughter's worldly success. After
moving to London, she pressured Harriet to adapt a more ostentatious
lifestyle in accordance with her fame, but she resisted, not wanting to
"mortgage my brain" merely for material show, preferring to save against
future need. The allegations of jealousy were real enough; of her mother's

response to her sudden popularity Harriet wrote: "My mother, who loved power and had always been in the habit of exercising it, was hurt at confidence being reposed in me; and . . . I, with every desire to be passive . . . was kept in a state of constant agitation" (1983, 1:249). Their relationship was troubled not only by the mother's simultaneous jealousy of and pride in her daughter but also by Harriet's desire both to win her mother's approval and to move beyond the compulsion to do so. Martineau's "devouring passion for justice" stemmed from the difficulties that plagued her early childhood; harsh nineteenth-century child-rearing practices reflected the mentality implicated in exploitation of the working class, in the plantation system of masters and slaves, and in the social tyrannies to which women were routinely subjected. Her commitment to eradicating injustices was more than childish resentment: as her perception of the dynamics of oppression grew more sophisticated, she was driven by "the conviction that communication between, [and] mutual education of, inferiors and superiors is the key to progress" (Myers 1980b, 77). As a result, "her lifelong hatred of irresponsible power, her pervasive interest in education and all forms of human development, her obsession with justice for all—workers, servants, children, women, slaves, the poor" found expression in the social causes she supported in her writing.[12]

The fame of Martineau's *Illustrations* not only established her career, it opened doors for her throughout the world. While touring America in 1834–1836, she met with President Andrew Jackson and members of Congress, she was courted by Northern abolitionists as well as by Southern plantation owners, and she was invited to move to Texas to "frame their Constitution" (1983, 2:52), an offer Martineau declined.[13] She considered herself fortunate that, along with visiting the great urban centers and social and political institutions of the New World, she also enjoyed access to the nurseries, kitchens, and boudoirs, which told another story of American life. Access also characterized her Middle Eastern trip ten years later, when her gender permitted her entrance to the wives' chambers in several harems while her international reputation secured her audiences with the harem owners. Such instances illustrate Martineau's unusual capacity to command professional respect in masculine realms (even in sexist societies) while preserving her respectability as a woman.

Signaling her late-blooming autonomy, she wrote to her mother this pointed declaration of independence from both familial strictures and gender limitations: "I fully expect that both you and I shall occasionally feel as if I did not discharge a daughter's duty, but we shall both remind ourselves that I am now as much a citizen of the world as any professional *son* of yours could be" (Chapman 1877, 91). In rejecting the role of the spinster daughter who stays at home tending to her aging mother, Martineau released herself from the passivity that earlier stymied her personal development and obstructed the performance of her public and professional duties.[14]

Harriet Martineau in 1833, by Miss Gillies.
The pose offers a subtle reminder of Martineau's deafness.

Courtesy of the Armitt Trust.

Sudden fame intensified the vigilant self-assessment so thoroughly in-grained in Martineau, as her extended diatribe against "literary lionism" il-lustrates (see 1983, 1:271–95). Celebrities—for instance, overnight successes like Martineau—were invited to social gatherings for the purpose of enter-taining the guests with displays of wit and erudition.[15] The "lions" of the season were in effect expected to perform for their supper in circles where they would not ordinarily have been welcome. Rejecting this custom, Mar-tineau instead held her own soirees, peopled by kindred spirits and literary intelligentsia rather than the rich and famous (1983, 1:374–75). Later, this independent spirit led her to refuse government pensions (offered several times throughout her career) that would have provided financial security, particularly during extended illnesses and old age, but that she believed would compromise her credibility as a political and social-problem writer.[16]

## The Middle Years: From Popularizer to Prophet

Writing the *Illustrations*—as its sometimes uncomfortable tension be-tween fiction and realism attests—convinced Martineau of her "utter inabil-ity to make a plot" (1983, 1:238). She argued that plots should be "taken bodily from real life" and, because a good plot is akin to prophecy, the writer's perspective must be omniscient; this, she claimed, is impossible. Her study of the plots of Walter Scott highlights her conflicted notions about fic-tion: "It seems as if one might trust to a novel growing out as it proceeds, in-stead of having the whole cut and dry before the beginning" (Chapman 1877, 214). Yet by her own admission, her mode of composition was spon-taneous, featuring no planning, no plotting, no revision or rewriting. Mea-suring her skills against Jane Austen—"a glorious novelist"—she concluded: "I *think* I could write a novel, though I see a thousand things in Scott and her which I could never do. My way of interesting must be a different one" (Chapman 1877, 199). But her protest that she could not sustain the omni-scient perspective required for handling a novel-length plot is inconsistent with evidence that Martineau was so deeply attuned to the spirit of the age as to be prophetically insightful—in effect, a social visionary. For example, one of the most striking features of her writing is her attention to various viewpoints—for, against, and everything in between—and her ability to il-lustrate their interactions and mutual interdependencies through characters and plot devices in her fiction, and through various rhetorical appeals in her nonfiction, all of which are integral to an omniscient perspective. This abil-ity was enhanced by a temporal focus, seen in her practice of drawing on past history and present circumstances to assess future direction.

In her analysis of Martineau's journalism career, Elisabeth Arbuckle draws a striking analogy between the alternative demands of creative writing and periodicals writing that resists the conventional dichotomy between fiction (involving a contrived plot fully comprehended by an omniscient narrator) and nonfiction (realism or truth reported by an objective observer):

In her many writings on social, economic, and political subjects, Martineau claims to see passing events as part of a Necessarian/Positivist design. By means of the imaginative qualities of her writing, including that for the *Daily News*, she brings events and issues to life. Thus most of Martineau's topics seem to be plots unfolding over time, and all her plots form part of a Necessarian/Positivist scheme of social progress. (1994, xviii)

Arbuckle's point highlights the idea that all narrative—whether fiction or nonfiction—performs the cultural work of recording history; journalism, of course, is a narrative particularly implicated in the making of history. Martineau, who not only wrote histories of the past but also recorded the events unfolding in the historical moment of which she was a part, proved to be particularly adept at recognizing the significance of the present in the context of past and future "plots."

By rejecting the argument that the popular association between masculinity and nonfiction genres proves that Martineau's was a "masculine intellect," I foreground a question that has characterized Martineau studies in her century as well as our own: was Harriet Martineau a feminist or not? The quickest answer to that question is no, if we bring to the term "feminism" a strictly twenty-first-century interpretation, but yes, if we regard her persistent presence in traditionally male-dominated genres as a practice manifesting feminist principles. Amy Schulman observes that "genres are not neutral classification systems but are part of a politics of interpretation. . . . Theories of gender and genre converge in their exploration of the problems of classification and the disruption of boundaries" (1993, 71). Schulman argues that women's work requires *relational* interpretation—assessment *in relation to* its sociohistorical context. Although genres do tend to reflect the worldviews of the dominant ideology, correspondences between the two are not inherent or fixed but socially constructed and are thus subject to being reconstructed; the boundaries are fluid, in constant flux, and defined according to whatever ideology is dominant at the time. This fluidity is highlighted by women writers who infiltrate genres traditionally closed to them—for example, Martineau ("serious" nonfiction prose), Elizabeth Barrett Browning (poetry based on classical themes), and Florence Nightingale (science writing based on empirical methodology)—thus eroding the boundaries delineating Victorian genres by refusing to conform to gendered guidelines.

One of Martineau's most notable characteristics was her compulsion for self-examination, which she of course applied to her writing abilities. She later wrote disparagingly of the *Illustrations,* claiming: "After an interval of above twenty years, I have not courage to look at a single number,—convinced that I should be disgusted by bad taste and metaphysics" (1983, 1:258). She completely dismissed her attempts at poetry writing—"I can't bear to think of it" (1983, 1:134)—while writing her one novel, *Deerbrook* (1839; it had moderate popular success and was much admired by such writers as George Eliot, Charlotte Brontë, and Elizabeth Gaskell), tested literary skills unused during the period of nonfiction writing following the *Illustrations*. Fearing her style was becoming "rigid and narrow" because she wrote nonfiction exclusively, she "longed inexpressibly for the liberty of fiction" (1983, 2:108). But despite this urge, she concluded that "I cannot write fiction, after having written . . . history and philosophy. . . . I doubted . . . whether I could ever again succeed in fiction, after having completely passed out of the state of mind in which I used to write it" (1983, 2:380–81). It may be that fiction writing taxed Martineau's time and skills in ways that nonfiction writing did not; her temporal investment in the latter was comparatively minimal and the remuneration more immediate and dependable, while the energy-drain of chronic poor health may have been another factor. Although she claimed that she wrote out of a "need of utterance" and never just to earn money, nonfiction writing offered a more reliable path for a self-supporting author in a perpetually uncertain market. Based on the fiction she did write, she might have been a fine novelist had she more actively cultivated fiction-writing skills. She continued to write occasional fiction throughout her career, her charming children's tales being particularly popular.[17]

But even if, as she claimed, her skill in fictional plot construction is weak, her characterizations (both fictional and nonfictional) are compelling. Such creations as Ella ("Ella of Garveloch")—Princess Victoria's favorite—and Margaret Kay ("Sowers Not Reapers")—Florence Nightingale's favorite—are among her most memorable characters. Illustrating her gift for nonfiction characterization are comments from readers who believe the author writes from personal experience: her piece on Manchester operatives ("A Manchester Strike," in *Illustrations*) must have been written by one who "spent all her life in a cotton-mill," claimed some, while her writing on servants *(Guide to Service)* convinced others that, despite her articulateness, the author must be "of very low origin,—having been a maid-of-all-work" (1983, 1:216). Martineau was both amused by such misperceptions and pleased that her depictions were so realistic.

Also notable is her lifelong pattern of turning virtually every personal experience into a piece of writing aimed at providing instruction by example. Her "Letter to the Deaf" (1834), for instance, counsels those coping with hearing impairments, emphasizing ways to cultivate independence and to avoid burdening others. Deafness involves more than aural deprivation and the attendant difficulties of communicating in society as a public figure; Martineau's impairment also involved the senses of smell and taste, of which she had limited experience: "for a few hours of two days of my life, during desperate headache, I have been able to smell and taste a little;—and odd enough were the sensations." Her pattern of transforming adversity is evidenced by her focus on the opportunity deafness affords for self-assessment: "I lost my hearing . . . at about eighteen,—when I was old enough to observe the effect on my intellectual and moral nature."[18] The effect, we may surmise, was an enlightening one, as were the two major periods of invalidism punctuating her adult life: during the early 1840s and again in the mid-1850s.

Her extended illness of the 1840s, during which she was confined to bed for over six years, provided opportunity for further self-assessment and, inevitably, publication.[19] Martineau's account of this illness, *Life in the Sickroom* (1844), offers encouragement and practical advice for the chronically ill on managing pain as well as on maintaining caretaker relationships. Extended illness and the inevitable contemplation of death caused her to explore the philosophical and spiritual aspects of invalidism as well: "The sick-room becomes the scene of intense convictions [including] the permanent nature of good, and the transient nature of evil" (1844, 1), the understanding of which, she posits, to a degree vindicates extended illness. Short illness or adversity brings sufferers to a deeper but usually transitory recognition of spiritual and philosophical truths, but they typically return to their customary ways once the discomfort passes. In contrast, chronic illness produces an "abiding and unspeakably vivid conviction of it, which arises out of a condition of protracted suffering" (2). Martineau advises caregivers and visitors to distinguish carefully between sympathy prompted not by selfless concern for the invalid but by their own fears; she denounces the tendency of the healthy to "lie" to the sick, however well intended. Instead, genuine consolation resides in compassion and a commitment to truthfulness: "Speak . . . the truth in love," she urges. "One who does this cannot but be an angel of consolation. Everything but truth becomes loathed in a sick-room. . . . [T]he sharpened intellectual appetite can be satisfied with nothing less substantial; the susceptible spiritual taste can be gratified with nothing less genuine, noble, and fair" (26).

*Life in the Sickroom* offers innovative advice that anticipates our modern perspectives on the health-promoting effects of nature and contemplative solitude.[20] Reigning wisdom dictated that invalids in particular be shrouded away from sunlight and fresh air for their own protection. As an enthusiastic sanitary reformer, Martineau vigorously promoted sunshine, clean water, well-ventilated houses, and simple cookery methods as the means to good health and social morality. She advocated the importance of a spirit-reviving view of nature from the sickroom window as crucial to the healing process and to one's spiritual regeneration. Writing of her own view through the window at the Tynemouth cottage, she reveals her heightened response to nature, which she studied day and night, marveling, "Should I actually have quitted life without this set of affections, if I had not been ill? I believe it" (55). She observed the changes in the sea by day and studied the night sky through her telescope, activities that served as a tonic: "To go from this spectacle to one's bed is to recover for the hour one's health of soul. . . . [T]he remembrance of such a thrill is a cordial for future sickly hours which strengthens by keeping" (56). This Wordsworthian valuing of natural scenes, to be fully appreciated in the moment as well as stored in the imagination for later pleasure, was a practice she cultivated for the remainder of her long life, from her release from this illness to her nightly communing with the stars from her terrace at The Knoll (as she named her Ambleside cottage) in old age. The idea that although "the outward man must decay, the inward man is . . . renewed day by day" (63) points, like everything else for Martineau, to the human capacity for perfection, which finds its most apt expression in communion with the natural world.

Martineau was also a student of *human* nature, whose ordinary activities she observed through her window as well. From this perspective, she re-marks, "how indescribably clear to me are many truths of life from my ob-servation of the doings of the tenants of a single row of houses; it seems to me scarcely necessary to see more than the smallest sample, in order to analyse life in its entireness" (85). Her unflagging optimism rose above the depressed spirits inevitable to long confinements, prompting her observa-tion that, although invalidism in a sense removes one from active life and thus the making of history, the experience enables one better to assess the relative values of worldly concerns. The lesson for her is clear: mundane busyness—in Wordsworth's phrase, "The world is too much with us"—pre-vents people from grasping what is meaningful and essential in life, while illness forces them to confront not only material concerns but spiritual and philosophical ones as well. During the contemplativeness afforded by illness, "History becomes like actual life; life becomes comprehensive as history, and abstract as speculation. Not only does human life, from the cradle to the grave, lie open to us, but the whole succession of genera-tions" (90). Martineau's study of nature and human nature from her sick-room window reflects not only her Romantic sensibility but her impend-ing Victorian agnosticism: of the Christian promise of an afterlife she observes, "till death satisfies us in regard to a local heaven, we may well be satisfied with that which lies all round about us" (103).[21]

*Life in the Sickroom* also highlighted her need for solitude. During her extended 1834 sea voyage to America, Martineau savored the tranquillity that followed the hard work and social whirl of the *Illustrations* period: "I have enjoyed few things more in life," she notes, "than the certainty of be-ing out of the way of the post, of news, and of passing strangers for a whole month" (1983, 2:6). Although an exceptionally active public figure, she relished the periods of solitude necessary to rejuvenate after a great creative effort. The analogy applies to illness, insofar as invalidism heralds the need for a retreat from an overactive life. Martineau particularly rec-ommended solitude for invalids, who were generally prevented from being alone out of caregivers' misplaced fear of morbidity or depression.

Letters from this period emphasize her appreciation for the benefits of nature and solitude. In a letter to Jane and Thomas Carlyle, she describes her Tynemouth work space, situated near an open window with flowers on the table and singing birds and blossoming gardens outside. With nature as inspiration, "We can hardly go wrong in this radiant universe," she wrote. "I hope it is no sign of disease to enjoy being quite alone as I do" (Sanders

1990, 56). Later she asserts, "I am best, on the whole, quite alone" (64), and in a letter to Milnes she admits that her solitude is "by my own desire" (67). But even in solitude Martineau made her mark on the busy village life around her, directing building projects and contending with social-problem issues: "Without leaving my sofa, I have had a well dug in the garden, and various improvements made in the village, and have been taking part against the intolerable bigotry of the clergy here,—men of the narrowest sort, who wring consciences atrociously." Chapman adds: "With the money placed at her disposition by Lady Byron she caused a drain to be laid the length of Tynemouth Street," while the new well not only "served the whole row of houses," it also served a moral purpose by keeping the maids closer to home and thus away from "bad company" (1877, 247). She advocated solitude for personal regeneration and self-assessment, anticipating our current interest in meditation and other self-healing practices. To publisher W. J. Fox, Martineau asserted that solitude actually improved her health—"I am rather better than usual, just now,—from being quite alone, which always refreshes me" (Sanders 1990, 70). Finally, she preferred solitude because "At the end of a bad day, I then feel that I have dimmed nobody's light,—given no trouble,—'consumed my own smoke', as Carlyle says. . . . [I] can do most when my trumpet lies still for weeks together."[22]

Far more controversial than her insistence on solitude is her assertion in *Letters on Mesmerism* (1845) that her long illness responded not to conventional medicine but to mesmerism, a popular pseudo-science of the period. The uterine tumor that confined Martineau to bed for nearly seven years was not relieved by any of the period's available medical treatments. When she tried mesmerism (at her physician's recommendation), her symptoms were relieved and she embarked on the most physically vigorous period of her life. This volume was followed by 1848's *Eastern Life, Present and Past*, for which she was labeled an infidel, primarily for such statements as: "for a long time I have been becoming aware how much Judaism owes to Egyptian predecession, and Christianity to both; and to heathen wisdom mingled with it . . . by the recorders of the Gospel" ("Eastern Journal," Chapman 1877, 255). Although radical, perhaps, to the general reading public, Martineau's thinking throughout this period represents a continuum evolving naturally and logically from the combination of her early influences, her professional life, her travels and illnesses, and her tireless self-scrutiny in pursuit of philosophical and spiritual insights.

Like "Letter to the Deaf," *Life in the Sickroom*, and *Letters on Mesmerism*, *Household Education* (1849), effectively a manual for cultivating nurturing familial environments, also relies on personal experience for its authority. The book begins with a disclaimer that denies her agenda is instructional, although she does offer the text as a model adaptable to the needs of individual families: "Let me declare here what I hope will be remembered throughout, that I have no ambition to teach; but a strong desire to set members of households consulting together about their course of action towards each other" (1). Her attitude is consistent with her concerns about education reform, based on the idea that, once introduced to the critical tools necessary for assessing one's situation, individuals benefit best by applying those tools to their own situations. Urging active participation by all family members—"all the members *are* included in the influences which work upon the whole"—she proposes to "write on the supposition that we are all children together—from the greatest to the least—the wisest and the best needing all the good they can get from the peculiar influences of Home" (10). Although her discussion emphasizes the middle class, which she terms "The Golden Mean," she includes everyone from the queen to workhouse inmates, incorporating women, children, invalids, and anyone else "rejected or slighted under former systems" (20).[23] Because all people receive their perspective on life from their own household education, which they in turn pass on to succeeding generations, "what a wide and serious subject it is that we have to consider!" (41).

Illustrating her concern with the effects of domestic environment on early child development, she asserts that any child who has strong support "can hardly fail of the best ends of life" (51). Martineau's allusions to her own childhood anxieties in *Household Education* reflect the lingering effects of a nonnurturing environment. Although she was provided with all the necessities of life, including religious and scholarly instruction, her example proves that material well-being offers no substitute for emotional nurturance. Her denunciation of the practice of breaking children's wills and calling it "child-rearing" stems from personal experience, not abstract theory. Her empathy for children is clear in her children's tales and in her advice to adults on child-rearing: offered despite her own childless state.

What she proposes in *Household Education* is radical: that all family members—including children—are equal and deserve respect, and that children's development into mature, moral adults is directly compromised by the typical family hierarchy, in which children are to be seen and not heard. Children who ask where they "come from" should be shown respect rather than lied to, as is the usual practice: "The deceptions usually practised are altogether to be reprobated. It is an abominable practice to tell children . . . a lie" (55). Children, like invalids, deserve the truth, since lying—even "for your own good"—represents the worst sort of role-modeling to the generation that will shape the future society. Further, children should be guided through the tragedies and disappointments inevitable in life rather than falsely shielded from them. Martineau rejects censoring children's reading, arguing that whatever is not understood will simply not "stick" and whatever they do understand should, again, be responsibly guided to prevent "mischief." Of bowdlerized literature she notes, "Purified editions of noble books are monuments of wasted labour," adding that an attitude of healthy mutual respect between parents and children is "an all-sufficient purifier" (229). Along with stressing the importance of carefully cultivating the imagination by highlighting its link with spirituality, she advocates good personal and familial habits of mind and behavior in order to meet "the needs of the social nature" (319). Martineau's progressive perspectives on child and family psychology anticipate fin de siècle developments in this field that continue to influence today's culture.

Subsequently, *Letters on the Laws of Man's Nature and Development* (1851), coauthored with Henry Atkinson,[24] made public her most radical claim yet: her rejection of religion for the philosophy of science. Science, whose principles were increasingly knowable through advanced technology and human intellectual evolution, gave shape and force to her necessarianism and positivism and promised liberation from the superstitions of myths and religions. Martineau rejected the dogma that an afterlife not only vindicates life's suffering but is the only authentic existence, positing that one who "cannot find full exercise for his moral nature in our actual life is below profiting by 'divine' intercourses. I am confident that the true moral life is found in going out of ourselves" (222). Living one's life motivated solely by self-gratification materially and spiritually (by stockpiling goods for one's corporeal comfort and good deeds against one's Judgment Day) signifies philosophical ignorance and arrogance, she maintained, whereas a life defined by service to human social progress is in harmony with nature and thus the will of God, and is itself a source of joy.

To Martineau, human dilemmas are resolved by necessarian positivism— "We feel a contentment in our own lot which must be sound because it is derived from no special administration of our affairs, but from the impartial and necessary operations of Nature" (284); we have but to align ourselves with Nature "and all the forces of the universe will combine to lift Man above his sorrows" (285). Martineau's early affinity with nature thus finds philosophical expression through her collaboration with Atkinson. She offered the manuscript to Moxon Publishing with the following disclaimer: "I think it . . . very striking and extremely valuable. It is, at the same time, daring to the last degree; and the public which certainly *is* ready for such works may not be *your* public." Publications from this period earned her criticism and condemnation she was never able to live down; but she never regretted having offered them to the public, as this letter attests:

> I am naturally of the most cowardly temperament possible; and in self-defence, as it were, I have clung through life to the unfailing security of seeking and avowing truth without any reservation whatever, as the only sure resting place of an anxious and apprehensive nature. It has carried me through life with fewer struggles than would have otherwise been possible.[25]

A crucial turning point serving as a prelude to the last active phase of her life, during which she reinvented herself yet again, the shift from religious dogmatism to a spirituality based on philosophy and science clarifies Martineau's mature identity.

From earliest childhood, religious influence was central to Martineau's self-concept. Her low self-esteem, exacerbated by morbid religious guilt, poor health, and family dynamics, was transformed by independence and professional success in young adulthood. Martineau regarded early childhood parroting of such maxims as "Dooty fust, and pleasure afterwards" (1983, 1:12) as a "bad sort" of religion proportionate to her emotional neediness; during childhood, "I was always in a state of shame about something or other" (1983, 1:15). As a Dissenter, she questioned religious platitudes that relied on faith alone for their efficacy. Her insights were precocious: as a child, she questioned the purpose of prayer—specifically, petitioning God for favors or to gratify desires—if God already has an unalterable plan in place, as church doctrine teaches. The perplexed, evasive response—that she was too young to understand such ideas—confirmed her suspicions that the adults in her life had doubts too, doubts considered dangerous to articulate. Because she was always ready to take risks in her pursuit of truth, Martineau's questing mind served her well as these important issues shaped an adult life often marked by invalidism and the contemplation of death.

The mature Martineau regarded Christianity's denial of the body and fear of God as "the Worship of Sorrow," charging that it was Christianity, not the advent of science and technology, that was responsible for the angst of nineteenth-century society: "The Christian superstition . . . has shockingly perverted our morals, as well as injured the health" (1983, 2:148). She regretted the years she spent in a perpetual state of guilt, longing for the afterlife that promised to vindicate earthly suffering. Having spent some time in "the atmosphere of selfishness which is the very life of Christian doctrine" (1983, 2:218), she was relieved to count herself among those who "enjoy their release from the superstition which fails to make happy, fails to make good, fails to make wise, and has become as great an obstacle in the way of progress as the prior mythologies which it took the place of nearly two thousand years ago" (1983, 2:356). Instead, because she believed in human perfectibility, she promoted the habit of self-assessment, which can reshape the world community, individual by individual. Hence she repeatedly recorded and published the fruits of her ruthless self-examination as a guide to others struggling with similar issues: not out of hubris, but as an offering, as her participation in a general discourse of self-improvement typical of the period.

## The Later Years: "The greatest literary engagement of my life"

As a result of the intense metaphysical searching of this period, Martineau—once "the last link of my chain snapped"—became "a free rover on the broad, bright breezy common of the universe" (1983, 1:116). This perspective anticipates her promotion of the three stages in human spiritual evolution outlined in her 1853 translation of Auguste Comte's *The Positive Philosophy:* mythology (worshiped in the ancient world), religion (worshiped in the early modern world), and science (which supplants both and promises the fullest realization of human development by situating spiritual responsibility within each individual). Martineau wrote in an age of social and religious upheaval generated in part by technological and scientific advances, and her gifts as both popularizer and prophet are aptly evidenced by her promotion of science as the new belief system: "the indispensableness of science . . . [is] the only source of, not only enlightenment, but wisdom, goodness and happiness" (1983, 2:330).[26]

Although her philosophies strained and in some cases terminated relationships, Martineau attributed her reprieve from death to the intellectual liberation they afforded. The invalidism of the 1840s was followed by ten years of robust health during which she toured the Middle East, hiking deserts and climbing pyramids. At home in Ambleside, exuding health and energy, she walked before sunrise, delivering her letters to the post office and arriving at a local farm before the cows were milked: "When the little shred of moon . . . and the morning star hang over Wansfell, among the amber clouds of the approaching sunrise, it is delicious," she wrote (Cone and Gilder 1887, 43). Of nature's powerful healing influence, she observes: "I almost wonder sometimes if anybody finds life what it is to me now,—in this paradise valley—without an ailment of body or trouble of mind for months together. I am now certain that I never knew before what health was."[27] This period of good health, followed by another near-fatal illness (this time heart disease), ushered in what proved to be the final and most prolific phase in her productive life: her career as a journalist. In the midst of this period, Martineau, having long been concerned about inaccuracies that circulated about famous people like herself, wrote her *Autobiography*, having it privately printed (to prevent editorial tampering after her death) and stored, to be distributed posthumously (as it turned out, over twenty years later). The *Autobiography* is a lively read, with Martineau's persona warm and engaging, although it offers more name-dropping than intimacy. While it serves as a valuable record of the Victorian temper and times, insight into the private character of the writer requires more careful reading.

One such insight reiterates Martineau's affinity with nature, most fully realized when she moved to Ambleside in middle age. As a young woman, "I went every fair Sunday morning over the wildest bit of country near Norwich . . . [to] a sweet breezy common, overlooking the old city in its most picturesque aspect" (1983, 1:144). This early connection with nature intensified following her six-year invalidism at Tynemouth, when "I felt a really painful longing to see verdure and foliage" (1983, 2:211).[28] A glimpse of greenery "made my heart throb . . . and bred in me a desperate longing to see more. I did not think I could have wished so much for any thing as I did to see foliage." Her desires were gratified in Ambleside, whose "mossy walls with their fringes of ferns; the black pines reflected in the waters: the amethyst mountains at sunset, and the groves and white beaches beside the lake had haunted me almost painfully, all spring" (1983, 2:219). Nature's effect on Martineau at this time was electric, transforming this virtual workaholic into a Lake District "local": "I was speedily instructed in the morality of lakers,—the first principle of which is . . . never to work except in bad weather" (1983, 2:220). To Ralph Waldo Emerson she wrote:

> For the first time in my life I am free to live as I please; and I please to live here. My life is now . . . one of wild roving. . . . I ride like a Borderer,—walk like a pedlar,—climb like a mountaineer,—sometimes on excursions with kind and merry neighbours,—sometimes all alone for the day on the mountain. I cannot leave this region. London must give way.

Urging Emerson to visit and meet her friends, the Arnolds and Wordsworths, she added that "the mountains are intimate friends of mine too, and *their* acquaintance I am sure you will like." Several years later she wrote of going back to work, "called hither by the commotion of the times," although she had no intention of leaving "my precious home" to do so.[29]

Toward the end of the *Autobiography*, Martineau describes her nightly communion with the stars, from which she "seldom or never came in without a clear purpose for my next morning's work" (1983, 2:415). She observes that one's relations with nature render inconsequential the temporal concerns of the world: "I experienced the full new joy of feeling myself to be a portion of the universe, resting on the security of its everlasting laws" (1983, 2:355–56). Her move to Ambleside represents less a retreat from public arenas than a synthesis of her life's varied experiences, all seen through the lens of The Knoll's peaceful environment: "I believe that, but for my country life, much of the benefit and enjoyment of my travels, and also of my studies, would have been lost to me" (1983, 2:415). While contemplating the stars, she relived her travels in America, Europe, and the Middle East, "all comprehended within my terrace wall, and coming up into the light at my call" (1983, 2:416). Although grateful for having moved among the most significant people, places, and events of her time, she asserts she would not exchange any of those "mere" pleasures "for one of my ordinary evenings under the lamp within, and the lights of heaven without" her beloved Knoll (1983, 2.417). A domestic environment in harmony with her professional activities and personal needs proved essential to her well-being, seen in her unwillingness to "let" her house despite repeated requests—"I stick to my own, more lovingly every year." In old age, she rated domestic tranquillity an even greater priority: "I do not suffer very much, as long as we can preserve perfect quiet," she wrote in 1867. "We have no cares or troubles in this house. All about me is love and peace." Poetry writing may not have been one of her gifts, yet the life she composed for herself in Ambleside was itself poetic: visitors termed The Knoll "'a perfect poem:' and it is truly that to me: and so . . . is the life that I have passed within it" (1983, 2:342).[30]

During her illness in the 1850s, when she wrote the *Autobiography* and prepared for death, Martineau's letters demonstrated the philosophical satisfaction of having lived life to the fullest, thus having no regrets about dying. Each letter from this period seems to be her last, and it is with some surprise that we find the following, written to Florence Nightingale, about her reprieve from impending death as the American civil conflict intensified: "I am not so eager [to die] . . . more from the American outbreak, which causes me to be seriously *wanted*. . . . My constant work on both sides of the Atlantic really puts down my personal feelings,—actually my bodily sensations,—more than I could have believed."[31]

Martineau's observation that certain influential people depended on the unique ties she maintained with the Americans she had met twenty-five years earlier attests to her lifelong commitment to the abolitionist cause. On this, the eve of the long-awaited Civil War, Martineau—casting herself as rescued from death's door because there was important work to be done—was so revitalized that her physical state became submerged in the excitement of this pivotal event in world history. The work seemed in fact therapeutic, regenerative rather than draining; to Fanny Wedgwood she revealed that her writing for the *Daily News* "is pleasant, while it satisfies my mind,—keeps off the temptation to feel useless" (Arbuckle 1983, 132). Recalled to life by the confrontation between the friends and foes of slavery, Martineau subsequently produced many hundreds of *Daily News* leaders on the American Civil War and related issues and contributed regularly to the *Spectator* and the American *National Anti-Slavery Standard* as well.

Paradoxically, this most objective of all her work concerns one of the great passions of Martineau's life—the abolition of slavery, one she was privileged to see realized before she died. From the American travel journals published early in her career to her *Daily News* leaders in old age, Martineau's participation in the American cause is central to her identity as a writer. Of her journey to America as a young woman, she notes, "The accident of my arriving in America in the dawning hour of the great conflict accounts for the strange story I have had to tell about myself" (1983, 2:61). Both personally and professionally, her American experiences established the framework for a lifetime of writing about slavery in its various forms: racial, sexual, and economic, all primary and consistent themes throughout her work. Of her journalism, R. K. Webb writes: "Her work has relevance, urgency, cogency, and impatience with muddled situations" (1960, 316), the last phrase offering a particularly important insight into her attitudes toward America, its people, its ideals, and its too-long unrealized potential.

Although Martineau wrote for various periodicals and journals throughout her career, the body of work she produced for the *Daily News*, more than sixteen hundred articles between 1852 and 1866, earned her the title "first and greatest of women journalists" (Arbuckle 1994, xviii). In her own words, this final phase in a long and prolific career represented "the greatest literary engagement of my life" (1983, 2:389). As a journalist, her influence was incontrovertible: "When I returned from the Continent," wrote *Daily News* editor William Weir, "her writings took me between wind and water, and went a long way towards determining the direction and character of my mind for life" (1877, 340). To this Chapman adds, "by having more or less formed the minds of her whole generation . . . she was enabled so greatly to influence her times." Perhaps not surprisingly, during this intensely public engagement, her personal concerns increasingly found expression through letters, demonstrating the clearest delineation yet between her private life and her public persona.

Two ideas are essential to evaluating Martineau's journalistic identity: first, the political expediency of anonymity and second, the assumption that nonfiction writing presupposes a masculine persona. Aside from a few early writings, Martineau never concealed her identity in print except as a journalist, as was customary in periodicals writing. She reveled gleefully in the public's speculation about the identity of the new *Daily News* leader writer, pleased that anonymity liberated her from the necessity of living up (or living down) to her literary reputation. Her early articles were "attributed to almost every possible writer but the real one. This 'hit' sent me forward cheerily: and I immediately promised to do a 'leader' per week" (1983, 2:406). Anonymity in print was particularly advantageous for Victorian women writers, who were thereby liberated from gender limitations to address, without censure, topics with the same authority that their male counterparts enjoyed. But within her first month at the *Daily News,* her editor advised her to forget about preserving anonymity as astute readers had already detected her identity through her distinctive style.

Martineau's example proves that, although women may not have been particularly welcome in the literary realm, it was possible to carve out a place for oneself, and to do so while retaining one's identity and without adapting a male persona. Uncorrupted by "literary lionism" as a young author, Martineau continued unswayed by public opinion, in praise or condemnation, as an old woman. Yet in this cautionary advice to young writers, in which she promotes intellectual self-reliance while warning that it exacts a high price, she implies that authorship is still a function, primarily, of the male identity: "I can assure any young author . . . that he need feel no remorse, no misgiving about conceit or obstinacy, if he finds it impossible to work so well upon the suggestions of another mind as upon those of his own. He will be charged with obstinacy and conceit, as I have been. He is sure of that, at all events" (1983, 2:161).

But although it is likely that Martineau's use of masculine pronouns simply reflects her capitulation to the accepted linguistic custom of the time, it is also true that males did not typically experience resistance to their thinking, writing, and publishing, although females certainly did, as Martineau well knew. Since readers of the *Autobiography* (from which this quotation comes) are aware of her gender, her "I" amid all those masculine pronouns invites us to consider the irony implicit in her situation as a female survivor in the predominantly male realm of literature in general and nonfiction writing in particular. Her insistence on establishing firm boundaries between her public and private lives, best seen in her attitudes about exerting absolute control over her *Autobiography* and correspondence, represents her understanding that writing, once committed to paper, becomes part of the public realm, to be edited or revised, read or misread, altered or censored. That her life, like her writing, went off "like a letter"—spontaneous and truthful—is a remarkable achievement during an age when literary lions were often themselves devoured in the feeding frenzies for which Victorian critics are famous.

One last text crucial to a consideration of Martineau's identity is her self-authored obituary, which reveals a woman unfettered by false modesty yet unblinking in her rigorous self-assessment:

> Her original power was nothing more than was due to earnestness and intellectual clearness within a certain range. With small imaginative and suggestive powers, and, therefore, nothing approaching to genius, she could see clearly what she did see, and give a clear expression to what she had to say. In short, she could popularize, while she could neither discover nor invent. (*Daily News,* June 29, 1876)[32]

Her modest assertion that the positive progress of humankind is something in which she was privileged to play a part elides the impact of her role in the formation of modern culture. Once she understood that her opinion was of international significance, Martineau groomed herself to be ethically worthy of that role, preferring to court controversy in the name of honesty rather than to "vegetate" in middle-class complacency or to become the pawn of any political persuasion. Since her fame and influence rivaled and sometimes eclipsed that of her contemporary male literary colleagues, Martineau's long exclusion from the Victorian literary canon raises some interesting questions for feminist inquiry. Her work and reputation deserve and require restoration, as any picture of the nineteenth century that does not include her influence is an incomplete one.

Martineau's mature identity is best summarized in her observation that "My business in life has been to think and learn, and to speak out with absolute freedom what I have thought and learned. . . . My work and I have been fitted to each other" (1983, 1:133). Her personal and professional lives were mutually inclusive, which accords with her pronounced impulse toward self-revelation. But she also exhibited an impulse to retreat into solitude, explained in part by her deafness and her intellectual pursuits and illustrated by her seclusion in Ambleside. Martineau's compulsion to transform private challenges into public tracts served as a kind of self-therapy that finds even in suffering a utilitarian purpose. Called historian and biographer, political economist and philosopher, the "first woman sociologist" and the "first and greatest woman journalist," Martineau might well have rejected such superlatives as lionizing. The extraordinary range of her interests, her expertise, and her influence perhaps provides the best key to this self-termed popularizer, whose genius resides in her ability to invent and continually reinvent herself during a century of unprecedented social change.

# 2

## Fancywork and Bluestockingism; or, Needles and Pens

She can deep mysteries unriddle / As easily as thread a needle.
—*Quarterly Review*

It is true, she was not much of a needlewoman. There is a tradition that the skeleton of a mouse was found in her workbag.
—**Harriet Martineau**

As we earnestly wish the authorship not to become known, I have used the mannish way of talking about needlework . . . . But you are not to support that I don't know better. . . . Few women of my time (amateurs) have done so much sewing as I, and with so much satisfaction.
—**Harriet Martineau**

What an advantage we have over sick gentlemen in this employment! One does learn of their netting sometimes; but somehow it sounds ridiculous.
—**Harriet Martineau**

## Needles and Pens

• The refinement of the separate spheres ideology throughout the Romantic and Victorian eras codified a gendered dichotomy in which needlework was exclusively linked with women "and thus opposed to the masculine world of public affairs," to which literary pursuits belong (Maitzen 1998, 63). That needle and pen were regarded as opposed to each other—with the former on the lower end of a hierarchical value system—clarifies the importance of needleworking to maintaining women's respectability, which was assumed to be compromised by "putting oneself forward" in print, in the public realm. For this reason, as a metaphor for the lives and work of Victorian women, needlework in its many varieties offers a rich text through which to study the status of women, both how they were perceived by society and how they perceived themselves.[1] Aside from the primary expectation that they marry and bear children, the other activity expected of women of all classes was first, that they learn how to sew; second, that some piece of sewing (preferably the entire workbasket) be kept nearby at all times; and third, that they never be caught with their hands idle when they might usefully be employed in needleworking.

Little girls routinely received sewing instruction when barely out of the toddler stage; having the work of their tiny hands scrutinized by adult women, who sternly unraveled crooked stitches needing to be resewn, was thought to be character building and a preventive check against troublesome behaviors bred by idleness. Although generally prohibited from formal education, generations of little girls learned their numbers and letters, their arithmetic and spelling, and their religious and social platitudes by working "samplers"—a symbolic commentary on the exclusively domestic purpose of girls' learning. A painstaking and time-consuming mode of learning compared with the chalkboards and pens used by boys, the practice suggests intriguing links between domestic and public, female and male, needle and pen: dichotomies aimed at delineating the spheres as separate but not equal, since the male component was presented as superior to the female. Thus is women's needleworking required yet denigrated; thus are women writers charged with impropriety for attempting to enter the public realm.

Regardless of their socioeconomic class, women were expected to sew throughout their lives, during childhood and girlhood, pregnancies and child-rearing, while employed (both inside and outside the home), and as far into old age as their vision permitted. No woman escaped with impunity the stricture to produce prodigious amounts of needlework, much of it necessary and useful ("plain sewing") but some of it "fancywork" which, if of limited practical use, provided visible proof of women's respectability. Highlighting the fact that women of all classes earned little or nothing from this laborious, time-consuming occupation, whether they worked for hire or merely for appearance's sake, Elizabeth Barrett Browning's heroine, Aurora Leigh, laments:

> The works of women are symbolical.
> We sew, sew, prick our fingers, dull our sight,
> . . . . . . . . . . . . . . . . . . . . . . . . . . . . . . . .
> This hurts us most, this—that, after all, we are paid
> The worth of our work, perhaps. (*Aurora Leigh* 1:456–57, 464–65)

Women who produced the requisite amount of sewing hardly had time for disreputable activities. For lower-class women, "disreputable" generally had sexual or moral connotations, while middle-class women must contend with notions of domestic respectability, which did not include a life

of the mind.[2] Neither class had the option to retreat to the garret to study
poetry, as Aurora did, or to the sickroom to translate Greek classics, as Elizabeth Barrett did (both upper-middle-class examples). Conversely, women
who produced books instead of buttonholes opened themselves up to
charges of neglecting their workbaskets and thus of compromising their
womanly role. The woman who could satisfy both sets of expectations was
rare—and overworked—indeed. Carol Wilson notes that needlework "is an
important device with which women writers complicate, subvert, or challenge the ideal of domesticity" (1997, 80), an idea illustrated by Martineau's claim that she is "excessively fond" of needlework even as she reifies the tradition that it is inferior to writing.[3] The relationship between
sewing as an outward representation of utilitarian respectability (produced
for private consumption) and writing as an expression of the inner, creative life (produced for public consumption) provides important insight
into Martineau's identity not only as a writer but also as a social activist.
Needle and pen, thread and ink, fabric and paper, stitches and words: all
are implicated in the linguistic and nonlinguistic texts produced by a
woman who was exceptionally prolific on both counts.

With a view toward broadening our understanding of the interplays between needle and pen in Martineau's life and work, I begin by examining
some of the recent critical dialog involving women, writing, and needleworking. These theoretical links facilitate an interpretation of Martineau's
dual training in literature and sewing as preparation for her role as a public
figure for whom skill in the domestic arts is integral to success in the literary realm. This dialog provides a framework through which to analyze
first, her textual contributions to the period's social-problem writing on
the desperate plights of exploited needlewomen and second, her stitched
"texts" worked for the benefit of various social causes. Together, they reveal Martineau's "need of utterance" as too compelling to be suppressed by
middle-class convention and too prolific to endure confinement in either
articulate or inarticulate mediums. Indeed, Martineau's prodigious need
strives to negotiate the limitations of both.

## Toward a Theory of Needleworking

Judging by the dearth of critical studies on needlework, there exists no
self-contained critical tradition by which to interpret the links between
women and writing and sewing. But there are contemporary scholars
working in this area, in disciplines as varied as feminist criticism, history,
art history, literature, anthropology, and folklore. What follows is a sampling of critical discourse on this topic which, in the absence of a co-
gent theory, offers some insight into the cultural traditions that defined women's domestic role and resisted their entry into public,
especially literary, realms. Recent critical work on knitting, embroidery, and
quilting demonstrates that these activities serve as powerful metaphors for

women's writing, particularly during the nineteenth century when women assumed an unprecedented public role as published writers. This scholarship reveals that the transition from needle to pen has a logic of its own, one that goes beyond metaphorical significance and resists conventional theory and methodology. In the absence of a unified theory, then, this discussion, in true needleworking fashion, pieces together the real and metaphorical connections between women's writing and sewing, between the tools that enable them to articulate—especially needle and pen—and between the verbal and nonverbal texts they produce.

A fruitful place to start is with a study aimed at constructing an epistemological framework for analyzing women's creative expressions, both linguistic and nonlinguistic. Folklorists Joan Radner and Susan Lanser, in their article "Strategies of Coding in Folklore and Literature," seek "to create a discussion between disciplines in order to evolve feminist theories that account for both literary and folkloristic texts" (1987, 413). They posit that, in women's texts—like writing and needlework, for example—"one can often find covert expressions . . . that the dominant culture . . . would find disturbing or threatening if expressed in more overt forms" (414). The interpretive theory designed to reveal those covert expressions incorporates such ideas as *appropriation; juxtaposition,* or the context in which the work is placed; *distraction:* Martineau's sewing visually distracts from her inner work of literary "composition" by conveying an image of respectability; *indirection,* like the use of metaphorical devices; and *trivialization,* "the employment of a form . . . that is considered by the dominant culture to be unimportant, innocuous, or irrelevant" (420), like Martineau's favorite medium, Berlin wool work. The final idea discussed in this article, *incompetence*—real or pretended—is a strategy Martineau refused to employ: unlike Brontë's Shirley Keeldar (a reluctant needlewoman) or Barrett Browning's Aurora Leigh (an inept one), Martineau was proud of her needleworking skill and regarded needles and pens as complementary, not antithetical, means of expression. Radner and Lanser's ideas provide not only the means for interpreting women's texts: they also emphasize that an interdisciplinary approach is crucial to analyzing them in a relevant framework.

Illustrating the idea that the messages in women's texts are often either covert or misread, Cecilia Macheski asserts that "there is no logical connection" between writing and sewing (1986, 100 n.19). Yet certainly connections exist, and the lack of logic may explain the difficulty in constructing a theory that accounts for two seemingly unrelated practices. A comparison of writing and sewing is made more significant by their being traditionally employed to maintain gendered divisions of labor—men write, while women sew—and, by extension, the entire social organization of Western societies. As a thinker known for resisting standard logic and a feminist theologian who aims to expose patriarchal constructions, Mary Daly demonstrates the gendered underpinnings of the reason-emotion dichotomy. Daly's lively linguistic analyses of the ways our language encodes

and perpetuates women's subjugation within patriarchy depends on rejecting the sort of logical processes typically associated with a classical (male-
oriented) education. Instead, her analysis thrives on a comparatively
"twisted" logic that suggests that the elusive links joining women with
sewing and writing are all the more profound for their compelling pervasiveness. By gathering in seemingly unrelated ideas in a kind of manic
word-association, like individual threads gathered into twists and spun
into a coherent fabric, Daly constructs meaning that illustrates how articulate and inarticulate mediums are not polarized, hierarchical, or inherently
value-bound but are profoundly interrelated. Traditionally, "articulate"
modes are verbal, either written or spoken, and "inarticulate" modes are
nonverbal, like music, and visual, like dance, painting, and needlework.
My interest in exploring methodologies for interpreting the intersections
of sewing and writing in women's lives is based on a rejection of that polarity, arguing instead that "inarticulate" modes of expression are legitimate texts written in codes that, once interpreted or translated, are as legi-
ble as any alphabetical language.

As a woman whose work was at times criticized through her gender (being a professional writer, a woman, and unmarried, her example was triply
negative), Harriet Martineau would have applauded Daly's analysis of the
term "spinster" as "She who has chosen her Self, who defines her self, by
choice, neither in relation to children nor to men" (1978, 3–4). While
spinsters were traditionally associated with spinning tales as well as thread,
these qualities were subsumed into the more contemporary definition of
"an unmarried woman . . . [a] woman past the common age for marrying
or one who seems unlikely to marry—called also *old maid*" (393). That the
term *spinster,* representing autonomy and creativity, has become synonymous with *old maid,* with the latter's insistent reference to one's marital
status—perpetual virginity, celibacy, and sexual redundancy—betrays cultural anxieties about women who produce books instead of babies.

But storytelling is also life-giving, giving birth to creative energy; spinsters spin stories as well as thread—spinning a yarn or story is the "creative
enterprise of mind and imagination" (Daly 1978, 389). The connection between the two ideas is emphasized by the Latin word *texere* (to weave),
which supplies the root meaning for both *textile* and *text;* ironically, *texts*
were historically written and read by men to maintain "the realm of the
reified word," while weaving and spinning were reserved for women and
girls, whose texts were almost exclusively nonverbal and, from this perspective, inarticulate, illiterate, and uncivilized (5). Echoing Martineau's
criticism in "Female Industry" (discussed later in this chapter), Daly observes that, although presented as the ultimate "reified" female text,
women's weaving "has been stunted and minimized to the level of the
manufacture and maintenance of textiles. . . .[T]he limitation of women to
the realm of 'distaff' has mutilated and condensed our Divine Right of creative weaving to the darning of socks." Martineau explores this point by

questioning the wholesale promotion of women's incessant needlework as long as it is not performed for remuneration and as long as it entertains no pretensions as an art form. Helen Diner's observation that "Knitting, knotting, interlacing, and entwining" may be female activities but so too is "entanglement in a magic plot" (Daly 1978, 400) highlights Martineau's example as a needlewoman/writer whose social-problem writing is not limited to spinning fictional yarns. More subversively, she offers explicit cultural criticism through her nonfiction periodicals writing designed to influence public opinion (conventionally regarded as a masculine genre) as well as through needleworked items for fund-raising bazaars, a more grass-roots approach to social activism (traditionally feminine). Martineau's eclectic approach to social reform insists on bridging, if not closing, the gender gap by which Victorian society defined itself.

Complementing Daly's linguistic analyses is the social/historical overview offered in Roszika Parker's study of embroidery, *The Subversive Stitch,* which dramatizes how gender-encoded language manifests itself in social classes and the types of needlework specific to them. Proving Aurora Leigh's assertion that the works of women are symbolical, needlework becomes itself a text in which we can read the changing history of the relationship between women and needlework as a reflection of shifting political ideologies. Parker investigates the "ideology of ease" created by a cultural attitude that both endorses and rejects women's idleness by promoting perpetual needlework. But while it is true that most women and girls sewed, regardless of their class, the *kind* of needlework they engaged in symbolized their class status. For example, lower- and working-class females performed the plain sewing necessary for most clothing and household items—essential but unglamorous—while upper-class girls were distinguished by their preoccupation with fancywork or embroidery, the purpose of which was, like their own lives, exclusively ornamental.[4] Parker notes that by the eighteenth century embroidery signified "a leisured, aristocratic life style . . . the hallmark of femininity" (1984, 11). Challenging the period's anxiety about women's proper role, notes Parker, Mary Wollstonecraft targets needlework as "a prime agent in the construction of femininity" (Parker 1984, 139), the solitariness of the activity encouraging self-absorption while its sedentariness renders women sickly. Perceptions of femininity depend on "false notions of female excellence [that] make them proud of this delicacy" (Wollstonecraft 1975, 171). Conceivably, the cult of female invalidism that parallels perpetual needleworking—itself a symptom of the social constrictions hemming women in on every side— might be seen as women's passive resistance to the useless ornamentalism they share with the needlework they create. As "good" women, their conformity with this lifestyle literally makes them sick, resulting in a grotesque realization of feminine ideology.

The early nineteenth century heralded a more complex attitude toward women's roles as the rise of utilitarianism and an increasingly critical attitude toward aristocratic decadence contested the "ideology of ease." The new morality of needlework "put to shame the selfish needle of the vain late eighteenth-century aristocrat" who sewed only for self-adornment (Wilson 1994, 168). Now, woman's needle served as a moral "compass, guiding family and nation on a steady course." But the standards of the new middle classes created a paradox for women, whose status as unpaid, unemployed symbols of males' economic prosperity conflicted with the values of usefulness and productivity. Roszika Parker asks, how can women be both fashionably idle and yet useful in a society "which scorned idleness and glorified work as the supreme virtue?" (1984, 154). The answer is, "They had their 'work'"—needleworking—and as long as they received no payment, women preserved their class status while negotiating the leisure/work dilemma.[5]

As a measure not only of class status but also morality, sewing "could be seen entirely in the light of their primary duty" (Parker 1984, 154): to serve their husbands and children or, for single women like Martineau, to supply the charity bazaars benefiting social causes. Employing needlework as a means for moral management eventually filtered down to lower-class girls, whose gains in education reform throughout the nineteenth century and well into the twentieth were repeatedly compromised by educators' privileging needlework instruction and practice (plain sewing for lower-class girls, fancywork and embroidery for middle- and upper-class girls) over academic courses. Despite outward signs of social progress, such tactics merely ensured the preservation of class and gender hierarchies, since girls were early trained to learn their social place and to remain within it, the concept of "upward mobility" being limited to men and the marketplace.[6]

A primary component perpetuating this class-inscribed needleworking ideology involved mothers who prepared their daughters to assume appropriate social roles. Because of women's economic reliance on men, their survival was "dependent on conforming to the feminine ideal" (Parker 1984, 129), which may account for Mrs. Martineau's strict attitude toward Harriet. Her daughter's dual handicap—she was reputedly plain-looking as well as deaf—perhaps led Mrs. Martineau to despair of Harriet's making the sort of match that would secure her economic well-being. Parker's summation of the complexities of mother/daughter relationships within feminine ideology is most appropriate to the complex relationship between Harriet and her mother: "The key to the hold embroidery and femininity established over middle-class women was that it became implicated in an intense relationship, shot through with as much guilt, hatred, and ambivalence as love" (130). Insofar as a mother experienced her daughter "as an extension or double of herself," training in and criticism of needlework "could be experienced as an oppressive forced bonding with the mother—a denial of the child's individuation" (131).[7] The conflicts between Harriet (whose coming-of-age was literary rather than domestic) and her mother seem intensified, rather than mitigated, by Harriet's fame as a writer. That her success was not of the "right" sort—ordinary domesticity, marriage, and motherhood—may have added to the antagonism.[8]

As a communal activity, quilting offers a distinct departure from the solitary act of embroidering. Like fancywork and plain sewing, quilting is also class-inscribed, having evolved among the lower classes who could not afford to waste even fabric scraps. Although quilting is more readily identified as an American, rather than an English, craft, critical analysis of quilting illustrates its relevance as a metaphor for domestic ideology on both sides of the Atlantic. The inclusion of quilt making in this discussion of Martineau, sewing, and writing proves relevant in several ways: first, she was herself a quilter (see Chapman 1877, 214) and second, quilting requires skill in plain sewing (piecing) and fancywork (quilting), both of which Martineau practiced.[9] These class-inscribed types of needleworking are incorporated in the same project—a project typically accomplished through communal rather than individual efforts; thus quilting reflects the broader American endeavor of equality and democracy, the "American experiment" that so captivated Martineau's interest. Further, quilting produces "texts" encoded with the American political and social ideologies that occupied much of Martineau's personal and professional energies. Not only can we read individual and family histories in quilts, which traditionally comprise scraps from favorite fabrics and pieces of clothing marking important occasions like weddings, births, deaths, and religious holidays, but we can also read in quilts the history of American culture during the era that realized both its greatest expansion and its most profound social restructuring—before, during, and after the Civil War.

For example, Carol Wilson notes that quilts serve as vivid "documents" recording such struggles as pioneering the West and the temperance and suffrage movements. But quilts had a more subversive use and, when hung outside houses ostensibly "to air," they also served as signals for the Underground Railroad, to warn fugitive slaves against dangers along the escape route and to "designate safe houses for runaway slaves" (1997, 81). A recent study, *Hidden in Plain View* by Jacqueline Tobin and Raymond Dobard, explores the roles played by African American quilters not only in the Underground Railroad but also in the history of this uniquely American art form. The study argues that many American quilt patterns are rooted in African textile designs, which often conveyed complex story lines laden with indigenous meaning. These designs were adapted for use in American quilt patterns as elaborately coded messages, serving as maps to direct runaway slaves to safety. As the commonest of everyday domestic objects, the sewing of which was central to women's activities, quilts represented a most unlikely, and therefore especially potent, medium for communication on which many lives depended. It is uncertain whether Martineau knew of this elaborate practice; however, given her abolitionist politics and her "womanish" love of needlework, she would have been delighted to learn that needlework could be turned to such wonderfully subversive ends. As these examples suggest, in their very ordinariness quilts represent highly potent texts, readable by those instructed in this admittedly specialized, yet hardly inarticulate, language.[10]

Ideological correspondences between quilting and women's writing are perhaps more logical than is true of other forms of needleworking. In particular, the piecing involved in organizing scraps or fragments of cloth into coherent quilt patterns (even "crazy quilts" have an organizing logic) extend metaphorically to the fragmented quality of women's daily domestic lives; this temporal fragmentation is suited to piecing quilts, an activity lending itself to interruptions. As wives, mothers, and nurturers whose constant availability to serve the needs of others was assumed and expected, women rarely had time or energy left over to write. For example, *Silences,* Tillie Olsen's study of the virtual absence of women writers throughout literary history, compares successful, published male authors who are required only to write (because women provide for their domestic needs) with women, whose time is spent in service to men, children, and domestic responsibilities. Olsen concludes that women's serving the needs of everybody *but* themselves, long upheld as their most admirable quality, is what accounts for generations of literary silences: hence the dearth of literary grandmothers.

Extending the needleworking idea to incorporate the enterprise of literary criticism, Elaine Showalter notes that the "metaphors of pen and needle have been pervasive in feminist poetics. . . . The repertoire of the Victorian lady who could knit, net, knot, and tat, has become that of the feminist critic, in whose theoretical writing metaphors of text and textile, thread and theme, weaver and web, abound" (1986, 224). As a metaphorical quilter stitching together the fragments of women's literary history, the feminist critic's work is predicated on the idea of piecing together cast-off scraps to create a coherent whole. For the writer as well as the critic, the idea of piecing "best reflects the fragmentation of women's time, the dailiness and repetitiveness of women's work" (228). Thus, the primary genres of women's writing traditionally tended to be short narrative pieces, poems or short stories, writing that could be managed in between domestic tasks. Similarly, although Martineau also wrote lengthier texts, her preferred medium—journalism—proved more amenable to a busy life filled with domestic as well as literary activities and marked by extended periods of invalidism. Whether by choice (as in Martineau's example) or necessity, the gendering of shorter genres as "feminine" has little to do with inherent linguistic or stylistic qualities and everything to do with the time constraints imposed on women by social custom.

This quality of fragmentation characterizes women's writing in longer texts as well. Harriet Beecher Stowe's incendiary *Uncle Tom's Cabin,* for example, was credited by some as virtually responsible for starting the Civil War by sharpening the ideological polarization already at work in America. The novel accomplishes this work by challenging genre expectations: it "does not obey the rules which dictate a unity of action leading to a denouement, but rather operates"—like a quilt pattern—"through the cumulative effect of blocks of events structured on a parallel design" (Showalter 1986, 237). Despite critical attacks on everything from its sentimentality to its politics and from its episodic structure to its social inaccuracies, Stowe's novel is unmatched in literary history in terms of popular impact, suggesting that perhaps the mainstream reading public (both men and women) is more attuned to fragmentation than to the seamlessness purveyed by the dominant ideology. Reading this text requires more than what Martineau calls "seeing through author spectacles," rendering it incomprehensible to those whom Stowe scathingly terms "that ignorant and incapable sex which could not quilt" (quoted in Showalter 1986, 238). Interestingly, a critic of Martineau's American travel writings terms them "precious patchwork,—for patchwork it may be called,—as everyone will perceive at once that the arrangement of her work into chapters and sections is a mere sham" composed of "agrarianism, abolition, amalgamation, Malthusianism, and radicalism, with a strong dash of egg-and-milk-ism" (Chapman 1877, 176). The examples offered by Stowe and Martineau suggest that their admirers are those able to perceive the subtexts underpinning much of women's writing, while those who "could not quilt," those outside the linguistic network defining women's texts, simply dismiss their work as inarticulate.[11]

Linda Pershing contributes an intriguing idea to these links between women, sewing, and writing in her discussion of invisible mending as a metaphor for women's triple roles as needleworkers, social protesters, and political commentators. As a type of needlework whose value resides in restoring to wholeness a tear or hole in fabric, effactually making the flaw disappear, the quality of invisible mending is measured by its unobtrusiveness: "the metaphor is essentially restorative. It suggests a type of preservation that is self-effacing . . . [and] calls as little attention as possible to the stitches or to the women who skillfully executed them" (1993, 343).[12] For Pershing, needlework represents a "'secret language of women' in which they are able to express their own convictions on a wide variety of subjects in a language that is, for the most part, comprehensible only to other women. . . . [S]ewing has long served as a medium for women's political discussion and statement" (338). Aside from Stowe and Martineau, other examples of needlewomen activists include feminist Susan B. Anthony, whose first public presentation of her women's rights platform occurred during a quilting bee, and abolitionist Sarah Grimké, who encouraged women to embroider "antislavery slogans and images on domestic articles, urging, 'May the point of our needles prick the slaveowner's conscience'" (Macheski 1986, 91). Even more subversive was Elizabeth Cady Stanton's rallying cry to dispense with needleworking altogether: "Woman has relied heretofore too entirely for her support on the *needle*—that one-eyed demon of destruction that slays its thousands annually; that evil genius of our sex, which in spite of all our devotion, will never make us healthy, wealthy, or wise." Stanton, no doubt, was one of many who regarded the advent of the sewing machine as, if not quite the death knell of the angel-in-the-house, at least the beginning of her liberation from enslavement to the "one-eyed demon."[13]

Cecilia Macheski offers another compelling example of how needlework is not only encoded as a text to be read by the "linguistically" initiated but stamped with the needlewoman's signature. Irish sweater knitters, whose male family members were primarily fishermen, developed highly individualized patterns, and "so unique was each knitter's code of stitches that should the wearer drown the sweater was relied upon to identify the body" (1986, 85). Aiming to establish an explicit connection between sewing and writing, Macheski attributes the evolution of needlework and of the novel to both "domestic necessity" and to "the special female perspective of the emerging artists. Thus, we should not be surprised that conventional historians . . . overlook the presence of an encoded language of either stitches or literary imagery and . . . see only the superficial pattern." Women's work, stitched or written, is "frequently dismissed as insipid or innocent, artificial or romantic, by those who have overlooked its feminine, or frequently feminist, subtext" (85–86). In her analysis of literary heroines' emotional states as reflected in their needleworking activities, Macheski observes that "The tedious but soothing rhythms of spinning, knitting, and sewing were the very pulse of women's lives" (86). Claiming needle and pen as the "new female iconography," Macheski concludes that women writers employ needlework imagery "to reflect, interpret, and enrich the lives of characters and readers alike," providing "a uniquely female signature" (98).

Offering a suggestive perspective that also highlights the relation between sewing and writing, Rosemary Mitchell analyzes the evolution of "female historiography" during the nineteenth century and "the development of history as a discipline" (1996, 189) through her consideration of women writers' histories of needlework. Noting that women writers "made an ambiguous use of the separate spheres ideology," Mitchell explores the differences between women's perspectives on history, presented as preservative and culturally and socially oriented, and men's version of history, which was traditionally "a false glorification of destructive values" (191). History writing features a unique lens through which to consider separate spheres ideology, specifically how the rhetoric of needleworking was employed to promote and critique social customs. Rohan Maitzen (1998) extends these ideas in her analysis of two other uses of needleworking imagery in relation to history writing: by critics, to denigrate history writing thought to be insufficiently masculine or rigorous; and by women writers, to present an alternative version of history that includes women and their activities. I do not here propose to discuss Martineau's history writing, work for which she was widely admired by critics and scholars of the genre; but the analogy between these ideas dovetails suggestively with my analyses of gendered ideologies, genres, and authorial personae, and of the complex relationship between needle, pen, and the life of the mind.

Although these explorations do not construct a conventional theoretical or methodological framework for analyzing the intersections between women, writing, and needlework, they reveal that a rich network of correspondences links the three. Most useful to Martineau studies, in my view, is Joyce Ice's (1993) idea of a process-oriented approach to analyzing women's relationship with sewing. Ice argues that understanding the *process* of sewing, in other words what women acquire through performing this act, is more pertinent to such an analysis than the substantive *goal* of sewing, the finished product. Linda Pershing, for instance, in her interview with a needleworker, notes: "As we talked together she often stitched, pausing with her needle poised in midair while she considered difficult questions, as though her mind and her embroidery were symbiotically fused" (1993, 327). Such fusion of articulate and inarticulate modes defies "logical" polarization of the two ideas. The same is true of Martineau, who claimed that her writing was spontaneous, committed to paper without drafting or revising; clearly, however, the hours spent needleworking also provided opportunities to rehearse her ideas while stitching, the activity or *process* serving as an alternative mode of drafting—invisible, unobtrusive, inarticulate, but no less prolific than more conventional means, like writing.[14]

The traditional assumption that men think logically while women operate out of their emotions (illogically) yields an alternative analogy: the connection between women's needlework and their written texts is amorphous *because* it by definition resists categorization according to conventional logic, which is not the same as being illogical. The elusive links connecting seemingly disparate discourses, both of which were essential to Martineau's identity personally and professionally, are not mutually exclusive. The idea that her domesticity precludes her role as a feminist prototype simply reverses the sexism of Victorian critics who attacked her *lack* of femininity as a woman who writes. Both perspectives fail to diminish the impact of a writer whose legacy resists reduction to an ideological equation. Like a quilt, Martineau's example is best read in the subtext underpinning the more ostentatious, less substantive, surface.

## A First-Rate Needlewoman

While careful to observe the rules of social decorum, the Martineaus were liberal in their determination that both sons and (to a lesser degree) daughters be educated. The Martineau parents raised their children "to an industry like their own;—the boys in study and business, and the girls in study and household cares" (1983, 1:27). This dual focus early established a basic pattern in Harriet Martineau's life, a life framed at its beginning and at its conclusion with sewing projects, with the busy years in between featuring a

dynamic interplay between pen—as a writer in the public realm—and needle, when prolonged confinements in the sickroom compelled her to sew
items for charity bazaars rather than to write social-problem articles. Although Martineau was relieved to be free of the limitations of marriage and
motherhood and identified herself most directly with authorship, she cultivated her early domestic training, of which she was markedly proud,
throughout her life. Yet she was also relieved when early publishing success
permitted her to put aside the needle (as an occupation) to pursue the literary career that was superior to needleworking in terms of intellectual stimu-
lation, personal satisfaction, and remuneration. Martineau gratefully acknowledged, however, that it was needleworking that enabled her to launch
her writing career by offering her a means of support during her literary apprenticeship. Throughout her life, needlework continued to represent a
measure of financial security in the event that her literary career, or the
health to sustain it, should fail.

Respectability was essential to the sort of middle-class family Martineau was born into, as was utility, economy, and prudence, and the image of young girls, eyes downcast, bent demurely over their sewing provided the most visible expression of this set of values. Martineau
internalized these values early, taking pride in managing her clothing allowance so well that she had money to spare for charity and books. During girlhood, she stretched her budget by sewing nearly every item of
clothing herself, from bonnets to silk-covered shoes: "I sewed indefatiga-
bly all those years. . . . I made literally all my clothes, as I grew up. . . .
The amount of time spent in sewing now appears frightful; but it was the
way in those days, among people like ourselves" (1983, 1:26). Writing in
retrospect, she admits to being "in truth excessively fond of sewing," an
activity that allowed for both socializing and, more important for Martineau, literary study and composition.

Although "respectability" is a term typically associated with sexual propriety and conformity to prescribed gender roles, the taint of what she
termed "bluestockingism" seems to have been nearly as great a cause for
concern. While she openly received formal and informal academic training,
she was not to display that learning, especially in public: "When I was
young, it was not thought proper for young ladies to study very conspicuously; *and especially with pen in hand*. Young ladies . . . were expected to sit
down in the parlour to sew,—during which reading aloud was permitted, . . .
but so as to be fit to receive callers, without any signs of bluestockingism
which could be reported abroad" (1983, 1:100; emphasis added). In other
words, a woman's intellectual pursuits were acceptable if confined within
the family circle, and Harriet was free to study Wordsworth and Milton,
Bentham and Malthus all she liked, provided she was occupied with sewing
while doing so and she was careful to cover up text with needlework should
callers arrive. "In Miss Martineau's youth," observes Maria Weston Chapman, "to say of a lady in England that she was a learned woman, was to

convey a disparaging meaning" (1877, 19). The matrix composed of
women's intellect, respectability, and needlework compellingly illustrates
the idea that acceptable private behaviors became unacceptable simply by
exposure to what George Eliot calls "the world's wife."[15] As a symbol of
womanly respectability, the needle was by far mightier than the pen,
whereas the pen, in fact, compromised that respectability—an attitude Martineau early disproved yet never ceased to negotiate.

As a young adult threatened by poverty for the first time in her life, Martineau employed her needleworking skills in more ways than one: in that
"season of poverty" (1830), she not only sewed for hire; she also "made and
mended everything I wore,—knitting stockings while reading aloud to my
mother and aunt, and never sitting idle a minute" (1983, 1:153). Important
to Martineau's development as a thinker and writer was the routine mind-
lessness of sewing, which afforded the perfect opportunity for "learning poetry by heart, from a book, lying open under my work. There was some saving in our practice of reading aloud, and in mine of learning poetry in such
mass."[16] The combined practice of intellectual exercise and domestic duties
("double work") established a lifelong pattern typical of a woman who refused fully to conform with the social expectations of these roles, yet who
was unwilling to relinquish either one, preferring instead to synthesize the
two. Not surprisingly, in her advice to "The Ladies' Maid" (1838), Martineau
recommends that servants, too, learn poetry while sewing, a theory practiced in her own domestic arrangements.[17] According to biographer Florence Fenwick Miller, "Her principles and her practice went hand-in-hand
in her domestic arrangements, as in her life generally, and her kitchen was
as airy, light and comfortable for her maids as her drawing-room was for
herself. The kitchen, too, was provided with a book-case for a servants' library" (1884, 136). Given that education reform for women of all classes
was a keen interest of Martineau's, women who occupied their minds while
sewing proved themselves superior, in her opinion, to those who wasted
time with idle gossip or self-absorption. Spending hours with the needle
may have been inevitable but allowing one's mind to grow lax as a result
was not. If women were to be thwarted in their need to acquire an education, then they must find ways to get what they needed subversively. Martineau's example is itself a case in point.[18]

Ever the nonconformist, Martineau took special pride in demonstrating
that intellectual women were not "unsexed," as their male critics charged,
but were capable of both "masculine" pursuits like writing and "feminine"
pursuits like needleworking. Indeed, the nondomestic literary woman was
an aberrant stereotype she resisted being identified with, proving that, despite her adult eclecticism, Martineau never relinquished her girlhood con-
ditioning in respectability. Public opinion, particularly where women writers desiring to retain respectability were concerned, was a significant issue.
In his advice to aspiring writer Charlotte Brontë, Poet Laureate Robert
Southey dismissed her literary gifts, urging her to look to the cooking

stove and sewing basket for creative release (Fraser 1988, 111). It is a testimony to the irrepressibility of Brontë's genius that today Southey's writing is all but unknown while she is immortalized through her strong-minded heroines, despite the brevity of her writing career.

Other literary examples illustrating the importance of domestic respectability for women writers include Jane Austen and Elizabeth Gaskell. Gaskell's energetic life as the wife of a vicar (with all the many parish duties that entails), as a prolific writer, and as a social reformer was punctuated throughout with repeated pregnancies and childbirths; but she was determined to "do it all." Of the unique conjunction between domestic responsibilities and the creative impulse, Gaskell wrote: "One thing is pretty clear, *Women* must give up living an artist's life, if home duties are to be paramount." Yet, she adds, "assuredly a blending of the two is desirable" (Hellerstein et al. 1981, 336).[19] Echoing Martineau, Gaskell notes that we must all find the work for which we are suited and "forget ourselves in our work." Gaskell's remarkable capacity to forget herself in her work is proven by her mode of composition, which was conducted at a table in the most trafficked area of her bustling household. In this way, she cultivated her "Individual Life" amid the noisy trappings of domesticity while conforming with expectations (in body, at least) that she always be accessible and available to serve the needs of others. Thus she wrote, with half-stitched muslin at the ready to cover her text should callers arrive and with one ear alert should a domestic crisis require her intervention. Far from a room of her own, Gaskell was fortunate to have a minute to herself; in contrast, no doubt her clerical husband enjoyed a private study in which to write his sermons in peace, buffered from the household din by his angel-in-the-house.

Another example is Jane Austen who, like Martineau, was an unmarried woman and of the respectable middle class. "Jane Austen herself," wrote Martineau, "the Queen of novelists, the immortal creator of Anne Eliot, . . . was compelled by the feelings of her family to cover up her manuscripts with a large piece of muslin work, kept on the table for the purpose, whenever any genteel people came in. So it was with other young ladies, for some time after Jane Austen was in her grave" (1983, 1:100–1). Rather than acquiring greater freedom through singleness, Austen wrote under a compulsion that suggests social reputation was doubly fragile for an unmarried woman who both writes and has a claim, by virtue of her class, to respectability. Sitting at her diminutive writing table, alert for the creaking door warning her to conceal her writing, the "Queen of novelists" was as subject to public censure as any slave to a master.[20]

As an unmarried woman, an "old maid" or "spinster" stigmatized (by the more vindictive among her male critics) as an unattractive "bluestocking," Martineau had a particular interest in proving that single women could live full, useful lives, lives of both the mind and the hearth. She was proud of her competence in both realms and irritated by those who assumed that her profession and her singleness precluded domesticity. She credited her domestic skills with saving her "from being a literary lady who could not sew; and when . . . I have been insulted by admiration at not being helpless in regard to household employments, I have been wont to explain . . . that I could make shirts and puddings, and iron and mend, and get my bread by my needle, if necessary . . . before I won a better place and occupation with my pen" (1983, 1:27). Needlework played a particular role in Martineau's winning a "better place and occupation" but, distinct from the lives of most Victorian women, it was for her a means to an end, not the end itself. Once her literary success permitted her to establish her own household, she was no longer bound by the provincial restrictions Austen experienced or by the constant visibility and availability required of Elizabeth Gaskell. But even in her own home, Martineau never relinquished her "womanish love" of needleworking.

These examples indicate that it was not only women's intellect or authorship that met with resistance, but also the challenge to respectability resulting from women's participation in the public realm. Prior to declaring herself a confirmed author, Martineau was aware that caution was a necessary component of literary composition, even in the privacy of her family circle: "my first studies in philosophy were carried on with great care and reserve. I was at the work table regularly after breakfast,—making my own clothes, or the shirts of the household, or about some fancy work; . . . and if ever I shut myself into my own room for an hour of solitude, I knew it was at the risk of being sent for to join the sewing-circle, or to read aloud" (1983, 1:101). As an adult, the high value Martineau placed on solitude derived partly from what seems like a virtual absence of intellectual privacy while living in her parents' house. But once she became a published author, the balance of power shifted radically. After her first publishing success in the *Monthly Repository,* her brother Thomas urged, "'Now, dear, leave it to other women to make shirts and darn stockings; and do you devote yourself to this.' . . . That evening," she adds pointedly, "made me an authoress" (1983, 1:120). That she was noticeably struck by the endearment—"(calling me 'dear' for the first time)," suggests a link between her emerging identity as a writer, which evoked fraternal affection, and needleworking's equation with feminine gentility, which, interestingly, did not. Further, her wording implies that authorship had less to do with her writing ability or even with her desire for a professional career than with earning her brother's permission to relinquish sewing for writing. Initially prompted to write by brother James, then excused from sewing (metaphorically, at least) by Thomas, having won her dying father's approval of her writing and been exempted from marriage by her fiancé's death, Martineau presents herself in these crucial, career-shaping early days as a respectably passive, unambitious young woman. But her swift transformation into a professional author aggressively pursuing reluctant publishers, confronting them face-to-face like "a man of business," suggests that her passivity was but a thin veneer masking a "need of utterance" too intense to be suppressed by middle-class convention.

Familial considerations included not only the opinions of Martineau's male siblings but also those of her mother. Chapman, who notes that as a child Harriet was "neither petted nor praised," reveals two incidents relevant to this juxtaposition of mother and daughter, needlework and literature. While adjusting her clothing prior to church, Martineau earned her mother's snappish admonition that "superior book-knowledge will never make up for being troublesome" (Chapman 1877, 7). This early inkling of her literary destiny prompted Harriet to ponder "All service-time and long after . . . whether she had book-knowledge"; ironically, what was designed to eliminate "troublesomeness" instead fixed the notion firmly in Harriet's mind. The second incident resulted from ten-year-old Harriet's frustration as she "stood with her face to the window to hide her tears, as the needle squeaked through the dingy gusset she was stitching" (Chapman 1877, 21). In a rare example of praise, especially meaningful at this moment of childish despair, her mother observed, "Why, Harriet! if you go on in this way, you will soon be the best needlewoman of us all." Mrs. Martineau's warmth at this crucial juncture provided a "ray of light and life; and she [Harriet] dated from it her success in all those little feminine handicrafts which then went by the name of 'fancy-work,' in which she so greatly delighted and excelled." These examples dramatize the mixed messages she received from her brothers' praise of her writing (resulting from her "bluestockingism") and her mother's rare approval, which privileged fancywork over "book-knowledge," and invite the conclusion that familial validation was predicated to a degree upon her ability to satisfy both sets of demands.[21]

Martineau's assertion that "if I had once conceived that any body cared for me, nearly all the sins and sorrows of my anxious childhood would have been spared me" (1983, 1:29) reveals a great deal about the conflicts that inevitably arise when the needs of the many outweigh, in true utilitarian fashion, the needs of the one. Martineau recalls a moment of clarity about family dynamics relevant to the needle-and-pen device: a friend "asked me why my mother sat sewing so diligently for us children, and sat up at night to mend my stockings, if she did not care for me; and I was convinced at once;—only too happy to believe it, and being unable to resist such evidence as the stocking-mending at night."[22] Diana Postlethwaite's suggestive observation that "For Martineau, the symbol of maternal care was not a loving embrace but a sewing needle" (1989, 591) highlights the prickly nature of this mother-daughter relationship and indicates that, as an autonomous adult, Martineau associated nurturance with the act of sewing for herself, her friends, and her favorite social causes. Chapman's observation that Mrs. Martineau, "always a severe mother," transformed into an "exacting and jealous" one with the advent of Harriet's literary success illustrates the mother's inability to conceal her critical attitude toward this late-blooming, ugly duckling of a daughter. Confronted with Harriet's literary and intellectual blossoming, Mrs. Martineau "again became as really unable to sympathise with her as when, in childhood, she had so fatally mismanaged her" (Chapman 1877, 93).[23]

What *was* well managed in this family was education in both domestic and academic disciplines. Proving the efficacy of this dual approach, the sewing instruction designed to signal perpetual respectability as unpaid labor proved to be essential to Harriet's economic well-being when the family business failed; sewing in turn led to the literary career whose roots were also established by her studies during her early years. Chapman notes that prior to the family's financial failure, Martineau's career gradually had been gathering momentum: "after having written . . . at least half a dozen octavo volumes, with fancy-work, needful needlework, and German literature crowded deep into the night, the way seemed to be opening to a successful literary career" (Chapman 1877, 42). But she was far from established as a writer and, left penniless and with few options, Martineau felt more secure at this juncture as a skilled seamstress than as a writer: "I hoped . . . that my needle would bring me enough for my small expenses, for a time; and I did earn a good many pounds by fancy-work, in the course of the next year,—after which it ceased to be necessary" (1983, 1:143). An unexpected benefit of poverty was the loss of gentility and with it the need to conceal her writing. The loss of income and social stature heralded a shift from rare moments snatched from sewing for writing to, eventually, the reverse. "I want to be doing something with the pen," she wrote to Frances Place in 1832, "since no other means of action in politics are in a woman's power."[24] Enabled by the initial success of her series to write full-time at last, Martineau became submerged in the frenzy of the *Illustrations'* composition and publishing deadlines, thus redefining the standards of respectability for an intellectual woman capable of earning her living by the needle as well as by the pen. The former promised obscurity, while the latter made her an overnight sensation and a political authority of international repute.

It was typical of Martineau—that is, the newly evolved Martineau—to confront the considerable problems facing a poor, single woman directly and aggressively. Although she initially spent long hours sewing—now for hire—her mind was hard at work planning the *Illustrations* project. Once she faced having nothing to lose, Martineau realized she had everything to gain by daring to articulate her dreams and ambitions and by taking steps to realize them. No longer a passive receiver whose life was dictated by fate and society, she was aroused and strengthened by adversity. Instead of "growing narrower every year," like the penurious spinster "Amazons" of Gaskell's *Cranford*, she rose to the challenge of economic independence: "So to work I went, with needle and pen. . . . It was truly *life* that I lived during those days of strong intellectual and moral effort" (1983, 1:145).

She realized literary success after a grueling, if comparatively brief, apprenticeship. Initially, she reserved her best energy for needlework, as that income was assured, if minimal: "During the daylight hours of that winter [1829], I was poring over fine fancy-work, by which alone I earned any money; and after tea, I went upstairs to my room, for my day's literary labour. The quantity I wrote . . . surprises me now. . . . Every night that winter, I believe, I was writing till two, or even three in the morning,—obeying always the rule of the house,—of being present at the breakfast table as the clock struck eight" (1983, 1:146–47). Her repeated assertion that during this period she "truly lived" is qualified by the revelation that she received little outside encouragement for her literary aspirations, which did not compare favorably with the more realistic and substantial prospect offered by needleworking. She therefore struggled to maintain the vision of her lofty literary goals, which had yet to be realized, much less to show proof of material gain.

For example, during a visit to London, though publishers' rejections of her proposals discouraged her, the prospect of securing work as a proof-reader promised employment that would replace needleworking drudgery with "literary drudgery," enabling her to support herself while pursuing recognition as a writer. But her mother suddenly recalled Harriet home, "to pursue,—not literature but needlework, by which, she wrote, I had proved that I could earn money" (1983, 1:149). Suppressing the rebellion Martineau undoubtedly felt (she was twenty-seven at the time), she returned to Norwich, from whence she ultimately launched her career.

Other instances of disparagement surfaced when she acquired a publishing contract that depended on her raising pre-publication subscriptions to the *Illustrations* series. While contacting family and friends, Martineau continued to field skeptical responses to her project. One relative sent "two sovereigns, and a lecture against my rashness and presumption in supposing that I was adequate to such a work as authorship, and offering the enclosed sum as his mite towards the subscription; but recommending rather a family subscription which might eke out my earnings by my needle" (1983, 1:168). The spirited Martineau returned the money, declaring, "I wished for no subscribers but those who expected full value for their payment, and that I would depend upon my needle and upon charity when I found I could not do better, and not before." As her response illustrates, her electrical transformation from middle-class passivity, in which she waited for life to happen to her, to a strong-minded, articulate writer whose faith in herself increasingly outweighed her insecurities, was nothing short of amazing.[25]

Once her writing career proved viable, Martineau rearranged her daily schedule to reflect her new priorities. Now, she reserved her best energy not for sewing but for writing: "it has always been my practice to devote my best strength to my work; and the morning hours have therefore been sacred to it. . . . I really do not know what it is to take any thing but the pen in hand, the first thing after breakfast" (1983, 1:191). So thoroughly did she identify with the image of herself as a writer, apparently, that she forgot the many years during which taking up the pen was a rare exception, since threading the needle was the norm. Success altered her life in a variety of ways; even the deafness that eliminated her from many of the observations and experiences crucial to a writer became less of a cross to bear. Responding to critics of her Malthusianism in "Weal and Woe in Garveloch," she quipped: "If any others should come whispering to me what I need not listen to, I shall shift my [ear] trumpet, and take up my knitting" (1983, 1:202). She parried critics' threats to her reputation for respectability not with words—heard, spoken, or written—but with her wit, her resilience, and her brandished knitting needles.

Writing never completely supplanted needlework, and the two interests became engaged in a dynamic interplay as Martineau's career continued to develop. After her return from America, she recalled an afternoon devoted to "darning stockings and brushing gown and cloak tails," secure in the anticipation of a cozy, uneventful winter following the extended exertions of writing and traveling. But publisher William Saunders interrupted the quiet domestic scene with his proposal that she serve as editor of a new political economy journal designed to capitalize on her recent *Illustrations* success. Debating the idea, Martineau turned from her domestic activities to reveal a sharp business sense: "If I do this, I must brace myself up to do and suffer like a man. . . . Undertaking a man's duty, I must brave a man's fate. . . . The possibility is open before me to showing what a periodical with a perfect temper may be: also of *setting women forward at once into the rank of men of business*" (Chapman 1877, 204; emphasis added). But Martineau, despite the vigor of these words, was not yet prepared to act without familial approval and left the entire decision up to brother James, who counseled against the editorship, which would have been a remarkable achievement for any literary newcomer, especially a young woman.[26] The incident signals a pattern of exchanges between Harriet and James that points to his jealousy of her professional success and to his rejection of her liberal radicalism, eventually culminating in their complete estrangement.

Chapman notes a series of entries in Martineau's journal illustrating the interplay between domestic and intellectual activities during this period: "Wrote notes, settled business, and am now going to darning and thinking. . . . Darned, but did not do much sober thinking. I cannot really think without pen or pencil or book in hand" (1877, 205). The admission reverses her earlier compulsion to employ sewing as a shield to conceal her thinking and planning. Her days were filled with business, both domestic and literary: "Back to the bank, and signed the transfer of stock. Mended my satin gown" (206). On another occasion, she "Mended and quilted till noon, very much enjoying my quiet over my own fire. . . . I bound and mended two pair of shoes, and darned a handkerchief. . . . Finished 'Pride and Prejudice'" (214). At this point in her career, the interplay between sewing and literature remained constant, although such was

A "thoroughly womanish" love
of needleworking. Courtesy of the
National Portrait Gallery.

Harriet Martineau in old age, needlework close at hand.

Courtesy of the National Portrait Gallery.

not always to be the case, since, as she was not to be England's first woman journal editor, her exact role as a literary social activist had yet to be defined.

## Bluestockingism: Social-Problem Writing

Not surprisingly, the needle-and-pen theme carries over from Martineau's life into her writing. Her needleworking expertise led her correctly to identify the sex of the author of *Jane Eyre,* a topic of intense debate in literary circles after its 1847 publication. The gender-evasive "Currer Bell," claimed Martineau, was definitely a woman, which was obvious from a minor but telling detail: "I had made up my mind . . . that a certain passage in 'Jane Eyre,' about sewing on brass rings, could have been written only by a woman or an upholsterer" (1983, 2:323–24). Needleworking finds expression in both Martineau's fiction and nonfiction writing, one of the earliest examples being the 1827 tale, "The Rioters." This cautionary tale against frame-breaking critiques the loss of needleworking skills among working-class women as a result of factory work.[27] Women factory workers unemployed during times of economic stress were unable to provide for their families as needlewomen because "they could not sew, . . . they could not knit" (65). Martineau blamed the industrial milieu for the general decline in needleworking skills, particularly among that portion of the working poor most in need of the craft. The decline of needleworking, for Martineau, paralleled the decline in family solidarity in the industrialized era.

Offering an alternative example is one of Martineau's most compelling fictional heroines, Dora Sullivan of "Ireland," who is distinguished in her community by her exceptional scholarship. But she voluntarily leaves school to spin wool in order to support her poverty-stricken family. She earns little for long hours of labor, although the hum of her spinning wheel comforts her distraught parents, suggesting that the mere gesture of putting aside books for distaff, replacing education with womanly domesticity, metaphorically begins to right the wrongs endured by the Irish people. As Dora's disastrous confrontation with feminine ideology unfolds, conflicts between needle and pen are heightened by her passive obedience, her inherent intelligence, and her exploitation by the men in her life. This narrative proves that a little bit of knowledge can be worse than none at all, prompting Martineau to conclude that universal education is the necessary prerequisite to resolving the relentlessly tragic "Irish Question" no less than the "Woman Question."

Needleworking plays a more central role in the tales "Jerseymen Meeting" (1834) and "Jerseymen Parting" (1834). In the first tale, the LeBrocq women, who have just completed a major washing and airing of all their handmade household linens, take in a blind wanderer named Stephen. Throughout dinner, Stephen "was sensible of the incessant motion of knitting needles all around him, in every interval of eating. All the four women were indeed knitting when doing nothing else; and Stephen felt rather awkward in the midst of so much industry" (1834a, 12). In return for their hospitality, the mercenary Stephen steals the linens produced by the LeBrocqs' "female industry," a devastating loss to the women who weave, sew, and knit all the household items themselves.[28] After moving to the mainland, Anne LeBrocq, seeking to earn a living by needleworking, fears "she must leave off knitting. . . . Nobody seemed to wear knitted smallclothes or petticoats in London, nor even shawls" (42). But there is more than self-conscious provincialism at work here, and the gender issues raised by traditional divisions of labor are highlighted by Anne's concern about earning a living in a country wherein "the men would condescend to such womanish work as tailoring." Illustrating the textual aspects of stitchery, Mr. Durell, a former Jerseyman also relocated in England, recognizes Mrs. LeBrocq's nationality by the distinctive stitching on the hem of her petticoat. Women are not the only ones, apparently, who "read" the subtle language of needlework.

In the sequel, "Jerseymen Parting," Martineau incorporates a metaphorical with the literal needleworking theme. "Knitting and Unravelling" is a pivotal chapter in which the texts' primary events crystallize and mysteries are solved, including Stephen's exposure as the linen thief. As proof that they forgive him, Anne and Mrs. LeBrocq teach him how to knit, thus forging a new friendship through needleworking practice that bridges gender and disability: "think of the benefit to Stephen to have such a resource! to have something to employ his hands" (1834b, 28). Knitting away, Stephen hears Mrs. LeBrocq's tears dripping on the knitting needles as she grieves for her lost son, prompting him to tell her of Aaron LeBrocq's whereabouts; thus is the mystery of Aaron's absence "unraveled" during the knitting lesson. Arriving to find the knitting abandoned on the table, Durell observes, "I was afraid you would find Stephen a bad scholar. . . . Offer to give Stephen a lesson in anything, and it always ends in his giving you a story instead" (42). Stephen admits he "never saw two people more in need of a story than these ladies." Demonstrating Martineau's own dual interests, the metaphorical links between knitting and storytelling (two ways of spinning a yarn) are particularly evident in the "Jerseymen" tales.[29]

Nonfiction articles such as "Female Industry" (1859) display an experiential dimension and understanding of domestic tasks specific to one who has been so trained. Needleworking skills give Martineau an advantage over male writers on the topic, who traditionally have little interest in and no experience of the activities of "'the spindle side' of the house" (1859b, 295) where women are employed with domestic tasks. Part of Martineau's aim in this article is to bring to the public's awareness the fact that "a very large proportion of the women of England earn their own bread" (294), with a view toward scrutinizing the prejudices and issues this unrepresented class of workers must confront in order to earn a living.[30] In her historical overview of Englishwomen and work, she aims to disprove the false "supposition . . . that every woman is supported . . . by her father, her brother, or her husband" (297). Martineau's acute insights into the economic plights of working women reflect a problem that continues to exist today: the devaluation of women's work. Rather than being assessed on its own terms and in the context of the national economy, women's work is taken for granted as unpaid labor performed in conjunction with the nuclear-family households necessary to the capitalist economic paradigm. The very absence of remuneration for housework fosters the idea that the work is as unimportant as the women who consent to do it. Seen in this context, Martineau's championing of domesticity does not, as some might argue, evidence essentialism or prove her lack of feminism; rather it asserts her recognition of the central place domestic labor holds in the broader realm of political economy.[31]

The history of women's work presented in "Female Industry" outlines women's consistent contributions to social economy from pre- to postindustrial society. In centuries past, she observes, women "plied the distaff" while tending herds; with the introduction of the spinning wheel in "every house and hovel," women were expected to spin during the "intervals of other business" (1859b, 296). Offering an early illustration of the idea that women's hands must never be idle, Martineau notes with some ambivalence that "'It stops a gap, and so must needs be,' was the reason assigned by the men." Even gentlewomen were not exempt from this stricture. Able to afford servants to perform their "plain" and household sewing, this class of women cultivated the craft of tapestry weaving and fancywork, the very uselessness of the occupation subject to Martineau's drollery: while others run her household, the gentlewoman oversees her garden and kitchen "without much interruption to the grave labour of stitching the siege of Troy, or the finding of Moses, in coloured wools or silks." Yet she does not deny that the combination of leisure and embroidery led to the creation of a specifically feminine art form. The aesthetic component, which she terms "the mystery of the silkwomen and spinners," adds to the ideological complexities inherent in the conjunction between women, leisure, and work and the unpaid labor of sewing. The aesthetics or "mystery" of needlework-as-art was compromised and nearly destroyed by the regulation and institutionalizing of male-dominated trades resulting from industrial capitalism. However, although the practice as a skilled craft declined as a result, the demand for qualified silkwomen outside the home created "one of the earliest branches of female industry" (297).

Most remarkable about these economic developments, Martineau argues, is that, despite great social changes, both the status of women and attitudes about the worth of their work remained static. The need for and the supply of female industry continues to increase, yet "our ideas, our language, and our arrangements have not altered. . . . We go on talking as if it were still true that every woman is, or ought to be, supported by father, brother, or husband: we are only beginning to think of the claim of all workers,—that their work should be paid for by its quality, and its place in the market, irrespective of the status of the worker" (298). The inevitability of social and economic changes in traditional divisions of labor mocks the "artificial depreciation" of women's work. Devaluation compromises the women who work for wages as well as those whose unpaid domestic labor is essential to the functioning of a capitalist economy, although it clearly benefits the men and institutions whose economic well-being depends on both. Of men's prejudice against working women, Martineau notes that "the jealousy of men in regard to the industrial independence of women . . . shows itself with every step gained in civilisation; and its immediate effect is to pauperise a large number of women who are willing to work for their bread; and . . . to condemn to perdition many more who have no choice left but between starvation and vice" (329).

Martineau's strong language—"to pauperise" and "to condemn to perdition"—draws on two ideas: *unpaid* sewing as a sign of propriety and the economic realities of needleworkers' lives. Although unremunerated needleworking was essential to women's respectability, as a paid profession it was popularly affiliated with falling and fallen women. The introduction of remuneration into the equation indicated, to some, a direct line to prostitution, since only those who were confined to the domestic realm, where their unpaid labor was not tainted by "filthy lucre," were secure from the vices and temptations of the marketplace.[32] This line of thought is worth scrutinizing, since most women knew some mode of needlework and therefore sewing was the most logical employment choice for those forced to work or starve. The profession's links with prostitution, real and metaphorical, are complex: many lower-class women (whose potential for sexual promiscuity was assumed by virtue of their class) sought sewing employment, ironically, because it was considered more genteel and respectable than factory or domestic work.[33] For this class, seamstressing signified upward class mobility. For middle-class women, employment of any sort for remuneration was a step down in social status, although in theory needleworking's association with respectability promised to preserve at least the pretense of gentility.

Regardless of their class backgrounds, women needleworkers were so severely exploited by this profession that many were forced to resort to occasional or "casual" prostitution to supplement inadequate incomes. Offering a potent commentary on the morals and manners of the time, those whose economic burdens were especially serious—perhaps they had children or ill, aging, and incapacitated family members to support—sometimes turned to "full" prostitution, the period's most lucrative profession for women, in order to meet their financial needs. Respectability forgotten in the struggle to survive, such women validated the stereotype linking the needleworking trades with prostitution; yet few social critics ventured to explore the socioeconomic dynamics underpinning the exploitation of these women in the period's economy. Martineau was one of the few who understood that economics, not immorality, lay at the root of the period's prostitution epidemic. The solution, she argued, resided in accepting women's need to work, in putting aside "the jealousy of men," and in helping women get the training they needed to find respectable employment through which they could earn a decent wage.

But men were not the only impediments to female industry: women themselves were also to blame for resistant attitudes toward working women. Martineau quotes the story of a shop owner who defied convention by hiring women to work at the counter of his mercer's (sewing notions) shop. Reasoning that women workers could surely measure and cut women's goods for women customers better than men could, the owner was surprised when business fell off as a result; interestingly, reinstating male sales clerks proved that women preferred doing business with men because they "could not trust the ability of their own sex. . . . [T]he ladies had no faith in female ability, even behind the counter" (1859b, 312). Given the increasing number of women employed in the public realm, which Martineau estimates at about one and one-quarter million, "The condition, claims, and prospects of such a section of the population ought to be as important and interesting to us as those of any class of men in the community" (320)—yet, curiously, they are not. The prejudicial social attitudes illustrated by women consumers refusing to buy from women clerks suggests how deeply ingrained is the inclination to devalue women's work and dismiss it as worthless or, worse, disreputable. This is exacerbated by the *theory* that conventional gendered divisions of labor are what distinguish unpaid from paid employment; in *practice,* a capitalist economy requires even women who work for pay also to work at home for free, an expectation not extended to their male counterparts.[34]

A typical rhetorical strategy of Martineau's is to point out the sensibleness of her argument, then to illustrate how certain people fail to perceive its logic—that readers may see themselves or someone they know in her example is gently implied—and finally, to offer a convincing example of the viability of the alternative perspective she proposes. The alternative she offers in "Female Industry" is the Lowell, Massachusetts, community of women sewing-factory workers. The four thousand cotton mill workers are so hardworking and self-sufficient that, together, they have built a church and a school and have established a periodical, the *Lowell Offering.* Despite their seventy-hour work weeks, these "literary spinsters"—she refers to their occupation, not their marital status—maintain neat, clean homes and tidy gardens, and they are always simply yet tastefully dressed; they read books, study music, and cultivate flowers, while "the Savings' Bank exhibits their provident habits" (323).[35]

Martineau contrasts the example of these New England factory girls with that offered in old England, where vulgar needlewomen scream "in the lane." Scrutinizing the sharp distinctions between the two, she concludes that it is not factory labor itself that "hardens and brutalizes the minds of men or women, but the state of ignorance in which they enter upon . . .[factory] life" (323). As she had noted in her introduction to "Mind amongst the Spindles" (1845), education and knowledge are what distinguish the cultivated from the vulgar, not economics or social standing. Emphasizing the synthesis of intellect and manual labor ("double work") underpinning the Lowell example, she characterizes these factory women as "wakeful and interested, all well-dressed and lady-like" (1845b). Compared with British needlewomen, the Lowell girls exhibit "superior culture. Their minds are kept fresh, and strong, and free by knowledge and power of thought; and this is the reason why they are not worn and depressed under their labours." She praises the "invigorating effects of MIND in a life of labour" as liberating, regardless of one's "outward circumstances."[36] Martineau's compulsion to make her writing instructive and informative reflects this conviction, yet her perspective on class standards is not without complications, either for Lowell's "literary spinsters" or for British needlewomen.

For example, the cultivated Lowell girls recite poetry and analyze Sunday sermons, while literature and music are their recreational activities. Betraying the middle-class association between femininity and respectability underpinning Victorian gender ideology, Martineau ponders, can English needlewomen be made as "womanly" as this? The very framing of this question radically equates education—rather than needlework—with feminine respectability, regardless of whether one sews for visual effect or for remuneration. But although the Lowell women are middle class in appearance and values and in the feminine accomplishments common to the leisure class, they are working class in terms of economic reality—they are, after all, confined within factories for seventy hours a week. Martineau praises the industry of these women, many of whom are working to put a brother through college or to pay off their father's mortgage, but remains silent about the likelihood that all this industry and accomplishment is for these women an end in itself, accomplished to serve someone other than themselves, and not the means for their own economic upward mobility.

As a solution to class and gender inequities, Martineau's combining middle-class cultivation and morality with working-class utility is a consistent theme throughout her writing, and it is both an innovative and a problematic one. Her alternative vision breaks through perceptions of class as innate and unchangeable, which is especially advantageous to the lower classes, who were assumed to be primitive and promiscuous. That the Lowell women prove to be not only educable but capable of cultivating aesthetic interests demonstrates Martineau's advocacy of wholesome domesticity along with education. But the Lowell example does not alter the fact that a lifetime of unrelenting hard labor does not compare with the leisured, graceful lifestyles bought by wealth and privilege. Perhaps a feasible explanation for the disparity lies in her implication that one *should* cultivate oneself (even if working class) and one *should also* work hard, keep busy, and practice thrift (even if wealthy). Martineau's idealistic example, comprised of the best qualities of both classes, serves as a model for a postindustrial society in which class privilege and class exploitation are less and less accepted as legitimate justification for social hierarchies.

While a compelling example, the Lowell community is utopian and unrealistic compared with the difficulties facing English needlewomen, who were often unemployed because of the sheer numbers of women desperate for work. If employed, they were overworked and grossly underpaid, enduring unhealthy working conditions with no job security or health or retirement benefits. Further, the ranks of poor and lower-class needlewomen swelled by an influx of middle-class women, like Martineau, whose sudden economic penury coupled with gentility created class divisions even among the unemployed. The situation of British needlewomen was further eroded by the cotton famine resulting from the American Civil War, causing the economic collapse of British mill towns. Another threat was the newly invented sewing machine, popular with factories and dressmaking establishments because it afforded cheap labor and required fewer "hands" to be employed (each machine replaces fifteen seamstresses, Martineau estimates). The sewing machine "will do great things," she predicts, but it will also "extinguish the craft of the poor needlewoman" (327). As the machines assume more refined sewing tasks through improved technology, and children replace women as a cheaper source of labor, needlewomen "can scarcely be worse off than at present" (328).[37]

According to Martineau, because the custom of teaching little girls how to sew resulted in great numbers of women seeking employment as needleworkers, the overabundance of workers diminished the quality of the work produced. She argues this claim from several standpoints: needlewomen are in serious straits and need immediate, practical solutions to their economic and employment problems. Given the many difficulties presented by the profession, her primary solution is that needlewomen learn other trades in which the demand for workers exceeds the supply—for example, watchmaking or china painting (as we now know, both options notorious for inspiring the "jealousy of men"). Women should have access to appropriate training and should not be prevented from employment on the basis of their sex. Another point concerns women's health, particularly their eyesight; women work for a pittance to serve the vanities of slaves of fashion, while the exploitation of "slopworkers" often results in their death.[38] What Martineau proposes is a complete revolution in the product and its production, calling for skilled needlewomen who know how to sew basic, well-fitted clothing for which they are not exploited and for which they are adequately paid.

Martineau posits that the needleworking trades are headed for extinction. Skilled needlewomen should be retained, while others should be trained in alternative occupations, including the operation of sewing machines; some should consider emigration while "the remnant of the poor sempstresses,—the last, we hope, of their sort" should come under the care of women philanthropists (328). Reminding readers of the specter of prostitution haunting working women, she argues that these "sempstresses" must be "kept out of the hands of the middleman . . . if some thousands of suffering women are to see their loathed occupation extinguished." Drawing on needleworking's popular analogy with morality, she notes that high-quality plain sewing is nearly a lost art, an art that some believe might be redeemed by instilling in its practitioners the moral virtues naturally accompanying meticulous work. This leads to a consideration of a report by School Inspector Norris, who recommends that half of the school day in girls' curriculums be spent practicing needlework, "for the sake of the effect on the girls' characters" (329). Needleworking creates the "quiet domestic aspect, . . . scrupulous cleanliness, . . . industry with repose, . . . cheerful relaxation of mind, . . . careful and decorous order . . . [by which] the character of the future woman is formed," Norris proclaims.

As evidence of the decline in both sewing quality and public morality, Norris notes with disapproval that girls who attend boys' classes show a marked *preference* for academic subjects and reject their sewing duties, indicating that they must be steered back to the needle and away from books for their own good. Thus is the practice of keeping girls occupied with needlework instead of challenged with academic subjects justified by the claim that sewing cultivates the moral and ethical virtues that will make them "good" wives and mothers.[39] The promotion of education reform for girls is not only suffused with the rhetoric of morality: it operates from the assumption that academics are antithetical to feminine morality and must be curbed for the sake of girls' morals and for the good of the nation. What Norris promotes is the sort of behavior management that trains the lower class to accept its penurious lot while embracing middle-class moral values: "as the girl is, so will the woman be; as the woman is, so will the home be; and as the home is, such, for good or for evil, will be the character of our population" (336). The nationalism implied by such a statement extends, as the century progresses, to incorporate the influence of domestic ideology over the entire British empire.[40]

Norris privileges girls' marriageability over education and employment, thus treating needleworking as part of education reform while drawing it into the service of the period's domestic ideology. His model curriculum offers girls less academic training than before, with more time devoted to sewing than to any other subject; in contrast, although herself an avid needlewoman, Martineau would never promote sewing at the expense of academics. However, she observes rather waggishly, Inspector Norris is a man, and it is women who "best know their own case" (336). Obstructions to women's progress must be removed at every level of society, from private family life to public institutions. Offering her own unique spin on nationalism, she concludes that women workers "will secure our welfare, nationally and in our home, to which few

elements can contribute more vitally and more richly than the independent industry of our countrywomen."[41]

Contrasting with the impressive historical scope of "Female Industry,"
the comprehensiveness of the issues it addresses, and its depth in discussing alternative occupations for needlewomen, Martineau's *Daily News*
articles on the plights of seamstresses target wealthy women and the husbands and fathers who pay their clothing bills. Thus, her focus shifts from
recuperating working-class women to educating women of the leisure class
about their role in the exploitation of needlewomen. Her 17 June 1856
leader boldly compares "the first and nobler Eve . . . in her native grace
and truth," whose nobility is evidenced by her desire for knowledge rather
than adornment, with "the last and degenerate Eve, masked beyond recognition" because enslaved by the tyranny of Paris fashions. Such "folly"
might be overlooked if it "left no calamitous results behind," but the tragic
conditions under which English needlewomen live and work as a result of
"continental despotism"—proving that "every fashion of dress has its martyrs"—amounts to a national disgrace. Offering an alternative appeal to
nationalism, Martineau rejects French fashions as fit only for "deformed
persons": "The question which concerns us is whether free England . . .
should condescend to mimic this barbarism of less happy countries. We
grieve that the ladies of England should embark in a competition beneath
their social standing." She concludes by evoking the cultural superiority
integral to Britain's great era of empire building:

> Would it not be more worthy of our free country, of our enlightened age, and
> of our national independence for our ladies to dress in some conformity with
> the principles of sense and taste, for the benefit of their own dignity, their
> husbands' fortunes, and the welfare of the working class, rather than to imi-
> tate and emulate the fantastic devices by which less happy societies strive to
> disguise and beguile their perils and their cares?

A daring strategy is to compare Queen Victoria with Florence Nightingale, two vastly different exemplars of aristocratic womanhood. The "fashionable follies" of some women, she observes pointedly, are directly responsible for the "depth of domestic offence" suffered by their
dressmakers. Martineau addresses "every woman, from the lady on the
throne to the shop-keeper's wife," asking that they—as rational beings
with hearts as well as brains—consider "the cruelty they inflict on everybody about them—by the selfish and hideous folly of their mode of dress."
She questions why, after the atrocities exposed in the reports of 1842 (parliamentary investigations published in "Blue Books") on the working conditions of needlewomen, exploitation of this group continues unabated:
"we profess compassion for needlewomen, and institute charities on their
behalf," yet fashions continue to be "ruinous to the dressmaking class" because of "ladies being in a hurry."[42] Since the concept of supply and

demand is central to theories of political economy, her approach targets those whose demand shapes the working conditions of needlewomen. Women who weep at the trials of protagonists in the latest sensation novels are, oddly, oblivious to the role they themselves play in destroying the lives of seamstresses by their selfish demands; compassion for real-life heroines, she charges, proves to be weakest in the rarified realm aristocratic women inhabit. Citing Victoria's power as a widely emulated and influential role model, Martineau asks: "Could not the first lady in the land be induced to sacrifice the lesser interests of the mode to the greater object of the lives and health of many thousands of dressmakers?" The query articulates publicly what she had noted earlier in a private letter:

> One grand fact is one which cannot be told publicly,—that the Queen has given an immense impulse to the evil . . . she was in such a desperate hurry for everything, and that, of course, made all other lofty ladies in a hurry too. She gave such short notice . . . that really her acquaintance had no choice between wearing old clothes and harassing the dress-makers. Many have been the deaths, and the losses of sight, and the lifelong shattering of health among dressmakers from the Queen's hurries.[43]

Distinct from her earlier reluctance openly to implicate the queen for perpetuating this damaging practice, the 1856 leader demonstrates no such reticence.

The June 1856 article concludes by offering a striking contrast between Victoria and her circle of fashionable ladies and Florence Nightingale who, herself of aristocratic birth, had just returned from nursing British soldiers fighting in the Crimea. Of fashionable ladies Martineau asks, "How can they look her in the face?" considering what she has accomplished, compared with the example of their own shallow lives. It is not dressmakers who are vulgar, as such women think, but the "frivolous women" themselves who are "vulgar in the highest sense." Martineau uses the opportunity to defend another maligned category of working women—nurses: "The women of whom Florence Nightingale is the exponent are at least equal to the highest class in London; while in the virtues and privileges of toil they are not surpassed by those who work for their bread." Referring to recent public debate on "the citizen character" of women, she observes that the plights of needlewomen prove that "so little fit" are upper-class women "for citizenship that they use such power as they have *to oppress*." As an antidote, she vows to continue exposing wrongs committed by wealthy women against needlewomen, the "victims of vanity, idleness, and pride."[44]

A more direct appeal to wealthy women, one that notably does not employ euphemisms, argues that, as a result of the demands of "the season,"[45] "scores and hundreds sink in sickness, in blindness, in madness, in death, from overwork at the needle. . . . [P]rostitution is fed by constant accessions from starved or overwearied dressmakers. . . . [T]he chief responsibility for this kind of suffering rests with the ladies" whose demands "regularly send a crowd of victims to the hospital, the brothel, the madhouse, and the grave" (*Daily News*, 13 January 1857). She observes that the sufferings of the dressmakers are well known, yet the system is perpetuated nonetheless: "The responsible parties, the fine ladies and their guardians, must . . . be prepared to answer for the fate of their victims." Claiming that the cost in human health and lives renders fashion as "barbarous as it is ugly," she concludes that "all men agree that there is no beauty in a style so far removed from nature and reason." Women who persist in wearing these fashions, in other words, do so for their own selfish vanity rather than to please men.[46]

On 26 June 1863 Martineau again targeted the role of Queen Victoria in the perpetuation of needlewomen's exploitation, particularly her capacity, as the most influential public woman in the world, to reverse that trend. She notes that Victoria read the "Report on the Condition of Our Dressmakers" published twenty years before, finding "something strange and almost incredible in the mode of life of the women who made the dresses which came to court." The report links the sufferings of needlewomen with the orders of their upper-class customers, yet such practices continue unabated. This was most recently evidenced by the death of a milliner, whose quarters during "the season" were so cramped and airless that she died from asphyxiation: "These are the things that are happening twenty years after that awakening which was to put an end to such enormities for ever. What, then, is to be done?" Rejecting gradual reforms in favor of "an explosion . . . which will astonish the world," Martineau proposes police intervention to expose the unhealthy and life-threatening environments of workrooms and to hold employers legally responsible for the deaths of their workers. Victoria "has only to speak her thought to shame or animate every customer of the West-end milliners"; of the more dramatic solution, police intervention, she concedes that "There is much evil in all such interference of law with private arrangements," yet in the absence of voluntary self-regulation, it becomes a necessary evil.

Whereas some of her *Daily News* articles on this issue assign culpability to upper-class women, others consider various points of view to demonstrate the complexity of the problem. Martineau systematically queries each party involved: "*What say the workwomen?* They say they must live, and by their needle. . . . They did not make the system; and the immediate consequence of any complaint would be their being thrown out of it" (*Daily News*, 19 January 1865). No protective trade organization exists by which they can petition for improved working conditions, much less to strike. "*What say the employers?* . . . They say they are in the hands of their customers . . . [and] they cannot get their bills paid." The "long-credit" system by which women take the clothing before paying for it directly affects the dressmakers since employers cannot pay workers if they themselves have not been paid. Finally, "*What say the customers?*" who are "shocked at all the overwork they hear of, and compassionate to all the spinal disease, blindness, consumption and nervous fever?" They deny personal responsibility but "Everybody knows that the customers are the dominant power in the shopping world."[47] Blame does not rest solely with the consumers but also with the men who pay their bills, since women of this or any class rarely control family finances. Envisioned as a complex process, some relief is possible if bills are paid on time so that employers may pay their seamstresses, who can then survive without resorting to prostitution.

Several articles highlight the activities of the London Dressmaking Company (LDC), an organization determined to meet the question of exploited needlewomen on practical terms: those of commerce. The LDC aimed to change the customary "long-credit" system as well as the problem of health-breaking overwork by limiting workers' hours and, daringly, refusing to accept dressmaking orders that could not be completed in a reasonable amount of time. Martineau is, as always, enthusiastic about schemes designed to remedy specific social problems, concluding "Here, then, is the opening through which it may be seen whether the pity and sorrow of English-women for the dressmakers is sincere and practical" (*Daily News*, 5 May 1864). A subsequent article on these "friends of the dressmakers" features a status report on the activities of the LDC, whose initial shareholders were also its customers, tangible proof of the efficacy of the enterprise. Demonstrating that reform is viable, association members were "as well dressed as anybody at the next drawing-room . . . [yet] have an easy mind about the people they have been employing": "No girl has sat up sewing through the night for them; nobody's eyes are the worse for them; no toil has been incurred for them which makes the illicit protection of selfish men—temporary and fatal as it is—too strong a temptation to be resisted." As a positive prototype, the LDC has the potential to eradicate the insidious long-credit system burdening other trades as well: "the influence of the company in substituting short for long credits between any class of tradespeople and their customers may carry blessings to other overpressed and sorely tempted orders of workers" (*Daily News*, 13 February 1865).

The invention of the sewing machine of course generated concern among various interest groups. Financially strapped needlewomen feared losing their positions, sewing establishments anticipated cheaper labor and faster production, and some working women sought alternative employment options. Martineau observes that, in an age notable for advanced technology, this machine is of "deep significance" to the period's shifting class and gender roles (*Daily News*, 31 August 1853). She first rejects the claim that sewing machines are responsible for the notorious poverty of needlewomen, since that has "existed from time immemorial" and then disputes that the machines foster unemployment, since "there are many employments remaining to be opened to women, much better for themselves and for society than driving the needle." She heralds the invention, like that of the "apparatus for washing by steam" (washing machine), as essential for freeing women from unnecessary drudgery and "unwholesome occupation." She focuses on the health issues associated both with the intensive sewing done by professional needleworkers and, echoing Mary Wollstonecraft, by women of leisure whose sewing serves a less tangible function. "There is something," she argues, "in the employment of driving the needle which makes it pernicious, even to the lady at ease in her drawing-room. . . . It seems clear that the day has arrived for sewing to be transferred from the human to the inanimate machine."

The release from drudgery promised by the sewing machine prompts Martineau to consider the present and future generations of women who work inside and outside the home, and to anticipate the establishment of working women's colleges to provide training in alternative occupations. On a distinctly feminist note, she concludes: "During the present rise in the social value of the human being, women are likely to be among the first to benefit." The timing of the advent of the sewing machine, in other words, could not be more perfect as women move away from unwholesome, redundant occupations and into healthier, more useful ones. Although offering little comfort to the "distressed needlewomen" now facing occupational transitions, the invention promises to decrease women's enslavement to the needle at home: "The sewing machine will soon put an end to the wasteful and unhealthy devotion of the greater part of women's time in domestic life to the needle" (*Daily News*, 9 January 1860).[48]

Martineau reviews another social reform organization, the Society for Promoting the Employment of Women, which solicited funds "to carry a certain number of unemployed needlewomen *of the higher class* through the winter" (*Daily News*, 18 February 1864). Martineau is consistent in her critique of this sort of "mischievous" charity, arguing that handouts offer only temporary solutions at best and at worst encourage false security; either way, charity avoids more substantial, long-term solutions. Further, the class considerations of the organization serve as a disturbing reminder that there is a pecking order even among the ranks of the unemployed and homeless, a category in which women occupy the lowest rung yet contend with other women for the few handouts and jobs available. Hovering over all are the persistent "perils [that] beset the course of young women who are idle by compulsion while hungering for bread," a dark reminder of needleworking's link with prostitution. The working women's colleges she glowingly anticipated in the 1853 leader have not yet become a reality; and, although she anticipates "cheerful study" in many academic fields, including, radically, "matters eminently important to women" like health, physiology, and economics, the discussion continues in future, not present, tense. Nevertheless, this leader, too, concludes on a strikingly feminist note, as she encourages liberal arts curricula designed to "enlighten and elevate the whole mind, and thus to raise the students to a higher rank not only of occupation, but of intelligence and character."[49]

Writing of avenues suitable for sociological inquiry in 1837, Martineau had observed: "I would only ask of philanthropists of all countries to inquire of physicians what is the state of health of sempstresses; and to judge thence whether it is not inconsistent with common humanity that women should depend for bread upon such employment. Let them inquire what is the recompense of this kind of labour, and then wonder if they can that the pleasures of the licentious are chiefly supplied from that class" (Martineau 1837, 306–7). Over twenty years later, "The Needlewoman: Her Health" (1860), published in *Once a Week,* rehearses these themes by focusing on employment-related health issues. Although the state of "distressed needlewomen" is deplorable, she asserts that "we may consider their position as already ameliorated by the introduction of the sewing-machine" (1860d, 596). In a negative comparison of humans with machines, she reiterates the inevitability of social transition in terms of employment: "It must be a mercy to stop the working of human machines, driven by the force of hunger, and disordered by misery. If the work can be done by an inanimate machine, it ought to be so done; and if the poor women ask what is to become of them, the answer is, that their lot really could not be made worse; while, for a large proportion of them, the new machine is an actual redemption." This article articulates more emphatically than the others the notion that needlewomen are literally a dying breed, not only because their trades are being transformed by technology but also because the ruthless demands of these professions as traditionally practiced compromise women's health, leading frequently to blindness and death. Martineau outlines the confined environments, poor nutrition, and lack of sleep, air, and exercise common to these trades, suggesting remedies that could easily be implemented in even the busiest workrooms. Because needlewomen are readily distinguishable by their outward appearance and carriage—"The eyes have a dead look . . . [and] the anxiety of the countenance tells the tale of an unnatural mode of life" (599)—, she urges: "We must not stop in our improvements till needlewomen are indistinguishable from the rest of the world on the ground of health."

The issues pertinent to women's health and emotional well-being—economics, prostitution, education, and employment—scrutinized in her writings on needlewomen demonstrate the ideological considerations of Martineau's interest in this primarily female occupation. Given the period's resistance to changing gender roles, her feminism—with its focus on women's economic autonomy, whether they are attached to a man or not—is quite radical. Martineau's needleworking articles illustrate that education is the primary motif underpinning her social criticism: educating upper-class women about the effects of their fashionable follies, upper-class men about the effects of the "long-credit" system and about the fates of seduced and abandoned needlewomen, philanthropists about the limitations of charity, employers about the destructiveness of exploitative working conditions, and needlewomen about alternative occupations that will enable them to be self-sufficient as well as intellectually stimulated. The image of Martineau committing poetry and political economy to memory during interminable hours of sewing during girlhood continues to provide an instructive lesson for those who would understand her idiosyncratic approach to Woman's Cause.[50]

## Fancywork: Social-Problem Sewing

As these examples show, Martineau's personal relationships with needle and pen coalesced in her writings on the plights of needlewomen. The dynamic was reflected in her private life, when prolonged illness periodically compelled her to relinquish her role as a woman of the press and rely on the needle as her medium for activism. Throughout her life she was a tireless advocate of social causes, although the state of her health often dictated whether her contributions would be literary or needlework. Her nearly seven years' invalidism spent in Tynemouth during the 1840s marked a period of seclusion contrasting markedly with the previous, career-making decade of writing and traveling. At such times, fancywork is a "solace to invalids and sorrowful people," she asserts. As an invalid, "my needle has been an inestimable blessing to me. . . . a tranquillising, equalising influence, conservative and restorative" (1860d, 597). More than a craft, needlework is an art for which she demands respect, "over and above mere toleration," and she rejects the hierarchy in which art is considered superior to craft: "If I say that it is somewhat like the gratification of the artist, I shall be told that it is infinitely better to paint or draw. . . . Each is good in its own place; and . . . I claim for the much abused fancywork (I include woolwork) . . . some respect." A letter to Elizabeth Barrett during the Tynemouth period reveals Martineau's profound attachment to her needleworking projects: "I am mourning over the approaching completion of a very long piece of woolwork which is to bring in a good lot of dollars for my abolitionist friends in America at their next fair" (Kelley and Hudson 1990, 8:248). Neither illness nor literary commitments superceded her affinity for needlework, wrote Florence Fenwick Miller, since "Not even in the busiest time of her literary life did she ever entirely cease to exercise her skill in this feminine occupation. In fact, she made wool-work her artistic recreation" (quoted in Cone and Gilder 1887, 51).

An 1840 letter to Chapman indicates the extent to which illness prevented Martineau from writing: "Garrison brings you 2 [pounds] from me, which I have earned by my needle for your society, being fond of fancy work, and fit only for it, in this my invalid state. . . . [T]here is in me no lack of willingness to serve our cause in any capacity" (Chapman 1877, 233).[51] Her letter to Catherine Macready expresses unqualified relief in giving up writing for needlework for the first time in ten years: "My dear friend, you cannot imagine how I enjoy my rest from the pen. I corrected my very last proof on Sunday night, and I feel pretty thoroughly sure that *I shall never write again.* You would be amused to see me, day after day, making baby-things for my sister Ellen" (emphasis added).[52] Similarly, a letter to Bulwer-Lytton asserts that "work" now refers primarily to needle-work—"how we women have the advantage in that blessed needlework!—besides which, mine stocks my charity purse," while in another to Elizabeth Barrett she confesses, "I . . . in shameful truth prefer needlework to all other pursuits whatever" (Sanders 1990, 83, 99). But this was not the first or the last time Martineau underestimated the physical tenacity overruling her various maladies: she was to live and write and sew for over thirty more years.

Martineau was especially fond of Berlin wool working, producing a piece Chapman singled out for praise: "[A] really remarkable piece of work, both for its great beauty and the amount of time bestowed upon it, was a table-cover, 'the four seasons,' of Berlin wool wrought into fruits and flowers, which was . . . the means of raising one hundred dollars for the cause" (1877, 246). Martineau was delighted to learn that the item was purchased for her friend Mrs. Charles Follen, widow of the German-born abolitionist at the forefront of the early American movement: "So many of my thoughts and feelings . . . are wrought into that table-cover, that I dreaded lest it should pass into unknown hands. But now—How much pleasure this has given me!" (332). Her assertion that the piece was as meaningful to her for the "thoughts and feelings" sewn into its fabric as for its material value in supporting "our cause" highlights the idea that, for Martineau, the needle-and-pen interaction involved more than merely outward signs of conformity with or resistance to social norms. Her comment suggests that both modes of communicating are necessary for her well-being and that together they comprise a network of expression that allows this exceptionally prolific mind the "need of utterance" it craves.[53]

Of Berlin wool work, Martineau's preferred medium, Roszika Parker writes that it "was the century's most successful commercial embroidery venture. . . . The patterns were promoted as 'tasteful' and the embroidery as 'easy.'" Yet this needlework was denigrated even as it was presented as a model for decorum: wool work "was both heavily promoted and constantly ridiculed" (1984, 170–71). Reflecting this tendency to devalue women's fancywork, Chapman observed that some "wondered how the great authoress could bear such a frivolous occupation," although she added that, during raffles, "the names most illustrious in the worlds of rank and philanthropy were rivalling each other" for possession of Martineau's needlework (1877, 332).

Interestingly, Martineau's recovery from the Tynemouth illness did not signal an instant return to writing, at least at her former pace. An 1846 letter to Elizabeth Barrett reveals a profound shift in her perspectives on work, personal well-being, and public duty. As she returns to literary productivity, she notes:

It is my desire to keep up that union of practical domestic life with literary labour which has been such a blessing to me ever since I held the pen; . . . I have a horror of a mere booklife;—or a life of books and society. I like and need to have some express and daily share in somebody's comfort: and I trust to find much peace and satisfaction as a housekeeper, in making my maids happy, and perhaps a little wiser . . . and in that sort of strenuous handwork which I like better than authorship. I am fond of [domestic activities] and across all these things, I see a pleasant prospect of congenial work. (Kelley and Lewis 1994, 12:52)

Part of her healing, apparently, included only a gradual return to literary labors, this time carefully tempered by a healthy balance of practical domesticity and intellectual pursuits. Her concern to strike a balance between the two indicates a radical shift in perspective stemming from her joyous release from the sickroom and evidenced in the philosophical quests of the 1840s and 1850s.

Eventually, improved health led her to move increasingly away from the needle toward the pen: "I have now to write a tale," she wrote to Chapman, "a little book for our great League Bazaar,—being too well and busy to do the fancy-work I had intended to send." She quips, "It is all I can do 'to keep my stockings mended'" (Chapman 1877, 244). Chapman explains Martineau's allusion to conservative abolitionists who, confronted by the double threat of social activists who are also women, demanded they give up political agitating and return to their homes: "Go spin, you jade, go spin! Better be mending your stockings!" No doubt the two friends—whose political activism was inseparable from their needleworking—shared a good laugh over the delicious irony of such an attitude, leveled as it was against women who refused to "suffer and be still."[54]

Martineau's second major illness paralleled the intensification of abolitionist activities in America during the 1850s. During this period she earned "lots of money" for the cause by producing fancywork, boasting defiantly, "I never countenance philosophers in contempt of fancy-work." Although Berlin wool work was now unfashionable, she continued to produce it, insisting, "I am equal to this sort of work, and not to anything requiring more sight and more attention. . . . If it brings you any dollars, well and good. If not, and you will kindly accept a rejected bit of work, do keep it, my dear friend, in memory of me."[55] Proud that her table covering "fetched 100 dollars for 'the cause' in America," she was also pleased to learn that it was purchased by "the chivalry"—abolitionist friends—who "presented it to my dearest friend,—Mrs. Chapman. Prettily done,—was it not?" (Sanders 1990, 141).

Some of her needlework was destined simply to brighten the lives of friends closer to home: "I am embroidering a cushion for [a friend] . . . bent on economy and plainness in every way; and I mean that she shall have one gay and pretty thing in her drawing room" (Sanders 1990, 141).

Florence Nightingale, expressing curiosity about this absorbing occupation, received a cushion worked by her fellow invalid, who wrote: "If you but once rest your honoured head against it, how pleased I shall be! . . . I am sure you will be so kind as to accept what I have had such pleasure in working for you." No needlewoman herself, Nightingale was "really overcome with the beauty of your present" and its proof "of your care and thoughts for me"; she expressed concern about the "trouble and fatigue it must have been to you." As a consummate needlewoman, Martineau especially appreciated a needleworked gift, like a cambric handkerchief from her niece Spring, which she vowed to use for an unusual, though characteristic, purpose: "I shall use it directly, and with great pleasure. . . . I have begun a large piece of woolwork, of a beautiful pattern: and it requires something soft to fold up in it, to prevent the canvas rubbing the wool. I shall cover it with this handkerchief and then I shall see it as I am working, and shall think of you: for I love your dear Papa's and Mama's little girl."[56]

During this second major period of invalidism, Martineau admitted:

> I have always had some piece of fancy-work on hand,—usually for the benefit of the Abolition fund in America; and I have a thoroughly womanish love of needle-work,—yes, even ('I own the soft impeachment') of wool-work, many a square yard of which is all invisibly embossed with thoughts of mine wrought in, under the various moods and experiences of a long series of years. It is with singular alacrity that, in winter evenings, I light the lamp, and unroll my wool-work, and meditate or dream. (1983, 2:414)

Although her attitude toward needlework is "thoroughly womanish," her words reveal that the very act of sewing signals a meditative mode, a virtual dream state concealed by the outward appearance of availability expected of respectable women. Rather than being distracted from her inner life as a result of the perpetual busyness demanded of women, Martineau early learned to adapt outward social rituals to serve her inner needs. Sewing represented various ideas to her: it offered a socially legitimate way to withdraw into her private thoughts and a time to study literature and plan writing projects; it had a practical use as a necessary domestic skill that could also be turned into remunerative employment should the need arise; and it signaled respectability, propriety, and gentility, each stitch confirming the decorous morality of the seamstress. Maria Weston Chapman evokes an image of Martineau that fittingly incorporates all of these factors: "indeed, as she sat in thought at her daily hour of rest, with her Berlin embroidery by her side, and her beautiful hands (hands that the rod of empire might have swayed!) folded across the newspaper on her knee, her whole presence instinct with high thinking and good-will, her whole expression so full of restful activity, it would have been difficult to find so impressive yet fascinating a presence" (1877, 272). Dinah Muloch Craik's praise of the needle as "a wonderful brightener and consoler; our weapon of defence against slothfulness, weariness and sad thoughts" (Parker 1984, 150) seems more appropriate to Martineau's experience than Elizabeth Cady Stanton's oddly phallic depiction of the needle as a "one-eyed demon of destruction."[57]

But even her high regard for needleworking was not without complications. Evidencing the conflict between literature and needlework seemingly inevitable for a strong-minded woman, Charlotte Brontë's Shirley Keeldar is "just about as tenacious of her book as she is lax of her needle" (Brontë 1966, 373). Martineau did not admit to this mutual exclusivity until late in life, when she openly expressed resentment against the occupation that claimed so much of her time. What proved to be her third and final major illness coincided with the intensification of another important social issue compelling her participation: the campaign to repeal the Contagious Diseases Acts.[58] Initially a prominent figure in the campaign, for which she circulated petitions, wrote articles, and generated support among influential people, the aging Martineau, because of declining health, ceded leadership in the repeal movement to social purity reformist Josephine Butler.

But, unwilling to abdicate what she termed obedience to "the inward witness," Martineau continued to contribute to the contagious diseases cause through needleworked projects. In a letter to Butler enclosed with her contribution for a fund-raising bazaar, she observed, "I assure you very earnestly that no one can be more thoroughly aware than I am that this is the very lowest method of assisting the movement. I can only say that I have adopted it simply because, in my state of health, no other is open to me. While you and your brave sisters in the enterprise have been enduring exhausting toils . . . I have been content to ply my needle when I could do no better" (Chapman 1877, 436–37). What makes her comments so striking is the assertion that needleworking is unequivocally inferior to writing— "the very lowest method"—which she undertakes only when ill health leaves her no other choice. Echoing her retort pronounced early in her career—"I would depend upon my needle . . . when I found I could not do better, and not before"—her words imply that her fondness for sewing, at least when dictated by ill health, is eagerly subordinated to a more efficacious means of articulation—her pen.

Yet the course of her career challenges her 1832 assertion that the pen is superior to the needle and "no other means of action in politics are in a woman's power." As a writer, Martineau's persistent presence in social and political realms established new conditions for exercising women's power during the Victorian era. But needlework served her political activism just as surely as writing did, giving her a decided edge over her male colleagues, who were denied the outlet of needleworking by social custom. At this late juncture, no doubt, resentment against the inconvenient debilities of old age underlay her stitches. "It was no dream I indulged in over my work," she noted, marking this instance as a distinct departure from those times in her life when needleworking was a welcome respite that fostered thoughts and dreams, rather than symbolizing physical defeat. She envisioned the campaign's successful outcome being tangibly worked into each stitch of this alternative text; she urges hope "as we ply our task, whether our labours be as high and arduous as yours, or as humble as mine" (Chapman 1877, 437). Although Martineau defended needleworking in theory and in practice, she also, somewhat ambivalently, perpetuated what I have called the false dichotomy that presents the pen as superior to the needle. Viewed in the context of Victorian gender relations and the values attached to them, she was of course correct.

Josephine Butler observed that even in her last days, Martineau "was always deeply interested in hearing in conversation the progress of our movement. . . . [H]er last finished piece of wool-work (her great relaxation) was the top of an ottoman" intended to be sold for the cause (Chapman 1877, 490). The piece, which was purchased for Butler by the Ladies National Association in the name of "The Martineau Memorial Fund," raised 156 pounds for the cause. Butler seems attuned to the idea that Martineau's needlework was not mechanical or mindless but "wrought with so many of my thoughts and feelings," as this admiring letter acknowledges: "Your ottoman, Mrs. Martineau, now stands in our drawing room looking brilliant, and useful and comfortable. It is much admired, and we tell with pride, who worked it. . . . [T]he amount of work in it . . . makes me feel myself unworthy that you should have bestowed so many precious stitches on me, . . . I love and value it with a peculiar tenderness."[59] Just before her death, Martineau wrote: "I must knit diligently. The baby has come (to a friend of my niece Harriet) before the blanket for the bassinet is ready" (Chapman 1877, 451). Chapman notes that her last finished work "was a cot blanket, knitted for a neighbour's baby, born on the 23d of January" (457). Illustrating her tenacity in both needleworking and literary realms, John Nevill adds, "when wool-work grew to be too great a strain on her eyes, she contented herself by knitting cot-blankets, one of which she left unfinished at the time of her death" (1943, 122), along with various unfinished writing projects.

The intersections of creativity and domesticity exemplified by Martineau's shifts between needle and pen provide a means for exploring gender and authorial identities as they coalesced in her life and work. She epitomized "The ease and mastery of a thorough needlewoman, who works out her thought on her materials," and for whom literary work and needlework were related activities (Martineau 1860c, 597). Perhaps needlework ensured Martineau the respectability potentially compromised by the suggestive innuendoes of "jealous" male literary colleagues; perhaps it offered proof that a strong-minded woman could also be feminine; perhaps sewing helped qualify her more outlandish nonconformities by asserting her claim to morality and decorum; or perhaps, as she claims, she simply was "excessively fond" of needlework, despite its inferiority to writing.

That the countless lengths of needlework Martineau produced over the course of her life were "invisibly embossed" with her thoughts provides a rich metaphor for her life and career. Far from a mindless activity or an empty social ritual, sewing for her manifested the creative and intellectual processes also expressed in her writing, a process yielding complex insights through the meditative state natural to sewing.

While Elizabeth Gaskell advocated cultivating the "Individual Life" somehow sandwiched between domestic chores, and Jane Austen carefully concealed it, subversively, under half-stitched muslin, Martineau claimed for herself the privacy denied most women by retreating to her interior realm protected by the emblem signifying propriety: her sewing. Each word she wrote, like every stitch she sewed, contributed to weaving the tapestry of her life: "I am oppressed with ideas and glad to find a vent anywhere," she wrote excitedly in 1832 at the start of a long and prolific career.[60] If her needlework was invisibly embossed with her unarticulated thoughts, her writing represents the linguistic translation of those thoughts. The dynamic interplays between needle and pen, fabric and page, texts of stitches and of words together reveal the mysteries of a silkwoman whose "need of utterance" was so compelling that its expression required articulate and inarticulate modes alike.

# 3

## America's Martyr Age and Reign of Terror

She was born to be a destroyer of slavery, in whatever form, in whatever place, all over the world, wherever she saw or thought she saw it.

—Florence Nightingale

The accident of my arriving in America in the dawning hour of the great conflict accounts for the strange story I have had to tell about myself.

—Harriet Martineau

I laughed more in the two years I was there than in all the 30 preceding.

—Harriet Martineau

### The Brewing of the American Storm

• Of the time in which she lived, Harriet Martineau observed with characteristic candor that there was a great deal to be said, and that she was more or less the person to say it. One of her primary literary and political interests was her lifelong fascination with the theory and practice of the American "experiment" as outlined in the Declaration of Independence and the Constitution: individual freedom, social equality, and political representation. From the travel journals published as a result of her 1834–1836 American tour to the hundreds of *Daily News* leaders and periodical articles about the Civil War and related issues written over a span of thirty years, Martineau's commitment to "my dearly-beloved Americans" is central to her identity as a writer and social reformist.[1] Indeed, her American experiences early established the ideological basis for a body of work guided by her desire to eradicate slavery in its various forms: racial slavery, seen in her abolition-themed writings; sexual slavery, illustrated by her focus on worldwide oppressions of women; and social slavery, demonstrated by her aim to educate the working classes about the forces creating and perpetuating their economic exploitation. Florence Nightingale's shrewd eulogistic assessment of her friend's overarching philosophy as a "destroyer of slavery" aptly mirrors every aspect of Martineau's life and career.

The first two publications resulting from Martineau's American tour were *Society in America* (1837) and *Retrospect of Western Travel* (1838). Both English and American observers keenly anticipated her assessments of American society, travel writing being one of the most popular genres of the period and Martineau being the most influential woman of the hour. *Society in America* aims at serious sociological analysis that measures America's practice against its stated principles, thus challenging genre expectations by offering scientific method rather than descriptive "picture writing." Although she stood by her innovative approach in *Society in America,* which she later claimed was better suited to an American audience, Martineau wrote *Retrospect of Western Travel* to satisfy readers (primarily British) interested more in entertainment than in analyses. My purpose in this chapter is to focus not on the American travel writing itself but on critical responses to *Society in America* and on her subsequent writing about slavery.[2] Of particular interest are two lesser-known texts: "Slavery in America" (1838), a southerner's critical response to *Society in America* that illustrates the pro-slavery attitudes and rationalizations shaping America's great civil conflict; and *The Martyr Age of the United States* (1839), Martineau's overview of the abolitionist movement that demonstrates her early affinity for the historical and biographical writing that characterizes her later career. Finally, a survey of selected articles, letters, and reviews written for the periodical press demonstrates the impressive range of Martineau's expertise in analyzing the complex issues related to slavery. I have chosen these texts because of their capacity to illustrate her cultural impact through her writing on this issue and to trace her growth as an abolitionist thinker and writer over the course of her career. My aim is first, more fully to establish her reputation as a highly influential voice to whom people from all levels of British and American society, regardless of their ideological persuasions, looked for insight, and second, to recuperate the remarkable status she enjoyed—both as a woman and a foreigner—as one of the most vocal participants in the transatlantic slavery debates. Critics praised or condemned Martineau, from the abolitionists who venerated her long after her death to those who, perceiving her politics as a threat to the South's "peculiar institution," threatened her life when they could not destroy her professional reputation. Either way, few in that era remained indifferent to her immense political influence. Martineau's assertion that her association with America "accounts for" her own history indicates that an analysis of this relationship is essential to a comprehensive picture of her life and work.

Martineau's symbiotic affiliation with American people and ideology was early proved by the intensity with which her favor was courted by

both pro-slavers and anti-slavers. Although at the time of her tour her reputation rested primarily on only one literary success, the *Illustrations of Political Economy,* Americans recognized the influential capacity of the "little, deaf
woman from Norwich" and opened their doors to her—or, in some cases,
shut them—accordingly.[3] Maria Weston Chapman noted that "What the old
over-civilised world would think of it all"—"it" referring to the American experiment in general and the slavery issue in particular—"was the natural
anxiety on both sides. Harriet Martineau was the representative to all, of the
mother country, which stood to them as the representative of civilisation"
(1877, 127).[4] But as the history of Anglo-American relations demonstrates,
not all Americans continued to regard Britain as the "mother country," and
there were many whose only interest in England concerned the economic
effects of its legislative policies on American institutions like slavery.

Neutrality on the slavery issue, even in a foreigner, was simply not an
option, and because her reputation as an abolitionist sympathizer preceded her, Martineau quickly found herself in a position of declaring publicly her stand on slavery. Although she professed her desire only to observe and specifically to stay out of American politics, she was early
marked as an important ally for whichever side could succeed in claiming
her support. Perhaps overstating the case a bit, she claimed: "I was a well-
known anti-slavery writer before I thought of going to America; and my
desire to see the operation of the system of Slavery could hardly be
wrongly interpreted by any one who took an interest in my proceedings"
(1983, 2:17).[5] Her remark reveals a disparity between the objectivity required of a social observer and her subjective commitment to the eradication of slavery. This conflict of interests is more fully revealed in the circumstances surrounding, first, her unusual decision to travel to America,
and second, the publication of her travel books.

Following the tremendous expenditure of energy required by her
marathon composition of the *Illustrations,* Martineau's decision to travel to
America seems more like a compulsion to experience another monumental
challenge than to rest from intensive labors. Despite her assertion that "My
first desire was for rest," she also posited that "it would be good for me to
'rough it' for a while, before I grew too old and fixed in my habits for such
an experiment" (1983, 2:3). The physical demands alone of such a journey
were formidable at the time, yet Martineau seemed revived by the very nov-
elty of the enterprise and, perhaps, piqued by its potential for danger.[6] Her
decision to visit America instead of the "beaten track" of the more conventional European tour seems surprisingly random, apparently prompted by
Lord Henley's observation that the Americans "have got at principles of justice and mercy in their treatment of the least happy classes of society which
we should do well to understand. Will you not go, and tell us what they
are?" (Martineau 1983, 1:270).[7] According to the *Autobiography,* this suggestion determined her destination and sealed her fate as a key writer on one of
the most pressing social problems of the century. Although she apparently

had no further relationship with Henley, his mild prompting at this pivotal moment in Martineau's life had profound consequences on her career.

But Martineau had, in fact, been thinking of an American tour well before Henley's suggestion in 1834, as her letter to William Tait a year earlier indicates. She proposed not only to undertake this journey but also to write the definitive account of the country: "If I am spared to come back, this country shall know something more than it does of the *principles* of American institutions. I am tired of being left floundering among the details which are all that . . . a Hall or a Trollope can bring away. . . . What I have said seems presumptuous. But the thing should be done, and I will do it."[8] Perhaps the contradiction may be explained by Martineau's lifelong compulsion to record, analyze, and publish her experiences, a tendency consistent with the period's valuation of empiricism and the philosophy of self-help. Yet Martineau's travel writing carefully distinguishes between self-revelation and the scientific understanding of, as she puts it, the *principles* by which Americans live. Highlighting Martineau's early affinity for journalism, Maria Frawley terms her travel writing "like investigative reporting," an idea illustrated by the dual publication of her travel journals: *Society in America,* designed to "test [America's] reality . . . against its ideals" through formal, public-oriented analysis, and *Retrospect of Western Travel,* offering a more personal memoir (1992, 14). Her assertion in *How to Observe Morals and Manners*—"what work on earth is more serious than this of giving an account of the most grave and important things which are transacted on this globe?" (1838a, 28)—emphasizes the moral and utilitarian underpinnings of all her literary enterprises.

An immensely popular genre of the period, travel writing tended to be descriptive rather than analytical, based on physical details that afforded little insight into cultural mores and social institutions. Prompted by her belief that a culture's deepest workings are revealed in its treatment of its most marginalized members, such as women, children, slaves, and immigrants, Martineau focused on American principles to emphasize the need for more in-depth analysis as a prelude to sociological understanding: "To test the morals and manners of a nation by a reference to the essentials of human happiness, is to strike at once to the centre, and to see things as they are" (1838a, 26). An essential part of how things are is the domestic realm, making her dual focus on public and private institutions innovative and, of course, controversial. Fresh from her first popular success as the writer of a series grounded in critical social analysis, she rightly perceived herself as the most likely candidate to provide a more substantial account of America than was currently available.[9] Perhaps, too, part of the appeal of such a lengthy journey was its promise of relief from family discord. Of her stressful state prior to the American tour she notes that, having been born with "a most beggarly set of nerves," she strove to cope with domestic tensions "but I could not hold my health and nerve" (1983, 1:251). Her subdued observation that friends "counselled my leaving home for a considerable time, for the welfare of all who lived in that home" (2:3) attests to the likelihood that family friction also contributed to her decision.

Accounts of the motivation behind publishing her travel journals are as contradictory as the differing explanations for what prompted her to travel to America. Despite her vow to write the definitive book on America, the *Autobiography* offers another perspective. Martineau goes to great lengths to justify publication while vigorously denying any original intention to do so: "I can truly say that I travelled without any such idea in my mind" (1983, 2:3). She refused all publishing advances and contracts offered before the trip, arguing, "I am sure that no traveller seeing things through author spectacles, can see them as they are." She drafted *How to Observe Morals and Manners* only to "oblige" a friend while en route to America; serving as a set of standards by which to assess social and cultural institutions, the book is today regarded as a pioneering tract of sociological methodology. It proved useful, of course, as a framework for ordering the varied experiences she encountered in America. As an inveterate journal writer who kept careful records of the people, places, and events of her tour, Martineau was incapable of looking through anything *but* "author spectacles," which is evidenced by the empirical orientation of much of her writing.

Following intense clamoring among interested publishers before leaving England, throughout her tenure in America, and on her return to England, she finally agreed to publish with Saunders and Otley. By way of explanation, she remarked, somewhat lamely, that rereading her journals simply led her to change her mind about her determination not to publish. The popular success of *Society in America* in 1837 led to the writing and publishing of a third book the following year, *Retrospect of Western Travel*.[10] "The other book succeeds so well," she wrote to William Fox, "that the publishers urge me to yield to the desire of the public, and give my personal narrative. There is no reason better than false delicacy for refusing; and so I am doing it" (Burchell 1995, 46–47). The disparity created by these varying accounts may never be resolved, although she was right to anticipate that the public's advance knowledge of impending publication would compromise both her observations and what Americans would permit her to witness.[11] Whatever her motivations, Martineau's significant contributions to Victorian travel writing offer an important resource for students of the period; as she herself was aware, witnessing America's "martyr age" was of such international import as to compel the publication of memoirs destined to instruct, to inform, and to influence public opinion on both sides of the Atlantic.

Martineau's abolitionist sympathies predate her American tour, as her early writing reveals. Susan Hoecker-Drysdale notes that her Unitarian background accounts for her early tendency toward abolitionism, citing her critique of slavery in several 1830 reviews (1992, 65). Slavery issues also find expression in an *Illustrations* tale, "Demerara" (1832), the primary source for which she was known as an anti-slavery advocate before the

American tour.[12] Martineau cast the plights of blacks enslaved on a British West Indies sugar plantation as both immoral, in terms of human rights, and illogical, in terms of political economy. "Demerara" dramatizes not only the sufferings of blacks but also the demoralization of whites through a system whose legacy involves depletion of the soil, the economy, and the people. Posed as an economic issue, slavery runs counter to a free labor system in that labor is secured through the purchase of humans whose only wages are subsistence (and that barely life-sustaining). Such an arrangement, exacerbated by the likelihood that freedom will never be earned, yields little incentive to work hard or productively, causing slaveholders to lose economically. But despite its dual appeals to both humanism and economics (she typically aims to address a variety of perspectives), "Demerara" earned Martineau a reputation more as an abolitionist sympathizer than as a political economist, at least in America. Setting an ominous tone for her American tour, the ship's captain was reluctant to let her go ashore in New York, fearing that the volatile temper of the slave debates would endanger the life of this opinionated foreigner. His caution, Martineau quickly learned, proved to be most appropriate.

## The American Experiment

Maria Weston Chapman, whose abolitionist fervor prompted her to depict Martineau's arrival more optimistically, noted that prior to this visit, "No English traveller had before visited the country with so brilliant a prestige. . . . [T]he statesman-like acquirements and literary success which had constituted her greatness at home were but few among many of the considerations that made her fame abroad" (1877, 98–99). Once in America, "There was not an eminent statesman or man of science, not an active politician or leading partisan, not a devoted philanthropist, not a great jurist, nor university professor, nor merchant-prince, nor noted divine, nor distinguished woman in the whole land who did not to the fullest measure of their natures pay homage to the extraordinary compass of hers" (105).[13] Although Chapman's hyperbolism requires readers' caution, the spirit of her comments aptly characterizes Martineau's reception.[14] But not everyone welcomed Martineau with open arms, and indeed many were angered by their failure to convert her to their way of thinking on the slavery issue, whether by persuasion, censorship, or threats. Anticipating the likelihood that her American tour would be dictated by hosts' attempts to screen or monitor her experiences, Ellis Gray Loring wrote this cautionary advice to her:

> The apologists for slavery in this country are thoroughly alarmed at your journey of observation. The author of "Demerara" is a formidable personage in the Southern States. . . . You are received with the most marked attention, writer as you are of the best anti-slavery tale ever written,—while a New England

man who should have written that work would have been . . . indicted and imprisoned. . . . But Miss Martineau is the world's property, and as she cannot be crushed, she must, if possible, be blinded. (Chapman 1877, 129)

Loring's remarks highlight the desirability of Martineau's witnessing real slaves—at work in the fields, for sale on the auction block, at home in their dwellings—before forming a comprehensive opinion on slavery as practiced in the South. Not surprisingly, Martineau acted on this crucial insight, conforming, as it does, with her sociological aims, her reliance on empirical observation, and her commitment to ascertaining the truth about American principles.[15]

Landing in New York shortly after a spate of anti-abolitionist rioting,[16] Martineau learned to her surprise that many Americans, especially women, were ignorant about issues threatening to test the values on which the country claimed to be based. Misinformation and misrepresentation abounded as abolitionists, colonizationists, and pro-slavers competed to sway public favor to their side.[17] When asked her opinion about interracial marriage, Martineau's reply—that she would not dream of "interfering between people who are attached . . . [or] with lovers proposing to marry" (1983, 2:15)—earned her the incendiary epithet "amalgamationist." Although her words had been deliberately misrepresented as actively promoting interracial unions, she unrepentantly insisted that legitimate marriage, no matter what color the parties involved, must surely be preferable to the sexual exploitation of black slave girls by white masters, a custom evidenced by the proliferation of mulattoes in the South. From this perspective, both interracial marriage and rape constitute amalgamationism, and what separates the former from the latter is simply "the priest's service" that makes legitimate the act that rape degrades.

The amalgamationist episode prompted warnings by concerned hosts to beware of remarks that could literally cost her her life. Many in those days were imprisoned for speaking their minds, some threatened with lynching, and others tarred, feathered, and murdered for far less candor than Martineau displayed. Her determination to give all sides of the debate a fair hearing was a necessary caution given the unsubstantiated rumors aimed at discrediting the abolitionists—many of whom were pacifist Quakers—cast by detractors as vigilantes and arsonists; generally, the period's riots, lynchings, and destruction of property were actually perpetrated by anti-abolitionist agitators, often of the "gentlemen" class. It is typical of Martineau not to mistake Americans' courting of her favor for genuine popularity; clearly, each group promoted a political agenda that would be greatly enhanced by her endorsement. Thus, while enjoying the best that America's socially and politically elite had to offer, she was keenly aware that this rarified vision of the country was a partial and highly selective one and insisted on visiting poorhouses, factories, prisons, and slave quarters as well as northern mansions and southern plantations.

Despite the dangers of professed abolitionism, her witnessing of lynch law (mob violence) in Boston during the second year of her trip convinced Martineau of the need to declare publicly against slavery. After landing in New York, Martineau's itinerary ranged from the mid-Atlantic states, through the southern states to New Orleans, then north up the Mississippi River to New England.[18] Because of her earnest desire to understand the South's social structure, her relations with her southern hosts were so cordial that some urged a return visit before she sailed for England. But it was in the North—not, as generally assumed, the South—that America's undercurrent of social unrest was most evident at this time. In genteel Boston, far from the notorious atrocities associated with rural southern plantations, Martineau learned of educated, socially committed whites like William Lloyd Garrison being pursued through the streets by crowds aiming to tar and feather him for his abolitionist politics. Similarly, privileged white women like Maria Weston Chapman—"where shame and peril are, there is she" (Martineau 1839, 72)—had insults and objects thrown at them by rowdies attempting to thwart their abolitionist gatherings. At one such meeting, with the doors bolted and an escape route planned in the event that the street crowds grew more aggressive, Martineau was asked to offer encouragement to those willing to give their lives for this cause. Striving with her reluctance to become politically involved, which would compromise her self-defined role as an objective cultural observer, and yet confronted by the social issue destined to shape the course of her professional life, Martineau remarked: "I will say what I have said through the whole South; . . . that I consider Slavery as inconsistent with the law of God, and as incompatible with the course of his Providence. I should certainly say no less at the North than at the South concerning this utter abomination" (1983, 2:31).

Despite these carefully chosen words, almost tepid in their strained effort at diplomacy, she had already made clear her position simply by attending this meeting, a conclusion likely to be reached by interested observers on all sides of the question. Rather than rest and relaxation, her motivation for this journey arose from her desire to avert middle-class complacency as a successful author in England by "roughing it" as a traveler in America. Inevitably, as Martineau later observed, "Having thus declared on the safe side of the Atlantic, I was bound to act up to my declaration on the unsafe side" (1838c, 2:163). Of her many experiences in America, *rest* was hardly one of them, particularly once the press exploited news of her remarks at the Boston Female Anti-Slavery Society. But there was no turning back for Martineau: "The mission of her life to the United States of America had begun; and with her, *words are nothing distinct from life*. The symphony predicts the coming strain" (Chapman 1877, 164; emphasis added).

The uproar resulting from the Boston meeting surprised even Martineau, who resolved not to be swayed by the bullying tactics of public opinion. While she became the darling of the abolitionists, attitudes toward Martineau outside of this circle shifted dramatically from the superficial lionizing she so adeptly detected to direct threats against her life. Newspapers throughout the country carried accounts of her declaration, most of them distorted and some, in Martineau's phrase, just plain "filthy." Demonstrating critics' tendency to discredit women writers' political involvement by attacking their femininity, one writer charged: "that unwomanly act of hers,—the delivery of a speech at an abolition meeting," is typical of what one might expect of "this Malthusian lady" (Chapman 1877, 172).[19] No longer welcome in the South, Martineau noted that southern newspapers now offered "mock invitations to me to come and see how they would treat foreign incendiaries. They would hang me: they would cut my tongue out, and cast it on a dunghill, and so forth" (1983, 2:46)— the jaded "and so forth" indicates that sophomoric insults and threats had become the norm. Some abolitionists were appalled at the notoriety they feared might injure the movement, while friends were concerned for her safety; socialites, to protect their reputations, shut their doors against her, no longer interested in courting the "lion" of the season. Unruffled, Martineau advised all concerned to "trust me to bear the consequences of saying abroad what I had long ago printed at home" (1983, 2:36).

The Boston episode is significant as the pivotal event separating superficial lionizers from those who would prove to be both lifelong friends and the crucial link between American events, Martineau, and her British reading public. Surprised to learn that the most venerated seat of learning and cultivation in America, Harvard University, was in fact crippled by its fear of nonconformity (in this case, abolitionism), Martineau marveled at "the subservience to opinion in Boston . . . [which] seemed a sort of mania" when measured against "the negro mother weeping for her children, . . . [or] the crushed manhood of hundreds of thousands of their countrymen" (1983, 2:39). Attitudes in Boston made such an impression on Martineau that twenty-five years later, when negotiating with American publishers for the release of her *Autobiography,* she wrote: "from what I witnessed in Boston, I should fear that there is little toleration there for freedom of thought and speech, and therefore a certain amount of peril to publishers."[20] Although northerners are assumed to have been against slavery, Martineau's experiences illustrate that the political dynamics were more complex, particularly during the early stages of the conflict. Many northern businessmen, for example, had economic interests in the "peculiar institution" and resisted any threat to their investments; others, like intellectuals Ralph Waldo Emerson and Margaret Fuller, dismissed the slavery issue as coarse and vulgar.[21] But Martineau was far too keen a social observer to accept class myopia—thinly disguised as either political economy or philosophy—as a legitimate excuse for avoiding issues of such magnitude as those confronting nineteenth-century America.

Martineau was aware that public floggings and lynchings were a reality in pre–Civil War America, regardless of one's nationality, sex, or color. In *The English Traveller in America,* Jane Mesick observes that possession of papers that might incite slaves to "insurrection, conspiracy, or resistance" against their masters was punishable by death (1922, 127)—a definition loose enough to include "Demerara" no less than the inflated newspaper accounts of Martineau's address to the Boston Female Anti-Slavery Society. Martineau knew that even the "vaguest suspicion" resulted in retaliatory acts without benefit of trial or concrete evidence. On the advice of friends and in light of a series of threats to her life, she arranged for the security of her papers (the journals in which she recorded all these events and that later formed the basis for *How to Observe Morals and Manners, Society in America, Retrospect of Western Travel,* and *The Martyr Age of the United States,* as well as Chapman's *Memorials*) and altered her travel plans to avoid potential confrontations. Martineau's remaining months in America were overshadowed by the constant threat of danger, while rumors of lynchings pursued her even into the free northern states. Far from immune to the fear generated by such threats, she noted that during this period she awoke each morning wondering if she would live through the day. The experience broadened her understanding of those who were so committed to the fight for human rights that they were willing to die for their beliefs: "I learned . . . to sympathise with the real griefs of martyrdom, and to feel something different from contemptuous compassion for those who quail under the terror of it" (1983, 2:55). Indeed, *The Martyr Age of the United States* proves that Martineau's "contemptuous compassion" shifted from sympathy to reverence for what she glowingly terms "these primary abolitionists."

The reverberating effects of her rather innocuous remarks in Boston dramatized the passions shaping the various viewpoints circulating in pre–Civil War America and sharpened Martineau's earlier reservations about the "peculiar institution." The compelling portrayal of dehumanization in "Demerara," written before she personally witnessed slavery, assumed a deeper, more impassioned cast in her writing once she attempted to interview field slaves who were too broken even to speak clearly, once she experienced the festive atmosphere of a slave auction during which lewd and suggestive "jokes" were employed to sell human beings, and once she comprehended that the large mulatto population bore compelling testimony to the systematic sexual exploitation of black women by white men for breeding purposes. In her travel notebooks Martineau wrote: "I have seen every variety of the poor creatures, from the cheerful, apt house-servant, to the brutish, forlorn, wretched beings that crawl along the furrows of the fields. The result has been a full confirmation of the horror and loathing with which I have ever regarded the institution, and a great increase of the compassion. . . . How Christians can exasperate one another under the pressure of so weary a load of shame and grief I can scarcely understand" (Chapman 1877, 131–32). Although clarity on theological issues remained unresolved for her at this time, Christianity's disturbing role in slavery no doubt contributed to the agnosticism defining her mature years.[22] As a young writer at the height of her popularity,

Martineau found that her empirical observations of slavery reinforced her earlier abolitionist inclinations, effectually sealing her fate as a vigorous participant at the forefront of Anglo-American slavery discourse.

## Society in America and "Slavery in America"

Back home in England after her American tour, Martineau was harassed only by hate mail, heavily weighted with dirt and rocks and sent postage-due from Boston, a disturbing reminder of the pettiness often shaping slavery debates. She spent a large part of the next thirty years chronicling what she termed "the martyr age" of the United States, its "reign of terror" or the events culminating in the Civil War, and the postwar Reconstruction period. As an emissary bringing American affairs before the British public, her "most earnest desire is that the facts about the Negroes (and also the 'Mean Whites') should be known as widely as possible in this country."[23] The 1834–1836 journey was the only visit she made to America, and the impressions that the country—with its professed ideals and unrealized potential, its people, and its painful social issues—made on Martineau accord with her commitment to "ascertaining and avowing truth: and the witnessing and being implicated in the perils and struggles of the abolitionists in the present martyr age of America has, of course, strengthened my convictions."[24] She later observed, "It was some years before I felt at all sure that I should not live and die in America. . . . If I had gone [back] to America, it would have been for the sole object of working in the cause which I believed then, and which I believe now, to be the greatest pending in the world" (1983, 2:84). But in fact she did work for this cause, using the means through which she exerted the greatest influence: her writing, both as a public figure of the press and as a prolific letter writer with an eclectic and broadly based circle of prominent correspondents.

Caught up in the intense revolutionary fervor of the turbulent 1830s, an era and a spirit coinciding with her own recent declaration of independence from familial and social restrictions, Martineau was powerfully inclined to devote her life to the American cause. But her aim was redefined once she returned to England, primarily due to the prolonged period of invalidism spent in Tynemouth. A letter to Chapman indicates that family issues also continued to plague her: "If I were well and had health, and if my mother's life were not so fast bound to mine as it is, I think I could not help coming to live beside you. Great *ifs,* and many of them. But I dream of a life devoted to you and your cause, and the very dream is cheering" (Chapman 1877, 232). As it turned out, it was not Martineau's abolitionism but her invalidism that supplanted the daughterly duties that must have become odious by this time; once preoccupied with her own health during the Tynemouth years, she could no longer indulge Mrs. Martineau's demands for her passive compliance. Fortunately for her daughter's personal and professional well-being, the aging Mrs. Martineau became the responsibility of her other children, freeing Harriet to participate fully in political realms (even from her sickroom) as the citizen of the world and the head of her household she had become. Testifying to Mrs. Martineau's tenacity, Martineau was nearly forty years old before her mother accepted, if not sanctioned, her autonomy.

Martineau's travel journals record her impressions, praise, and criticisms of America's institutions as measured against its professed values. Her critique emphasizes the ideals of equality, liberty, and freedom, ideals that were in practice systematically denied to all but a comparatively small number of privileged white men. The fact that women were excluded from legal, economic, and social arenas—seen in "The Political Non-Existence of Women"—as were blacks and other minorities and poor whites—as discussed in "The Morals of Slavery" (both in *Society in America*)—proved that "liberty and justice for all" was, in practice, liberty and justice for a select few. Although she believed that Americans possessed the qualities necessary for realizing democratic ideals, she posited that the American "experiment" was a failure and would continue to be so as long as slavery of any sort was permitted to exist in the land of the free.

Readers on both sides of the Atlantic anticipated with great interest the publication of Martineau's American travel books. Both those who embraced and those who rejected her social politics eagerly read her impressions of America, her unflinching assessments of its political leaders, and, of course, her critiques of attitudes toward slavery, which varied so widely across the country. Not surprisingly, the threats posed by her American travel books generated a lively critical response, illustrating the impressive scope of Martineau's political and popular influence. Writing to Chapman in 1837 about the pending reception of *Society in America*, Martineau noted: "I thought the book would ruin me; and this thought was confirmed by the importunity which has been used to prevail upon me to keep back some things which it was supposed I might say. I kept back nothing which it was in my heart to say" (170).[25] Her anticipation of critical furor proved well founded: "The newspapers and the Boston aristocracy are perfectly frantic against me. . . . My book has suddenly widened the split in the democratic party. I tell you this as American matter of fact, not as belonging to myself. I had done with the affair, when I sent away the last proof" (Burchell 1995, 47). Her arch disengagement from responsibility for her readers' responses openly acknowledges her political impact while presenting her book as nothing more than a mirror for the political reality already at work in America. Not surprisingly, some were inspired while many more were angered by the images reflected in *Society in America*.

For example, Chapman notes, "The press of the United States was well-nigh unanimous in taunting England with her goodness and greatness, which is called by every abusive name, and took the occasion to brand her personally with every ill epithet which she least deserved. She was a 'hard,' 'cold,' 'pitiless,' 'Amazonian,' 'masculine,' 'incendiary,' 'radical,' 'amalgamationist'" (1877, 183). She adds, however, that certain newspapers throughout New England resoundingly endorsed her friend's critique, indicating some hope that the American press would yet redeem itself from the ideological corruption Martineau had detected. Although she later termed herself a popularizer, Martineau never courted *popularity,* preferring to cultivate objectivity and analytical accuracy in her recording of the history unfolding around her. Truthfulness, a quality she particularly valued, often proved to be at odds with the popular trend of lionizing public figures (like politicians) whose fame did not depend on morals and ethics. In fact, she demonstrated that truth was instead symbolized by communal scapegoats like William Lloyd Garrison (who was imprisoned as a "low criminal" with a five-thousand-dollar ransom on his head), in whom society found a useful target for its own impotence. Of her friend's criticism of America's political leaders, Chapman wrote: "Herein . . . lay the secret of the public rage when the fact appeared that the illustrious stranger . . . had not found [America's public] men themselves illustrious; while she bore with the greatest composure to be laughed at for pointing out the despised youth Garrison as the great man of the age" (1877, 153). Martineau's courage in citing him as a martyr, coupled with the shrewd insight demonstrated by her assessments of those in "official" power, signify a depth of understanding far beyond the comprehension of a mere popularizer.

One American reviewer of *Society in America* rejected Martineau's analysis by invoking the ideological chasm separating England from its former colony, in the process dismissing her gender, her nationality, and her presumption in offering constructive advice: "Does a woman of circumscribed education and recluse habits feel herself competent to teach a whole nation,—a nation that did not think the wisest and the greatest in *her* land capable of giving them sound instruction? Did we not separate ourselves from them because we felt in advance of them? Did we not show ourselves superior, in physical strength and moral strength?" (Chapman 1877, 175). The phrases "circumscribed education" and "recluse habits"—both conditions expected, even demanded, of "respectable" middle-class females— elide the innate intelligence behind the success of the *Illustrations,* the work whose popularity accounts for Martineau's position as a writer of international authority. Illustrating the threat she posed by the very vigor of its condemnation, the review concludes, "We must warn our readers to consider this woman's advice as mischievous and pernicious in the highest degree" (177). Far from anticipating America's Civil War, this writer seems still to be fighting the Revolutionary War.

Another review targets her sociological methodology. In its review of *Society in America,* the London *Times* (30 May 1837) set the tone for several decades of literary dueling with Martineau that eventually involved the *Daily News* and aptly illustrated the period's resistance to innovative work by women writers.[26] Following an aside about her "indifferent grammar," the article critiques her departure from "a simple and vivid description of what she witnessed in the new world" (like Hall or Trollope, no doubt), charging that "the parade of what is called philosophy" that replaces it "is indeed one of the most preposterous and burlesque exhibitions that we have long met with." Yet in its criticism that the text "is essentially fragmentary," the review highlights the very qualities for which Martineau's work is today praised. Her "mapping out [of] 'the morals' of America . . . as they ought to figure according to the principles which she imbibed before her visit" the writer terms "dogmatical arrogance" rather than a logical measuring of America's practices against its stated principles.[27] Perhaps it is the idea of a *woman* writer who employs scientific method (rather than flowery adjectives) to which this critic objects. This "she apostle" offends by her presumption as a writer, as an original thinker, as a social scientist, and as a woman who not only participates in a traditionally male realm but also rewrites the standards governing it.

Yet despite attempts to dismiss her commentary as "dogmatical" or "pernicious," Martineau remained a force to be reckoned with. She was aware that her severest critics were "among those who were too hasty to do me justice at first, and mistook my real love and interest for their country for a traveller's carpings." Consistent with her stand on the superficiality of lionizing, Martineau eventually saw her criticisms vindicated by the "fall of [America's] public men, one after another, in precise accordance with their pithlessness on the one great subject of slavery."[28] That her influence was cause for concern was evidenced by the virulent tone of "Slavery in America, Being a Brief Review of Miss Martineau on That Subject, by a South Carolinian [Sims]," printed in 1838.[29] A substantial (eighty pages) rebuttal to Martineau's *Society in America,* this tract takes issue with her criticisms of "one of the most interesting and important domestic institutions of the south" (preface), beginning with the title's implication that, in America, *society* is synonymous with *slavery.* Contrasting with Martineau, who signed her real name to her writing about America, this author retreats behind the custom of authorial anonymity, allowing him to ridicule her reputation, appearance, and physical limitations with impunity. His attack ranging from insults ("Nothing escapes her tongue. . . . [S]he is too talkative to listen, and too dogmatical to learn" [16, 28]) to sarcasm ("Still the wonder grew / How one small head could carry all *she* knew" [16]) and from classist slurs ("she was a decided leveller" [17]) to attacks on her credibility (her opinions are "at the expense of truth" [18]), the writer urges Martineau to look to society in the North and in her own country before presuming to criticize southern slavery. Aside from its vigorous denunciation of—and thus, demonstration of—Martineau's influence, this pamphlet is significant for illustrating popular justifications for preserving the South's "peculiar institution."

For example, according to the preface, "The errors into which Miss Martineau has been led by a pre-existing prejudice and a partial acquaintance with the facts" are what necessitate publication of this tract, which aims to provide the public with "a faithful criticism of the glaring misrepresentations and absurdities contained in her *Society in America*." That the Englishwoman is "strong-minded, bold, disputatious, . . . a monstrous poser who declaims constantly . . . [and] who comes to teach, not to learn" (16, 58) ignores Martineau's professed aim to observe and learn, not to teach—first, as a traveler keen to witness the American experiment and second, as a writer compelled to record all she experiences. The charge that "Her ear is open to all that may be said against slavery; all that is said in its defence, she dismisses as not worth hearing" (25) is disproved by her aim to do that which the tract's writer seems unwilling to do: to hear all sides of the arguments—hence, her spending most of the first year of her tour in the southern states—and empirically to witness all levels of American society, from the White House to the cotton fields. There is, of course, some truth to the reviewer's claim, since slavery under any circumstances was not, in Martineau's view, justifiable.

As the article unfolds, the charge of closed-mindedness might be made of its writer, whose defense of slavery relies on the skewed logic of conventional, self-serving justifications. For example, he argues that blacks are inherently inferior, whether they are slaves or free, and that the abolitionists are immoral for challenging the "natural," divinely ordained social order. Since blacks are lazy thieves at worst and suited for the lowest forms of labor at best, emancipation proposes to elevate them to a condition to which they are not entitled (26–27). The "Southerner" rejects Martineau's claim that slavery breeds mental illness, arguing that it is the "general inferior activity of their minds," not slavery, that predisposes blacks to insanity (35). In contrast, Martineau argues that "general inferior activity" stems from legal and social prohibitions against educating blacks and from the accumulation of mental anguish and physical suffering resulting from enslavement and chronic hopelessness. The South Carolinian's assertion that there are "few people so very happy, hearty, and well satisfied with their condition, as the southern negro" (29) testifies to the writer's conviction that slavery is an unqualified good.

Martineau's appeal to humanitarian values was lost on those who justified the systematic dehumanization of an entire race under the guise of moral protectorship; similarly, her appeal to liberal capitalism held little weight with those accustomed to getting their labor for free. One point the author does concede to Martineau concerns the "illicit and foul conduct of many among us, who make their slaves the victims and the instruments alike of the most licentious passions" (38). But although agreeing that the sexual exploitation of black females is both a "perversion of their morals" and "dishonorable," the writer shifts from the idea of victimization to a more telling expression—"the female prostitution of the south" (39). Presumably, he judges prostitution comparable to the sexual exploitation of slave women; but the analogy fails for several reasons. The writer casts whites (the "superior" race) as the guardians of blacks, yet white men's rapes of black women merely extend the physical brutality underpinning the slave system in other regards; guardianship is hardly synonymous with exploitation and abuse. Further, prostitution implies some measure of autonomy on the woman's part, at least when compared with slave women; prostitution (termed, interestingly, "white slavery") may not offer an enviable lifestyle yet, in general, prostitutes earn money and are comparatively free to participate in the marketplace. As a result, many prostitutes were better fed, better dressed, and healthier than their "angelic" counterparts. Slave women, in contrast, received no material benefits and were forced to remain in their situation and submit to rapes; worse, their primary purpose—as breeders for the masters—compelled them to endure repeated pregnancies often followed by separation from their children, who were sold off as property. The Eurocentric morality posing as racial "guardianship" pales next to Martineau's haunting invocation of "the Negro mother weeping for her children," mulatto and illegitimate though they may be.[30]

The analogy most fully breaks down with the writer's assertion that this kind of amalgamationism produces some highly desirable consequences:

> The result of illicit intercourse between the differing races, is the production of a fine specimen of physical *manhood,* and of a better mental organization, in the mulatto; and, in the progress of a few generations, that, which might otherwise forever prove a separating wall between the white and the black,— *the color of the latter,*—will be effectually removed. (40; emphasis added)

In other words, once "superior" white genes subsume "inferior" black genes, "the eye ceases to be offended," rendering racism no longer a problem and ethnic cleansing the path to social morality.[31] Despite women's essential role in the process, this rendering eliminates women and the sexual outrages they endure from the equation, their primary link in the production of "fine specimens" erased by the generic term, *manhood.* In quick succession, this writer blurs the boundaries between slavery and prostitution, between the perversion of and the guardianship of morals, between sexual exploitation (rapes, pregnancies, illegitimacy) and the creation of "fine" specimens of manhood, and between black and white. So entrenched is his perspective that the possibility that black racial tendencies might overtake the white seems not to occur to one whose belief in white supremacy precludes any other potential outcome.

The article does not address what effects the shining new race envisioned by this writer will have on the southern economy, which depended on slave labor to produce cotton as well as to produce mulattoes to be sold at auctions. It also fails to acknowledge Martineau's discussion in *Society in America* of mulattoes, whose plights were exacerbated by their being rejected by blacks and whites alike. This reviled category of humans specific to slave culture demonstrates the dispensability with which human life was regarded by the South's "peculiar institution." Mulattoes of both sexes were considered unmarriageable as neither race would accept them; to Martineau, mulatto women offered a particularly poignant illustration of the system that created them yet has no place for them. Termed "quadroons" in New Orleans, mulatto women were groomed to be mistresses of rich white men; sexually valued for their exotic color yet unmarriageable for that very reason, quadroons often lived materially comfortable yet socially outcast lives serving as concubines to white men and mothers to their illegitimate children. Mulatto men were often reviled and oppressed by blacks in the ways that blacks were by whites and were generally regarded as unsuitable marriage partners for women of any color. Another complication was created by the custom of white slave-owning fathers favoring their mulatto children by freeing them, prompting redoubled legislation virtually ensuring the impossibility of any person of color ever "earning" freedom.[32]

"Slavery in America" is significant for its representative pro-slavery perspective and especially for its illustration of Martineau's impact as a writer whose political influence aroused such incendiary reactions. The length and vigor of this "review" of *Society in America* in itself speaks for proslavers' concerns about Martineau's impressions of American institutions and the effects of those impressions on the American and British reading public.[33] The American South, whose economy depended on slave labor in general and the English cotton trade in particular, naturally was anxious to strengthen its political and economic ties with England against the impending civil conflict. "Slavery in America" also anticipates the protests of anti-abolitionist clergymen and politicians against women abolitionists outlined in Martineau's *The Martyr Age of the United States*. Responding to the double threat of class and gender issues, the South Carolinian charges that Martineau—a "leveller"—"discusses the rights of man, and—heaven save the mark!—the rights of women too, with her chambermaid, when she cannot corner a senator" (58). Recalling what we might now term the "peculiar institution" of women's conduct books, Chapman notes that Martineau "was told the abolitionists were unsexing woman," prompting a renewed interest in disseminating tracts outlining "her appropriate moral sphere" (1877, 139).[34] Stunned by the prospect presented by abolitionism's race and gender collaboration, one American man objected, "But, dear Miss Martineau, is it possible you think women have the same duties and rights as men?" Excessive attention to this point suggests that many critics' objections were as much to the gender of *Society in America's* author as to the book's politics.

Along with gender, physical disability provided another basis for criticism. Employing the tactic peculiar to critics of Martineau who seemed, despite all their rhetorical strategies and intellectual posturing, still uncertain about having won their point, the South Carolinian concluded by attacking her deafness: "She gets nothing from her hearer, for she does not hear him. . . . That she has never listened while in America, is evident from these volumes; though I doubt not that a great many words have gone through her trumpet" (1838, 58). British reviews condemning her work on the basis of her disability were even more sophomoric. A review of *How to Observe Morals and Manners* proclaims that a forthcoming companion volume entitled *How to Talk*, "by a promising pupil of the Deaf and Dumb Asylum, is only delayed by Mr. Knight's not being yet able to find a deaf and dumb compositor to communicate with the author" (Croker 1839, 61). To these critics, her deafness apparently had some bearing on her capacity to write analytically: "Considering that there are but two *blind* travellers extant, and only *one* that we know of, stone *deaf*, we cannot but wonder where Miss Martineau has collected all this valuable information" (65). Chapman counters such childish ridicule presented in lieu of literary criticism by claiming that Martineau's

> powers of observation were enlarged by greater exercise than other persons undergo, for her deafness compelled a persistent course of inquiry,—a more careful inspection and a more thorough examination. . . . [Deafness] obliged her also to take the precaution of being always accompanied by a friend. This gave a double strength to her testimony; for although one may be presumed to be sometimes mistaken, in the mouth of two witnesses every word is established. (1877, 104–5)[35]

A far more novel review of her American travel books reproaches Martineau for her "robust health and tough nerves" and for her ability to

> race through the country with the frame of a mosstrooper for toughness of muscles and wiriness of frame, with being able to wade through a stream and sit in her wet clothes without fear of disastrous consequences, and overcoming difficulties which the stoutest male travellers considered almost insurmountable. . . . We do not object to Miss Martineau's health. We wish every woman on earth could boast of such hardiness. But we do object to such scamperings over strange lands for the purpose of procuring materials for a book which is to vilify the very people who give her the freedom of the country. (Chapman 1877, 173)

Given her lifelong preoccupation with her health, in which she confronted conditions ranging from extended bouts of invalidism to vigorous walking tours, this droll assessment no doubt amused her. The charge that her purpose was "procuring materials for a book" recalls her concern with minimizing any intentions on her part that might be construed as materially or professionally oriented; the term "vilify" unfortunately misses her many praises of America while focusing on the critical analysis that is integral to any sociological assessment. True of all her critics of *Society in America*, this writer's response demonstrates that, at the time, travel memoirs were not expected to offer serious, coherent cultural analyses such as Martineau aimed for but only to praise scenery and local customs. Martineau's analysis of the disjunction between the theory and practice of American ideology is prompted not by a "traveller's carping" but by her sincere desire to see the country—as a viable model for the "new" world—live up to its fullest potential.

Not all reviews were negative, although those are the ones that provide the most revealing evidence of Martineau's political impact, and Chapman's assessment is a case in point. Chapman was indefatigable in her devotion to abolitionism and in her defense of Martineau. As an authority on both, her assessment of the book nearly forty years after its initial publication is worth noting:

> [It] is not only by far the best book of travels in that country, in the judgment of the best qualified Americans and Englishmen, but it must needs remain of permanent value as a picture of the United States towards the middle of the nineteenth century. . . . Its fairness, its largeness and accuracy, the truth and beauty of its impartial reprehension of all that was bad and its sympathetic admiration of all that was good, are not only universally acknowledged among intellectual Americans at the present time, but they were so at the very period of publication, when moral opposition was at its hottest. (168–69)[36]

Chapman's claim that Martineau's travel writing was distinguished among other examples of the genre reflects the writer's focus on American society, its social institutions, and its people. She actively sought out the American experience from the high levels to the low, and was particularly pleased that, together, her professional fame and her gender permitted her access to segments of American society generally denied most foreign visitors. As a political economy writer, her fame secured her contacts with high-level government officials; as a woman, she was granted access to the domestic interiors not likely to attract or be accessible to male travelers. Because the state of a country, to her mind, is reflected as much by its domestic relations as by its political ones, she considered herself fortunate in her opportunities for such comprehensive cultural observation. Finally, that her writing was banned in the South renders even more significant the defamatory remarks of "Slavery in America" and other reviews, remarks presented as "truth" dependent on the aggressive censorship of alternative opinions. But thanks to Martineau's resilience, controversy and adversity only served to bolster her purpose: "If the abuse consequent on my books has any effect, it is to make me love the better part of the people more, and to draw them towards me."[37]

Writing of Charles Dickens's 1842 visit to America, Martineau applauds the trend for British notables to travel there, particularly for its capacity to influence public policy:

How I rejoice at the spreading of the fashion of liking the Americans! . . . I
cannot but wish that the slavery subject may come full under Mr. Ds view,—
tho' it will not, if any management of the aristocratic part of society can prevent it. . . . One conversational condemnation from him would do more for
the abolition of slavery than years of action of most people. . . . [A] word
from Boz given as occasion arises, should speed the downfall of the system.[38]

But "Boz" lacked Martineau's sociological commitment, having been
warned not to make Martineau's mistake of critiquing America because
"Americans can't bear to be told of their faults" (Dickens 1974, 3:157).
Dickens did write about America (the novel *Martin Chuzzlewit* and travel
memoir *American Notes*), but his account of the country avoided the sort of
detailed social analysis distinguishing Martineau's: "I know nothing in Humanity so beautiful as the domestic classes of America," she observed,
"those good and serene and happy people who abound, but whom he
[Dickens] seems not only not to have seen, but not to be in the least aware
of" (Burchell 1995, 73).[39]

Despite Americans' sensitivity to criticism, especially from a foreigner
they wished to impress favorably, Martineau's perception of her role remained focused on truthfulness and accuracy, traits consistent with her developing career as a journalist and investigative reporter. As an American
writing about her country's disappointing "experiment," Chapman offers a
harsher assessment of American hypocrisy than that permitted Martineau
when she observes that "men with the Bible in one hand and the Declaration of Independence in the other sold slaves to raise money to evangelise
the Hindoos and to send standards to the Poles. . . . [T]hese inconsistencies
. . . reduced the nation to moral idiocy" (1877, 174). Although as a public
figure Martineau's credibility depended on a more temperate, diplomatic
treatment of the issues, her private correspondence demonstrated an alter-
nating rage and despair over the American situation that plagued her for
decades. But truth often compromises diplomacy and, as a columnist for
the *National Anti-Slavery Standard* (1859–62), Martineau was eventually
asked to stop sending contributions, her politics having become unpalat-
able even to some abolitionists.[40] As her relationship with American ideology evolved throughout her professional life, conflicts not only between
abolitionists and anti-abolitionists but also within the abolitionist movement itself further refined Martineau's political ideology. Her early alignment with Garrisonian viewpoints, reflected in *Society in America*, strengthened as "Woman Question" debates were employed to discredit the
participation of women like herself and Chapman in public discourse. Not
surprisingly, the Garrisonians remained firm in their gratitude to Martineau's courage to speak with conviction and authority, attributing much
of the success of the movement to her and posthumously erecting a statue
in her honor. Chapman credits her friend with "The ultimate rehabilitation
of a race and the redemption of a continent," citing Martineau's influence

as "one important link in the chain of causes still producing happy effects" (1877, 165). Of her own role as compiler of the *Memorials,* Chapman wrote, "I have only to . . . show the impression she made on her contemporaries." As this sampling of critical responses to *Society in America* illustrates, the impressions she made ranged from animosity to gratitude, proving that her work rarely met with indifference.

## The Martyr Age of the United States

According to historian David Turley, "the decade from the mid-1830s to the mid-1840s was the highpoint of transatlantic abolitionism as a functioning international enterprise" (1991, 196–97). Britain's interest in the American situation, he adds, was keener even than in its own slavery problems or in the notoriously persistent international slave trade. Although the economics of slavery was a primary issue, this "transatlantic abolitionism" also had a religious basis:

> Anglo-American abolitionism became a major component of the larger transatlantic internationalism of middle-class Protestant benevolence alongside temperance and the search for international peace. Activism was rooted in a widespread confidence that the English-speaking peoples shared a set of common religious and moral perspectives to the benefit . . . of their own societies and the rest of the world. (197)

The "confidence" of Protestant sects extended to Unitarianism, the dissenting, socially committed theology in which Martineau was raised. Yet these two religious ideologies proved to be strange bedfellows: Unitarianism's dissent not only from conventional theology but also from conventional abolitionism is consistent with its status as a radical fringe group that was itself traditionally marginalized. In America, the division within the abolitionist movement between conservative Evangelicals and radical Garrisonians was one Martineau found particularly compelling. The same was true of English Unitarians who, concerned about improving the status of any maligned or oppressed group in society, "developed links with the more radical Garrisonian wing of American Abolitionism" (Turley 1991, 203). The split was dramatized at London's 1840 Anti-Slavery Convention, where women delegates—expected to remain "politically invisible"—were denied seats on the main floor, prompting Garrison boldly to sit in the women's gallery. As a Unitarian and as an activist for race and gender rights, Martineau's support of American abolitionism dovetailed naturally with the Garrisonian viewpoint, beginning with her American tour and continuing through subsequent friendships and literary collaborations.[41]

Of the "cursed and doomed institution of Slavery," Martineau asserts that she was privileged "to witness the opening of the martyr age of its reformers; and I am thankful that I did" (1983, 2:56). The rhetoric of martyr-

dom, often employed in her early American writings, provides the theme
for a lesser-known book also resulting from the American tour. Based on
Chapman's yearly reports compiled for the Boston Female Anti-Slavery Society, Martineau's *The Martyr Age of the United States* (1839)[42] offers a historical overview of the abolitionist movement and of those individuals who
were real and potential martyrs for the cause. This early collaboration between the two women initiated a rich professional and personal alliance
that spanned four decades.

Her writing eloquent, her language spiritualized, and her tone at times
reverent, Martineau observes: "There is a remarkable set of people now living and vigorously acting in the world"—who, despite their diversity, "act
as if they were of one heart and of one soul . . . directed toward a noble object" (1839, 3). First and foremost is William Lloyd Garrison, "one of God's
nobility" (7), jailed, tormented, and ridiculed for his radical abolitionism,
which included publicly burning a copy of the Constitution (its wording
permits slavery) and his insistence on immediate, universal emancipation.
Garrison published the abolitionist newspaper, the *Liberator*, from 1830
until the abolition of slavery in 1865 and was a lifelong correspondent of
Martineau's. Other martyrs include Prudence Crandall, driven from her
home for establishing an integrated school for "young Ladies and little
Misses of color" (13); David Child, husband of feminist abolitionist Lydia
Maria Child, ostracized for his abolitionist politics, particularly his shrewd
insights on the "Texas Question"; Maria Weston Chapman, educated,
beautiful, and privileged, who preferred a life courting danger and controversy as "Garrison's lieutenant" to the social ennui typical of her class;
Quakers Angelina Grimké, who freed the slaves she inherited and devoted
her life to eradicating slavery, and Lucretia Mott, who was active in both
the abolitionist and feminist causes; and abolitionist newspaper editor Eli-
jah P. Lovejoy, whose lynching-murder at his office put to the test two primary American values: freedom of speech and freedom of the press.

Martineau demonstrates that martyrdom assumes various forms, from
imprisonment to loss of home and employment and from social ostracization to loss of life. With acute insight, she rightly perceived that America's
reign of terror, peopled by abolitionists and vigilantes, slaves and free
blacks, socialites and politicians, dramatizes similar forms of oppression
evident in every society throughout the world, including her own: "Slavery is as thoroughly interwoven with American institutions . . . as the aristocratic spirit pervades Great Britain" (4). Ludicrously misplaced in a democratic system, aristocratic notions distort American ideology, from the
South's "peculiar institution" to Boston's social conservatism and sterile
intellectualism. But she remained optimistic about the American experiment despite the economic ironies of the situation: "Dark as American affairs look now, I have as strong a confidence as ever that the nation will
justify the hopes of their best friends—which means something very different from gratifying the vanity of their moneyed aristocracy."[43] Another

daring analogy developed in *Society in America* compares southern plantations with Middle Eastern harems: both have a "chief" or legitimate wife as
well as various subordinate wives or mistresses, servants, and slaves all sexually serving one master. But for Martineau, the Middle Eastern example is
preferable to southern plantations: odious though she finds the custom to
be, harems, at least, do not pretend to be other than what they are. In contrast, the social structure in America hypocritically hides behind the duplicitous, self-serving masks of monogamy and Christianity, with both the
northern and southern "peerage" citing democratic principles while claiming aristocratic privilege.

Also "thoroughly interwoven" into the social fabric of America was the
gendered division of labor that represented for some social stability and for
others the ideological complement to slavery. Analogies linking the exploitation of women with that of people of color at the hands of powerful
white men initially drew proponents of the abolitionist and feminist movements to work together, since "men hate those whom they have injured"
(Martineau 1839, 71). Demonstrating early links between the two is Garrison's ambitious prospectus to the *Liberator:* "As our object is *Universal*
Emancipation—to redeem woman as well as man from a servile to an equal
condition—we shall go for the Rights of Woman to their fullest extent"
(Martineau 1839, 54). Commenting on the segregation of women at London's 1840 World Anti-Slavery Convention, Garrison observed, "After bat-
tling so many long years for the liberties of African slaves, I can take no
part in a convention that strikes down the most sacred rights of all women"
(Pichanick 1977, 95). Garrison's protest was modeled after the first General
Convention of Women, held in New York in 1837, whose delegates ruled
that racial segregation in churches was immoral. To counter this prejudice,
the women pledged to take their seats "with the despised class" in any
church in which segregation was practiced (Martineau 1839, 52). The clash
pitting women abolitionists against the clergy proved to be a significant
chapter in the histories of women's rights, racial equality, and religion.

Such examples illustrate that the most outspoken opponents of race
and gender equality represented two of the most powerful, culture-shaping
institutions of the era: religion and politics. When the New York Convention delegates announced their support of the more aggressive abolitionist
activities of men, vowing to "honor their conduct" through sympathy, sacrifice, and vindication (Martineau 1839, 53), the General Association of
Massachusetts Clergymen formally censured the women abolitionists. Arguing that "deference and subordination are essential to the happiness of
society, and peculiarly so in the relation of a people to their pastor," clergymen expressed alarm about the general "alteration . . . taking place in
the female character" in the form of self-reliance in political and social
matters.[44] Resolutions that Martineau termed "worthy of the dark ages"
denounced women abolitionists, targeting in particular the Grimké sisters.
"It is wonderful," wrote Martineau with profound irony, how many ser-

mons of the period conclude "with a simile about a vine, a trellis and an elm" (54).[45] But the clergy's tactics failed, from the low (publicly accusing women abolitionists of unchaste, heretical, and unchristian behavior) to the absurd (sprinkling cayenne pepper on the stove in the women's meeting rooms so they could not hear speeches for the coughing caused by polluted air). Even back in England, Martineau continued to be implicated in these events: "The clergy have begun a regular warfare against the women, offering resolutions against their activity . . . and preaching against the *teaching* of women—aiming pointedly at the Grimkés and myself" (Arbuckle 1983, 9). It was the clergy's attempts to discredit women abolitionists, she claims, that prompted Garrison's "taking up the Rights of Women" in both the *Liberator* and at public assemblies; far from eradicating the problem, notes Valerie Pichanick, the formal pastoral condemnation itself "made feminism an issue in the antislavery campaign and split the abolitionist movement" (1980, 94). In their aim to intimidate women back into their homes, the clergy's actions contributed to the division within the abolitionist movement, resulting in the formation of the National Anti-Slavery Society, which opposed women's participation, and the American Anti-Slavery Society, the Garrisonian wing promoting the emancipation of women and blacks.[46] That the clergy presented itself as society's moral, ethical, and spiritual compass while belittling socially committed women and denouncing the freeing of slaves (both posing threats to a capitalist economy) offers remarkable commentary on the complex social, religious, and political ideologies of the time.[47]

The second Convention of Women, held in 1838 in Philadelphia, proved that even the city of brotherly love was not immune to the insidious influence of racism and bigotry. Hosted by liberal Quakers and held in the newly built Pennsylvania Hall, whose doors—particularly on this occasion—were open to people of all colors, the convention was besieged by threatening crowds of anti-abolitionist agitators. After several days, during which the city officials refused either to intervene or to protect the women, violence broke out, resulting in the burning of Pennsylvania Hall as well as the Orphan Asylum for black children, a "circumstance which most clearly indicates the source of the rage of the mob" (Martineau 1839, 73). Such instances of racist mob violence in the North's most cosmopolitan cities—New York, Boston, and Philadelphia—dramatized social problems too complex to be arbitrarily delineated by the Mason-Dixon line.

A man whose example links the realms of religion and politics is Unitarian abolitionist Dr. Charles Follen, an unconventional clergyman in that he specifically "advocated the agency of woman in social questions" and rejected their mandatory domestication in the name of morality and social propriety (Martineau 1839, 54). Instead, Follen posited that abolitionist work is the highest of earthly callings: "It is, indeed, a proof of uncommon moral courage, or of an overpowering sense of religious duty and sympathy with the oppressed, that a woman is induced to embrace the unpopular, unfashionable, obnoxious principles of the abolitionists." Follen's words emphasize the irony implicit in casting women as society's moral gatekeepers while denying them agency to perform this role outside as well as inside the domestic circle. Indeed, he claimed, the formation of the Ladies' Anti-Slavery Societies was crucial not only for the realization of abolition but "still more as an indication of the moral growth of society." Celebrating the same spirit of assertiveness that conservative clergy found so objectionable in women, Follen argued that through abolitionist work women were finally breaking down the boundaries of the narrow lot permitted them by men and assuming their place in the work of society. By observing that "it is woman, injured, insulted woman, that exhibits the most baneful and hateful influences of slavery" (56), Follen highlights a crucial point: that the values of the period's domestic and maternal ideologies were blatantly compromised by the slave system, which demanded chaste monogamy of white wives, whose offspring inherit the father's property, yet expected sexual compliance from black women, whose offspring were sold *as* property. Exposure of this double standard threatened to dismantle domestic ideology in its suggestion that women's roles are not, after all, divinely ordained, but are determined by men for the convenience of men. In Martineau's view, Follen's "martyrdom" stemmed from his dismissal as professor of German from ultraconservative Harvard University, which disapproved of his abolitionist politics.

The attitude toward women's participation in abolitionism demonstrated in these clerical examples finds its complement in political circles as well. An example of political martyrdom is illustrated by John Quincy Adams, former president and, in 1838, a Massachusetts congressman. Revered in some circles for his family's contributions to establishing the republic (his father, John, was the second American president), the aging Adams was ridiculed by political opponents as a doddering old man foolishly attempting to, in the phrase of his mother Abigail, "Remember the Ladies." Martineau records Adams's words for "the millions who owe to him the patient and intrepid assertion of their constitutional rights in the martyr-age of the republic" (Martineau 1839, 77).[48] Adams challenged his congressional opponent, a man who rejected as inadmissible political petitions signed by women abolitionists, objecting that such "discreditable" departure "from their proper sphere" (the domestic circle) is ruinous to the national character. Adams retorts that politicians use "erroneous, vicious" principles to exclude women's participation in politics and to dismiss the intensifying threat posed by abolitionist debates, thus negating the will of legitimate citizens. Like Follen, Adams casts the issues in a spiritualized light: "women are not only justified, but exhibit the most exalted virtue when they do depart from the domestic circle, and enter on the concerns of their country, of humanity, and of their God. . . . [It] is a virtue of the highest order" (78). Such appeals to religion and womanly virtue effectually challenge those whose claim to know the mind of God leads them to promote mundane patriarchal values "in His name," whether from the pulpit or the congressional floor.[49] Jane Tompkins's observation that novels like Stowe's *Uncle Tom's Cabin* are, "as a political enterprise, halfway between sermon and social theory" (1985, 126) pinpoints the very anxieties demonstrated by the religious and political resistance to social change outlined in Martineau's text.

Reiterating the religious overtones of debates contested from churches to political halls and involving people representing an array of vested interests—the very term "martyr" having profoundly religious connotations—Martineau concludes *The Martyr Age of the United States* by urging readers to support through "reverent congratulations . . . the spiritual potentates of our age" (1839, 84). The time for such encouragement is now, in the midst of the struggle, rather than after death, when it will be too late, since theirs is a living martyrdom. Five years later, Martineau's spiritualization of the issues intensified as events continued to build toward the war that was still decades in the future:

> . . . these *primary* abolitionists. How they stand!—more and more majestic, through all defection and adversity of every kind,—upheld, (it must be so) by God's own hand! This world has not such a spectacle elsewhere. In the sublime faith they impart, all fear and doubt vanish, and the whole race is seen on its march to Heaven gate. We may be thankful to live in their age. (Arbuckle 1983, 53)

Interestingly, Martineau speculates with some regret about the political implications of the martyrdom that had threatened her personally while in America: "I was sorry that I was not the victim . . . because my being a British subject would have caused wider and deeper consequences to arise. . . . The murder of an English traveller would have settled the business of American Slavery . . . more speedily than perhaps any other incident" (1983, 2:56). Despite her almost reckless approach to the American tour as an adventure, albeit one in which spirited abandon was early tempered by the sobering realities of empirical observation, the acute insight of such a remark was not false bravado. But it was her unanticipated yet inevitable career as a journalist, particularly as the American affairs expert for the *Daily News*, that proved to be the ideal vehicle through which to settle "the business of American Slavery."[50]

## The American Affairs Expert and the Periodical Press

Martineau's journalism career, begun in earnest in 1852 when she became a regular leader writer for the London *Daily News* and continuing to within a few years of her death, focused more on American issues than on any others, international or national, of the period.[51] Although on an occasional basis she had always written for the periodical press—her 1822

literary debut was in the Unitarian periodical, *Monthly Repository*—
Martineau's regular contributions not only to the *Daily News* but also the
*Spectator, Edinburgh Review, Macmillan's,* the American *National Anti-Slavery
Standard,* and others marked a period of literary productivity that was remarkably prolific even by Victorian standards. Her topics included American congressional politics, presidential elections, Reconstruction, the economics of the cotton market and alternative cotton sources, boycotting
slave-produced goods, and the slave trade, to list just a few. Martineau's
thwarted ambition to live in America and work for the abolitionist cause
found apt expression through periodicals writing during this most productive and gratifying period of her life and career.

Given her strong identification with her "dearly-beloved Americans,"
their democratic "experiment," and their "peculiar institutions," it is no
accident that the greatest flowering of Martineau's career as a journalist
coincided with the intensification of the American conflict. Her assertion
that her early exposure to the Americans directly shaped her own
history—"the strange story I have had to tell about myself"—is reflected in
the renewed vigor of the civil conflict in the late 1850s, which propelled
the invalid writer from the sickroom to the next phase in her career. Writing to Florence Nightingale of her role as American affairs journalist for
the *Daily News,* Martineau wrote: "I heard . . . a high political judgment
that the *Daily News alone* keeps this country right on American affairs,"
concluding "That *any* thing *like* what he said should hang on my life
makes me willing to live longer." Soon after, she reveals that she no longer
passively anticipates death, "partly perhaps because . . . [of] the American
outbreak, which causes me to be seriously *wanted.*"[52]

Letters surviving from the 1855–1856 period demonstrate dramatically
the degree to which Martineau's ties with American interests effectually
served as a lifeline, in a sense securing her another twenty years of life. Her
frequent assertions of despair over Americans' mishandling of their affairs
and of disgust at exposures of corruption in the North as well as the South
color the conclusion of the *Autobiography.* Her earlier anticipation that
America would realize its vast potential had dimmed, much as she believed
her vision of the world dimmed as death approached. But she was wrong
on both counts, and as the American situation intensified during the late
1850s, Martineau's letters assumed an optimistic, reinvigorated tone.[53] To a
"dear friend" she wrote, "I think the state of the world helps to keep me
alive,—especially the American part of it. There is so much work to be
done! . . . and I continue to be able to do it, . . . being sustained by it. . . . I
must help while I can; and the doing so seems to lengthen out life." Subsequent letters show that the *Times,* a perpetual irritant to Martineau, played
a key role in her rejuvenation: the *Times* is "abominable about American
slavery. . . . I need not tell you I am the opponent in *Daily News.*" Stung
into action by this old rival, she was soon too busy counteracting the
harm wrought by "that rotten old oracle" to dwell much on death; of her
reprieve, she boasts that she does "Pretty well for a dying person!"[54]

As the American drama unfolded, Martineau's energy rose in proportion. The long period of ennui preceding the resolution of slavery, paralleling her own physical illness and confinement, was now poised to erupt into Civil War, an event of worldwide significance: "How remarkably the fortunes of the civilised world have suddenly become dependent on the great question of free and slave labour. . . . The success of the antislavery cause . . . in America now would do more for human peace, progress, welfare, and happiness, than any other thing that could happen." Despite her assertion that her head, "the old jar and cucumbers," continued to cause her pain, she sewed for abolitionist fund-raising bazaars, wrote *Daily News* leaders, and generated circulars and petitions, participating in world events, as she did in the past, from her own home.[55] A visit from Lord Houghton during this period reveals that Martineau's physical health was tenuous at best, although her hold on life strengthened through her vicarious participation in international affairs. Of her wavering condition Houghton wrote, "She may die at any moment, or live many weeks. . . . I left Miss Martineau nearly insensible, and hope she may pass away without more suffering. But with all her illness she writes three times a week, in the *Daily News*, admirable articles. What vigour and spirit this shows!" (Nevill 1943, 113). According to John Nevill, who claimed she averaged a leader a day, Martineau was more prolific even than Houghton imagined.

The *Daily News*'s rivalry with the *Times* originated in an ideological split, the *News* being characterized as "in favor of free trade and social justice" while the voice of the *Times* was both "powerful" and "conservative" (Arbuckle 1994, xii). When the issues dividing British sympathy between the American North and South became personalized through their deleterious effects on the British cotton industry, the *Times*, representing the "voice of the 'old planter interest'" in Britain (Pichanick 1977, 216), cultivated a backlash against northern abolitionism in favor of supporting southern interests. Although the *Times* was not exactly opposed to the abolition of slavery in principle, in practice such a move, it argued, would have disastrous effects on the British economy. Thus did England's sympathy, through the influence wielded by its two primary newspapers, waver between the dichotomy Martineau strives to negotiate in all her writing: human rights issues and economic concerns. Of her writing for the *Daily News*, she assures a friend that "the articles on American affairs . . . are mine. By their being constantly supposed to be by Americans, you may fairly trust to them; and I think you will find them more hopeful than the contradictory and *meddling* articles in the *Times* and *Saturday Review* which are full of mistakes of fact, and some inconceivably gross."[56]

A sampling of Martineau's *Daily News* leaders on America reveals her remarkable range of expertise, her no-nonsense, uncompromising style, and her sharp and subtle political consciousness. Because of their capacity to reveal vacillating public attitudes, she found presidential elections a topic of special interest throughout this period. Her 25 March 1853 article discusses President Pierce's inaugural address, which established him as "in favour of maintaining that 'domestic institution,' the buying, breeding, and selling of black slaves." She sees a test case for Pierce's standards in the treatment of black seamen from European and other countries, who land in states where, by law, they are arrested as runaway slaves because of their color. South Carolina was particularly notorious for this practice, vowing to "continue to prevent the ingress of free persons of colour as she would persons labouring under contagious diseases, and foreign paupers and convicts." Martineau's discussion highlights the extreme degree to which racism infested America's cultural and legislative bodies, dramatizing the magnitude of a problem that was hardly confined to its geographic boundaries. She concludes that President Pierce's noninterventionist stance toward foreign seamen, a passivity effectually perpetuating the "domestic institution," indicates what may be expected from him concerning "the master-evil of his country."

Another leader from the same period addresses ways to prevent the economic collapse threatened by immediate emancipation. Martineau considers the economics of each slave-produced product in turn—sugar, rice, tobacco—and settles on cotton as the primary, because the most lucrative, crop. Yet although her arguments are couched in economic terms, Martineau repeatedly proves herself to be more than the political economist on which she built her early fame. Her overriding impulse is always humanistic, therefore a leader designed to placate those concerned with economic disaster as a result of abolition typically concludes, as this one does, with a reminder of more immediate concerns. Responding to Professor Calvin Stowe's claim that the average price of a slave has increased as a result of England's demand for cotton, she observes: "It is not pleasant to think that the moral sense and judgment of any portion of our countrymen are under coercion by commercial interests" (22 April 1853). She insists that Britain's role in the perpetuation of American slavery, whether through the desire for cotton or for profit, can reasonably find resolution simply by looking elsewhere for the product: "[T]his is the one way in which, without offence or mischief, we can bear our share in the extinction of remaining negro slavery, and save our national peace and commercial independence from a certain degree of peril." She devoted many articles to the topic of cotton, including her ongoing exploration of alternative suppliers like India, Egypt, Australia, and New Zealand to compensate for the loss of the American product.

Aside from British consumers' demand for cotton, Britain was also implicated in American slavery through manufacturing. Many articles reveal the effects of the cotton shortage on factory districts like Lancashire. Approximately three-quarters of the cotton milled in English factories was imported from America; with southern ports blockaded and in the absence of alternative suppliers, entire factory towns were virtually shut down, leaving many thousands without subsistence.[57] Again, Martineau warns, "It is time we were getting cotton from other places; and by this time next year we may be wondering that we did not do it before the great American crisis occurred. There has been clear warning of it for above a quarter of a century" (1 February 1860). Leader by leader, her tone grows more urgent: "The time is past for any attempt to ignore the risks. . . . A radical change is now inevitable" (10 February 1860). Although estimates, in the absence of statistics, are the primary measure available to us, the idea that two-thirds to three-quarters of all cotton imported into Britain for manufacture was slave-produced in America compares provocatively with the idea that more than two-thirds of American slaves were provided by Britain through the Bristol-Africa-America triangle alone; Liverpool formed part of the other primary triangle. The implications of this connection are beyond the scope of my discussion yet worth bearing in mind in terms of the complex Anglo-American relationship over slavery, still vital nearly a century after their mutual estrangement.

Several leaders mark the visit of Harriet Beecher Stowe, whose phenomenally successful *Uncle Tom's Cabin* won her an enthusiastic welcome in England; others raise lesser-known issues in Civil War history. A 2 January 1860 leader discusses southern secessionists' agitation, including the circulation of pamphlets implicating the Irish poor as "friends of the South" who burn abolitionists' factories and granaries. Already disenfranchised by England and America, the Irish immigrants—if this propaganda is to be believed—are said to do anything for money and revenge. Speaking as one who knows "what the barbarism of the extreme South is," Martineau illustrates how conflicting interests play on the dissatisfactions of "the poor and uneducated whites." The article reiterates her solution to the economic drawbacks of emancipation proposed nearly thirty years earlier in "Demerara":

> the Southern slave-owners would at once increase their property, secure their safety, and recover the many social blessings they have surrendered, by simply making hired servants of their negroes. Payment of wages, instead of supplying subsistence, and admitting a change of masters, was the simple method by which the slaves of half the Union were emancipated; and little more would be necessary in the grosser condition of Southern slavery. (2 January 1860)

Martineau more directly challenged English complacency about its involvement in American events by offering examples of visitors to America who were persecuted as abolitionist sympathizers (19 January 1860). Although they were British citizens, these people were not protected by the public prominence Martineau enjoyed; therefore, they actually experienced the treatment only threatened against her during her visit. Other examples of persecution include poor immigrants, book publishers and sellers, and even governesses among those suspected of being abolitionist agents, the spread of anti-slavery literature being a primary concern for censors. Such incidents contrast oddly with the impending cotton famine, as she notes with characteristic irony: "It is plain enough that while they are hanging Wesleyan Ministers in groups, without trial, and burning alive booksellers from the North, . . . they are not likely to send us much cotton. . . . [W]e have not an hour to lose in rendering ourselves independent of the issue. The question of cotton supply has become the very first social and economical question in English society" (28 September 1860). Martineau's repeated focus on the cotton supply in the *Daily News* reiterates her enduring concern with resolving both the "social and economical" issues that, in her view, dehumanized blacks and demoralized whites.

In 1865 both the Civil War and, once again, Martineau's health began winding down, yet she kept her *Daily News* assignments while relinquishing all other writing commitments: "*Daily News* work is so easy, and so very interesting and so important now that all the world finds and admits that we have been right throughout about American and other affairs, that I have every intention to go on while I can with journalism." A year later, she continued to write about America's Reconstruction period: "I still hold on to *Daily News,*—anxious to carry on the American case as long as possible, . . . American reconstruction . . . is a most anxious and important subject, and nobody who has not been in America understands it at all thoroughly."[58] More than thirty years after her journey, Martineau continued to regard herself as a primary authority on American affairs; more importantly, so also did her editors and her reading public.

Elisabeth Arbuckle notes that "Martineau's writing on American affairs [had] decisive importance" (1994, ixii), particularly when the effects of the Civil War on the cotton industry caused British sympathy to waver between the Unionists, abolitionists, and Confederates. Going against the tide of economics-based opinion, *Daily News* editor Thomas Walker, who thoroughly relied on Martineau's expertise in American affairs, "held firm" for the northern cause, encouraging her to keep readers focused on slavery's human rights issues. Her claim that her life had been extended through her role in the American conflict—pain and death were "put down" because she was "seriously *wanted*"—was affirmed by subsequent *Daily News* editors, who asserted that her leaders checked the false propaganda circulated by the influential *Times*. A later editor, Sir John Robinson, eulogized Martineau as the reporter who alone "kept public opinion on the right [pro-North] side" throughout this tense period (Arbuckle 1994, xii). The point is a crucial one since, as the earlier jockeying for her political favor during the American tour demonstrated, the war's outcome depended in part on British sympathy, and Harriet Martineau directly influenced that sympathy.

Martineau's professionalism and self-confidence irritated some critics, although it resulted not from hubris but from her commitment to ascertaining and disseminating truth. She observed that while she had been on the *Daily News* staff, "the truth has been told freely and fully about American affairs: and now we are seen to have been right all through,—*and we alone*" (Arbuckle 1994, 206). As a journalist, she strove for objectivity in reporting, yet she clearly struggled with this issue where abolition was concerned. Openly acknowledging her manipulation of the reading public, she asserts, "My principle in the case is to say all that can truthfully be said for them (the Northerners) on this side; and to speak the whole plain truth (as far as relevant) to them on the other side. . . . Of course this is the way to be unpopular on both sides: but . . . [i]t is the only way I see to do any good" (Arbuckle 1994, 214–15). Given the pro-South bias in the *Times*, she felt compelled to employ any approach that cultivated British anti-slavery sympathy instead. Her mission and the means of accomplishing it were clear: "I have to sustain . . . the virtuous people and their cause, and to expose the weakness, as well as the ignorance and guilt of the . . . Secessionists. *Daily News* has an influence there beyond all calculation" (Sanders 1990, 194).

While she was regularly producing *Daily News* leaders, she also wrote occasional extended analyses about American affairs for journals. "The Slave-Trade in 1858," published in the *Edinburgh Review*, addressed this international problem as it affected the American situation. This disturbing chapter in the history of slavery casts America as the foremost test case on which the eyes of the world are focused, just as Karl Engels regarded Britain as the representative model for industrialized society in *The Condition of the Working Classes in England* (1848). Yet, in Martineau's view, America did not stand alone on this issue, in terms of bearing sole responsibility for the institution, its perpetuation, or its eradication:

> Never were we and they more bound to each other in a common duty and a common sentiment than now. When we speak of the American people, we are thinking, first, of the sons and daughters of the founders of the Republic, and next of European immigrants who have entered the Republic as sons by adoption. . . . [T]he turbulent classes which have sprung from the one great corruption of the American polity . . . would be cowed at once by the mere reappearance of the old spirit which raised a group of colonies into a great nation. (Martineau 1858, 585)

Martineau's evocation of the original Pilgrim spirit by which America was founded echoes Elizabeth Barrett Browning's 1848 poem, "A Runaway Slave at Pilgrim's Point," whose fugitive narrator employed the same compelling device.[59]

The tone of "The Slave-Trade in 1858" attests to Martineau's renewed vigor and commitment to life. She firmly believed that America possessed the spirit necessary to eradicate slavery; recalling the ideological energy resulting in the founding of the United States, she termed the impending conflict America's "Second Revolution." But whether America would prove capable of rising to its greatest challenge remained to be seen: slavery "has lowered their reputation, degraded their national character, barred their progress, vitiated their foreign policy, poisoned their domestic peace, divided their hearts and minds; and may ultimately explode

their Union. . . . The opportunity of regenerating the Republic, and regaining the old place of honour among nations, is now present and pressing" (586). Although she accepts the argument that slavery exists in
America because England introduced the practice during the colonial period, she rejects the perpetuation of a system that the country clearly is
capable of eliminating: the outcome of the Revolutionary War, in which
the fledgling country defeated the powerful British empire, offering a
compelling precedent. Because England plays a pivotal, continuing role in
America's civil problems, Martineau envisions a "cordial alliance" between the two countries aimed at eradicating slavery. Early recognizing
the exploitation of Britain's working classes, Martineau drew a striking
analogy between plantations and the industrial milieu. "Not one of your
efforts is lost upon us," she wrote in 1838 to Abby Kelley of the Massachusetts Anti-Slavery Society. "You are strengthening us for the conflicts
we have to enter upon. We have a population in our manufacturing
towns almost as oppressed, and in our secluded rural districts almost as ignorant, as your negroes. These must be redeemed" (Chapman 1877, 223).
From the mature perspective of "The Slave-Trade in 1858," her insight
was prophetic and suggestive.

Similarly, an 1862 article that surveys prominent players in the slavery
debates also draws on Martineau's American experiences of a quarter century earlier. "The Brewing of the American Storm" is notable for its assessment of such statesmen as James Madison, John Calhoun, Chief Justice
Marshall, Bishop White, Henry Clay, and Daniel Webster.[60] The article
marks the occasion of the abolition of slavery in Washington, D.C. on 16
April 1862, the "day the American republic ceased to be a slaveholding
power" (Martineau 1862a, 97). Determined that the magnitude of this
event not be overlooked or downplayed, she asserts that the American
storm has been brewing since the early days of the republic and that the
inevitable outcome has always pointed to civil war.

Several people discussed in the article were acquaintances of Martineau's during her American tour. Bishop White deserves special mention
as one who "was as sensible as every good clergyman must be of the rav-
age which the institution of slavery was making in the religion of the
country" (98). Former president James Madison, a disillusioned coloniza-
tionist, agreed that, in their haste to justify slavery as divinely ordained,
"the clergy perverted the Bible, because it was altogether against slavery"
(99). And Andrew Jackson, whom Martineau credits with having "put
down" early secessionist agitation in South Carolina, "practically counte-
nanced the citizenship of negroes" (100), although he was himself a slave-
holder. Defying the stereotype of southern racism, Jackson is remembered
"by the black race as their patron, by the abolitionists as a witness to the
rights of the negro, and by the slave-holders as an ignorant functionary."

Martineau's memories of these men enhance the article's effectiveness, a
reminder that empirical evidence was the period's most compelling persua-

sive argument. For example, so certain was South Carolina legislator John Calhoun that the South's "peculiar institution" would triumph that he assured her personally that "the subject of slavery would never be mentioned in Congress" (102). Calhoun's posturing in the streets of Charleston "as if he were the ruling prince" was aptly met with the realization of Martineau's assertion that "Slavery was doomed," as was clear to most by 1862. Offering a complementary northern perspective, Martineau recalls predicting the "inevitable rupture of the Union" to American writer Catharine Sedgwick, who protested that "the sacredness of the Union . . . precluded its dissolution from being even imagined" (103). Martineau responded that forces more sacred than the Union are at work in the world, thus "If the will of God is against slavery, and your constitution involves it, which 'must give way'?"

Other personal anecdotes strengthen her credibility as an expert on American affairs, one who does not write merely as a conveyor of information but who also had direct, firsthand experience with the people of whom she writes. Daniel Webster addressed her as "My dear woman" and, familiarly "laying a strong finger" on her arm, urged: "don't you go and believe me to be ambitious" (105); indeed, she observes, it was his ambition to be president that led him to compromise his principles once too often, resulting in his political downfall. Of her acquaintance with Judge Story, whose anti-slavery politics caused him to be "passed over" for a seat on the Supreme Court, she notes: "For hours together we have discussed the inevitable issue of accumulating compromises" (106)—like those engineered by Kentucky senator Henry Clay. With Clay—"Of the whole company I knew him best"—she argued against the colonization schemes: "I had occasion, more than once, to show him that he went too far." She rejects the claim that the impending civil war was "undreamed of" because "It was discussed with me, a quarter of a century ago, by every man and woman I met in the United States who had any political knowledge or sense. . . . [L]et us not incur the charge of either ignorance or hypocrisy by saying that the Second American Revolution was not foreseen long ago" (107).[61]

Martineau offers an entirely singular perspective in "The Negro Race in America." Published in the *Edinburgh Review* in 1864, the article notably focuses not on white public figures, slave owners, or abolitionists, or on economics or even slavery, but on "the character and probable destiny of the negroes" (Martineau 1864, 203). By tracing the history of African Americans from the pre-Revolutionary era through the Civil War, the article highlights blacks' contributions to the Republic while focusing on education and literacy as fundamental to their emancipation and adaptation as free citizens. "Hope" is the key term here, a quality Martineau believes will continue to increase "in proportion as they find means of expressing their experience and their aspirations" (205) for themselves. Aimed at showing that, although blacks have been officially silenced they have not been rendered passive, her examples include Elizabeth Freeman ("Mum

Bet"), the former slave woman whose lawsuit challenging the wording of the Constitution led to the abolition of slavery in Massachusetts; blacks' responses to the duplicitous colonization schemes, which promised liberation but delivered further enslavement; the 1831 Southampton (Nat Turner) Massacre; and a dramatic increase in the number of runaway slaves resulting from tighter legal restrictions on people of color, especially mulattoes. Although the violence underpinning most of her examples testifies to blacks' desperation, there is also plenty to arouse hope in this population, if only by illustrating that, in some, the passivity engendered by slavery and racism backfired, breeding energy, spirit, and social activism instead. Accordingly, she singles out runaway slaves for special praise: they are "always the best and brightest specimens, for obvious reasons. . . . These successful fugitives . . . show that negroes are capable of taking care of themselves" (213, 217), even while eluding armed men, horses, and bloodhounds intent on tracking them down.

Along with examples of inspiring role models from African American history, Martineau discusses education as another medium for instilling hope and as the key to progressive social change. Literacy, even at the most fundamental level, posed such a threat to the slave system that laws were enacted forbidding the education of blacks. But not all were illiterate, and those who could read—perhaps, for example, house slaves who had access to the master's newspapers—established a system of communication between plantations, functioning as a type of underground railroad for the transmission of knowledge. "As passengers could go North by this means," she observes, "so news could come South" (214). Martineau's essay critiques white Christians who flatter eloquent blacks in order to persuade them to preach a particular brand of Christian doctrine to other blacks—one that instills fear and teaches that unquestioning obedience to the master is God's will—"the Christian hope of these people is, in truth, an indulgence of vanity in being petted by the Being they cringe to in prayer, and an exultation in an expected deliverance from whatever vexes them. . . . [T]he leaders of the worship are tools of the masters" (215). "The Negro Race in America" also features school integration in Boston; a slave woman who escapes with her infant by leaping over ice floes on the Ohio River (echoing an episode in *Uncle Tom's Cabin*); the New Bedford Convention of free blacks, who assemble annually to assert their patriotic allegiance to America, vowing to continue to do so throughout the conflict dividing oppressors from oppressed; and blacks' exemplary performance in the military, presented as evidence of patriotism and self-sufficiency. These examples from the past and present lead to a consideration of "the great speculation—what the future of the negro will be in America" (221). She details at some length reconstruction as modeled in the Sea Islands of South Carolina, where deserted plantations have been taken over by the government to teach and train former slaves to be self-reliant. The success of the experiment proves what Martineau had been saying all along: that paid labor motivates workers to a healthy competitiveness, which in turn benefits employers through superior performance and production, yielding profits for all concerned: the complete antithesis of the slave system.

As a product of Martineau's mature years, "The Negro Race in America" both echoes earlier works—the historical motif, the focus on present education and future hope—and demonstrates a depth of understanding that does not depend on spiritualizing or sentimentalizing the issues. The article is impressively written, strong, wise, full of admiration for the fortitude blacks displayed while enslaved and for the determination and courage they display now as they confront the challenges of freedom. Some of her observations are quietly ironic, for example, that the colonizationists' persecution of Garrison was itself responsible for the birth of the abolitionist movement: "The Colonization Society was of Southern origin, . . . formed avowedly in the interests of the slaveholders. . . . When they fined and imprisoned Garrison for saying what was proveably true, they destroyed their own cause to set up his" (209–10). Similarly, the southern secessionists found that the war destroyed the very system it was supposed to preserve: insofar as "the object of secession was to extend and perpetuate slavery, . . . emancipation has been its direct consequence" (242). Other remarks demonstrate that the aging Martineau was as incendiary as ever: there is no doubt, she claims, that "the tottering state of the 'peculiar institution,' which, while declared to be perdurable, *like Christianity,* was ready to fall at the first shock from without" (239; emphasis added). Although she leaves the theological criticism at that, perhaps out of respect for her Christian abolitionist friends, she was never able to reconcile herself to a religion that turned a blind eye to slavery and bigotry while ostensibly promoting compassion and love. She anticipates the time when blacks will speak for themselves and to listeners of all races, and she supports any measure that will lead them to that stage. What the future holds, through education and opportunity, is hope: "Such a revolution in negro history as is now taking place cannot but animate the minds so long depressed by the deferring of their hopes; and the highest ability of the class may well appear on the surface in this great crisis of their fate" (225).

## The Redemption of a Heretic

Her strong connections with prominent Americans provided one reason why editors looked to Martineau during the American crisis. Chapman, citing the letters and private journals Martineau made available to her for the writing of the *Memorials*, remarks on "how deeply her American intercourses touched her heart and mind. . . . [T]hey kept alive . . . the recollection of the years during which she had cherished the purpose of living with them in their own land" (1877, 365). News of her near-fatal 1850s illness prompted Garrison and the Boston Female Anti-Slavery Society to compose this official acknowledgment of Martineau's contributions to the cause while she was still alive to receive it:

> *Resolved,* That, since the briefest historical retrospect of the last quarter of a century would be imperfect without an expression of feeling in view of one great and holy life which the world has seen so unreservedly and strenuously devoted to the welfare to mankind; and since that whole noble life . . . has peculiar claim on *our* hearts, we feel privileged by our cause, to express to Harriet Martineau, while yet there is time, our deep, affectionate, and reverential gratitude for the benefit of her labours, the honour of her friendship, and the sublime joy of her example. (Chapman 1877, 365–66)

Garrison is as eloquent about his indebtedness to Martineau in this private letter:

> [T]wenty years ago, caricatured, reviled, hated, and ostracised as I was universally, . . . words of sympathy and approval were to me as cold water to the thirsty spirit. . . . Those you gave me . . . at the risk of social outlawry, popular contempt and indignation, and pecuniary loss. . . . [Y]ou thus sublimely took up the cross, 'despising the shame,' and have ever since been the unfaltering championess of justice, humanity and freedom, on a worldwide scale.[62]

His allusion to Martineau as Christlike is noteworthy in view of her disavowal of organized religions, particularly Christianity. But Garrison was no dogmatist: rather, he applauds her challenge to Christians to align their practices with their principles. He rejects her ostracization at the hands of "a hireling priesthood and a corrupt church"; he respects and admires her skepticism, her "conscientious dissent and honest doubt," and offers this most appropriate praise: "Conformity is never a virtue, *per se.* Heresy is the only thing that will redeem mankind." Having been pilloried his entire adult life for going against the grain of popular opinion, Garrison understood the wages of passionate commitment to ideals one is compelled to realize.

As it turned out, much of Martineau's best work on American issues was yet to be written at the time of Garrison's comments. Over ten years later, in one of her last *Daily News* leaders (9 January 1866), a jubilant Martineau celebrates the publication of the final number of Garrison's thirty-five-year-old abolitionist newspaper, the *Liberator,* made redundant by the successful conclusion of the Civil War and the freeing of the slaves. The article traces the history of the *Liberator*—from its inception, during which Garrison asserted, "I am in earnest . . . I will not equivocate—I will not excuse—I will not retreat a single inch—AND I WILL BE HEARD"— through its happy demise. She attributes the beginning of hope for enslaved blacks to the knowledge that "somebody was astir on their behalf in the Free States." Garrison's message was one of "peace and patience"

designed to quell slave uprisings and resulting vigilante violence, although he eventually conceded that war was the unfortunate but necessary means of eradicating slavery. From his ill treatment at the hands of
rowdies in Boston, where "he was dragged through the streets . . . with a
halter around his neck, and the tar-kettle heating at the end of the
march," Garrison went on to become the "MOSES of the coloured race, to
whom they looked . . . to bring them out of bondage."

Having realized his abolitionist ambitions with the help of heretical
women like Martineau, Garrison singles out her exemplification of
women's untapped potential: "by the force of her intellect, the scope of
her philanthropy, and the vigor of her writings in behalf of liberty and justice on both sides of the Atlantic, [she] placed herself among the foremost
of public benefactors, and vindicated the equality of woman with man by
a method as practical as it was conclusive." Martineau's example emphasizes the feminist dimensions of Garrisonian abolitionism, which had yet
to be realized after the Civil War and which subsequently occupied Garrison's energies as a franchise and temperance activist. Long reviled as an
"incendiary, fanatic and madman," Garrison is amused to find public disfavor suddenly transformed, so that he is now regarded "a good man, a
worthy citizen, a true patriot, and very much of a Christian!"[63] Garrison
never forgot the significance and the timeliness of Martineau's guarded remarks at the 1835 Boston Ladies' Anti-Slavery Society meeting, noting the
"immense moral courage" and "true martyr spirit" compelling her to speak
her mind and "disdain all subterfuges": "Having then taken up the cross,
you shall henceforth wear the crown."[64] Biblical rhetoric, typical of both
pro- and anti-abolitionist discourse, illustrates the protagonists' perception
of this civil conflict as a holy war. It is a mark of Martineau's impact on
American affairs that those whose martyrdom she earlier chronicled now
return the favor. Offering support and unflagging friendship during her
most controversial periods, Garrison's letters—all the more poignant in
that they are personal, not public, testimonials—eulogized Martineau during her life just as Chapman's *Memorials* did after her death.

On a more objective note that reflects American sentiments toward
Martineau other than those of her two friends, the *New York Independent*
published this death notice in 1876:

> The news of Harriet Martineau's death will have awakened in many minds in
> America a long train of retrospective thought. . . . Miss Martineau came to
> our shores in 1834 . . . preceded by an honourable reputation as a writer on
> political economy and an earnest advocate of freedom for the slave; and, as
> she did not hesitate to avow her sentiments, she was . . . frequently placed in
> disagreeable, and even dangerous circumstances. . . . [T]he clearness of judg-
> ment and fidelity to conviction which marked her whole career appear most
> strongly in her course in America, and for this Americans of to-day cannot
> but honour her.[65]

In 1884, Martineau's memory was most satisfactorily honored near the site of the Boston Female Anti-Slavery Society meeting that so profoundly altered the course of her life. Through the efforts of Maria Weston Chapman, a statue was commissioned, to be sculpted by American abolitionist Anne Whitney. During the unveiling of Martineau's statue, the speaker observed, "Miss Martineau has the great honour of having always seen truth one generation ahead. . . . The first element in Harriet Martineau's greatness is her rectitude of purpose, by which was born that true instinct which saw through all things."[66] Never a stranger to controversy, Martineau's nonconformist attitudes during an era defined by social upheaval earned her the martyrdom she attributed only to those active in the front lines of America's great civil conflict. Clearly, her modest assessment of herself as no more than a popularizer is eclipsed by her foresight as one who, instead, apprehended truth at least "one generation ahead."

# 4

## "I Would Fain Treat of Woman"

I would fain treat of Woman,—and shall do it in some form,—or in many forms; for there is much to be said upon it.

—**Harriet Martineau**

While so many women are no longer sheltered, and protected, and supported, in safety from the world (as people used to say), every woman ought to be fitted to take care of herself . . . that she may possess herself in all the strength and clearness of an exercised and enlightened mind, and may have at command, for her subsistence, as much intellectual power and as many resources as education can furnish her with.

—**Harriet Martineau**

Any pretence of horror or disgust at women having to work, is mere affectation in a country and time when half the women must work in order to live. . . . [T]he anxious solicitude of fathers . . . looks like a mistake when we learn how small is the proportion of women who can be genteel,—if gentility consists in doing nothing appreciable.

—**Harriet Martineau**

I think the want of a leading object is the greatest and commonest misfortune of young women.

—**Harriet Martineau**

## Female Industry

• Florence Nightingale, eulogizing Harriet Martineau in an 1876 letter to Maria Weston Chapman, assesses her friend's life and work along two primary lines: as an anti-slavery activist and as a woman of "religious feeling" (Chapman 1877, 480). The former is self-evident, "slavery" by Martineau's definition not being limited to racial issues but extending to class and gender as well; but the latter point raises interesting questions: not the least of which is how Martineau might respond to being termed religious after years of notoriety as an avowed agnostic. Citing such examples as *Eastern Life, Present and Past* (the 1848 travel memoir for which she was branded an infidel) and "Sowers Not Reapers" (the *Illustrations* tale featuring a compassionate portrayal of the "drinking woman," Margaret Kay), Nightingale asks, "what higher religious feeling (or one should say instinct) could there be?" She defines "religious feeling" in terms of what Martineau would call the "most serious business of life": as "the sense of good working out of evil, into a supreme wisdom penetrating and moulding the whole universe;—into the natural subordination of intellect and intellectual purposes and of intellectual self to purposes of good, even were these merely the small purposes of social or domestic life." Her use of religious rhetoric when speaking of Martineau seems misplaced but in fact aligns comfortably with her friend's "religion" of work and social reform.[1]

Of Florence Nightingale's cosmology Sandra Holton writes: "physical and moral purity were a single and absolute value. . . . For her the ultimate moral imperative was to understand God's ordering of the world in the laws of Nature. Morality and religious life involved for Florence Nightingale largely rational and secular exercises" (1984, 61). This interpretation accords with Jane Tompkins's analysis (1985) of the links between domesticity and religion in the life and work of Harriet Beecher Stowe. Tompkins challenges the ideas of domestic oppression and angel-in-the-house passivity by positing that for women like Stowe, cleanliness is indeed next to godliness. Martineau might object to the religious rhetoric, but she firmly believed that the universe is ordered according to scientific (in other words, natural) principles that are increasingly knowable through advanced technology and intellectual evolution, and that one of the most basic of those principles is domestic order (hence the link between domestic *science* and the natural order). From her perspective, the most mundane skills assume philosophical connotations, serving as a path to spiritual liberation by shaping a domestic microcosm mirroring the universal macrocosm. This view seriously complicates the stereotype equating domesticity with oppression.[2]

Thus, it is Nightingale's last phrase—"the small purposes of social or domestic life"—that particularly interests me in its capacity to spiritualize Martineau's life and work, implicating her social activism—from the loftiest philosophical speculations to practical instructions on animal husbandry[3]—in Nightingale's idea of religion. Because domestic issues affect the lives of everyone and basically define the few employment options available to mid-Victorian working women, Martineau devoted a considerable portion of her writing to women's work and education and to such legal issues as wife abuse, divorce and property acts, and infanticide. Her writing on women's issues depends on the idea that the domestic skills heralded as woman's "true" mission have the potential to empower, rather than to oppress—: or, at the very least, to bridge women's domestic space to the world of work outside the home. Martineau draws a sharp distinction between domestic skill and drudgery, citing chores like plain sewing and laundry as work best accomplished by sewing and washing machines. Women had long used domestic skills as a means to work outside the home, and Martineau was concerned with facilitating the next step in women's progress: their move into more skilled, more intellectually challenging, and more lucrative employment. Like many pre-first-wave feminists, Martineau appropriated separate spheres notions used to keep women in their place—domesticity, inherent nurturance, and maternal instinct—and employed them for quite another purpose: to argue that these are the very qualities that justify women's participation in the marketplace, an insight crucial to understanding the feminism implicit in what our contemporary scholars might otherwise regard as *essentialism*.[4]

Virtually all of Martineau's writing is politically oriented, both fiction and nonfiction, especially her periodicals writing. Martineau routinely employed her literary skills on behalf of marginalized groups, so that her pen was itself a primary tool for political activism. She signed petitions for Josephine Butler's campaign to repeal the Contagious Diseases Acts, for Sophia Jex-Blake's lawsuit against the medical school at Edinburgh University,[5] and for the Married Women's Property Bill generated by Barbara Bodichon and Bessie Rainer Parks. And, although she believed women had a long way to go before the vote would do them any good, she also signed petitions for the Women's Suffrage Committee. She was skeptical of extending the franchise to women at this point in history because, without education and intellectual and economic autonomy, she feared that women would remain the political pawns of the men on whom they were dependent.[6]

Martineau also opposed the admission of women to the Commons' galleries in Parliament as silly and frivolous—as R. K. Webb puts it, "a nuisance to M.P.s and a disadvantage to the wiser women who knew that a serious cultivation of political interests was better done at home" (Webb 1960, 181). She saw the potential for women who have nothing to do turning this token privilege into another excuse for a fashion display, giving women who were serious political activists a "bad name" by relation. She also denounced public feminist grandstanding: she disapproved "of the tone used by some of the public advocates of Woman's Rights," and detested "all setting up of idols, and all proclamation of Rights" (Sanders 1990, 115; 167). Her alternative method was to promote the period's work ethic, urging women to find the work they are suited to do and do the best they are capable of, for themselves, for society, for the benefit of all women everywhere. Talk unaccompanied by action is just talk, just as the franchise without an educated, evolved political consciousness liberates no one. Through a survey of selected representative texts, this chapter looks at some of Martineau's many contributions, as one of those serious political activists, to raising public consciousness about the status of women and the sorts of cultural and legal changes required to promote their cause. An examination of her efforts to formulate and to resolve the period's Woman Questions reveals that Martineau's identity as a woman writer and social reformist was directly shaped by the gender issues affecting all women, thus implicating Woman's Cause as another central theme in her life and work.

"Every girl has an innate longing, we are confident, for the household arts, if nature had but her way," Martineau asserts in "Female Industry" (1859b, 316)—a statement certain to set the teeth of present-day feminists on edge. Yet her perspective reflects an approach designed to appease conservative gender ideologists while providing women with opportunities for change and growth. Martineau's feminism, like that of Mary Wollstonecraft and the Garrisonian abolitionists, relied on appropriating separate spheres gender ideology as the means to an alternative end. Wollstonecraft's "republican motherhood," for example, argues that educated women make better mothers who in turn produce better citizens, while the Garrisonians reject the charge that abolitionist activism is unwomanly and un-Christian, claiming instead that it is the most womanly and holy of mundane activities women can undertake.[7] Contemporary feminism takes a dim view of such essentializing, seen in the characterization of Martineau as an antifeminist by those who regard her example as evidence of her "auxiliary usefulness" to the oppressive male hegemony.[8] But as chapter 2's analysis of the relationship between writing and needlework in Martineau's life shows, the role of domesticity in Victorian women's lives was more complex than the term *oppression* alone suggests. The equation of domesticity with oppression, especially popular since the second-wave feminists of the 1960s–1970s cited unpaid housework as a primary locus of women's oppression, fails to account for several alternative possibilities: some women *like* housewifery and take pride in cultivating those skills, others locate sites for feminism *within* domestic activities that afford a specifically female epistemology (like quilting), still others, like Martineau, seek to dismantle the sexual division of labor altogether, arguing that *everyone* depends on domestic economy and therefore everyone should be self-sufficient in terms of domesticity and economics.

Martineau's egalitarian notion of the centrality of domesticity to happy, healthy lives for both men and women extended to the community and broader society by collapsing, or at least weakening, the boundaries of separate spheres. Everyone, male and female, can and should know how to bake custards and sew on buttons as well as farm and keep cows and read, write, and think. Martineau's utopian vision sought to move beyond gendered divisions of labor to embrace a gender- and race- and class-free humanism; in this, both then and now, she swims upstream against historically specific currents whose social contexts are wary of such an encompassing vision. "The true rule in this case is that every human being, of both sexes, and all complexions, countries, and races, should be permitted and incited to do whatever it can," she wrote in the *Daily News*

(9 January 1860). "Capacity is the only just limit to the industry of any person whatever; and no one class or person can decide on the capability of another. 'A fair field and no favour' is the rule of justice and honour in the field of industry." But she also had a keen sense of timing: that so much of her writing was devoted to the causes of racial slavery, working-class poverty, and women's issues demonstrates her awareness that gross legal and political inequities must be remedied before a truly egalitarian humanism is tenable. That twenty-first-century culture is little nearer to egalitarianism than the Victorians attests to Martineau's insight that time-liness is crucial to the success of social reforms.

Martineau's resistance to gendered divisions of labor is seen in her par-ticipation in both male and female realms and in her refusal to choose be-tween the two. She broke important ground by steadily exemplifying throughout her life and career the stereotypically female qualities of sexual propriety, decorum, and domestic skill (minus the passivity) and stereotyp-ically male qualities of professional credibility, social influence, and liter-ary skill (without the acerbity often associated with literary men during this period). Admittedly, Martineau's admirable tenacity as a woman mov-ing about in a man's world, sans pseudonym, seems disappointingly un-dercut by some of her more conventional, or contradictory, attitudes, like the one from "Female Industry" previously quoted (1859b, 316). For this reason, her feminism needs to be assessed on its own terms and in its his-torical context rather than made to conform with our contemporary para-digms. Such an approach enables us to focus on what her gender politics does accomplish rather than on how it disappoints. Her economic and so-cial independence, her professional success and strong-mindedness, her formidable self-sufficiency and the range of her influence in political cir-cles: these are factors contributing to her image as a feminist icon. As Janet Courtney writes, "Her own so justly-respected personality . . . [ is] the best argument she could have used" in support of Woman's Cause (1933, 202).

Oddly, however, rather than viewed as evidence of her feminism, Mar-tineau's resistance to and rejection of any person, idea, or behavior com-promising Woman's Cause, particularly the more insipid forms of popular sentimentalism that romanticize women's inferiority, earned her labels ranging from latent lesbian to asexual to jealous to sexually frustrated. Such biologically reductive labeling indicates that the question of Mar-tineau's feminism has not yet been adequately addressed. A more relevant point to explore is whether she is simply full of blatant contradictions—rather difficult to believe of a woman of her intellect—or whether our defining concepts are too narrow to accommodate what she has, in fact, contributed to Woman's Cause. Critics' restless inclination to compart-mentalize Martineau's sexuality deflects critical focus from the quality and impact of her writing and politics as, in the public arena, it keeps Woman Question debates mired in the realm of sexuality, reifying the popular idea that women are bound by their biology. The speculative focus on

Martineau's sexuality reflects critics' need to account for a strong, gifted, intelligent, energetic reformer as a social aberration: certainly not, in herself, a viable role model for Victorian or contemporary feminists. I aim to move beyond biological determinism and to present Harriet Martineau as a thinker, a writer, and an autonomous individual whose success was due not to sexual frustration but to her self-proclaimed "need of utterance" and her prodigious intellectual and literary ability.

## Women in Fiction

Martineau's feminism is best seen in her own example, in her critiques of famous women of the period (see chapter 5), and in her writings that promote Woman's Cause. Shifting focus to the latter, this chapter addresses prominent themes that are less autobiographical and more representative of Martineau's concern with broader feminist issues, communally, nationally, and internationally. Valerie Pichanick notes, "It is rather surprising that Martineau failed to create a new image of woman in literature. In spite of an outspoken belief in equality, Martineau's fictional women . . . were rather conventional heroines" (1977, 29). Yet if Martineau did not create a fully realized ideal of liberated womanhood in her fiction, one free of contradictions, excesses, and faults, neither did any of her contemporaries construct such a model, although many tried. On the other hand, her scrutiny of often unquestioned social dictums performs the crucial work of illustrating which qualities promote Woman's Cause and which impede it. For this reason, Martineau's women characters are worth studying as critiques of the period's gender ideology, just as her abundant nonfiction writings on women's work, education, and legal status (discussed later in this chapter) critique biased laws, analyze existing institutions, and propose viable reforms to benefit women.

Martineau created compelling illustrations of women and girls whose characterizations foster our understanding of her feminism. This includes women whose qualities she regarded as admirable and worth emulating as well as those who, trapped by blind, unquestioning obedience to convention, perpetuate demeaning stereotypes while wasting their lives and diminishing the quality of the lives around them. Arguably, the examples illustrating negative stereotypes are even more revelatory than the positive role models in terms of their instructive capacity. Bearing in mind Pichanick's objection to "rather conventional heroines," conventionality is, in fact, what forms the basis of Martineau's critiques of gender ideology. The women characters who are most passive or pliable are those most likely, in her tales, to "come to a bad end." This pattern overturns Victorian gender ideology, as does Martineau's singular mode of describing her characters. Generally, in a striking contrast with most writers of the period, Martineau resisted describing her women characters' physical qualities, thereby compelling readers to focus on more substantive values when assessing their worth. Although some of her female characters convey a sense of beauty, it is their responses to life's challenges and their moral integrity that construct Martineau's alternative definition of attractiveness, which goes beyond the sexual and physical appeals leading to biological reductionism.

Several tales in the *Illustrations of Political Economy* (1832–1834) offer early examples of women characters that alternately promote and impede Woman's Cause. The opening scene of "Cousin Marshall" features a tenement fire and the death of a poor widow whose younger children are placed with relatives, while the oldest boy and girl are relegated to the dreaded workhouse. Typically, the tales analyze an aspect of political economy needing reevaluation and reform: here, the workhouse and poor-law systems and their effects on women and children. Of all those victimized by the ineptitude and inadequacies of poor-relief systems, orphaned girls are at the greatest risk, and young Jane Bridgeman's example dramatizes the workhouse's capacity to corrupt morality rather than to alleviate poverty and homelessness.

Until her mother's death, Jane's poverty, though a hardship, is not marked by immorality: for example, inappropriate sexual relations; this quality casts her as one of the "deserving" poor, which enhances the drama of her subsequent "fall" into the "undeserving" class. But the innocence and purity with which she enters the workhouse, rather than protecting her, instead render her particularly vulnerable to negative influences; Martineau's treatment anticipates Elizabeth Gaskell's works questioning the crucial distinction between girls' sexual ignorance (lack of knowledge) and sexual innocence (lack of experience) and the potential for disaster resulting from an inadequate understanding of that distinction.[9] Workhouse inmates range from cases like Jane, people who genuinely need sanctuary and protection, to those in a chronic state of poverty and unemployment, and include the criminal element as well as prostitutes who use the system when incapacitated by venereal disease or pregnancy and unwed mothers rejected by their families. Jane's fate is typical of what resulted from the workhouse's indiscriminate blending of naive children with indigents, criminals, and diseased prostitutes.

The privileged Miss Burke, whose purity is not compromised by poverty or orphanhood, visits Jane at the workhouse and is shocked by the mismanagement she finds there. Concerned about the "want of proper distinction" between the deserving and undeserving poor, Miss Burke reflects on popular stereotypes of workhouse inmates, noting "We are too apt . . . to regard all the poor alike, and to speak of them as one class" (30). The significance of this point, so aptly clarified through Jane's example, is revelatory, but it alters neither her present situation nor her fate. Although a minor character, Miss Burke offers an alternative to the self-centered and materialistic, vain and superficial females typical of her class. Despite her lofty lifestyle, she chooses to call at the workhouse rather than at the homes of frivolous socialites, illustrating the philanthropic movement that permits respectable women legitimately to leave their homes and to put their "superior" morality to practical use in the community.[10] Miss Burke is sensitive to, rather than repulsed by, the plights of the poor and demonstrates keen insight into the systematic perpetuation of poverty in this class: "It is rather hard upon the poor . . . that we should complain of their improvidence when we bribe them to it by promising subsistence at all events" (52). Her words articulate Martineau's conviction that charity perpetuates, rather than resolves, poverty by fostering a false sense of security; at best a temporary solution to chronic social problems, charity should be limited to emergencies and other crisis situations and replaced with the education, training, and work opportunities necessary for permanent self-sufficiency.[11]

Once released from the workhouse, Jane exhibits qualities associated with moral contamination: she resists hard work and displays vanity—considered especially inappropriate for poor girls and a sure sign of impending sexual fallenness—by complaining of her shabby bonnet and longing for a new one. Her position working for Farmer Dale promises economic independence while restoring her to a wholesome environment defined by hard work, utility, and sound morality. But charity has made her lazy and vanity (absorbed, apparently, from her exposure to prostitutes) makes her flirtatious; she is seduced into sexual consummation by promises of marriage and abandoned by her lover to deal with the consequences herself. Rejected by her Aunt Bell, who is too intent on exploiting the poor-law system to help her niece, Jane finds sanctuary with Cousin Marshall who, in contrast, prides herself on never having accepted charity, no matter how financially distressed.[12]

But Jane seems doomed by the negative influences set into motion by poverty, and she is arrested and returned to the workhouse, an environment distinctly at odds with her desire to reform her life.[13] Chastened by her experiences, Jane "would much rather have gone into service and tried to atone for what was done, than remain to be the pauper-wife of a man who had cruelly deceived her,—who would not marry unless he could be caught,—and who, being an unwilling, would be probably an unkind, husband" (108). This perspective offers startling commentary on Martineau's attitudes about marriage and sexuality: forcing Jane into marriage, which some claim is the only way to rectify the social sin of premarital sex, would only compound her troubles and further unravel a social fabric already compromised by such perversions of nuclear family ideology. Despite the considerable difficulties she faces, marriage is not the solution, nor is charity or the punitive workhouse.

The most unfortunate outcome for a girl like Jane is the one that Cousin Marshall dreads and that is sadly realized: "Her good cousin feared . . . that this misery might drive her to habitual vice . . . [and] she would become a castaway from her family forever" (108). Permanently stigmatized by circumstances not entirely of her own making, Jane is prevented from both legitimate employment and legitimate marriage; she fulfills the worst expectations of the stereotype and becomes a prostitute. As for the other women characters, Aunt Bell seems appropriately punished for cheating the system when her husband abandons her and she is compelled to move into the workhouse herself, with all her children. Cousin Marshall, whose moral stability is a guiding force throughout the tale, struggles economically all her life and dies a poor woman, thanking God for a "blessed life." Although Martineau implies that it is this woman alone who rises to the challenge of living a penurious life without resorting to bitterness, immorality, or deceit, Cousin Marshall, rather than earning respect from her community, suffers ridicule for her determined self-sufficiency when she could have asked for charity at the workhouse. If Cousin Marshall's example is a moral triumph, it is an ambivalent one, particularly since her only recompense for suffering in this life is the spiritual reward promised in the next.

"Cousin Marshall" raises various gender-related issues: the feminization of poverty, seen in the women characters struggling to support their families; the irresponsibility of men who abandon their familial obligations, whether unmarried (in Jane's case) or married (in Aunt Bell's); and the corruption of young girls by their exposure to the vice of a system that ostensibly protects them. The poignant image of Cousin Marshall, who dies alone in extreme poverty, somewhat pathetically thanking God for what blessings we can only imagine, offers a rather anemic consolation for undertaking suffering. There but for the grace of God and her wealthy family, perhaps, goes Miss Burke, proving that only the privileged can truly be angels-in-the-house; other women either die or take to the streets. Neither extreme permits women economic autonomy, independence, or freedom from want.

Dora Sullivan, the heroine of "Ireland," offers one of Martineau's strongest characterizations, although again not without complications. Dora is a more fully realized character than those presented in "Cousin Marshall," and the behaviors she models are more realistic than the extremes of Cousin Marshall's saintliness and Jane's corruptibility. That her docile obedience is presented as her most prominent quality makes her fall into criminality especially tragic, a device that effectively promotes Martineau's critique of the damage perpetrated on all women forced by custom into the unnatural mode of passive angel. Of the many social problems Martineau addresses in "Ireland," the most important is the significance of education as the prerequisite for social change. That Dora is both the primary woman character and the only one in her family who is literate is suggestively innovative on Martineau's part, particularly in view of the tale's outcome. Lacking Jane Bridgeman's naive susceptibility, Dora struggles to reconcile her book learning with unquestioning obedience to the authority figures whose limited vision leads to her ruin.

The daughter of poor tenant farmers, Dora is the "most promising" of the village students, and her scholarship pleases the priest and her proud parents. Her decision to leave school to support her destitute family while waiting to marry her fiancé, Dan Mahony, establishes her character as gifted, selfless, and compassionate. But Martineau offers Dora's feminine qualities not so much to admire as to scrutinize in terms of the dangers inherent in internalizing damaging gender strictures. Among the qualities Martineau critiques in Dora are her docility and passive obedience. Her intellectual superiority—her skills in reading and writing assume an almost mystical, magical quality to her illiterate parents—is undermined by her womanly submissiveness to priest, father, and husband, who contribute directly (albeit unwittingly: they are ignorant, not malicious) to her destruction.

Events leading to her demise are set in motion when she is asked to sign a legal document for her father. Counting on her unquestioning obedience, Mr. Sullivan proves his lack of discernment between knowledge and critical thinking by commanding Dora to write: "hold the pen and write as you're bid, and show what a scholard [sic] Father Glenny has made of you" (9). Dora glances over the document and warns her father against its potentially duplicitous wording, but in his hubris he dismisses her concern, to Overseer Teale's satisfaction. This pivotal scene, which anticipates a letter-writing episode that perpetuates the family's descent into outlawry, proves Dora's concern valid when Teale seizes their livestock, plunging the family further into poverty.

But Dan Mahony suddenly appears to rescue Dora and her family: "You trust me, Dora, don't you," he asks, "as the priest gave leave?" With these words, the noose tightens as Dora's innate intelligence is compromised by cultural, familial, and religious strictures demanding her acquiescence: "it had never entered her head to doubt—love having thus far been entirely unconnected in her mind with thoughts of the world's gear" (24). The marriage earlier delayed for economic reasons is now vigorously promoted for those same reasons, with Dora positioned between her needy parents and the strong, ambitious fiancé promising to help her family. As a result, Dora's "filial duty, religion, and love, all plied her at once in favour of an immediate marriage."

Dan's youthful energy, fueled by love for his young wife and compassion for her defeated parents, manages to stabilize the family, yet all is lost when they are again outwitted by Teale and left homeless. Enraged, Dan, "in a tone which none dared disobey" (43), orders all their belongings destroyed to prevent seizure by Teale; he hides his pregnant wife and her dying mother in a cave, and the two men become outlaws, determined actively to thwart the system designed to destroy them. Sick and despairing, Dora gives birth alone, her only company her mother's corpse. Traumatized by the crush of these events, Dora is later unable to remember the "circumstances connected with the death of her mother and the birth of her child" (73).

Dora again is made the instrument of the men in her life but this time with more tragic and irreversible consequences. While Dan's career as a renegade mercenary intensifies, Dora withdraws into silence and passivity, mechanically obedient to her husband's order that she write a threatening letter to a British army official: this is nothing, he engagingly assures her, but "writing a slip of a letter, my darling, because it's you that will be doing it neat and pretty" (77). The letter is traced to Dora, whose hiding place is found out; she is arrested for treason and jailed with her infant while father and husband pillage the countryside. In effect, the squalid conditions of jail merely extend her confinement in the cave and her steady retreat into her own murky psychological depths; Dora's health strains under the burden of her child's ceaseless wailing, and she passively watches her infant waste away, a tragic monument to feminine ideology. The values of filial obedience, wifely submission, and maternal ideology Dora Sullivan represents are thus perverted by father, husband, and authoritative political institutions, as well as by her priest.

The gravity of Dora's situation intensifies when Father Glenny, who takes her infant to healthier surroundings, realizes how completely this former model girl has been broken by her circumstances; he is struck by "her utter indifference" toward her trial (122). Proving her thorough victimization, "She made no preparation. . . . She had nothing to confess, nothing to ask for, no messages to leave, no desires to express" (123). Demoralized by grief as she hands her child over to the priest, she observes, "I forget all about my child's coming to me, and I don't think I care much about its going from me" (124). Refusing the priest's blessing—"No blessing, father, to-day! It has never done me any good"—Dora cuts all remaining ties with the life she has known, in effect anticipating her transportation for life as a convicted criminal. One by one, each relationship is severed and each quality that individualizes her is compromised, until all that remains is expatriation.

Although Martineau presents Dora as thoroughly blameless and a consummate victim, whose numbness indicates not her "unnaturalness," as the priest thinks, but a mode of surviving the unendurable, Dora's lethal combination of passivity and intelligence typifies the social expectations placed on all women. Her collapsed response to her tragedies suggests that she is powerless to meet adversity, although this is not surprising, given the forces ranged against her. But Dora does defend herself at last, in the presence of men and the institutions they represent: men who not only failed to protect her but who aggressively contributed to her destruction. Dora stands up for herself, not by thieving, like her father, nor by brutality, like her husband, nor by praying, like her priest, but by exercising the one gift all have admired, some have exploited, and others have suppressed: her literacy.

As she is led from the court, Dora overhears this oddly incisive remark from an old acquaintance: "If she had never been taught to write . . . this murtherous letter could never have been brought against her" (125). The observation prods Dora to break her silence. In a stirring monologue worthy of the moment, she demands, "Is there no language to threaten in . . . but that which is spelled by letters?" She posits that, even by destroying all schools, ink, and paper, "you will still find threats inscribed wherever there is oppression" (125–26). Her pointed demand—"When do prosperous men plot, or contented men threaten, or those who are secure perjure themselves, or the well-governed think of treachery?"—highlights the real source of rebellion and unrest: cold hearths, unemployment, starvation, and homelessness resulting from absentee landlordism, unscrupulous overseers, and a political hegemony indifferent to the plights of the Irish poor. That the judge remains unmoved matters less than the fact of her long overdue articulation, with its suggestive metaphor casting Ireland and its people as the text on which has been written the oppressors' every unjust act for all the world to read. As the court dismisses Dora and the truths she represents, so too does England dismiss the Irish, whose tragic problems are less indigenous than imposed from without. Nevertheless, Dora's character demonstrates that the power of literacy—written and spoken—poses a distinct threat to political hegemonies that cannot be ignored, even in a woman. That Dora's learning, optimistically symbolizing Ireland's potential to overcome its social problems through education, instead makes her a political scapegoat is the ultimate irony in this tale that rehearses the vexed "Irish Question."

The character Dora Sullivan, damned by the words written in her own hand, doomed by conflicting value systems promoting female passivity over male assertiveness, adds another component to Martineau's feminism. Despite her strong qualities, Dora is defeated by custom; like her creator, she negotiates between the intelligence associated with the masculine realm and the social strictures demanding female decorum. But unlike her creator, whose literacy produces thousands of pages of text pleading for social justice and whose life and work articulate a profound "need of utterance," Dora's transportation to a penal colony effectually silences her as a threat to social cohesion more insidious even than robbing or smuggling. "Ireland" hauntingly illustrates the exploitive relations on which imperialism depends: as England exploits Ireland and Overseer Teale cheats the poor farmers, so also do Mr. Sullivan and Dan Mahony use Dora's education to further their own ends at her expense. Martineau's perspectives into the interlocking race, gender, and class dynamics of imperialism in this early tale anticipate her progressive insights on Anglo-Indian relations later in her career.

"For Each and for All" features a striking departure from the foregoing characterizations by investing an aristocrat with the qualities that promote Woman's Cause. But Lady Frances is no ordinary aristocrat: daringly, Martineau endows her heroine with a rather controversial past. Prior to her marriage, Lady Frances, or Letitia, was a stage actress, a profession linked with "loose" women and prostitution. A woman putting herself forward in the public eye had no claim to respectability; since many actresses were pursued by wealthy admirers with whom they shared unchaperoned late-night suppers, sexual indiscretion was assumed integral to the general stereotype. But Sir Henry, a widower with grown children, is confident that everyone in his circle will accept his new wife; accordingly, although ruthlessly scrutinized on her arrival, Letitia's unpretentious manner with people of all classes quickly earns her their respect. Because of her inferior class and her experiences outside the rarified atmosphere of the aristocracy, Letitia exhibits a natural social grace most find endearing, even as it challenges strict observations of social caste.

Letitia's progressive insights are tested at an elaborate ball where, although she is much admired, she keenly remembers her own Cinderella origins. She is struck by the disparity between the "peers within and paupers without; careless luxury above and withering hardship below" (15). Like Dora Sullivan, Letitia interprets society as a text inscribed by privilege and poverty: "This is too deep a page for my reading," she says to her husband, "and not the easier for my having been in both conditions myself." But it is precisely her experience in both realms that suits her for philanthropic work, now that she finds herself in a position of some influence and power. Theirs is a marriage of love rather than convention or convenience, although Henry is forced to contend with gossips' claims that Letitia is an opportunist, interested only in his money and a luxurious lifestyle. For her part, Letitia, echoing her creator as well as the ubiquitous Mary Wollstonecraft, had resisted marriage as legalized slavery akin to prostitution, while the aristocratic lifestyle earns her contempt for its idleness and self-indulgence. Prior to marriage, Letitia argued that there was "little enough of rational freedom at the best in the condition of a wife, and that a woman's only hope of that which the marriage law at present denies her rests in the steady principle as well as the enlightened views of her husband" (18–19).[14] Henry demonstrates his "enlightened views" by assuming a government post in order to serve society. That their shared social commitment is Letitia's condition for accepting his marriage proposal both proves her lack of opportunism and attests to Martineau's interest in envisioning alternatives to the inequitable marriages commonly seen. Both Letitia and Henry are exceptional characters from opposite ends of the social spectrum, and their union challenges and redefines the limitations of conventional marriage.

Proving that a woman can be both intelligent and respectable, Lady Frances is opinionated and strong-minded and admired because of those qualities. She is critical of social and economic disparities and full of suggestions about remedying them. Interestingly, Letitia also expresses deep convictions about acting as a high calling rather than the debased pursuit it was assumed to be: "I dared not at once give up the calling which nature had sanctified to me, without providing for my race being served in an equal proportion in some other way" (33). One of the "other" ways open to few outside the peerage involves access to fine art: "They who perceive not that the fine arts are the fittest embodiments of truth and beauty are unconscious of the vastness of the department in which they would have man remain unserved" (34). On a related point that illustrates Martineau's aesthetics of realism, Letitia observes that the poorer classes exhibit "the most rapid vicissitudes, the strongest passions, the most undiluted emotions, the most eloquent deportment, the truest experience" comprising the "true romance of human life"; yet "these things are almost untouched by our artists" (127). She is also concerned about persistent attitudes condemning the arts, which she regards as avenues leading to "truth and beauty" as well as to respectable professions for women: "There is a kind of discredit belonging to them; so that it requires a very strong inducement to tempt people of great talent to engage in them" (65). Indeed, it is her profession and her experience of both poverty and wealth that so deeply sensitize her to the "true romance of human life."

Like all the *Illustrations* tales, "For Each and for All" offers expository conversations in which characters debate political economy from various perspectives. Most such conversations in this tale feature Letitia, whose activities bring her into contact with shopkeepers, aristocrats, rectors, and peasants in discussions about divisions of wealth and labor according to class. She puts her ideals to work in the community, not only in defense of the arts but in more tangible ways, like befriending the old rector, Joel, and helping people find solutions to their material difficulties. Although in terms of political economy this tale is unusual, its focus on alternatives to the inequities of conventional marriage, on the importance of supporting the fine and performing arts and making them accessible to working-class people, and on the breakdown of the caste system so damaging to a healthy society are welcome additions to discussions of profit and distribution. Letitia's character is especially finely drawn, making her an important entry in Martineau's cast of strong and compelling female characters, each contributing, in her way, to Woman's Cause: whether to celebrate women's abilities or to expose social injustices.[15]

Several *Illustrations* tales feature brief sketches of women characters whose qualities contribute to this emerging picture of Martineau's feminism. "The Charmed Sea," the story that caused her works to be banned in Russia, highlights two distinct types of women: the embittered Polish exile Sophia and the stoic Siberian peasant Emilia. Sophia, whose fiancé is conscripted by the Russian army, undergoes a dramatic transformation from an optimistic bride to a vindictive "old-maid." The primary object of her hate is the Russians, under whom the exiles suffer as virtual slaves. Consumed by hate, Sophia wishes she were a man, to shoot, hunt, and fight against the Russians, whose political aggressions deprive her of present comfort and future security.

Sophia refuses to be comforted, observing: "I am wiser now, and shall not go back into the old state. I see things as they are, bleak and bare, and soulless" (37). Sophia's mother observes that this degree of anguish exceeds the cushion of optimism by which she is herself sustained: "I have faith because I have not, like you, been tried beyond my strength" (39). Yet while it is true that there are limits to what humans can endure, Sophia's obstinate, unfeminine rage seems disproportionate to her loss. Hers is a disappointment of plans, a delay in their realization, not the actual losses—usually death—suffered by many of her compatriots. Her example dramatizes the plight of women raised to no other goal or expectation in life than marriage and motherhood; in the absence of those roles, Sophia's life has no meaning, her character has no definition. Without a man to lend her social status, Sophia is incapable of seeing beyond immediate difficulties to envision alternative ways of perceiving herself and her role in society. Once her fiancé is restored to her, Sophia instantly reverts to her old self, disproving her claim that she is forever changed by her experiences and verifying the centrality of marriage to her self-definition. Over all, she is less pitiable than self-indulgent in her inability to rise above her own disappointments and to participate in the more profound vicissitudes of her country's political crisis. In Martineau's view, concern for the greater good of society over one's personal traumas is a primary characteristic of those who promote Woman's Cause.

In contrast, Emilia—who possesses the masculine skills Sophia covets—is a woman who experiences the rather dubious benefits of marriage. This enigmatic Siberian peasant, unable to understand the language of the Polish husband to whom she has been joined, prefers silent endurance and action to words, prompting her husband Paul to work her like a pack animal.[16] A genuine survivor of the unforgiving Siberian wilderness, Emilia—her real name is rejected as too difficult to remember and replaced by her husband with one of his choosing—makes arrows, hunts and dresses the kill, performs all the domestic chores, waits on Paul and caters to him as he lolls about, praising her industry but never offering to help. In a revealing conversation between Paul and Taddeus, Sophia's brother, gender exploitation is cast as an aspect of imperialism that peasants mimic by practicing on each other. To Paul's bragging about Emilia's amazonian hardiness, Taddeus asks, "what she can do like a woman?" Paul responds, "Cook my dinner, and keep my house warm, and wait upon me." "So this is to be a woman, is it?" asks Taddeus, to which Paul replies: "Yes . . . as for the other things you value so much,—the power of thinking, and reasoning, and all that—where is the Polish woman that would not now be better off without it?" (51–52). Paul's remark rehearses the argument that educated women suffer more keenly under oppression for their knowledge, an idea Martineau refutes in her introduction to *Mind amongst the Spindles*. In a revealing comparison, Paul notes that Emilia "is more like a faithful dog," while Sophia, lacking a man, is "like a hunted tiger-cat" (69). Presumably, once the lack is filled, she too becomes "more like a faithful dog."

But Emilia is much more than an obedient pet; her plodding packhorse demeanor belies the unerring senses and sharp instincts of rugged self-sufficiency. That her bondage to Paul is termed a marriage is revealing, although Emilia, disturbingly, seems to accept her fate as inevitable. Together, the two women characters offer suggestive perspectives on women's lack of identity and autonomy without men to define them (Sophia) and on the superiority of female endurance even when handicapped by a parasitic male, as in Emilia's example. Despite the cultural displacement of this tale, its analogy with the institution of marriage in mid-Victorian Britain invites a striking comparison, as do the parallels between women—whether of the conquered or the conquerors, they share the subjection of the Polish prisoners—and slavery. The depictions of marriage offered in this tale, in which able women are bound by false notions of their function as servants to men, are as bleak as the Siberian wilderness in which they are set.

Another woman compromised by marriage is Hester of "Berkeley the Banker." Like Dora Sullivan, Hester is a model young woman whose artistic gifts lead her to employment as a book illustrator. Her wedding and move to London make her a sort of local hero whose example seems to prove that feminine decorum leads to upward mobility. But demonstrating instead that marriage is often the source of women's troubles rather than the solution to the Woman Question, Hester—separated from home, family, and community and now the exclusive property of her husband—finds herself joined to a spendthrift whose improvident habits keep them poor and whose meanness prevents her from any social contact. Edgar's covert activities surface when he most uncharacteristically allows Hester to visit home and sends her off with a stack of money to spend. Delighted to visit old friends and bolster the community's sagging economy by generously spreading her new wealth around, Hester soon learns that she has been duped by a cruel husband who provided her with counterfeit money.

When Hester confronts Edgar, he determines to "implicate her so far as to secure her fidelity" (2:70). To that end, he sends her on errands that make her an accomplice, and the more he demands her participation, the sicker she becomes as her wifely obedience—which conflicts with her own code of ethics—propels her into criminality. Whereas Dora Sullivan's weakness is her obedience to men and their institutions, even when she sees where it will lead, Hester's is her persistent romanticization of husband and marriage. That her marriage proves false is an idea she cannot accept; miserable with and without him, Hester wastes away until the fraud is exposed and Edgar imprisoned in Newgate, where he awaits hanging. Interestingly, in a dramatic illustration of the "political invisibility" of women, Hester is not implicated in his crimes after all because "she was regarded as being under her husband's control, and neglected by the law as an irresponsible person" (2:124). The regressiveness of such attitudes actually works in the wife's favor in this case, although she returns home alone, understanding finally that her love was not reciprocated, that she was used in a way that turns her community against her by exploiting her popularity and goodness, and that, without marriage or motherhood to recommend her, her once enviable life essentially ends in disgrace. Hester's example is one of many throughout Martineau's works that criticizes the practice, if not the theory, of marriage and the biased legal and social laws perpetuating gender inequities. Hester is not a legal criminal but an unwitting social one, stigmatized for the remainder of her life as a result of her association with a man she is bound by law and custom to obey. The tragic fates of such characters may seem artificially exaggerated, yet they aptly illustrate women's lack of legal protection and their susceptibility to social ostracization.

Although some characters are so marginal in their narratives as nearly to lose their ideological impact, the issues they represent are thematically consistent with Martineau's views on women. "Briery Creek" rehearses the temptations presented by luxury items in a community whose citizens struggle to maintain adequate subsistence. In a culture defined by the conspicuous consumption of goods, the poor see much to desire that is beyond their means, a dynamic provoking jealousy, resentment, and even criminality. In this tale, ironically, conspicuous consumption is most vividly displayed by the very people who ought to be modeling self-restraint: Rector Hesselden and his wife. Newly assigned to Briery Creek, the Hesseldens are class-conscious, moralizing Christian literalists who reject all liberal thinking, from scientific enquiry to socialism. A townswoman pointedly observes, "I can never make out . . . why so many of these very strict religious people dress so luxuriously. . . . Here is this lady, . . . dressed after such a fashion" as to turn the heads of local girls (106). Desiring to convey a more elevated image, poor girls work to buy clothing that is inappropriate for their lifestyle and their class. Rather than setting a positive example as a female representative of Christian values and principles, Mrs. Hesselden betrays her rigid dogma by not practicing what she preaches (the female Brocklehursts in *Jane Eyre* come to mind here). Connections between poor girls, stylish clothing, and prostitution were promoted endlessly throughout the period, as the ruling classes asserted their right to displays of wealth that were denied to working-class people. Martineau addresses these issues in her articles critiquing upper-class self-indulgence, particularly the "fashionable follies" of rich women and the bad example they set (discussed later in this chapter).

Jane Farrer in "The Farrers of Budge Row" illustrates a variation on the theme of women's dependence on men for their fates. A spinster at thirty-five and the only one of her father's children to obey his edict not to marry, Jane reaps no rewards for her compliance and even endures punishment for it. Poised between a married sister—who is apparently repaid for her disobedience by perpetual pregnancies—and a university-educated brother forced to keep his marriage a secret, Jane spends her lonely days keeping the books for the family business. "I hope God will be merciful with me," she observes caustically, "since I have been under another's bidding all my days" (13–14). Jane's remark is quite radical, considering its conflation of daughterly duty and religious dogma with an ill-concealed resentment rather than the passive acceptance regarded as "natural" to "good" women. When her father dies, leaving her an inheritance tax she cannot pay, Jane emigrates but drowns in a shipwreck. Tied to her father in life and in death by the effects of his actions and those of gendered economic and social systems, Jane Farrer's wasted existence leaves her bitter and narrow, a caricature of the socially displaced spinster subject to ridicule and derision and a more realistic portrayal of the type, no doubt, than Gaskell's gentle *Cranford* Amazons.

"Sowers Not Reapers" features Margaret Kay, the "drinking woman" that impressed Florence Nightingale, as a character who exposes the problem of alcoholism among working-class women.[17] Aimed at critiquing the Corn Laws, the tale outlines the circumstances created by legislation designed to help some (domestic farmers, specifically landholders) at the expense of others (consumers, particularly the working class and poor).[18] The destructive potential of the Corn Laws, which prohibited importation of competitively priced grain and forced people to buy expensive domestic grain or starve, is fully realized when famine, drought, and unemployment dovetail to create widespread poverty and starvation. Exacerbating this situation is the availability of cheap gin, which serves as a substitute for unaffordable food. Martineau presents Mrs. Kay as a loving wife and mother, loyal and generous to the point of self-annihilation in that she gives her share of food to her family while she numbs herself with gin. In Martineau's presentation, Mrs. Kay is a model of womanly sacrifice whose alcoholism figures as tragic proof of her goodness, rather than as a character defect or moral weakness.

As Margaret's alcoholism and the anorexia resulting from starvation and malnutrition compromise her health, John Kay urges his wife to relinquish the habit. But reformation comes too late, and although she achieves sobriety, Margaret dies as a result of the outer- and self-inflicted deprivations marking most of her life. Readers are invited to interpret her sober death as a triumph, yet this triumph comes with a disturbing price: like many angels-in-the-house devoted to family and self-denial, Mrs. Kay dies attempting to realize the impossible tenets of domestic ideology. Of female intemperance, Martineau wrote to Justice Story: "Depend upon it these cases will occur while women are what they are"—that is, forced into unnatural lifestyles at all class and economic levels (Culver 1984, 476). Further, while Margaret Kay's dying words condemning poverty's destructiveness criticize Corn Law legislation, her story also highlights a widespread social custom that demands another sort of accountability: the custom of dosing young children with laudanum (opium dissolved in alcohol), serving as a "cure" for physical maladies and bad behaviors and as a surrogate baby-sitter.[19] As a child, Mrs. Kay was regularly dosed; later, in her struggle to feed her family with insufficient resources, she employs gin as a substitute for food: particularly dangerous in view of the addictive pattern instilled by her own childhood "dosing." Intended as only a temporary measure to cope with inadequate food, gin proves so comforting in the face of chronically desperate circumstances that it quickly becomes a habit. Given Nightingale's assessment of Mrs. Kay's character as "religious," the insidious effect of chronic poverty on the "deserving poor" dramatized in this tale may spiritualize Margaret Kay's suffering, but it offers no solution to the indiscriminate waste of human lives wrought by political posturing and by ignorant, unscrupulous medical practices.

Ella of "Ella of Garveloch" and "Weal and Woe in Garveloch" is perhaps the most fully and satisfactorily realized of Martineau's women characters, although, again, not without complications. The title character of (then) Princess Victoria's favorite *Illustrations* tale, Ella combines many of the best qualities of the foregoing examples and models a woman worth emulating. Although her hard peasant life is not an enviable one, Ella's example illustrates Martineau's commitment to reaching middle- and working-class audiences with her message of social equity and reform. Representing hard work, honesty, and thrift, Ella is best characterized as a woman who triumphs over environmental challenges and gendered social prejudice. After her mother dies in childbirth, "the whole charge of the family had rested upon Ella" (19). At twenty-five, Ella, whose fiancé is seeking his fortune elsewhere, becomes the official head of her family of brothers after their father's death. She is a woman of "extraordinary energy, and one who deserved all the respect and love with which her brothers could regard her"; her "stern demeanor and masculine gait" (23) belie her capacity to nurture her young brothers—especially her favorite, the simpleminded Archie—as if they were her own children. Combining the qualities of maternal nurturing and paternal protection, Ella devotes herself to Archie's emotional and physical well-being, which requires constant supervision.

Ella also earns the respect of her "laird," the absentee landlord whose property she farms, but not before having her appearance scrutinized and assessed: Martineau's rare capitulation to the period's focus on women's appearance, although one in which she turns the custom to an instructive purpose. Initially, the laird imagines Ella "as corresponding in outward appearance to the elevated idea which was given him of her character" (19). Quite unlike the ladies in his circle, whose fashionableness and leisure are vaguely equated with virtue, Ella looks older than her years, the result of farming and fishing in this barren, unforgiving environment, thus "it was with some disappointment that he looked upon her for the first time. . . . [T]here was nothing at first sight to attract a stranger." Ella's appearance— tall and gaunt, her clothing unflattering, her feet bare, and long hair hanging loose—attests to her tenacity in living in a place where little survives, much less thrives. Yet the laird is impressed by the "strong expression of her eye, and of her weather stained features" (20) as well as by the confidence and clarity of her proposal to rent and work the land and fish the surrounding waters. Still underestimating her capacity to endure, he warns, "That is scarcely a woman's business, Ella. It brings toil and hardship to the strongest men" (22). Unintimidated by superior class, by the male gender, or by hard work, Ella responds: "It is my business, your honor; and it is not the blackest night, nor the stormiest day, that can weary me, thanks to Him that gives strength where it is wanted" (22–23). Going against custom, Ella not only reigns as head of household over her brothers: she also is the one who conducts business arrangements, usually of her own initiating, with landlords, overseers, ships' captains, and merchants, all of whose derisive or disparaging comments she patiently endures. Ella is no feminist "declaimer" with an agenda to promote: rather, she sees the work needing to be done and simply does it. This in itself, Martineau implies, is sufficient to earn Ella the respect she so clearly deserves.[20]

As in the tale "Ireland," Ella too must contend with a middleman, the overseer Callum, who is cunning and manipulative and who resents her because "There is no bringing her down" (26). He grudgingly admits she is a model tenant, yet complains that she is not humble enough for his taste. Constantly on the alert for any infractions of the rules by the tenants, he treads lightly with Ella, a woman "remarkable for strict honor; . . . she seemed so guarded on all points, that he began to think it prudent not to expose his authority to more mortifications" (73). But Callum is determined to "bring her down" because of the very unassailability of her character; further, because the laird clearly favors Ella, Callum feels he has been bested by a woman whose strength, determination, and character outweigh his own. He finds one mode of revenge through tormenting defenseless Archie in Ella's absence and another is in seeking out legal loopholes that would compromise this hardworking family's fragile economic framework.

With the return of her fiancé, Angus, from overseas, Ella "shed tears as if she had been broken-hearted" when he renews the vows she has long doubted. "They that have called me proud and severe," Ella says, "little knew what a humbled spirit I bore within me." For most of her twenty-five years, she gave to her brothers "the love I could not spend as a wife . . . how glad I was that my cheek withered, and that years left their marks upon me, that I might fancy myself more and more like their mother indeed" (117–18). Putting aside her loneliness, her burdens, and her fears of her lover's falseness, Ella relinquishes one role after another to Angus, and her strong, quiet character becomes softened, seemingly relieved to recede into a subservient status now that a man is in charge. But before criticizing what might be perceived as a disappointingly predictable narrative convention, I suggest that Martineau has two aims in presenting this powerful character as a tough survivor who also has distinctly feminine qualities: first, to demonstrate that women can rise to any occasion and can accomplish both roles according to gendered divisions of labor without compromising either one; and second, to demonstrate the potential for an equitable marriage in the union of Angus and Ella. Ella relinquishes burdens, not power, to the man who wishes to share her life rather than to master her or to deprive her of the very qualities that attract him to her.

"Ella of Garveloch" ends abruptly with the marriage of Angus and Ella, who set off together to buy her the bonnet whose style announces she is now a married woman, an item she is most anxious to acquire. Although the first example of feminine vanity in her character, the bonnet represents an important signifier of women's status and respect in the Garveloch community. Ella has proven her ability to head a household, to raise a family, and to provide subsistence, and her union with Angus represents the possibility of a marriage based on equality. Bearing in mind the laird's concern with Ella's appearance, Martineau's mild feminization of Ella does

not undercut her strong characterization because she has chosen a mate
less interested in "bringing her down"—or, for that matter, in putting her
on a pedestal—than in being her partner. Pleased by Ella's statement, "I
propose trafficking in caps," Angus also delights in her skill as a fisherwoman: "there was no more fitting occupation for such a woman as Ella
than fishing: but then, there were few such women; . . . here was an employment requiring strength, presence of mind, dexterity and patience; it
was therefore a fitting employment for such a one as Ella" (171).

The sequel, "Weal and Woe in Garveloch," features the now-prosperous
Ella and Angus, living in a big house with their impressive brood of ten
children. Displaced from the fishing boat to home and hearth, Ella's energy apparently finds expression in excessive childbearing. The family is
portrayed as thrifty and hardworking, qualities that serve them well when
the thriving local economy suddenly collapses. This tale, with its gentle
Malthusian urge to coordinate population size with available food supplies, with a view toward potential shortfalls in the latter, earned Martineau condemnation by critics who expressed shock that an unmarried
woman should presume to discuss matters not in her area of experience or
expertise: sexuality, marriage, and motherhood. The tale also outlines the
trials of Katie Cuthbert, a young widow regarded as "the lady of the island" because of her superior education, her "title to distinction" (6). Although her learning does not make her life as a net-weaver any easier, it
does earn her communal respect: "There was a sober truth in the judg-
ments she formed of people and of circumstances, which was all the more
impressive from the modesty with which she held her opinions, and the
gentleness with which she declared them." The expository conversations
shared by Katie and Ella reveal striking disparities in women's fates in the
absence of men and assert Martineau's view that, married or not, women—
especially educated, modest, and gentle women—*must* make such topics as
childbearing and -rearing, birth control, and infanticide their business and
emphatically *not* leave them up to men.

Garveloch's burgeoning population reflects a time of plenty that quickly
transforms to penury when hard times strike the community. When Magis-
trate Mackenzie mildly observes, "There is no need . . . to offer bounties for
the increase of population," Ella agrees: "I think not indeed . . . . It seems a
thing to be checked, rather than encouraged" (44). Spoken by one who has
so thoroughly won readers' goodwill, this is a remarkable statement; Ella
represents perpetual motherhood, yet she also encourages restraint from
considerations of political economy, albeit (in her case) after the fact.
Mackenzie observes that hard times leave people with little inducement to
marry and bear children who then suffer from want of food, a theme
played out in the tale's subplot involving Ella's brother Ronald and Katie
Cuthbert. As she struggles to feed her four young children, Katie is courted
by Ronald, who suddenly decides that to marry and, inevitably, produce
more children, would be to sin against an already overburdened social

economy. The two lovers sadly go their separate ways, struggling on alone through their respective economic difficulties. In the very absence of its articulation, the need for theories and methods of birth control is obvious in this example of people who can envision no alternatives between celibacy and procreation, much less for providing for already existing children. That the lack of such options results in the institution of marriage itself coming under scrutiny offers a daring social criticism. Social hypocrisy is perhaps nowhere more evident than in the pressure to marry and procreate in a culture that ostensibly promotes family values but is ultimately uninterested in supporting those values in times of economic dearth.

Katie Cuthbert's penurious situation compares significantly with that of Ella, whose excessive childbearing is in part balanced by her careful frugality. A conversation between the two women introduces a delicate issue that poses religious tenets against Malthusian population theories and both against the powerful impulse toward marriage and procreation. Katie observes, "Since Providence has not made food increase as men increase . . . it is plain that Providence wills restraint here as in the case of other passions" (96). Postulating a radical interpretation of social theory as a medium for realizing God's will, Katie concludes that deprivation, fever, and death "are the tokens that unlimited increase is not God's will." Ella, ensconced in her bustling, overpopulated household, remarks that each individual has a responsibility to society not to bring into it lives that burden it or that cannot be provided for. Although Ella speaks of the "undeserving poor" who rely on "the dole" to support their families, Katie's unfortunate situation begs the question of how to keep a socially and economically disadvantaged family together in a social system based on nuclear (two-parent) families. Stung by the contrast in their fates, Katie pointedly exclaims "Ah, Ella! did you consider this before your ten children were born?"[21] As Jane Bridgeman's tragic example proves, some of the "undeserving" poor were once "deserving" before social circumstances altered their course.

This remarkable conversation turns to considerations of other countries that endured famine conditions, particularly China and India, where infanticide was practiced to balance population with food supplies.[22] The shift from questioning the "Providential" dictum to "be fruitful and multiply" to advocating social responsibility through reproductive restraint is radical enough. But Martineau pushes this thinking even further by dramatizing the links between religious superstition, ethnocentrism, the perpetuation of poverty, irresponsible or inappropriate childbearing, and criminality (infanticide) resulting in the eradication of humanity's most precious resource: its children.

The radicalism of "Weal and Woe" should not be underestimated—it certainly was not by Martineau's critics—primarily because its ideology strikes at the heart of the period's thoroughly gendered social institutions. With the rise of the Woman Question and the intensification of women's resistance to the narrow roles to which they were confined, social hegemonies struck back by reasserting that woman's subordinate role is due to her biological destiny, a function that must not be compromised by such "dangerous" practices as higher education, employment for remuneration, and professions for women: not to mention birth control. Martineau does not directly suggest that excessive childbearing deters the cultural progress of women, but she does so indirectly by urging a utilitarian consideration of its impact on the greater good of society, which implicates the deserving and undeserving poor as well as the middle and upper classes. Serious gender issues infiltrate this tale, thinly masked by the broader concerns that pose private desires against public welfare.

But although the tale does not criticize Ella's prolific childbearing directly, the fact remains that perpetual pregnancies, confinements, and child-rearing prevent women from cultivating interests other than the domestic. Martineau argued that it is the duty of every individual to cultivate "to the utmost" his or her capacities, an idea most women were excluded from through compulsory and repeated childbearing. On the other hand, even within the separate spheres framework, Ella does not lose her strength, individuality, or power through marriage but instead earns the respect of those around her. Other *Illustrations* examples portray female characters whose strengths and weaknesses are compromised by their relationships with the men they have been conditioned not only to obey but to be dependent upon. Ella, whose character is supported by but not dependent upon Angus, offers an alternative both to the woman whose circumstances require that she go through life alone and to the woman made invisible by her absorption into the identity of the man to whom she is attached.

Throughout the two tales, Ella's powerful presence eclipses all the other characters; she is one of the most compelling and memorable of all Martineau's characters. The conclusion to "Weal and Woe" offers insight into Martineau's vision of ideal womanhood:

> [Ella's] mind and heart were as remarkable for their freshness in age as they had been for their dignity in youth. Inured to early exertion and hardship, . . . [s]he was never known to plead infirmity, or to need forbearance, or to disappoint expectation. She had all she wanted in her husband's devotion to her and to his home. . . . She had, from childhood, filled a station of authority, and had never abused her power, but made it the means of living for others. Her power increased with every year of her life, and with it grew her scrupulous watchfulness over its exercise, till the same open heart, penetrating eye, and ready hand, which had once made her the sufficient dependence of her orphan brothers, gave her an extensive influence over the weal and woe of Garveloch. (139)

Martineau's associating "living for others" in the domestic realm with power, wisdom, and influence in the community recasts women's role as a source of power rather than oppression, a primary theme in her writing about women. However, as her nonfiction writing on the status of women indicates, domestic empowerment is not an end in itself but is, rather, only the first step to the educational, economic, and employment parity that will lead women to full participation in the realm outside the home as well.

Martineau illustrates the effects of gender ideology on young girls as effectively as she depicts the wisdom of an aging matriarch. Motherless Mary and Anna Byerly of *Five Years of Youth; or, Sense and Sentiment* are the scandal of the neighborhood with their worn shoes, torn stockings, dirty skirts, and bonnets used to transport kittens, strawberries, and flowers: all of which, "of course, inspired a stranger with disgust." Although their widowed father tries to rein in the girls, he is preoccupied at best, prompting neighbors' gossip: such slovenliness in appearance can only indicate two girls who are careening down the path to moral destruction or, at least, unmarriageability. But despite the similarities in their childhood environment, Anna develops into a sensible young woman concerned about the well-being of others, while Mary, who is emotional and self-centered, is the bane of her father's existence.

*Five Years of Youth* anticipates what becomes, in the 1840s and 1850s, a popular literary convention: motherless daughters whose future is compromised by no maternal guidance and by a father who is indifferent or inept. This children's story dramatizes the importance of proper training for young girls, training that steers them away from wild, unfeminine ways as well as from the sort of vain self-absorption in one's appearance and emotions that Martineau—and Wollstonecraft before her—decries. The tale's thematic parallel with Jane Austen's *Sense and Sensibility* illustrates the contrasts between sisters whose differences sharpen as they mature, prompting one to insight and wisdom and the other to insipidity and sentimentalism. A dichotomy analyzed and critiqued by social thinkers from Wollstonecraft to Mill, *sense* is the quality that will liberate women from the artificial gendered constraints preventing their cultural progress, while an existence defined solely by *sentiment* perpetuates prejudicial female stereotypes. Martineau's distinctions between the two are integral to her perspectives on famous women of the period (see chapter 5).

The tale "Jerseymen Meeting" and its sequel, "Jerseymen Parting," feature Anne Lebrocq as a character whose innovative, *sensible* solutions to social problems nearly land her in jail. Because the Lebrocqs, recent émigrés from Jersey, are uninstructed in the complex tax system practiced on the mainland, Mr. Lebrocq inadvertently breaks several tax laws and is sent to debtors' prison, unable to pay the exorbitant fine. Recalling Dora Sullivan's writing ability, Anne in her naive simplicity writes a letter to the king, employing rational rhetoric at odds with the tax system's explicit lack of logic. But no reply is forthcoming, leaving the family disillusioned with the legal and political systems by which they are exploited and punished rather than protected.

Meanwhile, amazed by the high price of tea on the mainland, Anne's practical solution is one learned in her native Jersey, that is, to pick and dry wild thornbush leaves to be mixed with the high-priced tea to extend its value. She packages the mixture for neighbors, who will come to buy covertly but refuse to acknowledge her in public; with the trust of the guiltless, Anne is delighted to have found a mode of contributing to the family economy and helping her community through this useful cottage industry. But her neighbors' coolness is explained when Anne is herself summoned to court for tax evasion, wild thornbush leaves, oddly, being yet another taxable item. Significantly, when the situation seems at its worst with her father languishing in prison and Anne set for trial, her earlier letter to the king finds its way into the judge's hands. Impressed by Anne's eloquence, by her simple honesty, and by her naive trust in the inherent justice of the British legal system, he releases father and daughter. Anne's example offers an alternative to that of Dora Sullivan, whose verbal eloquence results in her ruin rather than her rescue from incarceration. On the other hand, the government's response to Anne's housewifely thrift—a quality so revered by domestic ideologists—proves that, like Dora's literacy, even the most innocuous of women's activities has its subversive side.

Of the influence and cultural impact of Martineau's fictional characterizations, Chapman wrote: "Every reader's memory will bear witness to the effect her criticism and her example have had on novel-writing. . . . [W]atchers by the springs of great social changes, can tell upon what multitudes fell the awakening music of her affirmation of all that is great, noble, and heroic in woman" (1877, 67). Citing such examples as Ella, Letitia, and Cousin Marshall, she asserts that "all the troops of the high-minded poor and the high-hearted lowly that rose from every pictured page, became the friends and educators of the young matronage of the United States. . . . [A]s illustrations of high character and lofty virtue and heroic endurance and uncompromising integrity, they possessed an incisive power." Martineau's promotion of Woman's Cause in her fiction is best seen in her depictions of qualities and behaviors worth and not worth emulating, a device that does not eliminate but specifically incorporates the domestic realm. The absence of a fully realized feminist prototype results from her more pertinent emphasis on the factors holding women back: including those she confronted herself, like girlish passivity, womanly docility, and obedience to patriarchal authority. This practice accords with the realism informing all her writing, a quality she prefers to the imaginativeness required by fiction. The absence of an uncomplicated role model reflects Martineau's approach to social reforms in her work and in her life, that is, to stay focused on practical solutions to immediate problems while never losing sight of "the big picture" of the status of women.[23]

## Women in Nonfiction

Martineau's fictional women characters illustrate that environmental circumstances often preclude social and economic autonomy, while her focus on the ways that women (and men, for that matter) perpetuate oppression by internalizing society's gendered strictures reveals a more insidious and effective way of keeping women in their place. Both insights are crucial to raising the status of women through exposing their plights, highlighting their abilities and potential, and positing viable avenues for social change. In chapter 2, I discuss Martineau's 1859 article, "Female Industry," which demonstrates the ways that social prejudice, both "the jealousy of men" and the mistrust of women consumers, hinders women needing to work for a living. Although my discussion of "Female Industry" focuses on the problems specific to needlewomen, Martineau also considers women in other fields, for instance governesses, women healers, cooks, dairy and agricultural women, miners and fisherwomen, domestics, artists and writers. Martineau's aim in this article is to combat prejudice against working women by outlining the history of women and work and by presenting a clear, logical case, based on census statistics, in which she exposes social resistance to working women as ludicrous, the numbers alone proving that the "working-woman question" is a moot point. This aspect of "Female Industry" provides a basis for the following consideration of Martineau's nonfiction writing as an important counterpart to her depictions of women in her fiction. That 1859 also marks the publication of Darwin's *Origin of Species* provides a suggestive link with Martineau's writings on the status of women, which invariably focus on the inevitability of social change and on the corresponding adaptive qualities necessary for survival in the modern period. At no time in history is this more clear than in the midst of the industrial era, when social roles and relationships were more intensely scrutinized than ever before. As ancient class relations broke down and certain traditionally female occupations phased out with the advent of industrialism, women's very survival depended on rejecting the passivity long presented as natural and normal to the sex.

Traditionally, aside from needleworking, many women needing to work outside the home sought positions as domestics. Considered a low form of employment, the domestic trades were popularly assumed to require no special skills other than what women already knew, like cooking, cleaning, and sewing. Problems arose when differing standards between upper-class ladies and low-class maids-of-all-work clashed, reflecting one of Martineau's pet peeves: girls' domestic training at home—in *all* classes—was so slipshod that few could accomplish the simplest household tasks for themselves, much less professionally.[24] Her critique of the effects of haphazard housekeeping on the British quality of life is consistent with the period's concerns about health and hygiene, morality, and nationalism. Martineau's criticism targets parents—mothers for poorly training their daughters and fathers for failing to secure them an education—employers, who do not themselves understand household management and who offer wages disproportionate to their demanding expectations, and education systems that are inadequate for preparing women to be economically self-sufficient. Because, as Martineau claims, "household education" involves everyone from the queen to the workhouse inmate, the present status and future outlook of women domestics is not surprisingly one of her primary concerns.[25]

Four ideas characterize Martineau's writing on women and work: her call for massive occupational reforms, her insistence on the need for the establishment of schools that offer both academic and practical ("common things") curriculums, her prediction that domestic labor as it has heretofore existed is bound (like the needleworking trades) for extinction, and her repeated references to Florence Nightingale as a prototype of the woman professional.[26] As an advocate for working women, Martineau challenges the universal complaint against domestics' ineptitude by posing two startling questions: "What do the heads of households think they have a right to expect in hiring domestic service? . . . What training have they [domestics] had which entitles their employers to expect them to be without fault of any kind?" (*Daily News,* 18 September 1861). Citing poor wages, mistresses' excessive demands, mistrust, and imperious attitudes as factors contributing to the high turnover rate in this occupation, she urges mistresses to "repose confidence, and show that they do. They must reward servants liberally."

Another theme is health, always for Martineau a primary indicator of the quality of one's work life. "The Maid of All Work: Her Health" posits that domestics "are conspicuously more unhealthy" than any other workers; since many enter the field straight from healthy rural backgrounds, she argues, it must be the working conditions that ruin their health. Paraphrasing Nightingale in *Notes on Nursing,* she observes that the requirement of perpetual availability to their employers is largely responsible for ill health in this group: "I have never known persons who exposed themselves for years to constant interruption who did not muddle away their intellects by it at last. . . . The female wards of [lunatic] asylums were filled mainly by servant-maids and governesses; and, above all, by maids-of-all-work" (Martineau 1860b, 465–66).[27] Perpetual availability is the curse of all women's lives, as women are to have neither an inner, creative life nor an intellectual existence independent of home and children; if they have no home of their own, they should devote themselves to someone else's domestic comfort. For this reason, Martineau presents women's need for solitude and privacy as essential for preserving their health, as she recognized in her Tynemouth days. With her empathy for the insults endured by domestic servants, her appreciation for the demands of domestic tasks, and her sympathy for women's struggle for independence, education, and economic autonomy, Martineau speaks with authority to and for this class of women. "She understood so thoroughly the theory of domestic service," wrote Chapman, that those who read her articles on the topic "supposed she must herself be a servant" (1877, 283).

These points anticipate 1862's "Modern Domestic Service," a more extended treatment of the issues introduced in the *Daily News* articles, and emphasize the theme of education she addresses in all her writing on the status of women. "Modern Domestic Service" examines the complaints of both employers and domestics, acknowledging that each has valid objections against the other side. Martineau notes that "the largest of all the classes of Her Majesty's subjects in England is the class of domestic servants"—just under 1,200,000 (1862b, 411). Such numbers make the status of female domestic laborers a serious consideration, as her interest in raising the standards of domestic economy on both individual and professional levels demonstrates. Martineau warns that the traditionally inequitable relationship between mistress and servant has shifted drastically with the social changes wrought by industrialization, and she urges careful reconsideration of these relations in order to resolve mutual dissatisfactions. So ill-inclined are young women to endure the insults and humiliations of domestic service that they would rather be needlewomen—another occupation in which women are notoriously overworked and underpaid—or, better, factory women.

One of the primary shifts in social structures resulting from the intersections of industry and democracy is the sharpened desire for independence among people of the lower classes. The constraints of domestic service compare unfavorably with factory life, which offers more freedom, better pay and nicer clothing, greater opportunity for socializing and leisure, a clear separation between work and home, and no strictures on receiving the attentions of "admirers." "In one word," Martineau neatly observes, "it is *independence* against *dependence*. The old aristocratic feeling . . . is well nigh extinct" (415). Rather than harkening back to the days when domestics were completely subservient and thoroughly humbled by their inferior position in life, "It would be more to the purpose to inquire of ourselves what we have done to deserve to be as well treated now as our grandparents were fifty years ago" (416–17). That she dares to assert that upper-class women must prove that they deserve loyalty and deference from servants who are overworked and underpaid offers a most telling commentary on the radically shifting class boundaries of the period.

What is remarkable to Martineau, given the number of domestic servants, is the complete lack of training and education preparing this million-plus class of workers for employment. She argues that, until workers are provided with adequate formal training, in academics as well as in the "common things," there is no ground for complaint on the part of employers. Thus her exploration of the status of women domestics segues into her promotion of education for girls of all classes, regardless of occupational pursuits. Significantly, mistresses also need an education, and she instructs them as well on alternative behaviors and attitudes to those of the past. The attitude of suspicion against the assumed propensity of servants to steal must be replaced with trust; wages must more adequately prepare domestic servants for old age, for which there is no provision other than the workhouse. Cultural enhancement is also desirable—like access to books, music, art, and socializing (as Lady Frances urged and the Lowell factory women demonstrate)—while cultivating a spirit of open communication between employer and employee promises to minimize prejudice on both sides. Over all, Martineau's message is a quite modern one: competition. If mistresses wish to secure good domestics, they must compete with the other options available to workers and meet or exceed the standards of those competitors. Although their "curriculums" may differ, the solution to the problems of domestic labor on both sides—education in how to be an employer and an employee—stresses the individuality of both parties, the breakdown of traditional class relations, and the resulting redefinition of working relationships.

Her conclusion to "Modern Domestic Service" envisions an optimistic future for an even more marginalized class needing work and a place in society. As working-class girls reject domestic occupations to join the industrial ranks, the positions they leave behind may be filled with poorhouse girls: "The greatest step taken will be when we can raise the lowest social class . . . —when we can replenish domestic service from schools which will have rescued pauper and ragged children from pauperism and raggedness" (439). Martineau's vision of a continually evolving society in which even the lowest category becomes upwardly mobile—and the nonadapting ruling classes extinct—neatly applies Darwinian theory to her analysis of social institutions.[28]

Although Martineau did not devote as much writing to the plights of governesses, the problems suffered by this group of workers may differ from domestics in kind but not in degree. The occupation of governess aligns with those of domestics and needlewomen in several ways: no formal training exists to prepare them for the occupation; they are notoriously overworked and underpaid, having no provision for illness or old age; and disturbingly high numbers of governesses end up in the workhouse or insane asylum. Further, this occupation reflects a class structure no longer viable in postagrarian society: most governesses were middle-class ladies attempting to preserve their gentility through economic hard times. They were valued for their superior breeding yet treated like servants, best seen in the expectation that they dress like ladies on a domestic's salary. Martineau's "The Governess: Her Health" outlines the poverty, social invisibility, and general ostracization of governesses, who permanently relinquish all claim to gentility by working for a living. Martineau agrees with education reformer Bessie Rainer Parkes that middle-class women are most at risk for poverty, as their only preparation for life is to be an economically dependent wife.[29] Should a lucrative marriage not come her way, the middle-class woman was ill-equipped to be self-supporting. Looking beyond present reality, Martineau draws an analogy between domesticity—"Women are made for domestic administration" (1860a, 268)—and the running of a school as schoolmistress, *administration* emphasizing her distinction between management skills and mindless drudgery. But a governess has no such autonomy, being expected not only to teach but to baby-sit, sew, and perform various tasks on demand; although regarded as a higher class of domestic servant, the governess never clearly knew her place since it changed according to the whims of her employer.

"The Governess: Her Health" indicts the Brontës' "love-lorn" governesses as an embarrassment to the profession, in which romance or upward social or economic mobility is the stuff of romance novels, not the grim reality of Victorian women's lives. Governesses "have no gratitude for the Brontës; and will have none for any self-constituted artist, or any champion, who raises a sensation at their expense, or a clamour on their behalf" (269). Martineau raises her own sort of clamor in the *Daily News* by asking, "When the Reports of the Governesses' Institution tell us of 99 unmarried ladies, old, infirm, and destitute, competing for an annuity of 20£ [pounds]; when there are thousands of such sufferers in the kingdom at this moment,—women brought up in comfort, and many in affluence, and now without a provision, without a home, without society, and without hope of any change for the better, are we to be told that nothing can be done?" Between the workhouse and alms, "Is there never to be anything more?" (29 November 1858). Despite the establishment of a women's employment agency and reading room at Langham Place, and the Governesses' Benevolent Institution, which aims to find alternatives to the workhouse for ill and aged governesses, the numbers in need far outweigh these few resources. Martineau accurately predicts the decline of this occupation, anticipating its replacement by college curriculums that would prepare women for teaching and other occupations.[30]

Education is, for Martineau, the ultimate leveler. To her, virtually all social ills are attributable to the absence or inadequacy of education; therefore, access to a comprehensive education is her immediate and universal solution to most social problems. Thus the theme of education underpins all of Martineau's writing on the status of women, beginning with "On Female Education," written when she was only twenty. The article contains the essential points of all her subsequent writing on education reform, although this early piece displays, interestingly, a distinctly Wollstonecraftian feminist ethic. "It is not so much my object to inquire whether the natural powers of women be equal to those of men," she begins placatingly, "as to shew the expediency of giving proper scope and employment to the powers which they do possess" (1822, 77). She firmly asserts, however, that there is no *biological* difference between boys' and girls' learning capacities, since "as long as the studies of children of both sexes continue the same, the progress they make is equal." Perceived differences between the two are social and artificial, as boys are encouraged to continue learning while girls are confined to "low pursuits," learning being thought "unbecoming" and inconsistent with female passivity. With sharp insight, she argues that the "natural" result of this artificial sexual double standard—the separate spheres dichotomy—is offered as "proof" that females are inferior to males intellectually.[31]

Like Wollstonecraft, who posited that empty-headed women will follow simpleminded pursuits, Martineau argues that women who have no "good aim" will express themselves through bad ones, like vanity, gossip, or worse. Typically, women "are gifted with faculties which they were not permitted to exercise, and were compelled to vegetate from year to year, with no object in life and no hope in death" (77). Having already equated women's role—almost exclusively a domestic one—with "low pursuits," she next illustrates that her promotion of domesticity is not without complications or ambivalence: "If 'great thoughts constitute great minds,' what can be expected from a woman whose whole intellect is employed on the trifling cares and comparatively mean occupations, to which the advocates for female ignorance would condemn her?" (78). Recalling Wollstonecraft's arguments in a similar vein, Martineau appeals to the idea that the roles of wife and mother carry a significant social responsibility and deserve not only respect but formal training through advanced education: "If we consider woman as the guardian and instructress of infancy, her claims to cultivation of mind become doubly urgent. . . . [W]e cannot be too careful to preserve our children from the effects of ignorance and prejudice on their young minds" (79). As for wives, she concludes, "I wish them to be companions to men, instead of playthings" (80). Despite her vigorous rejection of Mary Wollstonecraft's personal example, Martineau repeatedly illustrates that her own gender ideology thoroughly aligned with that of this feminist foremother.[32]

Nearly forty years later, women had slightly better education opportunities than before, but little had changed in terms of gender-biased attitudes. "What Women Are Educated For" critiques the "happy complacency" and "amiable magnanimity" of philanthropic men who dictate the standards of women's education: they still assume "that the grand use of a good education to a woman is that it improves her usefulness to somebody else. . . . [They] think they have said everything when they have recommended good intellectual training as fitting women to be 'mothers of heroes,' 'companions to men'" (1861b, 175–76). No longer willing to soften the impact of her feminism on this point, Martineau counters: "the first object of a good education is to improve the individual as an individual. . . . Till it is proposed, in educating girls, to make them, in themselves and for their own sakes, as good specimens of the human being as the conditions of the case allow, very little will be effected by any expenditure of pains, time, and money." She concludes, interestingly, by indulging in the very "declaiming" on the subject of "women's rights" that she elsewhere rejects: "[let us] uphold the claim of every human being to be made the most of . . . and the female sex is redeemed. Women will quietly enter into their 'rights,' without objection on any hand, when those rights consist in their being more reasonable, more able, more useful, and more agreeable than ever before, without losing anything in exchange for the gain" (179).[33]

As the example of governesses illustrates, middle-class girls were particularly vulnerable to social prejudice against educating women. Low-class girls knew from childhood that they must work for their living; upper-class girls had no need to. But middle-class girls were "neither educated nor provided for like their brothers; . . . if they do not marry, they must work (unprepared by education as they are) or starve" (*Daily News,* 17 November 1859). Martineau urges parents to provide for daughters just as they do for sons, noting that the number of destitute middle-class women "has far outgrown the scope and powers of charitable societies. . . . The first step is to perceive that the problem is now simply an educational one." The problem of what to do with "redundant" women—those not redeemed by work (if lower class), by marriage (if middle class), or by money and power (if upper class)—highlights a basic incongruence between the period's conflicting values of individualism and utilitarian conformity or, in Martineau's terms, *independence* and *dependence*.[34] But she also argues that women cannot wait passively for men to validate them; instead, they must take action on their own behalf: "We do not conceive that any appeal to fathers to provide better for their daughters, in comparison with their sons, will be of much practical use . . . till the women have established the fact of their own capability, and their will to be independent. All sorts of people have to show what they can do before obtaining free scope to do it" (*Daily News,* 17 November 1859), as she well knows from her own experience.

Martineau condemned "artificial" methods of dealing with the social anomalies presented by "distressed" or redundant women, like charitable societies or the emigration schemes popular in midcentury, in which superfluous women were encouraged to settle in the colonies. Although she was not entirely against such schemes, she considered them at best temporary solutions to chronic social problems requiring more substantial long-term solutions. The problem so glaringly highlighted by the spread of industrialization was, particularly for women, lack of education: "The difficulty with us is that an effectual education is not obtainable by any woman without extraordinary efforts and tact on her own part; and by few is it obtainable at all" (*Daily News,* 23 November 1859). Here, the nexus between poverty and education hints darkly at the specter of prostitution haunting all of women's undertakings: "The retribution comes in the poverty and helplessness of thousands of women who could have supported themselves if allowed a fair chance of study, and means of training. . . . . The question is, throughout its length and breadth, an educational one."

Martineau also promoted the education of industrial-class women, a class compromised by limited access to educations that would enable them to enhance the quality of their lives and to elevate their standards of living (*Daily News,* 26 November 1855). She rejected the reigning stereotype that the uneducated are inherently immoral and argued that, by providing low-class women with education in employment and domestic skills, good taste and morality would infiltrate all levels of society. She praised a school whose classes were scheduled around women's work hours in an industrial town; initially resistant, the women became excited and interested, while the combination of work and school instilled in them a sense of pride and accomplishment. As she argued in her analysis of "The Lowell Offering," the state of mind workers bring to their labor shapes the quality of their lives and the work they produce, which in turn reflects on the employer. Intellectually challenged, inquisitive minds enable workers to thrive in environments that might otherwise oppress them.[35] The article concludes by encouraging wealthy women to sponsor industrial-class schools in their communities and to "spread the example far and wide," a philanthropy worthy of the great Florence Nightingale herself. But despite her optimism, a leader written eight years later reveals that little has changed for this class of women in terms of education opportunities, prompting her to write yet again on the "existing neglect of the special functions of industrial women . . . the very large class of hunger-bitten women who are one of the reproaches and perplexities of our time" (*Daily News*, 9 July 1863).

Collectively speaking, Martineau's daring commentary on the status of women of course did not go unnoticed, and she was compelled to address the objections of those seeking to preserve outmoded gender relations. Responding to a letter to the editor from "Paterfamilias," who argues that girls' education is unfeminine, she counters that the issue is not a matter of *femininity* but of *masculinity*, specifically, with the potential for girls' education to "interfere" with the boys' education. Martineau pounces excitedly on the writer's charge that the labor market is already overstocked: "Here . . . we come at the truth. What are the brothers to do if the sisters are taught to work? There it is! There we arrive at the last, the deepest, the most flagrant popular objection to letting women be properly taught any branch of profitable industry" (*Daily News*, 9 January 1860).[36] The jealousy of men and of women proves to be a persistent theme: "It really appears as if there might be more mortification to the workers from their own sex than from men. The more superficial and conventional . . . look down on women, however highly educated, who work" (*Daily News*, 2 November 1860). As she reminded readers repeatedly, these issues point not to future change, but to changes already present in society: "The question of the industrial independence of women has already been settled. . . . [T]he education of women cannot go on to be what it has been. . . . We must fit our daughters, as sensible men fit their sons, for the real business of life, and not let them fail of the means of subsistence for want of arts which we should have enabled them to learn." Demonstrating her keen awareness of the profound impact of industrialization on society, she concludes that "when the women of England are more soundly and rationally educated, we shall properly understand and appreciate this industrial movement in its causes and in its effects." Women fitted "for the real business of life," those who rise to intellectual challenges and fully exercise their potential as active participants in society, by association elevate the status of other women. There is no reason, in her view, why any woman should be prevented by social prejudice from doing the same.

Other articles tackle more precisely the issues of funding and curriculum reforms, again calling into question the qualifications of men who presume to make these decisions for women: "How can the general run of gentlemen know young girls' minds enough to judge what they can learn and do, and what they ought to learn and do, and how their daily life should be trained?" (*Daily News*, 30 September 1865). Girls' education is best managed by "cultivated, sensible, capable, experienced women . . . [who are] better qualified than the best-intentioned gentlemen," particularly during the crucial formative years "which determine the character of . . . womanhood." Not only do children need their mothers to be educated: the times require curriculums featuring "Natural Philosophy" and other academic subjects (beyond "common things") in order to provide "the foundation of the material welfare of the household." Thus is modern science harnessed to the domestic sphere, anticipating the development of "domestic science" later in the century. Finally, she objects to a scheme for a new school for one thousand boys, arguing that for every five hundred boys educated, five hundred girls should be educated as well (*Daily News*, 24 November 1865).[37]

So far, this discussion of Martineau's nonfiction writing on the status of women highlights the unprecedented changes in women's work occurring by the mid-nineteenth century. Those fields traditionally open to women—governessing, needleworking, and domestic service—were being phased out by new occupations in industry, while a few persistent women only gradually progressed in professions in the arts and sciences. The primacy of education reform in favor of girls clearly seemed, to activists like Martineau and Bessie Rainer Parkes, the single most crucial factor outweighing all other considerations in the promotion of Woman's Cause, both to remedy current problems and to prevent future problems. At this point in the history of female industry, nursing provided a timely solution to women's need for economic autonomy that neatly combined education, occupation, and job security.[38] Throughout the 1850s Florence Nightingale earned fame for her work in the Crimea and for her efforts, through the War Office, to promote hygiene reform in the military. Nightingale's personal example as an exemplary professional woman and her interest in social and moral reform through improved standards of hygiene dovetailed perfectly with Martineau's reformist sensibilities. The professional collaboration between these two women included Martineau's tireless championing of Nightingale, whose name she invoked frequently throughout her periodicals writing and whose example illustrates what she believed all women can and should aspire to.[39]

From her earliest writing on the topic, Martineau presented nursing (like teaching) as a vocation requiring a commitment beyond merely earning a subsistence, since to do otherwise creates "nothing short of a curse to the rising generation" (*Daily News*, 5 July 1854). She traced the history of nursing, including the religious underpinnings of organizations like the Sisters of Charity, and urged secularizing the profession to avoid religious factioning, to standardize training, and to regulate healing practices.[40] Aside from full nursing programs, she also proposed that some basic nursing skills be incorporated into the "common things" in existing girls' curriculums as well. Proof of the timeliness of the nursing profession is offered by the example of Nightingale herself: "There is an instance at Scutari at this moment of what the administrative faculty of a woman may be. Theoretically, every woman is a nurse. Florence Nightingale is not only a nurse, and the means of educing the nursing power in others, she manifests in addition an administrative ability which would be eminent in any executive department whatever" (*Daily News*, 29 February 1856). Martineau repeatedly emphasizes that this "most womanly of professional occupations" (1860e, 8) is both a science and an art and therefore requires advanced formal training. Further, she encourages a vision of the nursing profession that incorporates women as administrators and, more radically, as physicians. Martineau called for nothing less than a total reconstruction of the relations between women and medical institutions and practices.

By promoting nursing as a legitimate and honorable vocation, Nightingale and Martineau confronted deep-seated social prejudices. Added to the usual prejudice against working women, resistance to nursing training for women evoked the stereotype of nurses as disease-ridden prostitutes and alcoholic camp followers; in a sense, *choosing* to work with the "base bodily functions" of complete strangers of the opposite sex stigmatized women even more than prostitution (the latter, at least, could be ascribed to mental imbalance or immorality). The image of depravity had a powerful hold on the popular imagination: "To be, to do, and to talk 'like an old nurse,' means to be . . . ignorant, superstitious, wrong-headed, meddlesome, gross, and disagreeable. . . . The image may be found in a multitude of works of fiction. . . . Let her retire behind the curtain to doze and booze and maunder out her queer notions about diseases and remedies. We have to study newer specimens of the same order of functionaries" (Martineau 1859c, 475). The stereotype, unfortunately, and the prejudice accompanying it, deterred potential probationers forced to confront familial and communal resistance to this occupation: "if a young woman . . . devotes herself to the care of the sick there is an outcry among the genteel about her low tastes, and among the conventional about her leaving her father's house for any independent occupation" (*Daily News*, 5 July 1854). As a result, the dearth of suitable applicants presented a chronic problem to the advancement of this profession, despite the best promotional efforts of Martineau and Nightingale.

The time seemed so perfectly designed for the transformation of nursing from a degraded to a respectable profession that women's reluctance to take advantage of the benefits afforded by nursing (all of which were offered at no charge to probationers, being supplied by the Nightingale Fund) hindered the profession's progress. Martineau aggressively replaced the old stereotype with the new, listing the criteria for suitable applicants in which morality, decorum, and temperance are implicit: "Women of

good health and good character, between 25 and 35 years of age," especially working-class single women, are the most desirable candidates (*Daily
News*, 25 June 1860). Screening was rigorous, with applicants required to
provide proof of age and marriage as well as a character reference; if they
were accepted, they received training, lodging and board, washing, clothing, and a small stipend. Placement and job security were virtually assured,
since "The pressing demand for good nurses renders the career of worthy
probationers secure." Proper motivation and attitude is crucial to this vocation—"We do not now expect good nursing as a fruit of heart-griefs or
*ennui*": a statement consistent with Martineau's denunciation of feminist
"declaimers" whose activism stems from personal problems rather than
utilitarian principles.

Considered in the context of her complaints against the dubious morality of male doctors attending women to whom they are not married (a
neat reversal of the same complaint used against nurses) and her advocacy
of female healers to attend women and children, her comment that "Our
countrywomen may now get possession of one part of their natural
domain—the sick-room" is less essentialist than radically feminist. With its
focus on education and morality, and its spiritualizing of women's social
obligations *outside* of the home, nursing presented a powerful counterpart
to the angelic "women's mission" keeping women in a state of dependence
and penury: nursing is itself "a mission for women, a vocation for them,
honoured, undisputed, and well rewarded. . . . As for those champions of
the sex who have most to say about a mission, we hope they will tell us
what woman's mission is if it be not nursing the sick. Those who are gifted
with the high female quality—the capacity for domestic administration—
may find full use for it" (*Daily News*, 23 February 1865).[41] Her *Daily News*
leaders on this topic present a revisionist image of nursing and angel-in-
the-house ideology: "The most natural, unquestionable, and fitting work
for womanly hands, head, and heart, is surely the tendance and treatment
of the sick and suffering" (*Daily News*, 31 January 1866). What makes this
seemingly essentialist perspective radical is its insistence that what ostensibly comes "naturally" to women now requires formal training and remuneration; thus can women professionalize nursing and find a market for
their home-bound skills in the working world outside the home.[42]

Not only did nursing offer a new vocation for women for which they
were eminently suited at a time when women needed to work and few options existed: it was one that was, or should be, free from the "jealousy of
men." Because the need for skilled nurses is so acute, "these are the palmy
days of the profession" when women have their pick of public or private
assignments, in England or in the colonies (Martineau 1865, 414). Martineau evokes a compelling vision of the effects of a visiting nurse who,
once her assignment is completed, leaves behind the healing influence of
good sanitary and domestic practices, which permeate the sickroom and
infiltrate the entire household. This influence continues to work on family,

home, and community long after she has gone, having the capacity to heal even social immorality. "Now is the time for women of enterprise, of benevolence, and of an independent spirit, to make a grand use of the best years of their lives," she urges, "to undertake the most splendid service ever offered to . . . women, and achieve an independence in a sure and speedy way" (425). The period's rhetoric of Woman's Mission, which renders women's confinement to the home a moral imperative, is here neatly realigned with such ideas as "independence" and "enterprise."[43]

An emphasis on the formal training of nurses depends on dismantling another stereotype: that women who could do nothing else became self-appointed nurses. "Woman's Battlefield" urges the need for regulation and training in the profession: "Wherever there are mothers and daughters and sisters," she concedes to the "women's missionaries" among her readers, "there will be more or less good nursing, as far as it can be taught by good sense and affection, in the common maladies which befall individuals" (475). But the kind of nursing she promotes "is an art based upon science." Recommending that nurses be single or widows without children to avoid conflicts of interest with their professional duties, she more daringly urges that they must also be free "from the prudery which is somewhat in the way of benevolent actions wherever it exists, and is wholly incompatible with the nursing office" (477). On the other hand, penitents (reformed prostitutes and fallen women) are undesirable candidates as "there must be no damaged character amongst them" to perpetuate old stereotypes.[44] Her concluding enthusiasm aims to overcome remaining objections with sheer rhetorical energy: "Open schools to women . . . and the sick of the next generation will not die by tens of thousands for want of good nursing. Disease will be checked on its first approach, and the morality of our day will be a theme which will take its place in history and speculation with the Great Plague and the Black Death. The doctors permitting and aiding, the women will achieve this victory" (479).[45] Her word choice again demonstrates how women reformists of the period appropriated the spiritualized rhetoric of Woman's Mission to argue that women are not the *least* suited to perform social work but the *best* suited. Thus hygiene reform became inseparable from moral reform, implicating social purity movements as well as education and employment reforms for women. Medical women—nurses and doctors—are now cast as elevated by their association with "base bodily functions" rather than degraded by them; they will go down in history, she predicts, as saviors of the human race.

Aside from her focus on employment reform and access to education, Martineau was keenly aware that some women's issues stemmed from their political invisibility. Although she argued that women need first to prove themselves in order to earn political and legal rights and privileges, she also understood that women's exclusion from political representation was not just unfair: it rendered them nonexistent in the eyes of the law.[46] Some women, those in life-threatening situations and at the mercy of cruel men, cannot afford the luxury of waiting until social attitudes evolve to a more equitable stage for women. As Woman Question debates became more aggressive, the plights of women who were beaten, starved, abused, even murdered with impunity by their husbands dramatized the extremes to which separate spheres ideology might be taken, convincing many, including Martineau, that legal reforms were as necessary as social reforms to ensure the advancement of women. Women were indoctrinated from childhood with the imperative to devote themselves to no other goal in life than dependency through marriage. Once married, they surrendered all property and earnings, even their bodies and their children, to their husbands; they had no legal rights. Whereas class issues entered into employment and education debates, brutality toward women and their total lack of recourse transcends class boundaries, making aristocratic women as powerless and unprotected as any woman of the pauper class. The high-profile legal cases of Lady Caroline Norton made public husbands' physical, emotional, economic, and legal abuse of women, to which the police and the courts generally turned a blind eye.[47]

Although Martineau argued that Victorian women had far more pressing concerns than the franchise to contend with, she also acknowledged the humiliation of "political invisibility" that women endured even as they worked and paid taxes like "real" citizens. That high-ranking government officials consulted Martineau about pending legislation, visiting her in her home and plying her with parliamentary Blue Books (official statistical information made available to the general public after the 1830s) even though she was not permitted to vote, is a rich irony indeed. More immediate and urgent, however, were the problems of married women, whose lack of identity under the law sometimes cost them their lives. Early in her tenure at the *Daily News* she denounced brutality against women and the ineffectuality of existing divorce laws: "Not a week passes without a report of some dreadful case of husbands, drunk or sober, ill-using their wives to a degree which, if practised upon brutes, would be followed up by the Society for the Prevention of Cruelty to Animals" (*Daily News,* 8 September 1853). Male violence against women prompted Parliament to pass a new law punishing such brutalities, but Martineau had little hope for its effectiveness: "a most painful, and by far the most pathetic, part of the business is the unwillingness of the wives to prosecute . . . .[because they] know not how their children are to be fed in the interval" if he goes to jail; they also fear his vengeance and increased brutality once released. Innovative, as always, in her design to influence (or shock) public opinion, Martineau questioned the very institutions on which society depended for its identity. How is it, she asks, that mistresses (denigrated as virtual prostitutes) in effect have greater freedom and better protection than do wives (valued because legally married)? "[T]he mistress is in a better condition than the wife. The mistress can free herself from her tyrant at any moment, while the wife has no escape. What say our moralists to this?" She condemns the Commission on the Law of Divorce, which proposes "to refuse divorce to women . . . altogether, except in cases of such rare atrocity as to constitute, practically, no exception at all; . . . . their strange doctrine is that such facilities are good for the husband, while yet the impossibility of divorce is good for the wife. . . . The husbands are the law makers; and the wife is dumb before the law, and Parliament, and the Commission which is to decide upon her interests."[48]

But the problems of wife abuse only intensify, prompting the passage of the Divorce and Matrimonial Causes Acts, which debated ecclesiastical versus civil court jurisdiction over marriage and divorce. "The spectacle is presented to English eyes every day of the advantage of concubinage over marriage," she protests (*Daily News,* 28 June 1854). The complex, expensive, lengthy process of divorce was cumbersome and prohibitive, especially for poor women, who wonder "why, if marriage with all its incidents and liabilities is common to all, the laws relating to it do not protect all equally. . . . [T]he profligacy of the vulgar rests with those who decree that there shall be one law for the rich and another for the poor"—and, of course, one law protecting men's interests and none at all protecting women's.

Of special interest to Martineau, given her many writings on female industry and economic self-sufficiency, was a husband's right to seize his wife's earnings. Martineau reports on the general meeting of the Law Amendment Society concerning the "unprotected condition of women under the law of England, and the prodigious amount of crime thence arising." She decries "the virtual reduction of wives to the state of slaves, when they have married bad men" (*Daily News,* 29 February 1856). Throughout her articles pleading for the rights of working women, she emphasizes the need for protective legislation for this group of workers, numbering several millions. But "The law was silent to the complaints" of both working and abused women. "The rule for Englishwomen in our time is— work," yet they continue to confront "the ancient jealousy which kept down female labour." Similar to her comparison between mistresses and wives is her assertion that a woman must choose between "celibacy, with freedom to work and enjoy its rewards, or domestic life, with total loss of control over her occupations and her earnings."

As her writing repeatedly attests, Martineau was not antimarriage, though she was quick to criticize the inequities of the institution: "something must be done, if we care to preserve the conjugal relation, instead of encouraging concubinage on the one hand and celibacy on the other" (*Daily News,* 26 March 1856).[49] But she also reiterated women's need to speak up, to "prove" themselves and make themselves heard, as a crucial factor in shifting the balance of power in women's favor. Parliament "could do nothing till women showed that they were dissatisfied with the present state of the law," therefore Martineau points triumphantly to a petition, signed by three thousand women, urging that "property shall continue in the hands of its owners, and earnings in the hands of the worker." Now that women have begun to make clear their case—"sensible women who have had the courage and the wisdom to speak for themselves"—Parliament owes them recognition if marriage is to be "redeemed from some of its worst snares and corruptions." She maintains that marriage should be an equal partnership, which it clearly is not in practice, and concludes with an analogy between slavery and marriage: "Other nations . . . may but too reasonably point to the condition of wives in England as one of sheer slavery, for anything the law does to prevent it."[50]

Martineau also addressed such issues as income equity, emigration, and the economic problems of single women. On equal pay for equal work, she asserts: "There will be not a few, we fear, who will cite on the instant several cases known to them where the work has been as hard, and the pay no greater; and will satisfy themselves with the conclusion that men do, and always will, pay less for women's services than for men's of the same quality" (*Daily News*, 2 April 1856). That comparable worth continues to be debated a century and a half later, unhappily, validates her claim. Emigration is another issue that she in part promoted, though with certain reservations. One of the period's more outrageous proposed "solutions" to the alarming numbers of women failing to meet the middle-class's economically dependent angelic ideal was to round up these social misfits and ship them to the colonies under the patriotic guise of expanding the empire. While willing to acknowledge the desirability of settling the colonies, Martineau questioned the dubious motivation behind promoting this scheme as particularly desirable for "redundant" women. Her argument poses "factitious methods" like emigration against working *with* the "natural laws of society"—in other words, political economy: "It would be easy to show that the sending off shiploads of any one class of people (and especially young women) to the colonies is a measure too artificial to succeed. . . . [T]he true way is . . . to apply ourselves to the opposite course—of removing obstructions to the working of the natural laws of society." If society worked with, rather than against "those great natural laws . . . there would be no starving sempstresses, no working to death of governesses . . . no shipping off of young women" to conditions worse than those at home in England. Like the workhouses, emigration schemes were notorious for lumping together diseased prostitutes, hardened criminals, and genteel spinsters in the same social category, and for functioning as a mass marriage market to enslave women in marriages of convenience for the sake of settling and populating the colonies. This practice vividly demonstrates the extremes to which the cultural hegemony would go in order to preserve the fiction of women's subordination and their relegation to only one acceptable role: that of wife.

Although dress reform may seem frivolous in comparison with these issues, Martineau presented it as a serious concern to women who were slaves to fashion as well as to women who were slaves in dressmaking workrooms. Martineau herself took pride in managing her clothing budget by dressing plainly; her no-nonsense advice to traveling Englishwomen, whom she urged to pack stout boots and clothing of functional brown holland, attests to her attitude that beyond its practical considerations, clothing should consume neither time nor money. She urged styles that are suited to the shapes and needs of women's bodies, that would promote rather than inhibit movement, and that were not hazardous to anyone's health. For Martineau, lack of pretension in appearance, whether one was attractive or plain, projects the message that women are more than the sum of their physical parts and is a prerequisite to social and political liberation. Women's refusal to continue to be infantilized by fashion "despotism" was an important factor in removing them from the "women, children, and idiots" category to which they were popularly relegated. Fashionable Englishwomen rendered themselves ridiculous by styles "not very English in taste," exposing themselves to ill health through inadequate coverage, excessively tight lacing, high heels, wide skirts with steel hoops, dresses weighing twenty pounds or more, and flammable crinolines.

Martineau's critique of popular women's fashions targets the sheer quantity of French-inspired dress: "the quantity is the marvel. . . . [These] flouncings and furbelows, . . . this vast circumference, . . . that yonder moving globular mass" have the capacity to knock unwitting pedestrians off sidewalks (*Daily News,* 17 June 1856). The worship of French haute couture demonstrates the "perils of ennui" common to wealthy women in civilized countries who, simply put, "have not enough to do," which "induces social and moral disease." As a result, they adapt French fashions, an "outrageous extravagance" that "encumbers the lightest, deforms the fairest, makes the plain woman ugly, and the ugly and beautiful alike grotesque. . . . It is unbecoming; it is expensive, it is inconvenient, it has no one recommendation" (*Daily News,* 17 July 1856). In another unflattering reference to girth, Martineau charges that "our ladies . . . look like walking wardrobes, from the weight they carry, and the amount of furnishings, one on the top of another" (*Daily News,* 13 January 1857). "Dress and Its Victims" details the "preventible mortality" of the "100,000 persons who go needlessly to the grave every year in our happy England, . . . killed by dress" (1859a, 387). Outlining what dress should and should not be, she regrets the "trains of funerals every year carrying to the grave the victims of folly and ignorance in dress" resulting from styles better suited to "a volunteer rifle corps or a regiment of Amazons rehearsing for the opera" (388–89). In her ridicule of fashionable women, Martineau's rhetorical drollery is relentless. Unsuspecting men have been impaled by exploding steel hoops; innocent children have been swept into oncoming traffic by "some unconscious walking balloon." As for the women who wear such fashions, they "are always in danger from fire, or wind, or water, or carriage-wheels, or rails, or pails, or nails, or, in short, everything they encounter" (390).

As consumers of such styles, women were unwitting pawns perpetuating their own oppression. The incapacitating features of Victorian fashion led logically to the cult of invalidism in middle- and upper-class women, and compare interestingly with the practice of Chinese foot binding that was so shocking to the West: both customs were designed to weaken women, to foster subservience and dependence, and to reify women's physical inferiority as evidence of their femininity and men's social status.[51] Fashion-conscious lower-class women raised other issues: since fashion was a privilege of the leisure class, such transgressing of class boundaries was condemned as vanity and deemed an indicator of girls' propensity to fall sexually. Inappropriately dressed factory girls sometimes lost limbs or even their life when excessive skirts got caught up in moving machinery; similarly, domestics endangered themselves by brushing past fireplaces and cookstoves while wearing voluminous crinolines. Finally, the problems of the needlewomen forced to produce these fashions demonstrate that both consumers and producers suffer from "fashionable follies."

Disgusted that stylish women perpetuate the myth of female vacuousness during a period when women were struggling for equality and political recognition, Martineau with keen insight denounced Victorian fashion and its proponents as high-visibility factors aggressively holding women back. Since fashion was a consuming interest to working women no less than to women who had nothing else to do, she rightly perceived that this was another issue about which the public's consciousness needed to be raised. She promotes dress reform, like the Bloomerism movement in America, as "thoroughly respectable, however it may be hindered and ridiculed by bigots and small wits" (*Daily News,* 21 October 1856). Everything about women's lives, even the "despotism" of fashions that prevent women from breathing adequately or standing on their own two feet, comes under the scrutiny of her feminist lens, revealing her keen awareness of the insidious degree to which weak-minded, dependent women are exploited by the very cultural values that ostensibly place them on pedestals to be worshiped.[52]

Martineau was committed to tearing down those pedestals, built as they are on "the old cant about the charms of woman in the function of a plaything or a slave," determined to replace them with "a rational recognition of the sober and serious duties and claims of this half of the human race in our own country and time" (*Daily News,* 21 October 1856). Over half a century after Wollstonecraft highlighted these same points, arguments about women's "natural" inferiority were still being rehearsed. "What sensible people"—like Martineau—"desire is, that all human beings should be as good as they are capable of being—that their powers . . . should be made the most of . . . instead of useless *a priori* argument about those powers in the case of woman." Appealing to the validating authority of science, she urged that Woman Question debates employ *fact* over the "loose rhodomontade" currently circulating: her own reliance on census statistics in discussing female industry offers a case in point. The importance of legal reforms in terms of women's earning capacity is clear: "many persons expressed surprise at the importance that female industry has assumed—at the amount of earnings that was in question. . . . [I]t is now too late to argue whether women can work, and whether they ought; and it remains only for their industry to be placed under the protection of the law, like that of men."[53]

As a single woman daily faced with the challenges and uncertainties of economic self-sufficiency, Martineau counted herself as fortunate among women in her ability to support herself as a writer. Although there were times when extended illness and other problems compromised her economic viability, she took pride in her steady refusal to accept a government pension. But hers is an anomalous example, and she pleaded eloquently for those single and widowed women "who, in every modern society, find it difficult to live, and almost impossible to place themselves in a position of comfort and enjoyment" (*Daily News,* 27 November 1858). Among this group are the elderly governesses and domestics and needlewomen whose years of hard work for little pay leave them no option for their final years but the dreaded workhouse. Martineau urges "a home, a maintenance, and a social position for unmarried or widowed ladies, who would otherwise be adrift and tempest-tossed on the heaving surface of society." In *My Farm of Two Acres,* she deplores the "unnatural mode of life endured by single and widowed women in confined circumstances, who pine away their lives in town" and considers viable alternatives for such women (1906, 8). One option is the establishment of Protestant convents where respectable "redundant" women might finish their lives honorably and safely, in community, rather than in isolation or in workhouse squalor. An alternative community is more secular: "I should like to see the economy of association made use of by women; to see them living in a sort of club-house, enjoying comfort and luxury, rather than dispersed in poverty among boarding-houses and schools" (Chapman 1877, 203). Martineau's vision of such a community is based on a rejection of patronage and class distinction, stressing instead simplicity and equality that will unite women through their common need.

Martineau's last professional involvement in Woman's Cause was through the campaign to repeal the Contagious Diseases (CD) Acts throughout the 1860s and early 1870s. Her links with Nightingale and the military, health and hygiene reform and its connection with public morality, and women's issues segued naturally into the social purity movement. By invoking the stereotype in which army nurses were assumed to serve the dual functions of health-care worker and prostitute, CD legislation directly undermined any progress realized by Woman's Cause in general and by nurses and other working women in particular. This demonstrates a powerful backlash against Woman's Cause that effectually mobilized British women to organize their protests into the comparatively unified movement we now call first-wave feminism. Nightingale observes, dryly, that CD regulation formally acknowledges that prostitution is a social necessity, not a moral aberration, and questions how the eighty thousand men hospitalized yearly for venereal diseases—not to mention the women confined to lock hospitals (specifically for the treatment of venereal disease)—are to be cured by an act of Parliament: "The thing is absurd." Viable solutions, based on Nightingale's extensive field research, already existed in the form of her proposed health reforms, specially adapted to the lifestyles and health issues of army men. But instead of employing her empirical evidence, proposed reforms were based on medical opinions "which don't address policy and morality." Like Martineau, she argued that as long as army men live in substandard environments—poor housing, inadequate clothing, nonnutritious food, with all the diseases that attend these conditions—and have nothing to occupy their free time, they will naturally turn to alcohol and promiscuity. The solution is simple: improve their standards of living and so too will moral standards improve, not only in the army but throughout the entire Empire.[54]

Nightingale's letters to Martineau throughout the spring of 1864 express her anger over the CD controversy, which peaks when she learns of a War Office proposal to screen and register prostitutes for army use, providing them with compulsory religious instruction designed to counter their immoral occupation.[55] Outraged at the acts' affront to women's civil liberties and at legislators' disregard of the scientific evidence that venereal infection is not gender-specific, Martineau wrote a *Daily News* article that served as "the first cannonade in the fight which became known as 'The Cause'" (Pichanick 1977, 24). Having so eloquently established that the "jealousy of men" was the factor most responsible for keeping women in a state of oppression—as even the revered Nightingale's difficulty in obtaining a hearing for her work vividly illustrates—Martineau was acutely aware of the implications of such legislation to working women as well as to conventionally house-bound women, an insight shared by reformist Josephine Butler. Since any woman, anywhere, regardless of her moral, economic, or social standing, could be arrested and held on suspicion of prostitution, the Contagious Diseases Acts concerned all women, not just camp followers.[56]

Martineau's 1864 *Daily News* article demonstrates her awareness that the social reforms she had vigorously promoted for decades were explicitly compromised by this proposed legislation: "It is an awkward and difficult state of things when legislation is necessary, or is sought without being necessary, on matters unfit to be brought under the eye of a great part of the public. The awkwardness and difficulty, however, are no justification to journalists for permitting the slightest risk of bad legislation which they may preclude by timely warning." In her role as a journalist, she believed it was her duty to inform the public about legislation currently afoot whose duplicitous wording threatened all women, wording "full of ill-defined or undefined terms, provisions for punishing unproved and unprovable offences, and for remedying evils which cannot be ascertained to exist. . . . . [V]ague, ineffective, and delusive as it is in its whole fabric, its passage would be a national calamity" (*Daily News*, 2 July 1864).

While the 1864 article features Martineau as a minority voice of protest in what was not yet a full-blown controversy—a position she was accustomed to—it represents the beginning of one of emerging feminism's most crucial battles. For many Victorians, a public health concern such as venereal disease was also a moral concern; but some insightful women recognized another issue: the deeply misogynistic bias underlying legislation that robbed all women of their civil liberties and made their bodies property of the state, subject to incarceration, detainment, and repeated pelvic examinations by men who were complete strangers. The article questions the efficacy of the proposed legislation when current related laws are not enforced, when alternatives have not been explored, and when men are cast as the victims of predatory, diseased females and not themselves as aggressors. Throughout her career, critics discredited, at times ridiculed, Martineau's criticisms of social institutions and cultural practices that compromise rather than protect women's rights, charging that her single, childless state rendered her positions untenable. But she as persistently demonstrated that her intellectual insights, coupled with her unassailable respectability, make her the perfect social commentator, particularly where women's issues were concerned. Accordingly, of her singular protest she observes, "It was sickening to think of such a work; but who should do it if not an old woman, dying and in seclusion? . . . . I felt that I should have no more peace of mind if I did not obey 'the inward witness' . . . yet it turns me chill in the night to think what things I have written and put in print" (Chapman 1877, 438).

Five years later, when she was retired from public life, Martineau wrote a series of letters to the *Daily News* signed "An Englishwoman," an aggressive barrage heralding the Ladies' National Association campaign to repeal the CD Acts. One letter posits that recent legal safeguards established for women have, through CD legislation, been set aside and replaced by liabilities: "Any woman of whom a policeman swears that he has reason to believe that she is a prostitute is helpless in the hands of the administrators of the new law. She is subject to the extremity of outrage under the eyes, hands, and instruments of surgeons, for the protection of the sex which is the cause of the sin" (*Daily News,* 29 December 1869). No longer willing to placate "Women's Missionaries" by diplomatic rhetoric designed to transform "Woman's Mission" into "Woman's Cause," Martineau asserts unequivocally what women's mission must now be if they are to protect themselves from an invasion that amounts to legal rape (by speculum): "The most sacred liberties of half the people of England are gone . . . and now it is the women, for the most part, who have to insist on their restoration. . . . [W]e see why it is that the Matronage of England is moved to avowal and action which it would have supposed impossible till these new perils became manifest." Concluding that the law protects men from women while offering women no protection at all, she urges the mothers of England to get involved in the protest in order to protect their daughters from outrage and their sons from vice. The impatience and disgust in her tone and language indicate an unwillingness, late in life, to employ diplomacy in order to convince, through logic and reason, those who have proven themselves illogical and unreasonable. With so little time and so few words left to her, Martineau in effect joins the ranks of the feminist "declaimers" who demand change and insist on it *now*.

Encouraged by an unprecedented sense of female community emerging from this episode, she posits that the establishment of the Ladies' National Association offers "reason for hopefulness . . . [because] an association now exists to which my countrywomen may resort for companionship in effort, for information and guidance, and for strengthening in the determination to stand by the personal liberties of every one of us" (*Daily News,* 30 December 1869). American women watched with interest the unfolding of this debate in England, keenly aware of its significance to the progress of women's rights and the threat it posed to all women everywhere. Eager to repay their British sisters who had campaigned for the abolition of slavery in America, American women now lent their support to the Ladies' National Association. Of this new national and international solidarity springing up around women's causes, Martineau wrote excitedly, "But what a prospect is opened for the whole sex in Old England! For the stronger and safer sort of women will be elevated in proportion as the helpless or exposed are protected" (Chapman 1877, 436).

Ray Strachey's study of first-wave feminism, *The Cause,* cites Martineau as one of the forerunners of the women's movement, one among many women who "contributed directly to its approach" from their individual spheres. "Long before any organisation was in existence," writes Strachey, "it is interesting to see, in their letters to each other, how a kind of freemasonry of understanding existed among them. They sought each other out, and . . . recognised each other" as ideologically like-minded (1978, 14). Rather than addressing issues like the franchise, which seemed so remote and premature, these women focused on "practical purposes," those appearing "more immediate and urgent," as sites for feminist reform (304).[57] Although the examples I have selected are only a portion of Martineau's prolific writing on women's issues, they make clear that she regarded education and work as essential bases for achieving gender equity. When she traveled throughout the Middle East in 1847, she was struck by the status of women there, particularly the wives, concubines, and slaves populating harems. Of ancient Egypt, she wrote, "The rank held by the women in old Egypt is a most striking consideration. . . . There seems to have been a real equality among the old Egyptians which indicates a degree of enlightenment which may make their lofty mythology not a *single* marvel" (Chapman 1877, 258). But in the Egypt she toured in 1847, she saw women who, to her mind, had been tragically wronged by the systematic prohibition of knowledge and activity in their lives. Far from access to education and occupation, the lives of harem women revolved around

sensual indulgence—eating, drinking, smoking, sexuality, inactivity—
while even the most socially elevated among them were the slaves and
playthings of men, a configuration strikingly similar to the status of "genteel" women in England. In this clash of ideologies between harem women
and Martineau—herself the embodiment of independence, of utilitarian
autonomy, and of physical and intellectual vigor—linguistic, moral, and
cultural differences were the least of their communication problems.

Contemporary scholar Leila Ahmed argues that harem life fosters female solidarity through offering an insular women's community; but to
Martineau it presents a grotesque illustration of patriarchy's power specifically to dismantle female solidarity by offering women community only in
and through their shared sexual enslavement.[58] Although Ahmed charges,
based solely on *Eastern Life, Present and Past,* that Martineau's is the worst
sort of ethnocentric orientalism in its misapplication of Western gender
standards to Eastern culture, a survey of Martineau's work, such as I have
offered here, points repeatedly to her concern that all human beings develop their capacities "to the utmost." Martineau's distressed response to
harem women was based on one idea—the same idea informing her fictional characterizations, the social causes she promotes in her nonfiction
writing, and her assessments of her women contemporaries—that is, that
being a strong-minded and informed woman and aggressively putting that
knowledge to work in the world for the benefit of humanity is the most
crucial prerequisite for the equality not only of women but of all society.
Such a standard is certainly humanistic, probably idealistic, but hardly ethnocentric. A viable example of female solidarity and community began to
take shape at the end of Martineau's life, when first-wave feminists, relatively liberated from such fundamental women's issues as work, education,
divorce, and property laws through the feminist activism of Martineau's
generation, undertook the next set of reforms obstructing women's
progress. But prior to that period, as the examples in the next chapter illustrate, community among professional women in Martineau's generation
was all but impossible in a culture whose perpetuation depended on keeping women in isolation, divided from each other and as enslaved to patriarchal institutions as any Eastern harem woman.

# 5

## "Not Fine Ladies,
## but True-Hearted Englishwomen"

I, for one, do not acquiesce. I declare that whatever obedience I yield to the laws of the society in which I live is a matter between, not the community and myself, but my judgment and my will.

—**Harriet Martineau**

Well, my dear friend, live long as we may, there is no prospect of a want of work for us. We have a scope and a call such as few women have. What *can* there be in the world's gifts to tempt either men or women aside from such a destiny?

—**Harriet Martineau**

Together with the well-worn and disagreeable talk about the Rights of Woman, we discard the sentimentalism of lack-a-daisical novelists who describe the position of women to be that of sitting in a drawing-room, beautifully dressed, with nothing to do but to make home agreeable to their husbands.

—**Harriet Martineau**

## The Personal and the Political

• As a prominent public figure, Harriet Martineau interacted with people from all levels of society, from heads of state and parliamentarians to slaves and workhouse inmates. Although her own reputation has slipped into comparative obscurity, many of her famous friends and acquaintances continue to be regarded as quintessential shapers of Victorian culture. Perhaps more than many of them, Martineau as a critic of Victorian society deserves recognition as a catalyst to post-Victorian debates and cultural developments. Martineau cultivated relationships (some personal, some epistolary, some intellectual) with a variety of artists, scientists, writers, politicians, and social activists, among them some of the most notable women of the period: writers Harriet Beecher Stowe, Catharine Sedgwick, Elizabeth Barrett Browning, Charlotte Brontë, George Eliot, and Elizabeth Gaskell; nursing pioneer Florence Nightingale; abolitionist Maria Weston Chapman; feminists Margaret Fuller and Mary Wollstonecraft; and social purity advocate Josephine Butler. Some of these women she never met personally: Martineau was born after Wollstonecraft died, and her relationships with fellow invalids Barrett and Nightingale, as well as with Butler and Stowe, were epistolary only. This chapter's focus on Martineau's wide-ranging and sometimes vexed relationships with famous British and American women offers a fruitful avenue for exploring her feminism. Martineau might well reject the idea of feminism as smacking of declaimers; however, if I define the term as any woman-centered approach to resolving social, economic, and political inequities based on race, class, and sex, her gender politics consistently prove her to be one of the great feminists of the period. Like other nineteenth-century feminists who recognized ideological analogies between the condition of slaves and the status of women, and like many feminist-humanists who view *gender* equity as the necessary precursor to *human* equity, Martineau promoted the welfare of all people beginning with what she knew best: the situations of women.

Her perspective on what women need to do in order to achieve equality depends on their capacity for self-discipline:

> It seemed to me from the earliest time when I could think on the subject of Women's Rights and condition, that the first requisite to advancement is the self-reliance which results from self-discipline. Women who would improve the condition and chances of their sex must . . . be rational and dispassionate, with the devotedness of benevolence, and not merely of personal love. (1983, 1:400)

Her own practice of self-discipline was exemplary, and it serves as a useful measure by which to assess her feminism as a woman writer. In 1833, while enjoying her first major professional success, Martineau crafted the following statement on the status of women:

> None of the many rewards of my humble exertions gratify me more than the appreciation by my own sex of my endeavours to prepare a way for them to more elevating objects and more extensive usefulness than at present. . . . Very few are called upon to make such a venture as I have thought it right to make. . . . If we could lay aside our selfish fears and scruples and affectations, and honestly set ourselves to discover what powers God has given us, and what we are to do with them, there is no power in man to condemn us to apathy and frivolity,—the only choice which is left us as long as we are content with either alternative. The true humanizing influence of woman will never be fully experienced till she becomes wise in thought, independent in action,

> and able to build up the charities in life on the foundation of principles ascertained by herself, instead of being taken upon trust. (Sanders 1990, 401)

The wisdom and clarity of this statement, particularly notable in a young and still unworldly woman, indicates an impressively developed gender consciousness that is radical—and thus urgent in recognizing that massive change is required *immediately*—yet tempered by an awareness that timeliness is essential for the success of social reforms. As in her writing on the situations of slaves in America, Martineau's stand on gender issues urges preparation on both sides: the dominant ideologists must be prepared to compromise while the oppressed must prepare for the transitions necessary to assume full citizenship. Preparation for civil autonomy, then, falls into three primary categories: education, legal and political reforms leading to individual representation, and shifts in both social ideology and in the balance of power. In order to understand Martineau's feminism as it manifests in her writing, it is important to regard these categories—at least initially—as sequential rather than simultaneous: education prepares and enables people to prove their worth; then, they must earn the franchise through intelligent and responsible citizenship; ultimately, and perhaps somewhat ideally, both will lead to favorable changes in social policies. In other words, women must first prove their worthiness to assume those privileges readily granted by men to men; and, although Martineau acknowledges the unfairness of this arrangement, her attention remains focused on promoting strategies for subverting that powerfully entrenched social custom.

The theme of education reform, the essential prerequisite to all other reforms, links the impressive variety of topics and issues she addresses throughout her long career. In *Household Education,* Martineau presents childhood education as the necessary foundation enabling people to cope with the problems inevitable to life. Yet "on no subject is more nonsense talked . . . than on that of female education," she notes. "Girls are not to learn the dead languages and mathematics . . . [because] the female brain is incapable of studies of an abstract nature,—that is not true" (1849, 240). On the contrary, she argues, "every girl's faculties should be made the most of. . . . [E]very woman ought to be fitted to take care of herself" (244). To survive in industrial society, every woman must have "the strength and clearness of an exercised and enlightened mind, and . . . have at command, for her subsistence, as much intellectual power and as many resources as education can furnish her with." The period's prevalent standard of educating women—if at all—for passivity and dependence clearly represents an ideology that is unrealistic and inappropriate for women in modern culture.

Her Ambleside neighbors, the Arnold family, provide a striking example of the tenacity of attitudes prohibiting certain kinds of education for women. Since two of the period's best-known education reformers were Dr. Thomas Arnold and his son, Matthew, Martineau found it remarkable that the Arnold women preferred to cultivate passive ignorance about two of the most pressing topics of the day—health and hygiene—rather than an "exercised and enlightened mind." The basis of her criticism concerns sanitary reform, on which she often lectured, but "As soon as Mrs. Arnold heard that I was going to treat of the *body,* she would not let [her daughters] come." Despite the advanced intellectual climate of this household, the Arnold daughters exhibited attitudes typical of most women of their class: "no one of them . . . ever had in her life a grasp of anything *real.* Words—words and sentiments unchecked by contact with external tests, make their lives one scene of busy idleness, pursued with the most astonishing complacency." My discussion later in this chapter of women she highly regarded—Florence Nightingale, Maria Martineau, and Josephine Butler—demonstrates the centrality of health issues to Martineau's perspectives on Woman's Cause. Indeed, sanitary reform provided the perfect medium through which women merged domesticity and morality with public, national concerns. Hygiene, of all things, offers one more example of the gendered standards separating the respectable from the unrespectable and, to her mind, social evolution from cultural stagnation.[1]

Martineau believed that examples of intelligent, strong-minded women were essential to realizing the legal and political changes necessary for women's progress. She claimed that "every woman ought to know the principles of the Government of her own country," despite and in fact because of women's political invisibility (Sanders 1990, 2). In 1837 she wrote:

> We hope to obtain a revision in parliament of all laws regarding Woman; to set a watch on all legal proceedings which relate to women; and to expose her whole state, from her bad nursery training to her insulted wifehood in palaces, and her wretchedness in prostitution. . . . The doubt is whether able women enough can be found to aid our beginning: *for women must work out their own redemption.* (Sanders 45; emphasis added).

The last sentence particularly highlights a shrewd and subtle political insight in its recognition that freedom and autonomy can ultimately neither be granted nor bestowed by those in power; rather—and this is a central idea behind Martineau's social politics—the oppressed must claim for themselves the status that is rightfully theirs. Her writings on slavery assert the same principle—true emancipation comes not from the whites but from self-validation; her admiration for runaway slaves ("the best of their kind") offers a case in point. This perspective anticipates John Stuart Mill's *The Subjection of Woman,* which argues that true liberation will result when women—not male parliamentarians—speak for themselves. Of course, as most of her writing demonstrates, the practical realities of patriarchal injustices unquestionably need aggressively to be addressed and legally remedied. Typically, the oppressed are too demoralized by their circumstances to generate sufficient energy to make themselves heard. However, that her gender politics maintains a lofty vision of universal parity along with attention to daily practical concerns reflects her ability both to envision "the big picture" and to appreciate the significance and the needs of the immediate historical context.

Martineau's entire life, personal and professional, was informed by political activism, compelled as she was by her "inward witness." As I have stressed throughout this book, she was one of the period's most active, pervasive, and prominent social-problem writers; all of her writing addressed the topics and issues of the period. Her activism continued through her needlework sold at fund-raising bazaars in support of various causes, while her correspondence with a stunning array of Victorian notables demonstrates her persistent politicking through appeals to friends, relatives, and aristocratic peers. Yet, despite her activism, she resisted feminist grandstanding: "I do not approve of the tone used by some of the public advocates of Woman's Rights; and I do not think that any good object will be attained by the formation of such a society" (Sanders 1990, 115). To Henry Reeve she asserted: "You are probably aware that I am of the old-fashioned order . . . as to what is admirable in women; . . . good treatment consists simply in giving their faculties fair play. I repudiate all abstract doctrines of rights,—all *a priori* arrangements for *giving* a position,—a position being a thing that must be earned" (164). This unusual perspective gives rise to claims that Martineau is an antifeminist while in the very process of capturing the paradox of her feminism: she dismisses feminist organizations and their demands for rights while also rejecting the false dichotomy of separate spheres ideology and the hegemonic structures on which it is based. In this, Martineau's thinking is so progressive that it anticipates a time, still unrealized today, when neither sex is bound by gendered concepts of human worth but by such ideas as universal equality and justice, what she terms "a fair field and no favour" (*Daily News*, 9 January 1860).

For the Victorians, transgressing the boundaries of gender roles constituted a direct threat to the established social order. Typically, men were associated with reason and discipline while women represented emotion and sensuality. Since the former carried more cultural weight, some early feminists posited that dismantling this gendered dichotomy by staking a claim for women's capacity to reason was the first step to achieving gender equity. From Wollstonecraft to Martineau to John Stuart Mill, social thinkers argued that women were forced by social custom and biological determinism into artificial standards of behavior and appearance, coerced into conformity by the threat of ostracization and compelled to economic dependency by a system that actively excluded them from education and employment opportunities. Some women attempted to satisfy both conditions, that is, to conform with cultural expectations as well as to cultivate their special gifts; as a writer, Martineau considered herself fortunate to have evaded the physical and emotional drains of marriage and motherhood, which left most women with little excess creative energy and virtually no social autonomy.

My discussion thus far has addressed predominant themes in Martineau's writing and primary interests in her life: needleworking as an activity essential to her creative process as a writer, the "American experiment" as an ideology with the potential to realize social equity, and fictional and nonfictional representations of women who promote and impede the progress of Woman's Cause and who demonstrate the degraded status of working women. All of these ideas are linked by their capacity to reveal Martineau's identity as a woman writer and as a feminist. Her relationships with famous women of the period provide an alternative and complementary perspective on the status of women. With a view toward tracing Martineau's gender politics over the course of her life, my discussion of her links with famous women follows a loosely chronological order. I begin with a feminist of whom Martineau disapproved—Mary Wollstonecraft—as a standard against which to measure her attitudes toward her midcentury contemporaries, women now commonly regarded as feminist prototypes. This and subsequent examples illustrate that Martineau's opinion on how *not* to be offers as much insight into her feminism as do those examples of women she regarded worthy of emulation.

In this focus on Martineau's attitudes toward her women contemporaries, I present her assessments of them as consistent with the framework through which she viewed society in general and Woman's Cause in particular. For her, the same standards of behavior apply to both private and public realms, an ethic leading to charges that her commentary is excessively harsh; in my view, this impression stems less from personal animosity than from Martineau's keen awareness of the seriousness of the issues Victorian women faced. I offer this discussion not to present her opinions of these women as necessarily representative of the general view but to highlight the standards she believed women must achieve in order to overcome popular prejudices obstructing their social progress. In my discussion of exemplary women, I include Martineau's niece Maria Martineau who, known by few outside the intimate Ambleside circle, is one of the women Martineau most admired in her life. Distinct from the vexed examples of some of her literary contemporaries, Maria Martineau, Florence Nightingale, Josephine Butler, and Maria Weston Chapman command particular attention as women who embodied and exemplified the strength of character and mind Martineau believed necessary to confront "the most serious business of life."[2]

### Mary Wollstonecraft

Mary Wollstonecraft offers a poignant example of intellectual brilliance compromised by passion and sensuality, and Martineau's critique of this early feminist provides important clues for understanding her gender politics. Although not a living contemporary of Martineau's, Wollstonecraft in her social and political theories influenced Martineau's intellectual development during her formative years. But as an adult, and despite—again, she might argue *because* of—her "disposition to honour all promoters of the welfare and improvement of Woman," Martineau asserts: "I never could reconcile my mind to Mary Wollstonecraft's writings, or to whatever I heard of her" (1983, 1:399). That Martineau, much of whose work aims to expose and eradicate oppressions suffered by women throughout the world, responded so adversely to the woman many regard as the founding voice of modern feminism, requires further exploration.

Martineau clarified her reluctance to identify herself with *feminist* issues—as opposed to her unwavering commitment to eradicating the *oppression* of women—in her discussion of Wollstonecraft. A "poor victim of passion," Wollstonecraft was detrimental to Woman's Cause because she paraded her private problems under the guise of political activism: "Nobody can be further than I am from being satisfied with the condition of my own sex; . . . but I decline all fellowship and cooperation with women . . . who injure the cause by their personal tendencies. . . . The best friends of that cause . . . speak from conviction of the truth, and not from personal unhappiness" (Martineau 1983, 1:400–1).

The differences between Martineau and Wollstonecraft do not arise from political or social theory but from the disparities between private and public practice, an idea informing virtually all of the former's writing about women. In Martineau's view, Wollstonecraft's tragic, and very public, love affairs, illegitimate children, and attempted suicide prove critics' charges that women can never be equal to men because they are chained to biological functions and excess emotionality. Martineau therefore argues that women in the public realm have a particular responsibility to behave in ways that will disprove notions of women's "inferiority" and instead illustrate their capacity for "cool-mindedness" and rationality. This perspective underpins her criticisms of Charlotte Brontë's novels (Brontë's strong-minded heroines are inevitably "undone" by love), George Eliot's highly publicized private life as G. H. Lewes's mistress, and Queen Victoria's prolonged deep mourning of Prince Albert's death (many years beyond the customary period) at the expense of her political duties.

From her earliest thinking about these issues, she believed that self-reliance and self-discipline were indispensable to promoting the welfare of women and to instituting social and political equality. Associated with masculinity, these qualities were generally discouraged in respectable girls: self-reliance was thought to be unfeminine while self-discipline seemed unnecessary, since many equated the opposite quality—pliability—with marriageability. Martineau also promotes affection, devotion, and benevolence of the "rational and dispassionate" sort as necessary for realizing improvements in the status of women. Since, in her view, women who both unquestioningly conform with (angels-in-the-house) or overtly rebel against (feminist declaimers) societal expectations perpetuate gender inequities, those who present themselves as rational, intelligent, and of course respectable prove their worth as responsible citizens. In this way, women can eradicate the negative stereotypes perpetuating their oppression, break down male prejudice against women, and remove obstacles preventing them from realizing their fullest potential as human beings. Martineau's emphasis on rationality in fact echoes Wollstonecraft, whose arguments promoting gender equity are based on the concepts of (masculine) reason and (feminine) passion, or sense and sensibility. In order to progress, women should cultivate the former and sublimate or eliminate the latter if they are to be taken seriously by those in power. Wollstonecraft's failing was her inability to practice privately what she preached publicly; that Martineau succeeded in doing just that often aroused antipathy among those with a less evolved capacity for self-discipline.

Martineau's perspective is not inconsistent with Wollstonecraft's arguments in *A Vindication of the Rights of Woman* (1792); both women share the daring opinion that, in practice, most marriages function as "legal prostitution" in that women exchange sexual compliance for material comforts provided by men.[3] Far less radical a feminist than posterity suggests, Wollstonecraft is sometimes criticized for not going far enough with her politics and, particularly, for proposing a brand of feminism that aims (or seems to) merely to create better wives and mothers rather than women who are individuals in their own right. Interestingly, Martineau's assessment of Wollstonecraft anticipates both this criticism and the more contemporary insight that the personal and political arenas are interchangeable where gender issues are concerned. In fact, just as Wollstonecraft's more conservative arguments seem designed to placate critics and cultivate allies by not appearing excessively radical, so too does Martineau urge caution in pursuing social changes she believed were premature: like the franchise for women or sexual liberation. But Martineau's complaint against Wollstonecraft is not political, it is personal; she had "no control over her own peace, and no calmness or content except when the needs of her individual nature were satisfied" (1983, 1:400). Wollstonecraft's personal tragedies and romantic entanglements earned her a notoriety that reinforced the notion that women are creatures of passion, not reason, which proves their inferiority and justifies their subordination. When, in her role as a feminist activist, Wollstonecraft allowed her personal life to become a matter of public significance, then she compromised Woman's Cause, despite her intellectual brilliance. According to Martineau's standard, Wollstonecraft was not self-reliant because she was perpetually compelled to be involved romantically and emotionally; she was not self-disciplined because these liaisons stemmed from unconventional, therefore scandalous, relationships that proved she was a slave to passion, not a rational woman in control of her destiny.[4]

In Martineau's opinion, the feminism of Wollstonecraft and her Victorian counterparts, "denouncers of the wrongs of women" (1983, 1:400), derived from personal unhappiness and disappointments rather than from a utilitarian, selfless orientation. To Martineau, an activism based on personal issues was worse than no activism at all in that it perverted the altruistic

ideals of social-problem movements. It is because of the scope and seriousness of these issues that she rejects women who "injure the cause by their
personal tendencies, . . . [they are] the worst enemy of the cause" they profess to plead (1:400–1). Although "allowance must be made for Mary Wollstonecraft" as well as for the "singular environment which determined her
course," Martineau resisted the tendency to valorize her, uncritically, as an
acceptable representative of women's rights.

On the other hand, qualities that *are* worth emulating, according to
Martineau, and characteristics that will promote women's rights are
demonstrated by "happy wives" as well as by "satisfied single women"
who are prompted not by an urge to vindicate personal wrongs but by a
desire for culturewide change. "The best advocates are yet to come," she
asserts, to be seen in the future female physicians, professors, artists, educators, nurses, writers, and businesswomen emerging throughout the
world (1:401). Unflaggingly optimistic on this point, Martineau believes
anything is possible for women who have access to education and training. Opportunity, self-reliance and self-discipline, benevolence based on
compassion rather than passion: these are to her the keys to transforming
the condition of women. "The best friends of that cause are women who
are morally as well as intellectually competent to the most serious business
of life": and this does not, to her mind, describe Mary Wollstonecraft,
whose feminist impact was dimmed by scandal. The unfairness of having
one's professionalism assessed according to one's private life was not lost
on Martineau, whose attempts to shed light on the institutions oppressing
women were ridiculed by critics as the ravings of a frustrated bluestocking;
but this awareness did not foster an alliance with Wollstonecraft. Instead,
to Martineau's mind, society's unforgiving stance toward gender nonconformity offers all the more reason why women must be doubly vigilant in
their private and public activities if they are ever to improve their status.
The extent to which the leading public women of her day meet or fail to
meet Martineau's standards for the best promoters of Woman's Cause
shapes the remainder of this discussion of "true-hearted" women.

## Abolitionists, Transcendentalists, and Evangelicals: The American Women

Martineau's *Autobiography* relates a brief yet revelatory episode that occurred during her American tour. Twice she visited the Sedgwicks, a family
of staunch northern Unionists, and for a time maintained a friendship
with writer Catharine Sedgwick. The episode concerns a confrontation between the two women in the midst of an otherwise idyllic walk, arm in
arm, along the "sweet Housatonic" (1983, 2:65). Martineau had suggested
that the dissolution of the Union might be the only way to abolish slavery,
an idea Sedgwick found so shocking that she actually withdrew from her
companion in physical revulsion. "The Union is sacred, and must be pre-

served at all costs," protested Sedgwick, whose worship of the "parchment idol" (64) (the Constitution) renders inconceivable Martineau's claim that the theory and practice of American ideology are emphatically not in accord.[5] The episode was instructive for Martineau in several ways: as she toured America, she learned that the slavery question was far more complex than a simple dichotomy (for or against), that many citizens confused patriotism with political myopia and class complacency, and that people's stands on the slavery issue—including her own—proved to be the single most decisive factor in the relationships she cultivated (or not) as a result of the American tour. These points are illustrated by her relationships with three of the most notable American women of the time: Maria Weston Chapman, anti-slavery activist, lifelong friend, and biographer; Margaret Fuller, transcendentalist, intellectual, and feminist; and Harriet Beecher Stowe, the evangelical abolitionist whose writing Martineau vigorously promoted through her *Daily News* leaders.

### Maria Weston Chapman

As evidenced by her various writings about the country over the course of her career, Martineau's lifelong fascination with the American experiment hinged on the disparities between its principles and its practices. The woman who best manifested the spirit of American ideology and who proved herself "morally as well as intellectually competent to the most serious business of life" was Maria Weston Chapman, whom Martineau met during her 1834–1836 American tour. Interestingly, the first exchange between the two women was distinctly inauspicious: Martineau, who spent much of her first year in America touring the southern slave states, received a letter from Chapman charging that the extent of her stay suggests she was being beguiled by her pro-slavery hosts. Martineau responded with defensive vigor, prompting Chapman's redoubled persistence in cultivating her alliance with the abolitionist movement. When the two finally met, Martineau was impressed both by Chapman's assertion that "My hopes are stronger than my fears" and by her striking appearance, "meant by nature to be soft and winning only, but . . . so vivified by courage, and so strengthened by upright conviction, as to appear the very embodiment of heroism" (1983, 2:28). Later, at that momentous Boston Female Anti-Slavery Society meeting, Martineau publicly declared her support of abolitionism, the significance of which was twofold: first, Chapman is the woman who pointedly challenged this self-styled sociologist—so intent on measuring America's theory against its practice—to align her own practices with her principles by taking a public stand. And second, the political radicalism marking the remainder of Martineau's professional life is directly attributable to the events of that day and their aftermath, all of which sharpened and clarified her evolving political ideology. As a prick to Martineau's conscience and an ideological comrade-in-arms, as effusive in her praise as she was sharp in her criticism, Chapman proved to be Martineau's best friend in the truest sense of the term.

Stunned by Chapman's personal charisma, Martineau initially feared that their friendship posed a danger to her recently acquired autonomy that "required my utmost moral care. . . . The discovery of her moral power and insight was to me so extraordinary that, while I longed to work with and under her, I felt that it must be morally perilous to lean on any one mind as I could not but lean on hers" (1983, 2:84–85). Given Chapman's aggressive abolitionism, Martineau's reservations were probably well founded, until, at least, the relationship was clarified as one of mutual respect and high regard. The concern Martineau expressed in 1837—"The doubt is whether able women enough can be found to aid our beginning"—is mitigated by Chapman's example. Martineau's admiration for Chapman reflects her excitement at finding a powerful female role model in an era when few women were inclined to risk social ostracization for their principles. Unequivocal commitment to principle was the first lesson Martineau learned from Chapman, whose priorities did not rest with beauty, dress, wealth, learning, or social prestige but with the eradication of slavery in America. High principles are what also drew Chapman to Martineau: "being what her works proclaimed her to be, I knew our lives could not fail to be of one substance, nor our lot of being cast in together" (Chapman 1877, 144). Chapman's words reflect the strong bond between these two extraordinary women that continued unbroken until Martineau's death over forty years later.

Perhaps the vague threat Martineau perceived stemmed from meeting Chapman at a point in her life when she had just "come into her own" as an independent woman; in some ways, that independence was not yet fully formed. Fresh from her phenomenal *Illustrations* success, which began with freeing herself from the trappings of middle-class complacency and culminated in international fame, Martineau seemed to recognize in Chapman's strong-mindedness an influence potentially detrimental to her newfound autonomy.[6] But while her wording suggests that Chapman's strong personality threatened to absorb or overpower her own, Martineau also noted that they had differences of opinion, "and that had not seldom happened" (1983, 2:85). Not destined to work side by side for abolitionism, the two women were united by their commitment to this cause though separated by an ocean, apparently worthy opponents who were also the best of friends. Their subsequent collaborations include a forty-year correspondence, which served as Martineau's primary link with American affairs during her *Daily News* years, 1839's *The Martyr Age of the United States,* Martineau's contributions to fund-raising bazaars and to Chapman's annual, the *Liberty Bell,* and Chapman's eulogistic *Memorials,* published as volume 3 of Martineau's *Autobiography* (1877). Her admiration for Chapman, the "most glorious woman I ever knew, or heard, or read of,—Garrison's equal and coadjutor," who evidences a "union of the highest intellectual and moral attributes," signifies that Chapman comes closest to realizing the sort of woman whose life is ruled by her commitment to the greater good rather than by her obsession with personal crises: "For twenty-five years she has been my study, first from a remote point, and then under the penetrating light of the strongest affection, and I certainly regard her as the most wonderful woman on record for power of achievement on the grandest scale."[7]

In *The Martyr Age of the United States,* Chapman is cast as one of the martyrs of the abolitionist cause. Like Elizabeth Gaskell, Chapman aimed to "do it all," serving as "Garrison's lieutenant," as wife and mother, as writer and editor, and as public speaker and political agitator. A "woman of rare intellectual accomplishment, . . . genius like her's cannot but take the lead wherever she acts at all; and she is the life and soul of the enterprise in Boston" (Martineau 1839, 27–28). Chapman rejected the "sinfulness of slavery" just as she rejected the charge that abolitionism is "unladylike"; she petitioned Congressmen to "remember that *they,* too, were women-born" (29); and, when ordered by the mayor of Boston to dismiss her abolition meeting, Chapman in turn ordered him to disperse the mob threatening from without. Clearly there was much for Martineau to admire in this woman whose beauty and charisma were matched by her contentious tenacity where abolitionism was concerned.

During the first twenty years of their friendship, Chapman consistently demonstrated her suitability for the "most serious business of life." That Martineau entrusted Chapman with writing her biography reveals a great deal about her esteem for her American friend. In an 1843 letter to Henry Crabbe Robinson urging the destruction of her letters, she observed: "there is no possible Executor whom I wish to admit to a sight of my private letters, my letters of affection, and I write no others" (Sanders 1990, 72). But by 1855, she had made Chapman her executor, handing over her private correspondence and journals in a singular act of faith and trust, charging Chapman with sole discretionary responsibility. Outlining the circumstances of her authorship, Chapman quotes a letter from Martineau, written during her 1855 illness: "I need not say that keeping up my friendship with you is more important than any business, and dearer than most pleasures" (1877, 1). Her tone suggesting that this might well be her final leave-taking of Chapman, Martineau assures her she will "try to work with you for such time as I remain" (2). Two months later, laboring to complete her *Autobiography* as ill health persists, Martineau asks Chapman to complete the work, prompting Chapman's vow "to show . . . what no mind can see for itself,—the effect of its own personality on the world."

Martineau's choosing Chapman to write the *Memorials* finalized the long-standing feud between Harriet and her brother James, who—curiously—fancied himself the most likely person to fill this role. Over the years, James's ambivalence toward Harriet became increasingly pronounced, resulting in her permanent break with this formerly adored brother. On James's unsuitability as her biographer, Martineau observed: considering the "intervals of 4, 6, and 7 years when he has not even *seen* me,—that he despises my books, knows none of my friends, or my habits, and very few of my opinions, and has never seen me for 20 years without insulting me,—he is not exactly the person to write my life" (Arbuckle 1983, 142). As Harriet's radicalism—including her highly publicized agnosticism—increased, James became proportionately resistant to his famous sister, thus widening the ideological breaches between them. As a woman, a foreigner, and a radical abolitionist, Chapman, in James's view, could not be more ill-suited to record his famous sister's life. Writer Constance Hassett argues that Martineau's choosing Chapman as her biographer was "highly political" and "clarifies the feminist basis of the women's mutual admiration" (1996, 379–80). Hassett's argument hinges on the idea that the spirit of anticlericalism is implicated in both feminism and abolitionism, which accords with the split in the anti-slavery movement over the status of women in political activism. Over all, notes Hassett, "Harriet's opinions strike him [James] as variations on the theme of insubordination" (395); as a result, James continued the feud long after his sister's death through repudiations, in print, of both Harriet and Chapman.[8] That Martineau chose "Garrison's lieutenant" as her biographer verifies how fully, as Florence Nightingale argued, her identity was implicated in the fight against slavery; thus, she selected the woman who best symbolized that spirit, the only woman who rivaled Nightingale herself in Martineau's estimation.

The two women shared more than a commitment to abolition. Martineau's letter to her cousin Henry Reeve highlights the feminist implications of Chapman's embodiment of American ideology. She marvels that Chapman's unmarried daughters exhibit none of the usual desperation typically linked with spinsterhood and is amazed that they go against the social grain *by choice*: "There you see a kind of American women who really are moulded by the spirit of their country. . . . [S]o many opportunities of marrying, in all manner of tempting ways: but they seem not to be disposed,—under the circumstances of the times. . . . [O]ne seldom or never sees a whole family so passing through life by choice" (Sanders 1990, 165). Following the conclusion of the Civil War, as the two friends grew old and Chapman's visits to England were more rare, they conveyed their affection and regard primarily through letters. These letters indicate a shared wisdom resulting from age and from a long and loving collaboration: "Farewell for to day, my dearest love," Chapman wrote, adding encouragingly, "patience and consolation to you, my dearest one! do we not see the reasons for every thing?—and accept and grow content?"[9] One of Martineau's last letters prior to her death concludes, "O my friend, I must not sink our hearts by words of farewell to-day. . . . Till our next greeting, then, farewell! I will attempt no more, for you know how entirely I am, as for half a lifetime, Your devoted H. M." (Chapman 1877, 455–56). The public and private communities of women over which Chapman and Martineau presided in their respective countries reflect feminine social influence and political power of a scope that hardly needed the franchise or any other male-sanctioned privilege to express or to manifest itself.

## Margaret Fuller

Margaret Fuller, author of the feminist classic, *Woman in the Nineteenth Century* (1845), aligned less with Martineau's assessment of Chapman than of Wollstonecraft: Fuller, too, was brilliant, articulate, and badly behaved. The two women met during Martineau's American tour, initiating a relationship that was complicated virtually from its inception: due, according to Martineau, to Fuller's "bad manners and self-delusions" (1983, 2:73). Proving valid this assessment through her own words, Fuller's remarks about Martineau in her correspondence reveal that her effusive praise, bordering on the dreaded "lionism," shifts abruptly to vicious denunciation and back again, often in the same passage. In 1836 Fuller wrote that she had been reading Martineau's work: "I find, with delight, that [she] has written on the very subjects I wished most to talk out with her, . . . I think more of her character when with her, and am stimulated through my affections" (Fuller 1983, 1:242). Fuller anticipated visiting Martineau in London, where together they would "see the best literary society" (1:243), yet just a few months later her mood was quite altered: "I suppose Miss Martineau says just whatever she thinks of the Bostonians as she does of all things and persons without regard to effects. . . . Little importance should be attached to . . . a person like her" (1:251). Given the timing, Fuller was perhaps responding to Martineau's unwanted notoriety, following the Boston Female Anti-Slavery Society meeting, as a reluctant abolitionist "declaimer."

Initially, Martineau and Fuller were "intimate friends." Martineau recalls the younger woman's "admirable candour, . . . her genuine heart, her practical insight [that] endeared her to me, . . . [and] led me to expect great things from her" (1983, 2:72). In turn, Fuller regarded Martineau as a mentor, a prototype of a successful woman author, with strong opinions on social and political issues: "She has what I want,—vigorous reasoning powers, invention, clear views of her objects," she wrote excitedly (*Memoirs* 1:153). "Never shall I forget what she said. It has bound me to her. . . . [W]e passed the barrier that separates acquaintance from friendship, and I saw how greatly her heart is to be valued" (1:152). Fuller effusively thanks God "for the purifying, elevating communion that I have enjoyed with this beloved and revered being. . . . May her path be guarded and blessed. May her noble mind be kept firmly poised. . . . I shall be cheered and sustained . . . by remembrance of her earnest love of truth and ardent faith" (1:153).

But their relationship barely survived the publication of *Society in America* in 1837, a book thoroughly motivated by Martineau's "earnest love of truth and ardent faith." Martineau was particularly wounded by Fuller's criticisms: "An immense letter from Margaret Fuller," she wrote in her journal. "Sad about herself, and very severe on my book. . . . I commit myself boldly, but . . . . I suffered a good deal from her letter" (Chapman 1877, 201). Counting herself among those who found Martineau's book unworthy of the author or the country, Fuller condemned her "presump-tuousness, irreverence, inaccuracy, hasty generalization, and ultraism. . . . Frequently I felt pleasure and admiration, but more frequently disappoint-ment, sometimes positive distaste" (1983, 1:307, 310). Her disapproval was twofold: first, she objected to the book's implied criticism of Bronson Al-cott through its negative analysis of transcendentalist philosophy; defend-ing Alcott, Fuller compared him, hyperbolically, with the philosophers of ancient Greece. A second, and related, issue was abolitionism, their ideo-logical disparity on which neither woman was willing to compromise: "I do not like that your book should be an abolition book. . . . [W]hy leaven the whole book with it? This subject haunts us on almost every page." She concludes by reaffirming her love and sympathy for Martineau, which she then undercuts by noting "the sympathy between us is less general than I had supposed." Fuller's drastic shifts in her attitude toward Martineau, even within the space of one sentence, are striking in the range of their emotional intensity, suggesting that her disappointment in the mentoring relationship she had earlier anticipated was keen indeed.

Fuller also, privately, denounced Martineau's *The Martyr Age of the United States,* which she pronounced "stained with credulity, exaggeration, and man deification as ever. She has placed her abolitionist friends in the most ludicrous light" (1983, 2:48). She concluded, ungraciously, that the American abolitionists would not object as they have no "good taste." Since emancipation was central to Martineau's ideology and anathema to Fuller's, the friendship between these two women—one a transcendentalist and one an abolitionist—was doomed from its inception.

Despite the breach in their relationship, Martineau enthusiastically rec-ommended Fuller's *Woman in the Nineteenth Century*—which she pro-nounced "Beautiful!"—to her friends (Arbuckle 1983, 85). But she was trou-bled by several aspects of Fuller's character, particularly her haughty perspective on slavery and her elitist, prima donna behaviors. Martineau greatly admired Fuller's intellect and feminist insights but regarded her po-tential as largely unrealized due to the transcendentalist class-consciousness defining her worldview. Living "in the most pedantic age of society in her own country, and in its most pedantic city," Fuller has limited herself by "pedantic habits of thought and speech" (1983, 2:73), thus betraying the values of the American experiment, of Woman's Cause, and of her own po-tential as a prominent intellectual.

As a transcendentalist, Fuller viewed the slavery question as coarse and vulgar: this Martineau "considered unworthy of her . . . from her regarding the anti-slavery subject as simply a low and disagreeable one, which should be left to unrefined persons to manage while others were occupied with higher things" (1983, 2:70). In light of the stellar example of Chapman, a woman of a quite different Boston circle who regarded abolitionism as holy work of the highest possible calling, Martineau was struck by the anomaly presented in the contrast between the two women. She pondered Fuller's later capacity to sympathize with and campaign for Italy's quest for independence and unification while remaining indifferent to the "struggle for the personal liberty of millions in her native republic" (2:71). "Haughty" and "complacent," Fuller represents the sort of "'gorgeous' pedants" who fancy themselves "the elect of the earth in intellect and refinement"; existing in the rarified atmosphere of philosophical speculation, they "looked down upon persons who acted instead of talking finely."[10]

In subsequent years, the relationship fully deteriorated; in Martineau's view, Fuller "made false estimates of the objects and interests of human life" (1983, 2:73): in other words, she favored a lofty philosophy over the more practical, humanitarian orientation engrossing Martineau. Martineau records Fuller's 1846 visit to Ambleside with rather more indulgence than that apparently demonstrated by her guest. Fuller's companions seemed to enjoy themselves, but Fuller "as evidently did not, except when she could harangue the drawing-room party, without the interruption of any other voice within its precincts" (2:252). On one excursion Fuller made clear her displeasure by refusing to speak to anyone, behaving more like a spoiled child than a mature woman. Interestingly, Fuller's account of her European tour in her *Memoirs* details her visit to Wordsworth and to nearby Ambleside (where Martineau lived), as well as to London, where she visited Henry Atkinson, Martineau's friend and coauthor, but she never mentions Martineau's name. Although Martineau's account may be seen as biased or defensive, Fuller exposes herself through her own words, in the letters and memoirs, as a precocious dilettante, whose piques were surprisingly— given her gifted intellect—immature.

Judging by such overt behaviors, Fuller was disappointed in Martineau as well; in Martineau's words, "I was so thoroughly common-place"— presumably through her links with abolitionism—"that she had no pleasure in intercourse with me" (1983, 2:253). When the two met in London prior to Martineau's Middle Eastern tour, Fuller "treated me with the contemptuous benevolence which it was her wont to bestow on commonplace people." Soon after, she concluded that Fuller's marriage, motherhood, and political activism promised to make "interesting and beautiful" what had previously "run to waste in intellectual and moral eccentricity." Writing to Ralph Waldo Emerson in 1852 after reading Fuller's posthumous *Memoirs*, Martineau noted:

> I had no idea that she was another instance of the old fate,—of a woman of strong nature, debarred from a home of her own, . . . . nor how very far she was from peace. How plain this becomes when we see her marry as she did. . . . Her terrible sufferings . . . seem all to have arisen from obvious transgressions of the laws of our nature. . . . Well: it is a life full of instruction, and of very sorrowful interest;—as thorough a revelation of woman's needs

as I know any where; and the most affecting, as being exemplified in one who should have done and enjoyed so much.[11]

Fuller's role as "the first American newspaperwoman and a major cultural critic" (Helsinger 1:38) attests to the professional and literary interests she shared with Martineau, yet these similarities bred animosity rather than allegiance. According to Elizabeth Helsinger, Fuller's relationships with other prominent figures of the day were also contentious; she "fascinated, repelled, and ultimately perplexed her contemporaries . . . [as was] evident even in the . . . tempering accounts of Emerson, Channing, and Clarke in the *Memoirs*" (1:38–39). Both Elizabeth Barrett Browning and George Eliot criticized Fuller's writing, although they felt—like Martineau—that her personal example was compelling, poignant and, in the end, tragic. Mary Russell Mitford termed Fuller a "strange, wild woman" while another called her a "sibyl in a straight jacket. Was it any wonder that she raved?" (1:40). These comments dovetail with Martineau's surprise to learn that Fuller was "another instance of the old fate": a woman of brilliance struggling to align her principles with her practice, a woman of the nineteenth century out of step with—because in advance of—the times.

Toward the end of her life, Martineau regretted that Fuller's early preoccupation with sterile intellectualism made her "insensible to the vital interest and importance of the life, events, and influences of her own country and people. It was a remarkable spectacle to those who knew her during her short visit to England,—the unconsciousness she manifested of the crisis through which the mind and heart of her own country were passing while imaginative literature, and an arbitrary ideal philosophy occupied her." But despite her resistance to involvement in American civil issues and the tragedy of her untimely death, Fuller briefly experienced life's "deepest interests . . . with which she was inspired and clothed in her last and crowning days."[12] The political consciousness that leads to social activism—which, to Martineau, outweighs abstract philosophies and theologies—distinguished Fuller's last years, when she, for a short time, realized the potential Martineau recognized back in 1835.

### Harriet Beecher Stowe

Harriet Beecher Stowe, the American evangelical abolitionist and author of *Uncle Tom's Cabin,* had no personal contact with Martineau except through letters and reviews, yet the two women shared many thematic and literary affinities. Stowe's 1852 novel so powerfully contributed to the intensifying American civil conflict that some—Abraham Lincoln, for one—credited the book itself with sparking the Civil War. Given her own experience with hostile threats resulting from her comparatively mild antislavery commentary, Martineau felt a strong connection with Stowe, who dared to enter the debate on such unequivocal terms as those presented in *Uncle Tom's Cabin.* This novel, she wrote, "has done more to popularise

American politics in England than all the slavery pamphlets ever written. People in this country now *feel* the importance of the one great problem that endangers social life in the United States, and are desirous of *understanding* all its bearings" (*Daily News*, 25 March 1853). Just as attitudes differed radically and unpredictably between the northern and southern states, so too were English sympathies far from uniform on the slavery issue.[13] Ever alert to the significance of history in the making, Martineau observed that Stowe's arrival in England is "no trivial matter" (*Daily News*, 12 May 1853). Several of her *Daily News* articles devoted to this writer attest to the importance of England's support of the cause she represents.

Martineau generously praises Stowe, delighting in the irony that this wife of a poor Midwestern preacher is being wildly lionized by the rich and famous of England "who had been charmed by her marvellous book" (*Daily News*, 9 May 1853). But there is no need to critique *this* example of literary lionizing, since it proves that "truth and humanity may gain from all ranks" and that "the genius of the New World may win [praise] from even the most select coterie of the Old." Relying as it does on the leveling effects of shared commitments to moral and social causes, this observation highlights the special importance attached to women's anti-slavery activities: "Slavery is a subject on which women may and should speak and act as freely as men, and if men do not speak and act as freely as they ought, women are quite right to choose their own method of expressing their own protest, individual or collective."

Stowe is "no fine lady," Martineau asserts, no great intellectual, although she does have many good qualities and "plenty of ability" (*Daily News*, 9 May 1853). Despite criticisms of the novel's accuracy in its depiction of slavery, Stowe's book nonetheless represents a timeliness that Martineau perceives far outweighs literary considerations: "The singularity of the case is that she has been made, unintentionally and even unconsciously, the apostle of the greatest cause now existing in the world." Despite its "grave artistical faults," the novel is truthful and objective, marked by an "absence of all self-reference" and written "because she could not help it"—all points congruent with Martineau's literary ideology, which itself stems from an irrepressible "need of utterance." The article concludes that this "most successful of living American authors" serves as the "embodied rebuke of the lovers of freedom and the advocates of popular government." All she says here of Stowe might be said of Martineau herself, whose popular success twenty years earlier reflected the timeliness of the Reform Bill–era publication of the *Illustrations*.

A 12 May 1853, *Daily News* leader reiterates the idea that the time is right for the emancipation of slaves as well as of women through abolitionist activism:

> [Stowe] now is the very first among those who ascribe her marvellous fame to the ripeness of the world for the subject on which she spoke, as she says, "because she could not help it": and her steady persistence in this view in the

midst of such an intoxicating whirl of success of every kind as would have turned almost any other head, marks her as a greater woman than all the genius of all the women who ever lived could have made her, without her honest simplicity.

The power of Stowe's book, she asserts, "is in its truth." But not all of her comments were positive. Privately, Martineau wrote to Fanny Wedgwood, "Poor Mrs. Stowe and sundry clergymen cut a wretched figure, don't they?" an attitude attributable to her criticisms of evangelicalism (Arbuckle 1983, 212, 213 n. 13). As the most famous and influential (white) female abolitionist in American history, Stowe's evangelicalism conflicts not only with Garrisonian ideology, which Martineau supports because of its feminist slant, but also with Martineau's secular enlightenment, which views Christianity as joyless and guilt-ridden, superstitious and self-indulgent and, together with capitalist ideology, directly responsible for the perpetuation of slavery.[14] Yet despite this fundamental ideological disparity, the two women remained friends through their shared commitment to eradicating the defining social problem of the era.

Stowe's subsequent novel, *Dred* (1856), did not enjoy the success or lasting fame of the earlier book, although its welcome was assured while her popularity was still at its height. Martineau's praise of *Dred*—"*as you ask for my opinion of the book,* you may like to know that I think it far superior to *Uncle Tom*"—emphasized her preference for realism in fiction: "I knew that with you, I should be safe from the cobweb-spinning of our modern subjective novelists, and the jaunty vulgarity of our 'funny philosophers,'— the Dickens sort, who have tired us out. . . . [O]ne will have no patience with any but didactic writing, after yours" (Stowe 1889, 308–9). Literary history shows, however, that didacticism, of which the once-timely *Illustrations* and *Uncle Tom's Cabin* are prime examples, fell into disfavor as literary tastes shifted to reflect social change.

Martineau urged Stowe to visit The Knoll, despite the former's ill health: "*Can't* you come? You are aware that we shall never meet if you don't come soon. . . . I hope to have breath and strength enough for a little talk with you. You could have perfect freedom at the times when I am laid up, and we could seize my 'capability season' for our talk" (Stowe 1889, 308). Although Martineau remembers meeting Harriet Beecher's sister Catherine and father, Lyman, while in America, she is uncertain about having met Harriet: "Did I see you (in white frock and black silk apron) when I was in Ohio in 1835? . . . I believe and hope you were the young lady." The tantalizing question remains unanswered, while another letter dating from this period proves that the friendship was destined to remain epistolary. Stowe wrote of her thwarted visit, "To have seen you, to have [talked] with you, to have had your sympathy and advice would have been very delightful to me and I can scarce reconcile myself."[15] As my discussion later in this chapter shows, it was perhaps best that this friendship was not further tested by the mentoring relationship Stowe (like Fuller before her) seems to anticipate.

In a letter to Chapman written when Martineau's professional career was virtually over, Stowe noted: "Please to tell Harriet Martineau from me that the expression of *her* approbation and sympathy, has been more to me than the *disapprobation of all who have disapproved in England. . . .* [T]ell her that I believe in the power of truth and justice."[16] The sentiment could not more perfectly align with Martineau's pursuit of truth in all her undertakings, an ideal designed to inspire more animosity than friendship among certain circles. Although initially Margaret Fuller regarded Martineau as a mentor, affection soon shifted to temperamental piques once Martineau's "low" commitment to abolitionism became clear. Similarly, Catharine Sedgwick "lionized" Martineau but rejected her challenge to the sanctity of the Constitution, even when millions of politically unrepresented lives were at stake. But when friendship resulted from a shared commitment to truth and justice—in the examples of Chapman and Stowe, a commitment that demanded no less than the abolition of slavery—powerful friendships and alliances were formed that defied geographic boundaries and the passage of time. In her *Autobiography* Martineau wrote: "I am pleased to find that in the South I am still reviled, as I was twenty years ago, and held up, in the good company of Mrs. Chapman and Mrs. Stowe, to the abhorrence of the South" (1983, 2:40).[17] Although she denied that her role in the American conflict even approached that of Chapman and Stowe, she was delighted that her name was linked with theirs: a claim to fame of which she was particularly proud.

## Fine Ladies and True-Hearted Englishwomen

The most celebrated of Martineau's Lake District neighbors was William Wordsworth, whose wife, Mary, she eulogized in *Biographical Sketches:* "There was something mournful in the lingering of this aged lady—blind, deaf, and bereaved in her latter years; but *she* was not mournful, any more than she was insensible" (1868, 86). Mary patiently buried her loved ones, one by one, yet she "liked life to the end." Martineau found much to admire in the quiet woman behind the famous poet laureate, a woman whose existence seemed eclipsed by the domestic minutiae of marriage and motherhood yet in whom she saw an admirable model of womanliness:

> By her disinterestedness of nature, by her fortitude of spirit, and her constitutional elasticity and activity, she was qualified for the honor of surviving her household—nursing and burying them, and bearing the bereavement which they were vicariously spared. She did it wisely, tenderly, bravely, and cheerfully, and she will be remembered accordingly by all who witnessed the spectacle. . . . She was the incarnation of good sense. (87)

Mary Hutchinson Wordsworth symbolized an increasingly rarified way of life immortalized by the Romantic-era writers and thus, a way of being in the world. Like Martineau, her life spanned the Romantic and the Victorian ages, both women preferring the Lake District's timeless natural beauty to the sooty cityscapes marking the progressive technological era. Also like Martineau, Mary promoted thrift and self-sufficiency, and she rejected the idea of charitable handouts in favor of teaching the poor how to "do" for themselves. "Young wives for half a century learned [from] . . . the example of the good housewife at the Mount" (92), notes Martineau. She might have added that the most influential woman in the world for over sixty years, Queen Victoria, could also have learned from Mary Wordsworth's humble example.

### Queen Victoria

The Victorian era might well be termed the century of women: it featured a woman leading the great British Empire out of the agrarian age, through industrialization, and into the modern period; it yielded the greatest flowering of women writers in literary history and the advent of women into other traditionally male-dominated professions; and it formulated the eternal battle between the sexes into a neat, self-contained Woman Question. Out of the Woman Question evolved first-, second-, and third-wave feminism, which continued to grapple with the complex gender issues the Victorians could ponder but not resolve. All of this suggests that Queen Victoria herself symbolized the rise of nineteenth-century feminism, though such was not the case. Although my purpose is not to analyze Victoria's feminism but to discuss her in relation to Martineau, it bears mentioning that the queen is today generally regarded an antifeminist, primarily for her refusal to promote women politically, although she was herself a political icon.

Known for her obsessive devotion to Prince Albert and her personification of the maternal angel-in-the-house, Victoria was also critical of the earthier aspects of conjugal life—particularly the inconvenience, discomfort, and embarrassment of pregnancies and childbearing. Victoria's attitude was surprisingly inconsistent with the pervasive heterosexual, nuclear-family, domestic ideology her own example codified. This suggests that what has been stereotyped as sexual prudishness marking the era that bears Victoria's name was in fact a thinly disguised resistance to the period's strict delineation of sex and gender roles, a resistance expressed even by its epoch-defining monarch.

Back in London after her American tour, Martineau experienced the excitement of Victoria's coronation. "We are all somewhat romantic about our young Queen, poor thing!" she wrote in 1837. "What chance has she of growing up simple and good? but she really is an exceedingly good girl at present" (Sanders 1990, 48). Victoria's sheltered girlhood, her youth, inexperience, and political naivete construct a dubious image of leadership potential that many overlooked in light of the unquestioned "sanctity" of royal succession. It was not until later in her career that Martineau dared openly to criticize Victoria for exploiting the "distressed needlewomen" whose cause Martineau championed. As was clear in the examples of Fuller and Wollstonecraft, Martineau disapproved of women who were placed by fortune or circumstance in positions of power and influence from which they might accomplish much good on behalf of the oppressed, yet who fail to do so out of a misplaced sense of their own importance.

Martineau recorded Victoria's coronation at Westminster Abbey, which she attended because "it was a clear duty to witness it" (1983, 2:121). She outlines the day's events meticulously, beginning with the overexcitement that woke her up far too early; by four in the morning she was dressed in "crape, blonde and pearls" and set off with her sack of sandwiches and shawl for the day's events. Because of the well-dressed, jeweled crowds thronging the abbey and her rather poor perch, she was able to see little of the ceremony and to hear even less, but she did observe the crowds and offers a lively description of this remarkable historical event. By some feat of acrobatics Martineau was able to glimpse Victoria's "enthroning": "Her small dark crown looked pretty, and her mantle of cloth of gold very regal. . . . The homage was as pretty a sight as any;—trains of peers touching her crown, and then kissing her hand" (2:125).[18]

But although she concludes, "It was a wonderful day; and one which I am glad to have witnessed" (2:127), she adds that the event had an unexpected effect on her: "It strengthened, instead of relaxing my sense of the unreal character of monarchy in England." All the pageantry could not conceal the fact that the monarch was no more than "a nominal ruler," making the festival "barbaric" and the ritual's theology disturbing: "There was such a mixing up of the Queen and the God, such homage to both, and adulation so like in kind and degree that . . . it made one's blood run cold to consider that this was commended to all that assemblage as religion . . . the most coarse and irreverent celebration that I was ever a witness to" (2:127–28). As a Dissenter, she was shocked at the superimposition of sovereign upon deity and apprehensive about how the Christian hegemony's political machinations would shape the new queen's reign. Her distaste for this link increased as her own theology shifted to agnosticism: "I can't pretend to countenance the pretence that the poor ignorant baby of a queen is a potentate," she wrote rather vindictively to William Fox in 1844. "That sham is to me the most fearful portent of all" (Burchell 1995, 77).

Martineau was initially impressed with Victoria, whom she described as "really pretty," with an "ingenuous and serene air which seemed full of promise" (1983, 2:120). But within a year her expression was melancholy, bold, and discontented, in accordance, Martineau posits, with the political intrigues that obstructed her every move. "I have never gone out of my way to see great people," she wrote, "but the Queen went abroad abundantly, and I saw her often" (2:119). She records seeing her at the theater during William Macready's performance of *King Lear,* during which Victoria rudely laughed and gossiped loudly to everyone's annoyance, although she was eventually silenced by the actor's compelling performance. Martineau implies that Victoria's melancholy demeanor was due to her unmarried state, since, once ensconced in marriage and motherhood, her "virtue" as well as her appearance flowers again. Seemingly, the only period of happiness for Victoria was when she was married, making her forty-year widowhood a dubious period in England's social and political history.

Although the two women never met, Martineau was known to Victoria as one of the nation's most famous and popular writers. As a princess, Victoria read and admired the *Illustrations of Political Economy,* in which her favorite character was the Scots fisherwoman, Ella ("Ella of Garveloch"); she also ordered Martineau's *Illustrations of Taxation.* Early in Victoria's reign, Martineau learned that, upon hearing of her series *Guide to Service,* the queen requested "that several hundreds of the forthcoming series" be ordered for the libraries at all the palaces.[19] All this was quite gratifying and attested to Martineau's influence in political circles; yet, it does not curtail her subsequent criticisms of some of Victoria's policies.[20]

Several of Martineau's *Daily News* articles mark significant events in Victoria's reign. A 30 November 1854 leader on the Crimean War expresses regret for the conflict but asserts unflagging support and loyalty for Victoria in the midst of political controversy. Martineau extols the queen's "strong soul," her bravery and courage by stressing her *public* maternal role: "We have all said to one another what a kind, motherly heart she has, and how the havoc of war must wound it." She emphasizes the necessity for this war—"She is right—we, her people, are right"—in terms that implicate government and citizens equally, thus relieving Victoria of sole culpability:

> Our Sovereign has afforded us a long period of moral repose, as regards our relation to the throne, by her personal virtues. We have neither been disgusted by vice, nor irritated by folly, in the highest personage and family in the realm; we have, on the contrary, had our peculiarly English persuasions and sensibilities gratified, by the honest English virtues which have flourished there through a period of seventeen years.

This record of honor and stability in itself, she concludes, justifies public support of Victoria's design to thwart the "aggressions of despots."

On Victoria's twenty-first anniversary as queen, Martineau outlined a retrospective of her rule. Although at the time of her accession "unbounded and absurd expectations were entertained," designed to dispel a mood of political gloom, a more realistic assessment attributes England's prevailing sense of optimism to her "personal qualities," her "personal virtues," her "faithfulness," and "her fidelity to the pledge . . . that her life should be devoted to the happiness of her people" (*Daily News,* 19 June 1858). The arti-

cle emphasizes the idea of a role model worth emulating as the truest measure of womanly worth: "we are disposed to value at its utmost the blessing
of a virtuous Sovereign, who is willing to help, instead of hindering us in
our work of self-government. This is her best prerogative; and other sovereigns will show themselves wise in proportion as they emulate it."

In terms of emulation, however, there was a significant point on which
Martineau critiqued Victoria, who displayed a weakness for "fashionable
follies" at odds with her influential position. In the *Westminster Review* she
wrote: "We doubt whether in any age of our national history, or on any
spot of the globe, a more indefensible mode of dress could be pointed out
than we have displayed before us": in, for example, fashion magazines
marked "Patronized by the Queen" (1857, 174). She charges that court
dress is a "monument of folly" and Victoria could single-handedly change
all this "by setting the example of a truly tasteful mode of dress. . . . She
might do it in a month . . . [and] put an end to the abuse." Similarly, in "A
Real Social Evil," Martineau condemns the wearing of crinolines and appeals to the "good sense" of, if not Victoria herself, then that of ordinary
English matrons: "If the Queen were known to discountenance . . . the
fashion of hoops which renders it but too easy to set women and children
on fire, . . . the evil would immediately disappear" (*Daily News*, 15 October
1861). Martineau urges her countrywomen "to be ready to follow the royal
example which we anticipate; or, if that should be wanting, to act without
it in that sphere of home in which every English matron is queen." If, as
the most visible woman in the world, Victoria can perpetuate silly or even
life-threatening fashion trends, so too can she reverse them by her example. This she did, soon after: motivated not by social conscience but by the
widowhood that shaped the remainder of her long life.

The sudden and untimely death of Albert from cholera in 1861 sent the
grieving Victoria into a prolonged seclusion that nearly wrecked the empire,
according to some political analysts. As her mourning went beyond the customary year and promised to continue indefinitely, the nation's sympathy
for Victoria began to wane. Martineau observed in 1861, "of course we all
fear for her brain. . . . [But] as long as there is an appeal to her *courage*, and
her official *duty*, she will probably do very well indeed" (Sanders 1990, 196).
Two years later, Martineau's letter to the *Daily News* editor entitled "The
Queen's Hospitality" addressed several criticisms of Victoria, including her
extensive mourning, which created considerable problems: "The continued
seclusion of the Queen so long after the expiration of the year of close
mourning is a natural and proper subject of regret; and the regret is so
widely spread as to warrant some expression of it" (*Daily News*, 18 March
1863).[21] Trade and politics suffered as a result, prompting Martineau to encourage Victoria to "exert her well-known strength of mind, and subdue her
own feelings to the duties of her function." Recalling her earlier appeal to
Victoria's "personal qualities," Martineau urges the queen to resume the
public duties her position requires of her, and to prove that public faith in

188 | THE HOUR AND THE WOMAN

her has not been misplaced. "She must not retreat now into a solitude of re-grets," Martineau emphasizes. "She must appear to us in that capacity, and in that spirit which no personal experience should affect or obscure—as a devoted sovereign among a devoted people." By 1865, Victoria's continued heavy mourning seemed simply self-indulgent and irresponsible. Privately, Martineau wrote, "The misery is that *(entre nous)* the Queen has made up her mind *never to meet her Parliament again.* A friend of mine who was here in the spring heard this from herself just before. The selfishness is the shocking thing. She says she is sure she should have 'some bad attack.' . . . All her ladies and gentlemen wish she would resume her duties. . . . Be-tween her wilfulness and the P. of Wales's idleness, the country has 'a black look out,' as some of the Ministers think."[22]

Publicly, Martineau employed subtle psychological insight by urging Vic-toria to put aside her grief and resume her official duties, if not for her own or her country's sake, then *for Albert's.* "One tribute alone remains to be paid to his honour," she wrote, and "it is his wife who has to render it" (*Daily News,* 2 September 1865). The tribute is Victoria's resumption of her official duties, presented as the ultimate selfless sacrifice by a widow whose grief perpetuates unrest among the living and, Martineau implies, the dead. "The promise was to be all a Queen to her people, whatever her lot, within herself, as a woman," and her continued mourning has broken that promise, prompting divisive speculation about a monarchy whose virtual absence has proven its own redundancy. Victoria's resumption of her duties is the tribute that will lay Albert to rest honorably, comfort the queen, quell parliamentary intrigues, and placate a restive populace: "one day of deep, holy, glowing satisfaction remains for her—the day in which she will render her highest and tenderest homage to his memory by resuming the crown-ing duty of her station in life." Martineau's rhetoric compares significantly with that of "women's missionaries"—but again, to an alternative purpose: Victoria's "crowning duty" is not her role as wife and mother but as the rul-ing monarch of the British Empire. Her personal and public reliance on Al-bert may be "natural" to domestic ideology but, given the queen's personal qualities and her public responsibility, his influence is not necessary for her to reign over an empire: "She will appear before the Legislature, not now aided by his hand, but supported by the strength of his conscience and the steadiness of his judgment . . . under pain of weakening the foundations of the throne. . . . [She must show] an example of true regality in her superior-ity to personal sensibilities when these conflict with duty."

Despite criticizing the current state of national affairs due to Victoria's mourning, Martineau reiterates the idea that, with or without Albert's presence, Victoria is a "true-hearted Englishwoman," and the nation now waits for her to resume this role. But such encouragement as Martineau re-peatedly offered in the pages of the *Daily News* was apparently unheeded. In an 1867 letter to Lady Elgin, six years after Albert's death, she observed, "It is sad enough that the Queen is roving the Highlands for ten weeks together while the affairs of the nation are in a critical state. It is most desirable that she should show some readiness to go home, and attend to business" (Sanders 1990, 215). Victoria's example compares with that of Mary Wollstonecraft in that both allowed personal issues to supplant public duty, thus reifying the biological underpinnings of separate spheres ideology and compromising their role as "true-hearted Englishwomen." Perhaps in no other example is the conflict between personal and political more vividly dramatized than in Queen Victoria.[23]

### Elizabeth Barrett Browning

The "cult of invalidism," now thought to reflect an unnaturally passive, sheltered lifestyle that literally made Victorian women sick, provided the initial impetus for Martineau's relationship with Elizabeth Barrett. From the early onset of deafness through the major periods of invalidism punctuating her life, Martineau learned that the discomforts and deprivations of illness also had the advantage of excusing her from time-consuming social rituals, allowing her legitimately to read, think, and write instead. The same was true for Elizabeth Barrett, a prodigious scholar often confined to the sickroom, from which she conducted relationships with the outside world that were primarily textual. Although both women suffered from legitimate physical ailments, they shared an appreciation for the irony that feminine ill health enabled them to pursue "masculine" intellectual pursuits. Eventually, Martineau's recovery prompted her to hike through the Middle East and to transform herself into a rugged Lake District "local," whereas Barrett relinquished the role of obedient invalid daughter for the marriage, motherhood, and political activism (like Fuller, on behalf of Italian independence) invigorating her mature years. Seemingly predicated primarily on their spiritual bonds as invalids, writers, and women, their friendship did not survive the radical shifts in their perspectives once their lives resumed outside the sickroom.

The two women never met but they did read and admire each other's writing, cultivating a literary friendship conducted solely through correspondence. Barrett wrote, "With all my insolence of talking of her as my friend, I only admire and love her at a distance, in her books and in her letters, and do not know her face to face, and in living womanhood at all" (Kenyon 1899, 1:227–28). The intellectual bond between the two invalids was immediate: "I have had a great pleasure lately in some correspondence with Miss Martineau, the noblest female intelligence between the seas; as sweet as spring, as ocean deep. She is in hopeless anguish of body and serene triumph of spirit, with at once no hope and all hope. To hear from her was . . . a pleasure and an honour to me."[24]

Barrett regarded Martineau as "the most logical intellect of the age—for a woman"; she shared her letters with friends, anxiously awaited Martineau's assessment of her poetry, hung her portrait in her room, and later defended Martineau against Robert Browning's criticisms. Writing to Mary Russell Mitford, Barrett admiringly termed Martineau "the most manlike woman in the three kingdoms . . . in the best sense of man, a woman gifted with admirable fortitude, as well as exercised in high logic" (Sanders 1979, 9), a compliment the poet also reserved for George Sand. Writing about Barrett, Martineau was equally generous with her superlatives: "What a wonderful woman she is!—her genial and glowing morale so self-sustained, regulated, and cheerily sympathetic under the inspiration of her . . . learning, and the *very* hard pressure of her suffering life" (Sanders 1990, 93–94). They sent each other copies of their work and exchanged critical opinions, although the mentoring position fell primarily to Martineau as the more firmly established writer of the two.

In her criticism of Barrett's writing, Martineau encouraged clarity and precision of expression, urging her to avoid obscure poetic constructions and to be "simple, direct and modern": "I see no bounds to what your writings might be and do, if you could alter this one peculiarity" (Sanders 1990, 98). But, clearly uncomfortable in this mentoring role, she protested, "I do feel it so absurd for me to be criticizing poetry to a poet." One of the texts Barrett sent Martineau for commentary was *Poems* (1844). Both Martineau's willingness to praise and her reluctance to criticize tempered her remarks. "I sickened at my rashness," she confessed, "[at] the deadly shame of the thought that I had undertaken to criticize you. . . . Indeed it is my more proper business humbly to receive from you, than to examine the quality of what you offer. . . . I saw at once . . . that you had made an immense advance on the former volume . . . in precision, in dignity and clearness. . . . I find ideas . . . which are grand, moving and beautiful beyond my power of acknowledgment" (103). Yet true, as always, to her "inward witness," Martineau adds that something is not quite right with this volume; unsure how to phrase the criticism, she attributes her reservations to her own limitations as a poetry critic. She praises the poet's sonnets and singles out "Lady Geraldine" as "glorious"—"I was *swept* through it" (104)—while "A Drama of Exile" is "exquisitely beautiful." Overall, despite a "certain mannerism," the "predominant impression is . . . of your originality. . . . Your mind is to me a new one: and its utterances are fresh as if no one had spoken poetry before you." Perhaps thinking herself better equipped to criticize the critics, she concludes that the reviews are respectful but inadequate to Barrett's achievements.

Published (anonymously) in the same year, 1844, Martineau's *Life in the Sickroom* was wrongly attributed, interestingly, to Elizabeth Barrett; both women regarded the error as a compliment to their quite different writing skills. Further, although many assumed that the book's warm dedication to another invalid (also anonymous) was written by Martineau to Barrett, that proved not to be the case.[25] Great changes awaited both women: Elizabeth met Robert Browning as a result of the publication of *Poems,* and Martineau's health suddenly and radically improved. To Barrett, she indicated that her priorities were beginning to focus on something other than either her literary career or her illness: "I plan no work at present. . . . [M]y longings are all for fresh air, beauty and idleness" (Sanders 1990, 109–10). Her New Year's greetings to Barrett in December of that year demonstrate an unabashed exuberance at leaving behind the sickroom to which her friend was still confined: "I *must* send you my New Year's hopes and desires for you,—my blessing for all your love and goodness to me during this great and kind old year, now departing. It has made you one of my chief benefactors . . . you are a warm, bright, substantial reality to me,—*a friend*. . . . You have given me ideas,—you have roused in me emotions, so far beyond your own former influence, and any other of a kindred sort this year" (Kelley and Hudson 1991, 9:305–6). Not long after, Elizabeth Barrett was similarly transformed from a cloistered invalid to an international celebrity. Writing to Martineau of her improved health and her newfound delight in sunshine and nature, Barrett wrote giddily, "there is no saying what foolish thing I may do." The "foolish thing" turned out to be marriage to Robert Browning and elopement to Italy, which Martineau pronounced "a truly wise act" (1983, 1:417).

Writing retrospectively in the *Autobiography*, Martineau was better able to articulate her literary criticisms of Barrett Browning than she had been earlier. Emphasizing the quality of realism so integral to all her literary undertakings, Martineau argued that a life solely of the imagination was appropriate only in certain contexts: "Her poems were to me, in my sickroom, marvellously beautiful: and, now that . . . my life has been transferred to the free open air of real, practical existence, I still think her poetry wonderfully beautiful in its way, while wishing that she was more familiar with the external realities which are needed to balance her ideal conceptions" (1:418). Life in the sickroom is a dream-state in which invalids read and write poetry through the opaque lens of laudanum, while "real" life is lived only by healthy people unimpaired by physical limitations. In other words, invalidism, which consumed so much of Martineau's time (according to Valerie Sanders, fully one-third of her life), in a sense precluded the realism by which she measured the worth of all things, from life to people to literature.[26]

An 1856 letter more explicitly articulates these points:

> I am persuaded that she [Barrett Browning] has not the remotest conception of what it is *to know* any thing, and therefore to (in the highest sense) *believe* any thing. . . . Her poetry is, I think very beautiful in relation to a particular state or stage of mind; but it has no element of durability in it. . . . Her faults are, I entirely believe, from her seclusion from life during some very important years . . . [which] caused her to live upon words, and feelings expressed only by words. Under an opposite training . . . I believe she would have been a vast genius" (Sanders 1990, 136–37).

To Martineau, women in all situations thrive when they have "double work"—intellectual and practical; Barrett Browning's rarified invalidism afforded her only the former. Illustrating their quite different orientations, the poet commented similarly on Martineau's literary talents, which she believed were wasted on histories, biographies, and journalism at the expense of her imaginative faculties.

Martineau seems not to have followed Barrett Browning's career as it evolved from the shadowy insularity of which she was critical to the "real, practical existence" of marriage, motherhood, and political activism she found praiseworthy in Margaret Fuller. Barrett Browning's poetry featuring conspicuous political and social themes—*Aurora Leigh* (1856) and *Poems before Congress* (1860), for example—reflect her personal liberation and demonstrate a depth of realism that should have satisfied even Martineau. The poet's writing on child labor, gender exploitation, the heroes of the Italian unification movement, and slavery demonstrates a far broader awareness of the "serious business of life" than the familiar *Sonnets from the Portuguese* suggests. Indeed, the literary ambitions and needleworking trials of Aurora Leigh resonate with Martineau's own experience of forging a literary career as a woman alone in London, while "Runaway Slave at Pilgrim's Point" vividly dramatizes the fate of unprotected slave girls like Ailsie, the American slave child that Martineau tried unsuccessfully to adopt, hoping to save her from sexual exploitation.[27]

Prior to meeting Elizabeth, Robert Browning regularly visited Martineau; like his future wife, he consulted her about his writing as a novice seeking a mentor in the successful and influential older woman. Valerie Sanders notes that the relationship between Browning and Martineau soured after she responded less than enthusiastically to his work: "He meant to take no more of her advice, whether on worldly or poetical matters, viewing her largely as a quasi-comic Amazon, who wanted to have women in Parliament, and wrote long, garrulous letters about stocking-mending" (1979, 10).[28] This turn iterates a pattern that was to plague Martineau throughout her professional career: asked by writers like Sedgwick, Browning, Barrett, and Charlotte Brontë to critique their work, she demurred, pleading that her skills as a nonfiction writer did not qualify her adequately to assess creative writing. Each time she agreed to such requests, prompted by pressure to use her influence to promote aspiring writers, her criticisms bruised egos and broke friendships.

Criticisms notwithstanding, Martineau also applauds Barrett Browning as a woman, a poet, and a positive role model for Woman's Cause: "A few really able women,—women sanctified by true genius . . . [like] Browning,—quickly repair the mischief, as regards the dignity of women" (1983, 1:352). Similarly, as Valerie Sanders notes, Barrett's "loyal defence of her friend in response to Browning's opposition reveals the strength of her trust in Harriet Martineau's mental and literary abilities—and her admiration for an Aurora Leigh type of woman, who could brave public opinion and pursue her chosen career of writing" (1979, 13). Sanders posits that, through their literary alliance, Martineau initiated the process of Barrett's liberation that was completed by Robert Browning, with the result that she was eliminated from the triangular relationship altogether. This assessment accords with my suggestion that the relationship between the two women was shaped by the specific circumstances each experienced during the 1840s, a relationship destined to cease once those circumstances shifted. In 1844—the publication year of *Life in the Sickroom* and Barrett's *Poems*—Martineau wrote to Barrett, "You have been in my mind, and your volumes open before me daily, and many times in a day: and you will ever be associated in my mind with a very peculiar season of experience" (Sanders 1990, 103). Read in retrospect, her words seem to point inevitably to an eventual parting of their ways.[29]

### Charlotte Brontë

It would no doubt surprise students today that Martineau's literary fame far eclipsed Charlotte Brontë's at the time of their friendship, begun around 1848, when public curiosity over the elusive identity of "Currer Bell" was at its peak. The mystery of *Jane Eyre*'s authorship particularly interested Martineau, as many readers believed she herself had written the novel. She found the novel so psychologically resonant that she suspected the writer must be an intimate friend. To Fanny Wedgwood she wrote: "Can you tell me about *Jane Eyre*,—who wrote it? I am told I wrote the 1st vol: and I don't know how to disbelieve it myself,—though I am wholly ignorant of authorship. I cannot help feeling that the writer must know not only my books but myself very well" (Arbuckle 1983, 95). Similarly, Martineau recorded that Brontë admitted that reading Martineau's semiautobiographical *Household Education* was like "meeting her own fetch,—so precisely were the fears and miseries there described the same as her own, told or not told in *Jane Eyre*" (1983, 2:324). Even before they met, then, the two women shared experiential and literary affinities. As was true with Elizabeth Barrett, Martineau was again cast in the role of mentoring the younger writer; also similarly, the friendship ended, unable to weather certain ideological differences. More explicitly than was true with Barrett, the marriage of the one and the candid literary criticism of the other combined to thwart the women's literary network even as they constructed it.

Based on a sewing reference in *Jane Eyre*, Martineau had already determined that Currer must be a woman, a suspicion confirmed by Brontë herself. In an 1849 letter, Brontë sent Martineau a complimentary copy of *Shirley* with a note in which she transparently referred to herself as "she," which was awkwardly crossed out and replaced with "he" (Martineau 1983, 2:323). This prompted Martineau boldly to send her reply addressed to "Madam," to which Brontë responds she would like to visit "one whose works have so often made her the subject of my thoughts" (Martineau 1983, 2:325). Ludicrously continuing the masculine pretense, Brontë wrote that *Deerbrook* "ranks with the writings that have really done him good, added to his stock of ideas, and rectified his views of life" (2:323). Her acceptance of Martineau's invitation to visit was also determined by her host to have been written by a woman, although the unexpected appearance of a six-foot-tall male visitor just prior to Brontë's arrival added comic relief to the highly charged anticipation of the moment.

Brontë was in fact neither tall nor masculine; her diminutive stature contrasted strikingly with her fame—"I thought her the smallest creature I had ever seen (except at a fair)" (Martineau 1983, 2:326)—as did her quiet grace and humility. Her purpose in calling on Martineau was twofold: to pay homage to the older woman and to seek her literary advice. In a spirit of unflinching self-assessment that no doubt endeared her instantly to Martineau, Brontë asked her to comment—not on her writing itself, but on reviews of her work, which she wished to understand and to benefit by in future. "She besought me then, and repeatedly afterwards," wrote Martineau, "to tell her, at whatever cost of pain to herself, if I saw her afford any justification of them. I believed her . . . perfectly sincere" (2:326). As her tone implies, mentoring once again resulted in a relationship sacrificed to honesty.

Brontë's impressions of Martineau during her 1850 visit to The Knoll demonstrate a shrewd insight into the latter's character:

> Of my kind hostess herself I cannot speak in terms too high. . . . [I] find a worth and greatness in herself, and a consistency, benevolence, perseverance in her practice such as wins the sincerest esteem and affection. She is not a person to be judged by her writings alone, but rather by her own deeds and life—than which nothing can be more exemplary or nobler. . . . Faults she has, but to me they appear very trivial weighed in the balance against her excellencies. (Shorter 1896, 442–43)

Brontë wrote to her father, marveling at the health, energy, and immense productivity of this period in Martineau's life, which contrasted with Charlotte's constitutional fragility: "As to Miss Martineau, I admire her and wonder at her more than I can say. Her powers of labour, of exercise, and social cheerfulness are beyond my comprehension. In spite of the unceasing activity of her colossal intellect she enjoys robust health" (454–55). To friends she wrote, "Miss Martineau I relish inexpressively. . . . [She] is certainly a woman of wonderful endowments, both intellectual and physical. . . . The manner in which she combines the highest mental culture with the nicest discharge of feminine duties filled me with admiration, while her affectionate kindness earned my gratitude" (457, 460–61).

But Brontë also admits to sharing "few of her opinions" and, of the controversial Atkinson letters, in which Martineau's agnosticism was made public, noted: "I deeply regret its publication for the lady's sake; it gives a death-blow to her future usefulness. Who can trust the word, or rely on the judgment, of an avowed atheist?" (Shorter 1896, 313).[30] Martineau is of course not an atheist, as both Charlotte and Patrick Brontë assumed;

Chapman accounts for the disparity by noting that Brontë unquestion-ingly "accepted, as it was natural for a clergyman's daughter to do, the clerical declarations that philosophy was atheism" (1877, 291). But even Brontë conceded that atheists deserve to be judged according to their ac-tions more than their words: "I do not feel that it would be right to give Miss Martineau up entirely. There is in her nature much that is very noble" (Shorter 1896, 277). Martineau, in turn, defended Brontë against charges of "coarseness"; to Leigh Hunt she wrote: "I have wondered what you and Mr. Lewes can have meant about there being . . . coarseness in Miss Brontë. How is it possible? . . . Is it not somebody else you mean? . . . A fairer specimen of the true heroic mind I never saw: large and strong,—gentle and composed,—meek and self-possessed. . . . [S]he is as opposite to the creature of passion and prejudice as to the marble-hearted self-seeker."[31] Martineau goes on to assert that she and Mr. Atkinson agree that truth seeking and liberal-mindedness are qualities nearly impossible to find in one person: with the exception of Charlotte Brontë (who would no doubt cringe at validation from *this* infidel quarter!). Ultimately, however, their friendship failed the tests of truthfulness and liberality in an episode whose repercussions extended beyond Brontë's death. Contrasting with Martineau's vibrant energy at this time, "poor delicate 'Currer'" found the literary criticism of her friend more difficult to digest than even her agnos-ticism, while Martineau was forced to concede that "coarseness" *is* a factor she must confront in Brontë's writing.[32]

As the infamous *Villette* episode reveals, the disparity between Mar-tineau and Brontë hinged not only on theology but also on their differing gender ideologies; their friendship was strained to the breaking point by Martineau's *Daily News* review of *Villette* (3 February 1853). Artistically, Martineau found much to praise in the novel, and the greatest portion of the review articulates those praises. However, in terms of moral principles, she argued, *Villette* is inferior to *Jane Eyre* and unworthy of the potential the author demonstrated in that book: "The author has no right to make readers so miserable"; its unrelenting "subjective misery" is oppressive, its foreignness is "strange," the characters lack goodness and their morality is questionable: "An atmosphere of pain hangs about the whole, forbidding that repose which we hold to be essential to the true presentment of any large portion of life and experience," an assessment consistent with her re-jection of feminist declaimers of woman's wrongs and of her promotion of self-discipline. A broader insight is Martineau's claim that the romance theme essentializes women—even a strong character like Lucy Snowe—as having only one object in their minds: "All the female characters, in all their thoughts and lives, are full of one thing, or are regarded by the reader in the light of that one thought—love." She predicts that readers "will re-ject the assumption that events and characters are to be regarded through the medium of one passion only." Another objection concerns the anti-Catholic bias of the novel: "She goes out of her way to express a passionate hatred of Romanism. . . . We do not exactly see the moral necessity for this (there is no artistical necessity)." Since Protestants and Catholics already hate each other "quite sufficiently," *Villette* irresponsibly adds fuel to the fire rather than providing readers with a compelling reason to convert to any organized religion.[33]

Martineau stood by her review, which she regarded as honest, constructive criticism: just what Brontë had requested: "I know," Charlotte wrote, "that you will give me your thoughts upon my book,—as frankly as if you spoke to some near relative whose good you preferred to her gratification" (Martineau 1983, 2:327). In overlooking Martineau's praises to focus exclusively on her criticisms, Brontë naturally was stung by her assessment: "she has hurt me a good deal . . . she and I had better not try to be close friends; my wish indeed is that she should quietly forget me" (Barker 1994, 720). She made the break final in a letter to Martineau, and the two never met again. Chapman notes that Brontë "had earnestly adjured Harriet Martineau to give her a full and frank opinion of her novel, *Villette;* and, however affectionately and thoughtfully given, it was only the more painful to the receiver, seeing that it confirmed the current and more roughly expressed opinion of the world" (1877, 292). Brontë viewed the matter quite differently, charging that Martineau's analysis was "so strangely and unexpectedly acrimonious, that I have gathered courage to tell her that the gulf of mutual difference between her and me is so wide" that the relationship must cease (Shorter 196, 368).[34] Mixing friendship with professional advice again proved dangerous for Martineau and hints at a type of "literary lionism" in which she was used by other writers for the promotion of their careers and rejected by them when her advice was not to their liking. Martineau's literary criticism, which was direct and honest without being "acrimonious," was consistent with the idea that she held women to an even higher standard than that applied to men, and with good reason: more clearly than most, she understood the stakes for which women were playing and the obstacles impeding their progress.

To Fanny Wedgwood Martineau wrote that *Villette* "is *marvellously* powerful, but grievously morbid, and not a little coarse"; she wonders "What has become of the old heroism which made our grandmothers bear their interior conflicts in silence and humility and cheerfulness? What apology *can* C. B. offer to 100,000 women,—especially governesses" whose private lives have become open to public speculation as a result of *Jane Eyre* and *Villette*? (Arbuckle 1983, 125). Her words recall an idea central to Martineau's feminism: that women writers and public figures are particularly responsible for promoting Woman's Cause in an unassailable fashion to a public strongly predisposed to resist sexual equality. Martineau's nonfiction writing repeatedly addressed the plights of working women who were associated with prostitution by virtue of having to earn a living; the image of the predatory governess seeking to escape poverty through a lucrative marriage was an unfortunate stereotype to which Brontë (however unwittingly) contributed. From this perspective, we can appreciate Martineau's concern that Jane Eyre's class-inappropriate romanticizing about the bigamous Rochester and Lucy Snowe's affiliation with M. Paul (both thinly veiled allusions to Charlotte's potentially adulterous relationship with M. Heger) do little to promote the cause of women simply trying to earn their bread honestly.[35] Critics' charges against Brontë's "coarseness" may well make present-day readers bristle, yet Martineau's reaction was consistent with her concern about the quality of individual contributions to the "big picture" of women's emancipation and with public perceptions of the difficult situations of working women.

Martineau deeply regretted the untimely death that prevented Brontë from writing another book that could "(as I hoped it would) enable her to see what I meant, and me to re-establish a fuller sympathy between us" (Martineau 1983, 2:327). Brontë's admirable "integrity," "noble conscientiousness," and "self-reliance" were somewhat compromised, in Martineau's view, by the "morbid condition of mind" attributable to the "unwholesome" physical and psychological environment in which she lived (she termed Haworth parsonage a "living sepulchre"). But though Brontë's judgment may prove on occasion to lack clarity, the "genuine spirit of the woman" was that of "humility, candour, integrity, and conscientiousness . . . unspoiled" by fame (2:328). With her death, "society has sustained an unexpected, as well as irreparable loss."

Martineau's eulogy of Brontë attests to her misunderstood aims as a critic and to her genuine admiration for the younger woman. Her obituary of Brontë, written for the *Daily News* and reprinted in *Biographical Sketches,* praises "this gifted creature . . . [whose] steady conviction was that the publication of a book is a solemn act of conscience. . . . In her high vocation she had, in addition to the deep intuitions of a gifted woman, the strength of a man, the patience of a hero, and the conscientiousness of a saint." Her moral strength was equal to the "intellectual force manifested in her works" (1868, 44–46). Finally, Martineau unknowingly echoes Brontë's earlier praise of her mentor: she "seemed a perfect household image. . . . She was as able at the needle as at the pen" (49), a paragon of womanhood in her synthesis of literary creativity with domesticity. Martineau's opinion of Brontë approached her admiration for Chapman and Nightingale, although the novelist's fragility prevented her from participating in the active world with the vital, forceful presence demonstrated by those women. Despite Brontë's many fine qualities, she lacked the physical and emotional stamina and intellectual foresight required of the sort of woman best able, to Martineau's mind, to promote Woman's Cause.[36]

## Elizabeth Gaskell

The misunderstanding characterizing the relationship between Brontë and Martineau did not end with the former's death, but was further fueled by the publication of Elizabeth Gaskell's *Life of Charlotte Brontë* (1857), by

Martineau's response to it, and by the flurry of contentious communications between Martineau and Gaskell, Charlotte's father, Patrick Brontë, and her husband, Arthur Nicholls.[37] Although Martineau questioned Gaskell's initial silence on the backlash against the biography—"I must say, I should like to have had *some* sign of humiliation and self-blame from Mrs. G., who appears to be only half sensible of the position in which she stands. . . . *Everybody* is talking about it"—Gaskell's concern to vindicate herself with Martineau soon placated her. "Mrs. Gaskell's readiness to do justice in all the particulars in which I have any concern is everything that could be wished. . . . She sent me Mr. Brontë's letter. . . . The old monster! Anything so appalling as one sentence in it I am sure I never saw come from a human hand. . . . I do mourn that Mrs. G. ever came in the way of that awful family."[38]

As two of Brontë's closest literary friends, Martineau and Gaskell experienced a connection that strengthened following publication of the *Life*. Gaskell wrote: "I am in despair about 'the public.' For some reason they seem to say such bitter and hard things about me. . . . I do not know what to do; but if Miss Martineau advises me strongly to do any thing, I have such reliance on her strong sense and warm heart that I believe I should do it." Another letter from Gaskell sought Martineau's alliance against the Haworth opposition; she reports that, when Mr. Nicholls "wrote in the authoritative style usual to him" concerning the *Villette* controversy, she responded with vigor that any future correspondence from him should be directed to her solicitor. Gaskell thanks Martineau for her help on the biography and apologizes for any "vexation or extra trouble" caused by the book's reception.[39] But despite Gaskell's deference toward her, Martineau remained critical of Gaskell's account of the *Villette* dispute, while Gaskell's referring to Martineau's philosophical alliance with Henry Atkinson as "an error" was poorly timed, to say the least.

The relationship between Martineau and Gaskell differs from those discussed thus far in that each was already an established writer, although an unofficial mentorship clearly existed. The two women traveled in similar literary circles and knew many of the same people: both wrote for Dickens's periodicals, for example, and both had experienced his cantankerous misogyny. Of Gaskell's literary merits, Martineau had plenty to say, both in praise and condemnation. "O! what a beautiful book it is!" she wrote of the *Life of Charlotte Brontë*. "Mrs. G's part is most charmingly done, I think,— allowance being made for sentiment now and then swamping conviction" (Arbuckle 1983, 153). *Cranford* also earned praise: "What a beautiful *Cranford* Mrs. Gaskell has given us again!" But *Ruth,* oddly, she condemned: "*Ruth* won't help us. All strewn with beauties as it is, it is sadly feeble and *wrong,* I think. Amidst much wrong, I think making Mr. Benson such a nincompoop is fatal" (125). Although *Ruth* has "much that is beautiful, there is much that is disgusting, and a good deal that is poor."[40] As a serious social-problem novel, *Ruth* dramatizes the fate of an orphaned seamstress; seduced, pregnant, and abandoned by her upper-class lover, Ruth is saved from suicide and befriended by the Reverend Mr. Benson. Although Gaskell's compassionate treatment situates the blame for unmarried motherhood in religious and social hypocrisy, and does so by drawing on the strength of the author's own impeccable reputation, some critics—Martineau among them—objected to the book on the basis of its distressing subject matter. *Ruth* dramatizes the plights of seamstresses, thus through fiction complementing Martineau's periodicals writing on the topic, but this is not sufficient to vindicate the novel; nor does Gaskell's timely use of nursing, which she casts as a vocation that redeems and, more important, *is redeemed by* the fallen woman, earn Martineau's approval. Ruth expiates her social sins by nursing during a cholera epidemic, drawing a powerful analogy between social needs and women's need to work. But Martineau was clearly drawn more to Nightingale's rejection of the link between "penitents" and nursing than to Gaskell's deliberate embrace of the two.

Martineau's objections to *Ruth* highlight an interesting distinction between realism, which she valued, and "coarseness," that which was perhaps a little too real for comfort. Gaskell's writing was directly influenced by Martineau's own combination of fiction and didacticism. Gaskell's success as one of the most prominent social-problem novelists of the period is traceable to the pioneering work of Martineau, as analyzed by literary historian Louis Cazamian (1973). Similarly, Monica Fryckstedt ("The Early Industrial Novel") attributes the development of the industrial novel, like Gaskell's *North and South* and *Mary Barton,* to Martineau's early fiction: for example, "The Manchester Strike." Making a more substantive claim, Simon Dentith argues that Gaskell's political economy continues where Martineau's left off: "It is only when the form does begin to venture on areas which are indeed 'economic' that . . . the claims of Political Economy [are] reasserted. Mrs. Gaskell, it seems to me, stepped across such a boundary in *Mary Barton,* and made amends to Political Economy in *North and South*" (1983, 192). If imitation is the sincerest form of flattery, Gaskell's writing pays eloquent homage to Martineau as her literary grandmother, a connection Martineau seems not to recognize.

Gaskell's social-problem writing incorporates the concerns of political economy, while focusing more on the human drama than on the didacticism Martineau was known for; in a sense, Gaskell accomplishes through her fiction what Martineau believed herself unable to do. Gaskell's persistence in treating the fallen woman theme throughout her career directly countered the romanticization of female sexuality presented by Brontë and other women novelists to whom Martineau objects. Aside from her writing, Gaskell was also involved in active "recuperation" of fallen women in her community. She not only wrote about social change, she actively participated in it, making her a stronger example of Martineau's ideals than Martineau credits her with. Yet this does not earn Gaskell a place in Martineau's circle of women worth emulating for their promotion of Woman's

Cause. Martineau seems to find more to criticize than to praise in Gaskell's work: "how entirely Mrs. Gaskell fails," she wrote. "Her personages are a museum of oddities" (Sanders 1990, 177). Martineau's aim as outlined in her preface to the *Illustrations*—to educate those most directly affected by economic inequities—found logical expression in Gaskell's working- and middle-class "museum of oddities," whose characters and events drama- tized the economic principles outlined in the earlier series. Critics labeled "coarse" the increasingly audible calls—like Brontë's and Gaskell's—for sexual justice for women and for men to take responsibility for the period's epidemics of prostitution, illegitimacy, and venereal disease; far from ac- knowledging the increasingly obvious need to confront these issues di- rectly, Martineau continued to insist that such outward manifestations of passion indicate the need for self-discipline. It is not surprising, then, that George Eliot, whose literary standards and intellectual stamina mirror Mar- tineau's but whose unconventional morality earned her disapproval, did not find favor in this pantheon of notable women, either.

*George Eliot*

By the time Eliot's star as a novelist began to rise, Martineau's career had shifted almost exclusively into journalism writing for the *Daily News* and other periodicals. Despite disparities in their moral standards, the two women actually had a great deal in common: aesthetically, both valued re- alism, particularly in novels; both "converted" from necessarianism to posi- tivism (Eliot admired Martineau's translation of Comte's *The Positive Philos- ophy* and Martineau made Eliot a joint trustee of a fund to promote Comte's work). Both wrote for the *Westminster Review* and shared an interest in phrenology and mesmerism and both experienced permanent breaches with beloved brothers who rejected them: Martineau for her agnosticism and Eliot for her adulterous relationship with writer and editor George Henry Lewes. As a child, Maggie Tulliver (in Eliot's semiautobiographical *The Mill on the Floss*) displayed a morbid religiosity to compensate for her low self-esteem, exhibited the intellectual precocity her school-bound brother lacked, was hampered by an ineffectual father and an overly critical mother, and was crushed by her adored brother's inability to love her un- conditionally: all patterns strikingly resonant with Martineau's experience.

Eliot's first impressions of Martineau hint inauspiciously at future dis- cord: she was "very kind and cordial but unhappily not able to stay long enough to dispel the repulsion excited by the *vulgarity* (I use the word in a moral sense) of her looks and gestures. . . . I honour Harriet Martineau for her powers and industry and should be glad to think highly of her. I have no doubt that she is fascinating when there is time to talk" (Haight 1954, 2:101–2).[41] When Eliot visited Martineau at Ambleside in 1852 (this is not even mentioned, interestingly, in the *Autobiography*), she revised earlier im- pressions: "Miss M is charming in her own home,—quite handsome from her animation and intelligence" (Cross 1885, 1:223). To John Chapman, Martineau wrote, "Miss Evans's visit was a vast pleasure"; she regrets she could not prolong her stay, although they did tour the Ambleside Building Society's model cottages. Eliot's *Middlemarch* heroine, Dorothea Brooke, with her innovative plans to provide affordable housing for the poor, finds a prototype in Martineau and her Ambleside cottage scheme. Martineau, who pronounced *Middlemarch* "the ablest book ever written by a woman," although "painful," seemed not to recognize herself in Dorothea, whose characterization pays homage to Martineau.[42] Eliot observed of *Deerbrook*, "I have read *Deerbrook*, and am surprised at the depths of feeling it reveals" (Sanders 1986b, 59). This lukewarm remark is curious in light of parallel themes shared by *Deerbrook* (1839) and *Middlemarch* (1860): the village doctor whose promising career is compromised by local political intrigues and the ill-fated romance resulting in marriage motivated by duty rather than love. The publication dates of the two novels strongly suggest an influence of the former over the latter that Eliot seems reluctant to acknowledge. Further, scholars have noted striking parallels between Martineau's account of the Reform Movement in her *History of England* (1849–1851) and Eliot's fictional rendering in *Felix Holt, the Radical* (1866), as well as between Eliot's title character in *Silas Marner* (1861) and Martineau's "The Hill and the Valley" (in the *Illustrations*). All this suggests that, in Eliot's case, Martineau played the role of mentor and literary grandmother without—as in the previous examples—formally being asked to do so.[43]

Eliot admired Martineau's writing: "After all she is a *trump*," she wrote, "the only English woman that possesses thoroughly the art of writing."[44] But like many prominent figures who admired Martineau in other respects, Eliot drew the line at the publication of the Atkinson and Martineau letters, calling *Letters on the Laws of Man's Nature and Development* "the boldest I have seen in the English language . . . but studiously offensive" (Haight 1985, 364). Martineau was especially sensitive to the harsh criticisms she endured for her collaboration with Atkinson, and Eliot's comments—which seem inconsistent with her own interest in philosophy, mesmerism, and phrenology—further complicated relations between the two women. Eliot also disapproved of the very concept of writing an autobiography—a consuming interest of Martineau's during the mid-1850s—claiming, "All biography diminishes in interest when the subject has won celebrity—or," she added more aggressively, "some reputation that hardly comes up to celebrity" (Sanders 1986b, 159).[45] Similarly, Martineau also had difficulty critiquing Eliot's writing without adding commentary of a more personal nature. Responding to critics' charges that Eliot's realism in *Adam Bede* was not literary in origin but taken from real life (in other words, ironically, too real to be believable fiction), Martineau condemned her lifestyle while defending her aesthetics: Eliot "has deplorable weaknesses,—as her present unhappy position shows; but *that* kind of weakness"—poor authorship—"is not in her line."[46] She also objected to the George Eliot pseudonym which, she felt, rather than concealing the scandal, added to Marian Evans's notoriety with the result that "the sale and circulation of *Adam Bede* were instantly checked when the authorship was known" (Arbuckle 1983, 187).

Eliot was the subject of some speculation between Gaskell and Martineau, who pondered the identity of the mysterious author of *Adam Bede* (1859). Both women admired the novel, even after learning the author's identity, but disapproved of Eliot's notoriously public private life. Martineau's "criticism of George Eliot generally betrays a sense of offended propriety," writes Valerie Sanders. "She found it hard to accept that a great novel could be written by someone with a morally dubious private life" (1986b, 22–23). Writing to Henry Reeve, Martineau observes: "I *am* sorry Miss Evans wrote it *[Adam Bede],* and should be glad to die . . . sooner,—if that could make it anyone else's.—I did not *like* her,—to my surprise,— after high expectation, and before she had any notion of Mr. Lewes" (Sanders 1990, 181). Indicating what was for Martineau the interchangeability of public and private standards of behavior, she concluded, "I admired her abilities, beyond expression; but I did not much respect, or at all *like* her. I do wish the secret had been kept." Eliot's antipathy toward Martineau's "vulgarity," clearly, was mutual.

Keenly aware of the controversy surrounding her reputation, Eliot regretted Martineau's inability to separate private life from literature intended for public consumption: the key ethic shaping Martineau's gender politics. "As to Miss Martineau," she wrote to Sara Hennell,

> I respect her so much as an authoress, and have so pleasant a recollection of her as a hostess for three days, that I wish that distant impression from herself and her writings to be disturbed as little as possible by mere personal details. Anything she may do, or say, or feel concerning me personally, is a matter of entire indifference: . . . the freer I am kept of all knowledge of that comparatively small circle who mingle personal regards or hatred with their judgment or reception of my writings, the easier it will be to keep my motives free from all indirectness and write truly. (Cross 1885, 2:108)

Ironically, such sentiments could not more perfectly align with Martineau's own commitment to the integrity of living according to one's "inward witness," regardless of the notoriety, scandal, and social ostracization that results.

Lewes's reputation, which was apparently dubious even before his relationship with Eliot, prompts Gaskell to wonder, "How came she to like Mr. Lewes so much? . . . [H]e is so soiled for a woman like her to fancy" (Uglow 1993, 463). Gaskell hesitated to dismiss Eliot altogether on the grounds of immorality, arguing that the superiority of her writing must reflect equivalent "possibilities of greatness and goodness." To Eliot herself, Gaskell wrote, "I should not be quite true . . . if I did not say . . . that I wish you *were* Mrs. Lewes. However that can't be helped, as far as I can see, and one must not judge others," she concludes rather lamely. Professional conflicts with Lewes prove that sexual impropriety was not Martineau's only objection to one of the foremost literary couples of the day. Eliot biographer Gordon Haight notes Martineau's strong aversion to Lewes, whose own study of August Comte, *Comte's Philosophy of the Sciences,* was published within weeks of her own translation; the competitive challenge was exacerbated by Lewes's negative review of the Martineau-Atkinson book. As a result, according to Haight, Martineau spread malicious gossip about Lewes and Eliot, prompting the latter to note, "Amongst her good qualities we certainly cannot reckon zeal for other people's reputation. She is sure to caricature any information for the amusement of the next person to whom she turns her ear-trumpet" (Haight 1985, 167). "Until her death," adds Haight, "Harriet Martineau maintained this irrational antipathy" to Lewes and Eliot. Perhaps her comment (in a *private* letter) that Lewes "finds it answer well to pick her [Eliot's] brains for his own book and his boys' education. . . . When will she find that out?" (Arbuckle 1983, 129) is petty, but it hardly amounts to "irrational antipathy," of which I have seen no evidence.

No doubt Martineau's standards of womanhood seem too strict or narrow for twenty-first-century tastes; yet she was a free-thinking, liberal-minded radical and it makes sense that her objection to overt expressions of female sexuality, given what was for Victorian women a highly vexed gender ideology, stemmed from her keen sense of timing and foresight more than prudishness. If, as she argued, the time was not right for the women's franchise, neither was it right for open discussions about female sexuality: over a century's worth of Freudian feminist backlash against first-wave feminism offers a potent case in point. Some intrepid souls, fortunately, chose to brave public resistance to this issue anyway; but to Martineau's thinking, the suppression of women by religious, familial, economic, and political institutions—a suppression based on biological prejudice—was so commonplace as to be insidious, demanding more immediate attention than sexual liberation.

Professional jealousy may have played a role in these literary relationships, although it seems more likely that the real struggle, as I outlined in chapter 1, concerned a relatively new problem for nineteenth-century women: the need to cultivate identities as *women* and as *writers* despite few literary grandmothers and, at best, haphazard literary apprenticeships. The example of derailed literary networking between Victorian women offered by Eliot and Martineau seems especially poignant given the many similarities they shared, biographically, intellectually, and professionally. But, unlike the other examples I have explored thus far, the relationship between Eliot and Martineau was not based on mutual admiration or friendship, nor did it involve—officially, at least—the mentor-apprentice dynamic; and, while competitiveness may have been a factor, that seems unworthy of either writer, since each was a firmly established professional in her own right. Perhaps each thought the other ought to have known, and behaved, better than she did; perhaps each felt the other gave Woman's Cause a bad name.[47] Yet as the following examples prove, William Clark's complaint that Harriet Martineau denounced "almost every distinguished woman . . . any one with whom she could possibly be compared" unjustly casts her as spiteful toward rather than critical of women she believed compromised Woman's Cause.[48]

## Women "of the heroic order"

Since she did not find fully satisfactory role models among literary women, who, then, represented to Martineau the true-hearted women embodying the highest ideals of Woman's Cause? Who are the women who refused to equate passivity with morality and nationalism, arguing instead that social activism is a sacred, womanly obligation? Who are the women Martineau viewed as the embodiment of womanliness—in its feminist, not Victorian, sense—once released from the stays and whalebones confining their bodies and the "mind-forg'd manacles" confining their intellects? For Martineau, true-hearted Englishwomen were not to be found among the literary women of the day, women who had many fine qualities but who yielded to the demands of the marketplace by producing romantic stereotypes—in their novels or in their lives—instead of independent role models. As the remainder of this discussion shows, the women Martineau most admired, along with American Maria Weston Chapman, shared three distinctive qualities: none of them were professional writers, all of them were committed activists in the period's social purity campaigns, and each one rewrote the angel-in-the-house script (a male fantasy) from women's perspective.

### Maria Martineau

Maria Martineau was neither a writer nor a public figure; content to be a "homebody," she supported Harriet Martineau's controversial ideologies and sought no fame on her own account. Known, if at all, only by association with her famous aunt, Maria was one of the few women thoroughly and uncritically venerated by Martineau. Born in 1827 to Harriet's brother Robert and his wife, Jane, Maria lived a rather unremarkable life in industrial Birmingham until she became companion to her aunt in 1855. As a child, she did, however, distinguish herself among the other nieces and nephews who, when asked what gifts they wanted brought back from America, passively demurred, shyly leaving the choice up to Aunt Harriet. But Maria boldly requested, of all things, a hummingbird's nest, which her aunt, true to form, succeeded in securing. Chapman wrote, "It was this child who, twenty years after, joined her in London, at the time that her recovery was pronounced hopeless, with the devoted determination of never leaving her again; who was unto her as a daughter, and who died by her side" (1877, 95). Destined to become her aunt's companion, secretary, nurse, housekeeper, and closest friend as well as her primary contact with the world outside The Knoll, Maria quickly proved herself capable of many undertakings, most importantly in her capacity to keep pace with Martineau's demanding schedule of literary, domestic, and social projects.

Maria's role as her aunt's staunchest supporter in both personal and professional realms is inestimable, particularly given the atmosphere of controversy Martineau perpetually generated. Judging by the examples discussed so far, Martineau's relationships with prominent women often tended to be contentious and reciprocally critical; the idea of women's literary networking seemed a remote possibility, which may reflect the mood of the period or the personalities involved or both. But Maria understood that Martineau's forays into mesmerism, positivism, and agnosticism aimed not at notoriety for its own sake but instead constituted her earnest attempts to resolve the philosophical conundrums she grappled with all her life. As she weathered financial difficulties, illness, and old age, Martineau's oft-stated "need of utterance" was matched by another need—the pursuit of the sort of philosophical resting place that enabled her to come to terms with the vicissitudes of life and death, fame and loss, and chronic illness—which she terms "the one thing needful" (1983, 2:335). Maria Martineau was herself a sanctuary, a safe and reliable haven, and her indefatigable support of her aunt during this crucial period marks her as singular among Martineau's circle indeed.

Martineau's enthusiasm for Ambleside's healthy environment is personified by Maria, who thrived in The Knoll's idyllic self-sufficiency. Martineau's letters throughout the 1850s are filled with references to her niece, who is "well and glorious . . . the picture of health" (Arbuckle 1983, 145, 198); Maria is "charmingly well and happy . . . [and] her family are delighted at her health and spirits,—a great comfort to me!" (Sanders 1990, 139, 195). Maria's "devoted determination" resulted in her excelling in a variety of roles, from housewife to secretary and from nurse to editor; her seemingly boundless energy spilled over into the community, which found in her a tireless worker, a dedicated nurse, and a selfless friend. Maria "is as well as can be," wrote Martineau in 1856, "and very happy among her poultry, and country pleasures of many kinds" (Arbuckle 1983, 148). "She teaches my maids . . . in the evenings, and 'hunts the waterfalls,' and loves the mountains in the mornings, and is in the finest health."[49]

In this household, skilled nursing and efficient domesticity were of a piece with hygiene and good health. As a nurse, Maria was a natural healer. She was "incomparable," "glorious," and "unsurpassable": "We are very happy,—my dear nurse and I," Martineau wrote; "[she] does somebody good every day of her life" (Sanders 1990, 133, 161, 151–52). Maria also proved adept at domestic skills, a topic on which Martineau was opinionated and exacting. Using her own household as a kind of laboratory, Martineau, with Maria's assistance, tested various new theories on health matters, like the importance of cleanliness, plenty of light, and well-ventilated rooms in the promotion of good health: all radical ideas for the time. Good cooking is essential for good health, she argued, equating "good" with simplicity, freshness, and nutritive value. Writing to thank Isabella Beeton for a copy of her book, *The Book of Household Management* (1861), Martineau observed, "It has given me a great deal of pleasure; and my niece, who relieves me of housekeeping and is a first rate housewife, declares the book to be very valuable indeed in the cookery part." For both Beeton and Maria, this is high praise from a pioneer enthusiast of sanitation reform. Maria also participated in less orthodox practices, like mesmerism; Martineau was delighted to learn that Maria secretly mesmerized her bedclothes, to ensure her aunt better sleep.[50]

Aside from her nursing duties at The Knoll, Maria was also active in the Ambleside community, tending the sick and even delivering babies: "What an effective brave woman she is! . . . By some instinct M. did exactly what was right," Martineau remarked following an impromptu delivery (Arbuckle 1983, 190–91). Maria seemed to dispense healing and peace wherever she went. To Bessie Rainer Parks, Martineau wrote that Maria spent "such a winter as I hope she will never have again,—nursing Miss Napier as well as me. For eleven weeks she walked daily 3 miles out and back again, to see Miss N," who was alone, sick, and unattended. To Sarah Martineau she added, "I do wish F. Nightingale knew her [Maria]; and then she would see one heaven born nurse,—somewhat like herself."[51] Even the "most helpless" local doctor—"He is a good natured and honourable man, but not very wise, and wholly destitute of resource"—bowed to Maria's superior judgment: "I suspect his awe of Maria's sense and knowledge makes him worse; but we have to rely on ourselves" (Sanders 1990, 191–92).

During this period, when Martineau was herself most in need of nursing and when much of her creative energy focused on sanitary reform and on championing Florence Nightingale's campaign to legitimize nursing as an honorable profession for women, she found in Maria the perfect prototype for Woman's Cause. Maria was domestic yet professional, an instinctual, compassionate, intelligent healer; she was open-minded and energetic and too busy for psychological morbidity, romanticizing, sexual scandals, or other behaviors that retard woman's social progress. To Nightingale, Martineau asserted, "I do think you would find her as near to your standard of a nurse as anybody in Europe." Later, following Maria's visit to Nightingale, Martineau wrote: "I can fancy that you now know what I mean in wishing that you had a Maria,—and what *she* means in longing to nurse you, as well as me. I verily believe that her excellent health and spirits are owing to her having what some people would call double work": intellectual occupation as well as practical or material activities. Maria enjoyed good health for the first time in her life—"a sort of health which implies happiness," thriving as she did in this idyllic environment with plenty of "double work" to challenge her.[52]

Further proving her indispensability, Maria was also a companion and a friend to her aunt. Together, they sat at the perpetual wool work coming from Martineau's seemingly bottomless workbasket. The sewing circle at The Knoll differed markedly from that of Martineau's childhood in that stitching now afforded opportunities to discuss ideas: "I find *that* a great resource, though my eyes fail me a good deal: It really is such pretty work! and Maria takes interest in it too; so we sympathize over it,—as well as over greater things" (Arbuckle 1983, 143). A significant point of sympathy was Maria's perspective on the family feud between Harriet and James Martineau: "Maria's frank declarations of James being throughout the oppressor, and I the victim, and that *he* had for ever closed all possibility of intercourse by making no reparation, and destroying our esteem" (142) vindicated the publicly maligned Harriet most satisfactorily. Despite Harriet's long history of controversy and idiosyncrasies, Maria rejected the reactionary condemnation of Martineau that some of her aunt's friends and relatives were so quick to dispense.

Materially, psychologically, and emotionally, Martineau's reliance on Maria gave her a much-needed respite from a long and busy life, allowing her to focus almost exclusively on writing during Maria's nine-year tenure at The Knoll: "Maria spares me everything *but* the authorship." Maria assumed Martineau's business and financial correspondence—she "does it perfectly well"—and copied out manuscripts and collated proof sheets (Arbuckle 1983, 137, 244). Her niece is a "woman of eminent sagacity and conscientiousness," Martineau pronounced with satisfaction, as adept in business matters as she is clever in protecting her famous aunt from the "Chattering Hopes and Advices" of the celebrity-hunters who seek her out: "I gratefully admit that I suffer very little indeed from that sort of plague. Maria wards it off, in fact."[53] Reiterating the idea of sanctuary, she wrote: "It was impossible to be more extensively and effectively aided than I was by her. She took upon herself all the fatigue that it was possible to avert from me; and I reposed upon her sense and spirit and watchfulness like a spoiled child" (Martineau 1983, 2:407). The enormous relief of turning control of her domestic and professional affairs over to one as trustworthy and capable as Maria was a new luxury to Martineau, who weathered one of her most difficult periods of invalidism during the late 1850s and early 1860s. Distinct from Chapman's comment on surrogate family roles, Martineau's dependence on her niece ("like a spoiled child") casts Maria as the mother, rather than the daughter, that Harriet never had.

Maria's presence at The Knoll enabled Martineau to produce some of the strongest writing of her career: in addition to various writing projects, including two books on India and collaborations with Nightingale on sanitary reforms, Martineau during this period wrote regularly for four periodicals—London's *Daily News,* the *Spectator, Once a Week,* and the American *National Anti-Slavery Standard.* Her prolific output she virtually attributes to Maria: "I live on,—month after month, by dint of absolute monotony of life (which I happen to like) and incomparable nursing," she wrote to Henry Grote. "My greatest pleasure is in witnessing the capital health and cheerfulness of my beloved Maria, under such a responsibility as the care of me. She *does everything well,*—as well as can be,—from cooking sick messes to revising my articles: and such a sense of power as she must have is a great sustainer . . . [of] our mutual attachment."[54]

Aside from letters and articles written at her aunt's dictation, few records of Maria's perspective survive to provide insight into her experience, about which Martineau consistently wrote so glowingly. Among the few remnants is a letter to Bessie Rainer Parkes marked "strictly confidential." She wrote to enlist Parkes's aid in averting any sudden shock to Martineau: specifically, by news of the anticipated death of her friend, invalid Florence Nightingale. Maria's sensitivity to and concern for her aunt is evident: "I have learned to know that I must save her, at any cost, from sudden shocks of all sorts." Prompted to write by persistent rumors of Nightingale's deteriorating health, Maria asserts that "when the end does come it will be a terrible grief to my Aunt . . . for there exists between them a very strong friendship." The favor she asks of Parkes is to telegraph her immediately if she learns of Nightingale's death, reasoning that "it would be safer she should hear it from me" than read it in a newspaper. Clearly demonstrating her professionalism and intellectual clarity, she concludes: "It is the fact of your being a woman of business that makes me feel more confidence in relying upon you in this delicate matter than I could in any one else."[55]

With her intense focus on health issues, Martineau was keenly aware of the need to replenish Maria's energy and to that end regularly sent her off to rest and recuperate. "I sent Maria away for a month . . . that she might be saved from the *need* of a rest and holiday," she wrote to Fanny Wedgwood. "It is of such consequence to spare nurses *before* they are injured! To my pride and pleasure . . . all exclaimed at the sight of her. 'Why, you *never* looked so well!' And I quite believe it,—she being of the heroic order" (Arbuckle 1983, 131). But although anxious to preserve her niece's well-being, Martineau found that Maria's absence created an emptiness in the household proportionate to her indispensability: "During the first week of M's absence I am to be alone. . . . I am always worse in M's absence, . . . as no one but M. can revise, correct proofs, and write *all* sorts of letters" (197). Unfortunately, separation from this infinitely capable woman who was so finely attuned to Martineau's needs was soon, tragically, to be permanent.

The great irony of Martineau's chronic ill health and Maria's blooming energy so repeatedly affirmed in letters from the period is that Martineau ended up surviving her niece by twelve years. The sudden shock Maria sought to prevent from undermining her aunt's health (Nightingale outlived Martineau by thirty-four years) actually came from Maria herself, who, in February 1864 succumbed to typhoid fever contracted while nursing sick neighbors. At first, Martineau seemed unable to absorb the implications of Maria's illness: "Her illness naturally makes me worse than usual," she wrote rather crabbily to her niece Spring.[56] But despair soon rendered her virtually inarticulate: to Erasmus Darwin she confided her "hopelessness about Maria. . . . [W]hile she *may* live, the chances are infinitely against it. . . . I *am* lonely therefore. I wish to be alone . . . till the suspense is over" (Arbuckle 1983, 248–49).

The suspense was over quickly, and condolences arrived from the many quarters that this remarkable young woman touched during her nine years at Ambleside. "I thought you would like to hear how many of the poor spoke of her to me today all with sorrow for her and for you, some with appreciation," wrote Jane Arnold. "Two mothers told me how she had stopped to notice and look at their children as she passed. What a remembrance she has left, of unselfish untiring exertion for others." And in the absence of Maria's letters or memoirs, this letter of sympathy from Martineau's nephew Russell compellingly indicates the reciprocal nature of Harriet's relationship with Maria:

> The loss of such a friend as you have had in Maria is the severest that one can be ever called to bear; and I am sure that you must feel that her place in your heart, if not in your house, can never be occupied by another. But you have the happiness of remembering that Maria's life has been perfectly happy in its self-devotion to you, and that her death has been a fitting end to so noble a life. To have attracted Maria's affections and given to her energy a fitting mission and to her life a serene happiness, is to you, I think, quite as legitimate a source of comfort, as it was to Maria that she was *able* to be useful to you.[57]

But the most poignant comfort of all came from Florence Nightingale, a public figure thoroughly bound up in Martineau's conception of the very private Maria: "Twice, when I saw her," wrote Nightingale, "she spoke of her life with you as being a 'privilege'—and when I said, Yes, I *do* think it *is* a privilege, I thought her face was like the face of an angel."[58]

Martineau survived the shock of Maria's death and continued to live and write, attended by various nieces and hired maids. Yet, according to John Nevill, "The loss of Maria, on whom she had grown to depend for so much, whose patient and unassuming devotion had been the mainstay of her existence, completed the ruin of Harriet's health" (1943, 117). More revelatory is Martineau's candid admission to Fanny Wedgwood nearly two years after Maria's death: "The truth is, the mainspring of my life snapped when I lost Maria, as I doubt not you understand; and I need not say more" (Arbuckle 1983, 257). As time went on, the need to "say more" surfaced, as in this remarkable 1867 letter to Mrs. Grote:

> For nine years my niece Maria and I lived in a companionship so close (from my illness) that few married people are so much and so exclusively together; and I verily believe that, in those years, there never was one passing moment

of discontent of either with the other. She was . . . the ablest woman I have known,—taking the whole course of a woman's duties into the account,—with vast knowledge, a stout and tender heart, inexhaustible sympathy, and a temper without flaw. She had splendid health, from the time she came here, and was so happy that her friends called hers "a radiant life." . . . I did shudder at heart as the thought of Maria being mortal shot through me, but her youth, and her perfect health seemed such a security for her outliving me! And so did her evident fitness and preparation for taking up Florence Nightingale's work. When she was dying, F.N. said she was irreplaceable. . . . This was—is the deepest grief I have ever known. (Sanders 1990, 208–9)[59]

Martineau's conception of the primacy of mutual trust and respect between invalids and their caretakers she had outlined twenty years earlier in *Life in the Sickroom,* in which she pleaded for patients' rights and responsibilities in quite progressive terms. With Maria and Harriet, the intimacy implicit in the healer/invalid relationship proved to be akin to marriage in that one's well-being was bound up with that of another: emphatically not a one-sided relationship of dependency but of mutual interdependency. Martineau's regard for Maria revealed a great deal about her attitudes toward female role models appropriate for the rising generation of women: models embodying Chapman's fierceness and compassion, Nightingale's consummate professionalism, and Maria Martineau's open-mindedness, intellectual clarity, and courage to act on untried ideas. Nightingale later echoes Martineau's marital analogy: "Few have been the friendships I have known, fewer the marriages, which appeared to me worth much. And of these few I have seen many cut short by death. Unless the union of two together makes their work better for mankind, I cannot call it worth the tie. . . . I always thought your union with her, fructifying for mankind, one of the noblest I had ever heard of. I am sure her sympathy with you was." Nightingale's empathy, through her letters of this period, reached across the miles permanently separating the two friends: "Believe that there is no one in this world who thinks of your great trial, and feels how insupportable it is, as I do. I think of you day and night. Would I could bear a part of it for you."[60]

Years later, as Martineau prepared for her own death, the impact of Maria's loss was still a prominent feature in her life: "—and now I desire nothing except in the languid way which is all I ever feel since I lost Maria. . . . I care as much for the great and the distant as ever" (Chapman 1877, 424). Chapman's sentimental casting of Maria Martineau as the daughter Harriet never had minimizes her role as the individual who virtually single-handedly managed the complex health, domestic, financial, and literary affairs of her aunt during one of the most professionally productive and physically debilitating periods of her life. The companionship and mutual regard shared by these two women was based on spiritual compatibility and a shared commitment to performing the work needing to be done. Martineau wrote: "She is something that one hardly meets twice in a life time,—for *power* convertible to any purpose, while steady in its virtue as the stars in their courses. . . . She is *the* member of the clan" (Sanders 1990, 141–42). As Martineau vigorously critiqued the Americans, not out of animosity but because she believed absolutely in their yet-unrealized potential, so too did she chide prominent women who compromised their abilities with questionable behaviors. Yet her ability to praise was equally generous and her eloquence unbounded when her high standards were not only met but exceeded. Such was the case with Maria Martineau.

## Florence Nightingale

Prior to the friendship between Martineau and Nightingale, which began around 1858 during one of the most politically active periods in Martineau's life, both women had variously expressed the philosophical perspectives they later found they shared. Like Chapman, Nightingale was gifted and privileged but, like Martineau, she preferred independence through singleness and vocation to marriage and motherhood; like both, she determined the path most meaningful to her and created opportunities to perform important work in the world beyond the drawing room, kitchen, and nursery. Distinct from Martineau's reluctant but passive acceptance of the inevitability of marriage, Nightingale actively discouraged suitors and resisted her family's aggressive tactics to get her properly married. Further, Nightingale's radical determination to legitimize nursing, an occupation conventionally associated with prostitution, venereal diseases, and alcoholism, speaks eloquently for her insight in recognizing a solution to two chronic social problems: society's need for skilled, formally trained nurses and women's need for respectable occupations. Aside from such strident behaviors as resisting the pressure to marry and aggressively pursuing a professional career, Nightingale's feminism was every bit as eclectic as Martineau's; it, too, requires a paradigm shift on the part of scholars aiming to understand her high status in Martineau's regard as one of the most exemplary women in the world.

As a writer, Martineau left behind many texts through which to explore her feminism. In contrast, although Nightingale did some writing, primarily on nursing, she was not a writer, per se: a notable exception being what is now regarded a feminist manifesto, *Cassandra*. *Cassandra* was written in 1852, during Nightingale's struggle to break free from the limitations of respectability and propriety that hampered any Victorian woman with professional ambitions.[61] The pamphlet demonstrates Nightingale's fitness for "the most serious business of life" by asking, "Why have women passion, intellect, moral activity . . . and a place in society where no one of the three can be exercised?" (25). While it is true that women were kept occupied with busywork, they were also prevented from more creative pursuits, since, "If she has a knife and fork in her hands . . . she cannot have a pencil or brush" (30). The family life with which women are to be content "is too narrow a field for the development of an immortal spirit. . . . This system dooms some minds to incurable infancy, others to silent misery" (37). Her appeal to the "immortal spirit" highlights a central tenet of Woman Question debates in which some argue that woman's role as moral gatekeeper requires her confinement in the home while others—Nightingale, Martineau, and Chapman, for example—claim that this very quality expressly suits her to work outside the home for the benefit of society.

Like Martineau, Nightingale viewed spinsterhood as a welcome alternative to the limitations of marriage as defined in their time: "true marriage . . . does not exist at present upon earth" (Nightingale 1979, 44). Like Wollstonecraft, who regarded marriage as legalized prostitution, and Martineau, who condemned the economic motivations behind many marriages, Nightingale also cited the powerful analogy with prostitution: "The woman who has sold herself for an establishment, in what is she superior to those we may not name?" (48). Given their similar views on the mindless social rituals that absorb women's lives, it is not surprising that these two prominent social anomalies became friends and collaborators. Arriving at the perverse realization discovered by Martineau, Elizabeth Barrett, and other women seeking privacy and solitude, Nightingale noted that nothing excuses women from perpetual availability but illness: "Bodily incapacity is the only apology valid." But her comment in a letter to Maria Martineau—"I have still something to learn every day of the invincible strength of inertia"—suggests the dual capacity of invalidism both to promote and to impede one's work.[62] Nightingale's legacy as an invalid (in need of nurturing) and a healer (by definition, a perpetually available nurturer) powerfully illustrates the ambivalent position Victorian women were forced by custom to inhabit. The cult of invalidism, real or feigned, thus provided a significant, subversive leverage by which the "weaker sex" empowered itself.

In the absence of other accounts of their friendship (the *Autobiography* had already been printed by the time they began corresponding), the extant Martineau-Nightingale correspondence offers an essential resource for understanding the mutual regard the women shared.[63] Early letters, formally addressed to "Miss Nightingale" or "Miss Martineau," soon shifted to "My dear Madam," then "My dear friend," and finally "Dearest friend." Their correspondence is characterized by news about business and professional matters, by reports on the status of their health, and by an absence of gossip and trivialities. Throughout the crisis of Maria's illness and death and its aftermath, Nightingale wrote weekly, sometimes twice-weekly, letters filled with sympathy and comfort for her grieving friend. Given her insights into the characters of Maria and Harriet, and the mutual professional interests and ethical standards the three women shared, Nightingale was no doubt best qualified to "nurse" Harriet Martineau, through loving words sent from a great distance, during the most debilitating crisis of her life.

One of Nightingale's first letters to Martineau aggressively takes issue with the idea of Woman's Mission and with various claims for the feminist and unfeminine implications of her work with "base" bodily functions: "I am brutally indifferent to the wrongs or the rights of my sex—and I should have been equally so to any controversy as to whether women ought or ought not to have done what I have done for the Army—though a woman, having the opportunity and *not* doing it, ought, I think, to be burnt alive." Martineau replied that she is sympathetic to the "Woman's Missionaries" in one sense: "To me it seems right that all people whatever should *do what they can do in natural course:* . . . everybody being allowed to do their best." But she is not at all sympathetic to the "setting up of idols, vindication of rights, and all unnecessary division of men's and women's work." Both women reject feminist dogma based on protesting the wrongs of woman, recalling Martineau's complaint about Wollstonecraft and her ilk, who undercut Woman's Cause by public displays of self-indulgence. For Nightingale as for Martineau, feminist action should be motivated by selflessness and a concern for the greater good rather than the desire to vindicate personal wrongs.[64]

Because the strong friendship between Martineau and Nightingale was strictly epistolary, Maria Martineau's visits to Nightingale provided an essential link between the two women, whose invalidism and professional commitments conspired to keep them apart. As she did with Chapman, Martineau collaborated on several writing projects with Nightingale, who provided the data collected from her field research (primarily during the Crimean War) while Martineau provided the narrative. The collaboration produced *England and Her Soldiers* (1859) as well as "Health in the Camps" and "Health in the Hospitals" (published in the American journal the *Atlantic Monthly* in 1861), along with letters to the War Office advocating simple preventive sanitation measures to avoid unnecessary deaths among the troops.[65] Theirs was an inevitable match: Nightingale had long admired Martineau's writing, while the latter's interest in personal, communal, and national health issues found a knowledgeable and sympathetic resonance in Nightingale's sanitary reforms.[66] As was the case with Chapman, perfect accord was unlikely between two such strong-minded women; Martineau wrote, "Where you and I differ it is because you are thinking of one thing (administrative rule) and I of another,—the principles of political conduct"—but their differences were as complementary as their similarities.[67] In both instances, differences strengthened, rather than dismantled, the women's relationship.

Both Harriet and Maria vigorously promoted Nightingale's *Notes on Nursing: What It Is and What It Is Not* (1860)—Harriet through various periodical articles and through her prolific correspondence and generous reviews: "(*Entre nous,* I am going to do my part by reviewing it in a broad way)," she confided to Erasmus Darwin (Arbuckle 1983, 187).[68] Accordingly, her review in *Quarterly Review* begins "in a broad way" by asserting, "This little book of Miss Nightingale's is a work of genius" (1860, 392). To Nightingale, she sent two infallible assurances of the book's worth: its controversy—

"It is the best possible sign . . . when offence is taken in the first instance"—and Maria's approbation: "'What a wonderful book it is!' Maria cried out yesterday" (Sanders 1990, 183). "It is as if nobody had ever before spoken of nursing. It is so real and so intense, that it will . . . create an order of nurses before it has finished its work. . . . Maria is writing to friends who have money, to show them what good they may do by putting this little book into every house where there are women of any good quality."[69] Demonstrating her conviction that improved living standards in the lower classes would be an immediate result of hygiene reform, Martineau distributed sixty-six copies of *Notes on Nursing* "among homely women, and poorish people who would not be likely to buy" (Arbuckle 1983, 190). She also appealed to those influential in the highest circles, noting, "Lady Elgin hopes to get the Queen's attention fixed on the Nursing movement,—which is just what it wants,—to be made what vulgar people call 'genteel.'"[70]

The professional collaboration between these two remarkable women is impressive for, among other factors, the apparent absence of friction that marked Martineau's relationships with some of the other famous women of her day. Nightingale's scientific approach to resolving social problems resonates with Martineau's positivistic belief in science as a means to eliminate religious superstitions and promote the evolution of civilization. These women were colleagues and friends, as concerned about promoting each other's work as about nurturing each other's latest personal health crisis. Together, they compose a compelling ideological match, prompting Pilkington Jackson to write admiringly, "How extraordinary that two ladies of this eventful period should have arisen out of the ranks of luxury, have thrown aside the tinsel and frivolities of fashionable life, put on the heavy armour of reform and done battle with the great impediments of the age."[71]

A contemporary critic, Charles Rosenberg, views Nightingale's social impact in terms similar to those I have employed to contextualize Martineau's historical contribution: "Nightingale's career is symbolic not only of woman's emergence from the strictures of traditional roles . . . but of a fundamental reordering of English society, of its forms and self-conceptions" (Rosenberg 1979, 131). Martineau, in her unpublished obituary of Nightingale, emphasized the combined values of respectability and social impact constructing her ideal of womanhood: Nightingale "was no declaimer" (like Wollstonecraft) "but a housewifely woman" (like Brontë); "she talked, and did great things" (like Chapman) (Sanders 1986b, 180). Her promotion of nursing as "the most womanly of Woman's work" (Martineau 1865, 425) reminds us that domesticity did not, for Martineau, signal the gender oppression assumed by second-wave feminists. As the highest praise she can bestow, womanliness equates with strength, energy, and intellectual vigor, the courage to act on innovative ideas and fearlessness in the face of controversy—like Maria Martineau—and is quite distinct from psychological morbidity or false romanticism. The "jealousy of men" who equate womanliness with passivity and invisibility she counters with examples of women who are domestic and feminine as well as fierce competitors in the public world. It was Nightingale who ended up outliving and eulogizing Martineau, for whom she also reserved *her* highest praise: "She was born to be a destroyer of slavery, in whatever form, in whatever place, all over the world, wherever she was or thought she saw it. The thought actually inspired her . . . no matter what, she rose to the occasion" (Chapman 1877, 479).

### Josephine Butler

Although this discussion effectually concludes with the example of Florence Nightingale, Martineau's association with Josephine Butler—one of the most prominent names in the rising generation of feminists—illustrates her direct legacy to first-wave feminism. As her life, health, and career wound down for the last time during the 1860s and 1870s, she cultivated no new close female friendships except with Josephine Butler (again, epistolary only), with whom she was involved in the campaign to repeal the Contagious Diseases (CD) Acts. Some discussion of Martineau's relationship with Butler serves as a fitting epilogue to the previous examples by illustrating her powerful social and political influence, which continued well into her seventies, and by demonstrating her willingness to court controversy yet again in defense of women's rights. Martineau's participation, written and needleworked, in this campaign stemmed naturally from her interest in health issues and sanitation reforms, her commitment to Woman's Cause, and her instinctive rebellion against institutionalized social oppression. Through the end of her life, Martineau was, in William Lloyd Garrison's term, a heretic, frequently a solitary voice of protest and often ostracized as a result of attending to her "inward witness." But she was not alone in her protest against the CD Acts' aggressive misogyny, and her relation to Butler illustrates Tennyson's observation that "The old order changeth, yielding place to new" ("The Passing of Arthur" 11.408) as the grandmotherly Martineau passed the torch to the next generation of feminist activists.

Recalling that Martineau's interest in these issues dated from the Tynemouth years, Chapman observed that Martineau's journal "records the strong feeling that moved her to the service of unhappy women, and her conviction that it must be, if possible, a part of her future life. 'If not,' she says, 'someone else will do it.'" This role was undertaken by "her honoured and beloved friend Mrs. Josephine Butler . . . and they wrought together through all the last suffering period of her life" (Chapman 1877, 427–28). Prophetically, Martineau early "felt the coming danger, and met it by correspondence with Florence Nightingale and other influential persons who had like herself been long aware of the growing evil; and in 1859 she met it by a series of powerful leading articles in the *Daily News*": to which the *Times*, not surprisingly, took the opposing stance.[72] Into this controversy came Josephine Butler, who demonstrated sharp social, political, and gender insights and an eagerness to put her resources to work for this cause. Butler focused on the plights of fallen women and prostitutes, many of whom she "recuperated" by turning her home into a refuge and halfway house. Martineau supported Butler's Social Purity Association, but it was their collaboration on the campaign to repeal the Contagious Diseases Acts that most directly brought together the aging, invalid author and the young, energetic reformer.

In November 1869 Martineau wrote: "One of my chief correspondents . . . [is] Mrs. Butler of Liverpool,—*the* Mrs. Butler. . . . I have given my name to the Committee,—(as has Florence Nightingale)." She notes that she obtained permission from the *Daily News* to reprint five of her leaders relating to the subject in pamphlet form, to be distributed by Butler's organization. Not having met *"the* Mrs. Butler" herself, Martineau relies on others' impressions: "F. Arnold says Mrs. B. is the most fascinating woman conceivable,—in appearance, manner, conversation . . . *quiet* to the last degree consistent with the interest of her conversation and ways,—and yet impulsive." Butler's combination of womanly propriety—she is "quiet"—with the vigor and tenacity required to prevail against male opponents and their institutions—she is "impulsive"—made her an exemplary promoter of Woman's Cause.[73] As a late-Victorian feminist prototype, Butler's contribution to Woman's Cause resided not only in her activism but also in her demonstration that women can be both feminine and political, compromising neither and redefining the standards for both.

Martineau's famous name on letters and petitions and in the *Daily News* contributed to the early success of the cause. In 1870, for instance, the women, for whom the franchise was still fifty years in the future, campaigned so vigorously against pro–Contagious Diseases politician Sir Henry Storks that his bid for reelection was defeated. The association's petition addressed "To the Women of Colchester," in Storks's district, appeals to the sanctity of the home, Christian morality, and the "eminent honour and security of our sex," which are compromised by Storks's assertion that prostitution is "a necessity." Casting themselves as "true-hearted Englishwomen" rather than "fine Ladies," the signatories—Harriet Martineau, Ursula Bright, and Josephine Butler—urged women to speak out in their homes and neighborhoods to influence "every Elector who values as an Englishman should, the sanctity of his home, the purity of his sons, and the honour and safety of his daughters" (see appendix for full text). The petition's rhetorical appeals to Victorian values illustrate the impressive range of political influence wielded by women despite not being permitted a representative voice in government. The episode verified what Martineau had said all along: that, while the franchise would be nice to have, women enjoyed considerable political influence without it.

Martineau's promotion of the CD campaign proved to be her last literary activism as age, illness, and debility increasingly curtailed her writing projects. Butler's assumption of the reins of the movement was timely and necessary, as the controversy was destined to continue until the laws' repeal in 1886, ten years after Martineau's death. In a compelling illustration of the era's persistent gender strictures, old age did not exempt her from charges of impropriety, nor did it tone down her feistiness: "I am told . . . that this is discreditable work for woman, especially for an *old* woman. But," she added with a prickly shrewdness undimmed by age, "it has always been esteemed our special function as women, to mount guard over society and social life,—the spring of national existence, and to keep them pure; and who so fit as an *old* woman?" (Chapman 1877, 400). She also supported Butler's campaign through her own considerable correspondence, here demonstrating an inclusive, proprietary attitude: "*Our* cause, - *the cause* which outweighs all others,—gets on thoroughly well. You must have heard of the triumphant result of Mrs. Butler's Evidence—given before the Commission." Martineau's earlier protection of Nightingale is mirrored in Butler's concern for Harriet's privacy and limited energy as an elderly invalid. Butler apologizes on behalf of "our committee," which used Martineau's name without her permission: "I pleaded that you could not give any *work* now to the cause, and might object even to this use of your name. . . . I engaged them to promise that you should never be troubled" by further requests. But Butler cannot resist adding, "Of course, we all felt that your name added force to our front ranks," acknowledging that, at seventy years old, Harriet Martineau was still a political force to be reckoned with.[74]

From the preface of *Personal Reminiscences of a Great Crusade*—significantly termed the "recital of our abolitionist struggle"—Butler acknowledges her debt to Harriet Martineau: "When, in 1872, I was summoned to give evidence before a Royal Commission to inquire into this question, I stated on the authority of Mrs. Harriet Martineau . . . that an attempt was made during the Melbourne Ministry to introduce this Parisian system into England" (1896, 7–8). Prior to the passage of the 1869 act, a "powerful protest had been raised" by Martineau, who "with all the shrewdness and enlightenment of a true woman and an able politician, had seen the tendency of a certain busy medical and military clique in this direction."[75]

When the women's petition was published in the *Daily News* (according to Butler, with two thousand signatures), "the conspiracy of silence" was disrupted (Chapman 1877, 435). Martineau observed, the "*Daily News* came out clearly and strongly on the right side before any other London paper broke the silence" (Chapman 1877, 435). Of this "unexpected and powerful manifesto," a parliamentary member observed: "We know how to manage any other opposition in the House or in the country, but this is very awkward for us—this revolt of the women. It is quite a new thing; what are we to do with such an opposition as this?" (Butler 1896, 20). Butler's description of her campaign, as she traveled from town to town generating support by raising public consciousness, sounds very like Martineau's notoriety as an abolitionist in 1830s America. Butler was similarly menaced by mobs of "hired roughs, and persons directly interested in the maintenance of the vilest of human institutions" (Butler 1896, 44). Recalling the Massachusetts clergy's campaign against women abolitionists, Butler recounts that her meetings, too, were forced to adjourn because cayenne pepper had been sprinkled throughout the room "in order to make it impossible for us to speak" (89). Throughout the *Reminiscences,* Butler refers to the repealers as "we Abolitionists," a term emphasizing ideological links between the emancipation of slaves and of women defining the century's sociopolitical landscape. Butler's assertion of Martineau's continuing influence—"When I mentioned Harriet Martineau as sympathising with them, a bright gleam passed over their faces, from town to town as I went"—attests to the social impact of women who respond unfailingly to the "inward witness."

In its obituary notice of Martineau, the *Shield,* published by the Ladies' National Association, observed that few people "realized the tremendous issues involved in the question, Shall the State sanction and protect prostitution?—or dreamed that in agitating, as they then believed, simply for the repeal of a cruel and indecent law, they were bringing to a crisis the whole question of the enslavement of the weak to the lust of the strong. Mrs. Martineau, however, appears to have fully realized the gravity of the situation from the very beginning" (Chapman 1877, 435). She foresaw victory but recognized the battle would be "fierce" and would not be handled quietly but noisily and publicly, with the result that Parliament and the general public became locked in a debate that refused to "suffer and be still." Writing to Chapman at the time of Martineau's death in words echoing Nightingale's eulogy, Butler asserted that she was "Faithful to the end to the cause of liberty, justice, and purity, faithful to the end to the cause of the white slaves of Europe as she had been faithful to the cause of the black slaves of America, so died Harriet Martineau, full of hope about our cause and of sympathy with the men and women who are working in it. A noble life followed by a noble death!" (Chapman 1877, 490).

## Feminism and Woman's Cause

The best friends of Woman's Cause, in Martineau's view, are those "who are morally as well as intellectually competent to the most serious business of life"; judging by the examples discussed here, few women achieved her standard. For Martineau, the unconventional private lives of Wollstonecraft and Eliot rendered undesirable feminist prototypes, despite their brilliant intellects. Extending the analogy, Brontë's candid portrayal of women characters who embody both respectability and passion—a point in her favor with contemporary feminists—for Victorians, unfortunately, reified the idea that women are incomplete without marriage and motherhood and that all working women are simply looking for a mate. Harder to understand is Martineau's flippant response to Gaskell, whose focus on fallen women and male sexual culpability established new boundaries for women writers and an important voice for poor working women. Gaskell wrote in the spirit and the tradition of Martineau herself, whose pleas for birth control in 1832 and condemnation of the Contagious Diseases Acts in 1869, with a variety of woman-centered writings in between, wielded particular authority coming from a prominent and respected woman. In the examples of Barrett Browning and Fuller, conflicting political consciences may account for the cooling in these relationships, and, although Martineau admired both women's commitment to Italian liberation, she was puzzled at their indifference to the social issues plaguing their own countries. Victoria, similarly, impeded rather than promoted woman's progress during this crucial chapter in feminist history by an extended mourning that many regarded as self-indulgent. In the words of a contemporary critic that highlight the pluralism of these perspectives, Martineau's work suggests she was and is "a more complete and, indeed, more modern figure than were the Brontës and Wollstonecrafts, whose emotions once flared and have now passed away" (Richardson 1984, 457). As a feminist, as in other realms, Martineau demonstrated a visionary quality, often unappreciated in her time and in ours, aimed at eradicating the fundamental biological prejudice underlying all women's oppressions.

Martineau's other professional relationships fared better when literature was either not involved or was a collaborative effort. Maria Martineau's "evident fitness and preparation for taking up Florence Nightingale's work" linked her with the two women Martineau most venerated: Nightingale and Chapman. Chapman provided "the most perfect proof within my experience of the possible union of the highest *intellectual and moral* attributes. Such a *nurse*, among other domesticities!" Martineau wrote in an 1860 letter to Nightingale (emphasis added).[76] As a term of the highest praise and one most emphatically *not* associated with prostitution, "nurse" illustrates Martineau's keen interest in health issues, like abolitionism, cast as a specifically *womanly* concern in its focus on social and moral welfare. The best promoters of Woman's Cause, then, are linked by their association with healing and restoration: Maria, Martineau's private nurse and Ambleside's community nurse; Nightingale, in whom the ideas of respectability, nationalism, morality, and hygiene reform coalesce; Chapman, healer of the fractured American Union; and Josephine Butler, midwife to first-wave feminism. Finally, in a telling analogy, Martineau earlier perceived her role as author in the preface to *Life in the Sickroom* to be that of a healer, declaring herself eager to "have the honour of being your nurse, though I am myself laid low" (1844, xv). Thus did the author herself also perform the work of nursing, a healing reaching across space and time through her words and texts.

Martineau's feminism stemmed from her recognition that what prevents Woman's Cause from progressing more than any other single factor is biological prejudice: prejudice linking passion, sexuality, and maternity with intellectual inferiority, irrationality, and "coarseness." But celibacy was not, for Martineau, a necessary condition of feminism; and, although she critiqued the state of marriage as practiced in the nineteenth century, she upheld the institution while rejecting the idea that it be mandatory for everyone. For her the crucial point is that sexual respectability has the power to promote Woman's Cause while scandal, however unfairly, impedes it. Simply put, in her view, women cannot get on with the "serious business of life" until they prove false the hegemony's expectation that they are destined, by nature, to fail. One of her more striking prophetic insights, which significantly pays homage to the maligned Mary Wollstonecraft, she addressed to Chapman in 1840: "You will live to see a great enlargement of our scope, I trust; but, what with the vices of some women and the fears of others, it is hard work for us to assert our liberty. I will, however, till I die, and so will you; and so make it easier for some few to follow us than it was for poor Mary Wollstonecraft to begin" (Chapman 1877, 233).

# 6

## "(Entre Nous, Please)"

### "Letters are the Thing"

The possibility of *letters* means that nothing is quite ended, that private self and public self will continue to shift and slide into one another, that each soul knows relationships which are many, not one, and complex, not simple.
—**Margaret Doody**

I have long been uneasy at the thought of how many valuable things I suffer to go out of my mind for want of energy to record them. . . . I will try whether I can reconcile journalising with ease and freedom of mind.
—**Harriet Martineau**

Post time is looked to for its sure freight of love and pity and good wishes. . . . Letters are one's best company on that day,—and best if they are one's only company.
—**Harriet Martineau**

When her literary activity ceased, her epistolary vigor continued, and she wrote long letters to her many friends on both sides of the Atlantic, thus keeping herself in sympathy with all the political and social movements of the day.
—**George Holyoake**

• As a literary grandmother to the generation of women writers emerging during the heyday of Victorian literature, Harriet Martineau pioneered virtually uncharted territory by openly shaping her identity as a woman writer. From her refusal to employ a pseudonym[1] to her experiments with form and content, Martineau resisted conforming with reigning genre and gender standards. She early demonstrated her inclination to write in a variety of genres, her restless "need of utterance" never fully satisfied with the confines of any particular one. Even her prolific periodicals writing, which features some of the finest work of her career, seems more worthy of a history or sociology text than of a daily newspaper. Not surprisingly, her extant private correspondence offers a wealth of insight not only into her identities as a woman and a writer, but also into her observance of public and private boundaries, the latter being always clearly signaled in her letters by "(*entre nous*, please)".

My focus on primary themes in Martineau's life and work demonstrates that, for her, all the world's a text to be read and analyzed, to be inscribed with needle and pen, in her endeavor to "edit" the society she helped to create through her social commentary. That her enviable ability to compose "went off," she asserts, "like a letter" offers an essential clue into the intersections of authorship, gender, and genre in this writer. Needleworking was one of the activities that replaced the drafting, revising, and editing processes with an alternative mode of producing texts whose early stages were worked out through codes of stitchery. As my discussion in this chapter will show, the act and process of writing letters served a similar purpose and as such provides further insight into Martineau's contributions to literary, social, and feminist history. Charles Darwin's assertion that "She never had occasion to correct a single word she writes, which accounts for the marvellous rapidity with which she brings forward her books" (Webb 1960, 41) hints, again, at the relevance of a process-oriented approach to analyzing Martineau's work through a focus on her letters.

An intriguing link with these themes is offered by her preoccupations with American slavery and with Woman's Cause. For Martineau, American society represented a page whose very blankness (in terms of a historical past) presented the perfect opportunity for righting the wrongs of Old World social injustices. Instead, however, the institution of slavery tragically reified those injustices, making emancipation the only means to align America's practices with its principles. Thus was the text of racism—in which social relations are based on the visual cues of skin color and physical characteristics and the cultural assumptions attached to them—superimposed on that of the "parchment idols" delineating American ideals. Here, too, the union of nonverbal with verbal texts became, for Martineau, inseparable; as the topic on which she produced more writing than any other, the American experiment aroused in her great distress and passion, although she never lost hope in the country's capacity to redeem itself.

Further, given that women comprise more than half the human race, Woman's Cause provided another text that incorporates all of these themes: public and private identities, women's work, and slavery and emancipation. Her writing—fiction and nonfiction, autobiography and epistolary— employs women as themselves texts to be read, analyzed, and critiqued, guided by her aim to transform women's subordination by exposing what impedes their progress and by proposing alternatives that will promote their

cause. Among her contemporaries, Martineau's subtle political consciousness found much to criticize, although she was as quick to praise and promote women "of the heroic order" as she was to resist feminist "declaimers." In her fiction, women's texts can both destroy and preserve as
well as expose injustices: Dora Sullivan is imprisoned and exiled because of
the threat her literacy poses, while Anne LeBrocq's letter earns freedom for
herself and her father; Lady Frances, having experienced both economic
realms, finds the disparities between rich and poor "too deep a page for my
reading." Martineau's nonfiction texts range from popular journalism to petitions, like the "Women of Colchester" poster campaign; such grassroots activism fueled changes in social attitudes and led to parliamentary legislation
benefiting women. Underpinning all her activities in this vein is her conviction that the public persona that individual women project is crucial to the
success or failure of the collective Woman's Cause.

This study of Martineau's impact on Victorian culture, both American
and British, domestic and political, reveals her to be a genuine original
who challenged critics' urge to categorize her through conventional gender dichotomies. One of the most pronounced of her idiosyncrasies is her
passion for letter writing and her fierce determination to preserve the integrity of her letters, the privacy shared by writer and recipient and, especially, freedom of speech. Interestingly, her method of composing the *Illustrations* and the *Autobiography*—"I did it as I write letters, . . .—never
altering the expression as it came fresh from my brain" (1983, 1:195)—was
true of all her writing, suggesting that a key to understanding Martineau's
personal and literary identities is her *mode* of composition no less than the
content. This chapter studies the epistolary format that she found so liberating that she even employed the form for many of her works intended for
publication; a related aim is to establish the act of epistolary writing as itself part of the process essential to her literary production.

Contrasting with Linda Peterson's claim that Martineau's resistance to
drafting, editing, and revising marks her as a masculine writer, I argue that
her mode of composition is not a gender issue but simply part of her creative process. When she was confined to the sickroom, needleworking became doubly important to that process, while in times of health, hiking
and walking provided an alternative. These were no mere strolls she took
during periods in her life when she was not ill: her hiking tour through
Scotland with James in the 1820s covered around five hundred miles; accused of scrambling across America "with the frame of a moss-trooper,"
she later hiked through Middle Eastern deserts to climb the pyramids and,
in middle age, amazed her Lake District neighbors by arriving at outlying
farms literally before the cows were up. Her reputation as a vigorous hiker
(up to ten miles a day) prompted her neighbor, William Wordsworth,
drolly to caution visitors against accepting her invitations to take a stroll.
An 1827 letter to Ellen Martineau offers an early indication of what is for
Martineau an essential link between walking and writing: "I have been

walking far and wide; from six to ten miles every day lately. . . . [It] does me good and helps on my writing, which is my chief object" (Sanders 1990, 11). Similarly, letter writing also served a creative purpose, offering an essential forum for testing and rehearsing her ideas prior to publication and for developing her political and social ideology.[2]

Another purpose of this chapter is to consider why the only genre legitimately open to Martineau as a woman—the novel—was the only genre in which she did not write (with the exception of *Deerbrook* and, arguably, her "historical romance," *The Hour and the Man*), although she was clearly adept in all the subsidiary genres contributing to the novel. Did she resist novel writing *because* it was expected of her as a woman? Did she tackle histories and journalism *because* they were forbidden to her as masculine genres? My related aim, then, is to explore the claim that genres and language are gendered: an admittedly convenient, though entirely fallacious, analytical framework fraught with anachronistic social baggage. This peculiarly Victorian perspective survives today in studies that claim Harriet Martineau's successes as well as her failures result from her writing in a masculine narrative voice and in masculine genres: even from her having a masculine mind. But *are* there masculine and feminine literary voices? How are they distinguished from each other? What makes language and genres gendered, or is gender-neutral language possible? Since such questions arise from dichotomized thinking, I suggest that current feminist scholarship, with its interest in collapsing polarized paradigms in favor of more fluid interdisciplinary approaches, offers a relevant alternative avenue of inquiry, that is, by considering the differences and similarities between personal and political language and analyzing where they overlap and to what end. Conceivably, this intersection might be the juncture wherein what Josephine Donovan terms a "woman-grounded epistemology" (1984, 100) reveals more fully than gendered dichotomizing what Harriet Martineau accomplished and has to offer us still.

By confronting the issue of gendered language and genres, my intention is to examine the premise that gender is implicit in our linguistic system, specifically the claim that women writers participate in the literary realm in proportion to their ability to conceal their gender by writing "like a man." That the Victorians viewed women writers in this light is easily attributed to a social system in which virtually every aspect of life was divided along gender lines; to cross from one to the other—women writers or men needleworkers, for example—constituted deviance and was ostracized accordingly. But although our culture has inherited this thinking, we are hardly bound to continue perpetuating it; indeed, contemporary work intended to recuperate so-called marginalized women writers is distinctly impeded by the suggestion that the degree to which a woman wrote "like a man"—or, alternatively, "like a woman"—represents the degree to which her literary reputation has survived. For example, the topic of the work responsible for launching Martineau's career, political economy, was typically dubbed masculine; this makes the writer herself "masculine," an idea used both to account for her unlikely success and to condemn it as unladylike. Mary Kelley writes that Catharine Sedgwick, despite her admiration for Martineau, felt that her writing about this subject "was not the loveliest manifestation of woman," although Martineau was able to transcend the taint by a personal "virtue" that made her "the embodiment of femininity" (1993, 34–35). Feminine virtue to some degree vindicates the woman writer's masculine presumption; but while such justification assuages the immediate problem created by the woman who is both virtuous and literary, it evades questioning the obvious challenge posed to separate spheres ideology by someone like Harriet Martineau.

Sedgwick's attitude is not surprising, given the temper of the time and popular prejudice against women reformists, whose activism was labeled coarse, unladylike, and un-Christian. So tenacious was this attitude that twentieth-century biographer Vera Wheatley presents "Demerara"'s focus on slavery as evidence of Martineau's masculinity: "Harriet Martineau's mind has sometimes been described as masculine in outlook and perhaps in this tale of slavery the first indication of such an outlook—logical, unsentimental, and far sighted—is to be observed" (1957, 99). With complacency that today astonishes, Wheatley unquestioningly accepts and perpetuates this anachronistic attitude, which she offers as *proof* of Martineau's literary credibility. Cy Frost articulates what Wheatley does not by asserting that the very act of writing, regardless of genre or topic, signified women's social deviance; by appropriating the masculine sphere, women writers threatened the integrity of the domestic sphere. To illustrate, Frost notes that even Harriet Beecher Stowe, despite her associations with domesticity and evangelicalism, was perceived as "immodest, and therefore deserving of the opprobrium due to any unreserved assault on the status quo. . . . Stowe 'forfeited her claim to be considered a lady'" (1991, 256) by writing of the "masculine" topic, slavery. Martineau's insistence that if men are not taking up the pen to address the problem of slavery then it is incumbent upon women to do so evidences her defiance of unsubstantiated or artificial gender strictures, particularly in light of more serious human rights issues.

Throughout this study, I have used Martineau's letters to illustrate her concerns with various issues, often expressed more candidly in her private correspondence than in writing intended for publication. In contrast, the following discussion considers the centrality of the epistolary genre to her mode of composition by analyzing the range of topics she addressed and the variety of her correspondents. The sheer quantity of letters in itself is striking: judging by the amount of correspondence that survived her strictures that it be destroyed, the sum total—were it available to us—would be staggering indeed. Epistolary correspondence was for Martineau a daily ritual, even during periods when she was too ill to write for publication; when she could not herself hold a pen, she dictated letters to a niece or companion. As productive a writer as Martineau was, she was an even more prolific letter writer, and so central was this form in her life and work, and so explicit and opinionated was she on the topic of letters and in the letters themselves, that a special focus on this genre warrants our attention. One way of arriving at an epistemology relevant to Harriet Martineau is to consider her letters in themselves a legitimate and especially revelatory literary genre. Acknowledging her dissatisfaction with her novel-writing ability, she asserted, "My way of interesting must be a different one" (Chapman 1877, 199); her ways of "interesting" include biography and history, philosophy and political economy, sociology and journalism, and autobiography and letters: if not the novel itself, then certainly all the components contributing to that genre.

## Toward a Theory of Language, Genre, and Gender

Very powerful organization indeed for a female, more like that of a male.

—Unknown observer, on Martineau's work.[3]

Writing of Harriet Martineau in *The People's Journal* in 1846, William Howitt's opening statement voices an assumption so common that it probably raised few eyebrows: "Harriet Martineau presents one of the finest examples of a masculine intellect in a female form which have distinguished the present age" (1846, 141). Howitt's phrasing indicates that a framework through which to account for a being who is intelligent and articulate despite being a female did not yet exist. "It is highly satisfactory that the vigour and grasp of female intellect should have found as practical asserters amongst the fair sex as female sensibility and imagination," Howitt continues, concluding that Martineau's example represents a "triumph for our dear friends of the Cinderella sex" (142). Clearly, Howitt's aim is to praise Martineau in the highest terms available—she thinks like a man—while at the same time staking an unassailable claim for her femininity: one hand may hold a pen, it is true, but the other holds a needle. Martineau may be striding aggressively through what most acknowledge is a masculine realm, but she never forgets her Cinderella origins: no doubt because she is never permitted to forget, even as a celebrity of international stature. She may have risen out of the ashes to participate in loftier realms, but she will never be more than a guest, since she can be relegated back to the scullery without notice. Howitt's brilliantly telling allusion to the Cinderella myth, evoking at best fairy godmothers and at worst female mutilation, provides a powerful metaphor illustrating the period's investment in perpetuating the separate spheres fairy tale that kept women universally oppressed.[4]

Similarly, in the very act of praising her accomplishments, an 1856 publication entitled *Eminent Women* contributes to this celebration of masculinity that has been presented, for more than a century, as scholarship on Harriet Martineau. The entry begins promisingly—"[F]oremost among the names of the female writers of Great Britain will be found that of Harriet Martineau," followed by what is, again, apparently intended as a compliment: "Her genius differs . . . from that of all other *litterateurs* in that she possesses an intellect which may be truly called masculine; and, for this reason, we place her at the head of the eminent women of our time" (9). Also again, the writer is anxious to assert that, despite "the vigour and grasp of her intellect, she is a true woman, and proclaims Home as peculiarly the female sphere of action." To anyone who views Martineau through the lenses of true womanhood and separate spheres ideologies, as this writer does, her promotion of domestic skills would seem, on a literal level, an attempt to expiate her social sins of intellectualism and economic autonomy. Yet as an examination of this issue in the broader context of her writing shows, the role played by domesticity is more complex than either separate spheres ideology or feminist analysis suggests. The author further asserts that Martineau recognizes "women's sphere of usefullness as domestic, and not executive": a point emphatically not true, considering her vision of governesses transformed into school administrators, of matrons as hospital administrators, and of women's health care being entrusted to women doctors exclusively. The entry's conclusion—"Her triumph . . . and the constant progress which she has made in self-discipline, self-culture, usefulness, reputation, and pecuniary ease, affords the greatest encouragement, and a noble example, to such as are endeavouring to struggle into light"—might be more worthy of Martineau's legacy were it not for the biologically reductive comments preceding it. Interestingly, the author claims that she lacks "that picture-writing . . . which now are the only certain guarantees of popularity": for critics throughout her career, sufficient justification for dismissing her work for its failure to conform with genre and gender expectations rather than analyzing it from a more relevant perspective.

Both selections aptly demonstrate how domestic ideology was employed to "excuse" Martineau's eccentricities as an unmarried, self-supporting woman writer, although her embrace of domesticity requires, as I have shown, a deeper analysis. Chapman's observation, "From the beginning, Harriet Martineau's anonymous writings have always been attributed to a man; her industry, judgment, and insight went so far to supply the want of what men learn in the university and the market-place" (1877, 38), better highlights the threat posed by her friend, whose intellectual vigor and economic self-sufficiency are attributable not to the university education or "old boy network" typically enjoyed by men but to her own native intelligence. What Martineau called the "jealousy of men" is nowhere more apparent than in the anxiety to account for the anomaly of a woman who was professionally more successful than most men and was so without access to male privileges.

As the example of Vera Wheatley proves, Martineau fares no better at the hands of some twentieth-century critics. Biographer R. K. Webb, whose *Harriet Martineau: A Radical Victorian* (1960) virtually shaped the last forty years of Martineau scholarship, perpetuates the myth of the masculine mind. Webb criticizes Martineau's judgment in choosing Chapman as her biographer—Chapman's apparently lightweight mind being no match for Martineau's masculine one—and speculates on "Miss" Martineau's lesbian tendencies without offering substantiating evidence. Webb's presenting her as a sexual anomaly, an idea as prevalent in 1960 as during Martineau's lifetime, implies that her literary success was "not normal" but an aberration of gender.[5] Deirdre David expands this thinking by arguing that Martineau's feminist impact was limited because she was full of contradictions: she was an intellectual woman yet "devoted to *passive observation* of a rapidly changing society in whose 'making' she believed she had no part" (1987, 31; emphasis added). Yet a look at the very first page of Martineau's *Autobiography* reveals her keen awareness of the prominent part she actively and aggressively played in the shaping of Victorian social history, seen in her vigorous assertion that her "somewhat remarkable" life requires a full autobiographical record; she knew this as early as 1831, when she first began organizing an account of her childhood; again in the 1840s, during her long illness; and again in 1855, when her conviction that she was dying prompted her to finish her autobiography. David's assessments of Martineau are themselves curiously Victorian, like her claim that Martineau's career was "defined by her auxiliary usefulness to a male-dominated culture. . . . [S]he embraces her subordinate status. . . . Her call is for women to be educated so they might clear-headedly, rationally assent to their subjugated condition" (31–32). But an analysis of Martineau's writings on women, such as that offered in chapter 4, reveals that her "call" was in fact only the first step in a process that promotes education and the professionalization of women's occupations as the means to prepare women to assume their place in the world *outside* the home. This "call" was not an end in itself but aimed toward an alternative end, that is, women's successful entry into professions requiring specialized training not associated with domestic tasks, like the fine and performing arts, business, and the sciences. David's claim that this "auxiliary usefulness . . . facilitates almost all her non-fictional writing" and "impedes her writing of fictional prose" (86) so entirely misses the point of Martineau's contributions that it ranks with the quaint assessments offered in 1846 by Howitt and in 1856 by *Eminent Women*.

Another way of accounting for the anomaly presented by Martineau is based on the assumption that language and literary genres are gendered. Writing of masculine and feminine authorial personas, J. Paul Hunter notes, "When men impersonate women there is often a certain trying on of roles, an experimentation with a possible identity, a personation tried but not a road taken. . . . Women writers, on the other hand, are more in a conscious position of cross-dressing, knowing that they can project a role for a moment but not take on a real identity" (1990, 272). Hunter's statement implies that language *is* gendered and the gender is male, placing male writers in a position of appropriating the feminine in a way that is not permitted to women writers, who are at best visitors in this gender-specific linguistic system. Contrasting with the limitations Hunter's perspective imposes on women writers, Alexis Easley presents this sort of gender role-playing as particularly liberating: "The assumption of male narration and male readership was almost universal. . . . Thus, women journalists often wrote in 'drag,' referring to themselves and their readers using masculine gender markers" (1997, 1). Easley accounts for Martineau's linguistic cross-dressing by claiming that "Only by attempting to write from an ungendered, depersonalized perspective could women come to be treated equally in all of the professions" (9), although what constitutes masculine "gender markers" (other than the obvious pronouns) or "ungendered, depersonalized" linguistic cues is not clearly defined. Nor do either Easley or Hunter explain the "universal" starting assumption that language and genres are male-oriented, an assumption begging for analysis in its capacity to negate entirely women's place in the linguistic system. Women have certainly been hindered in their contributions to hegemonic culture, but they have contributed nonetheless, through both articulate and nonarticulate modes; even an oppressive patriarchal culture could not eliminate women's participation in and influence on the linguistic system.

Similarly, Gaby Weiner accepts the "universal" masculinization of language as inevitable, attributing Martineau's literary success to her capacity to adapt her feminine perspective to masculine linguistics. Referring to "Female Industry," Weiner does make some attempt to illustrate how this might work in practical terms: "This article was written anonymously, as were many of her newspaper and journal articles. Harriet Martineau often implied that her articles had a male author (see above 'us, the breadwinners'), presumably to give them added weight" (1983, xiv). By claiming that Martineau's including herself among "us, the breadwinners" necessarily indicates a masculine association, Weiner assumes that only men work and ignores the primary point of the article, evident from its very title: that well over three million of "our countrywomen" *are already* the breadwinners, among whom Martineau counts herself. Since both men and women writers of the period wrote anonymously for periodicals and used inclusive pronouns in addressing the reading audience, it is unclear how this dynamic masculinizes Martineau but does not feminize, for example, Charles Dickens: unless, of course, we accept the assumption that language is masculine-oriented. Martineau's formidable literary reputation, making her anonymity virtually impossible to conceal in print, hardly needed any "added weight" to carry her points.[6]

Extending this line of thought from language to disciplines, Linda Peterson claims that Martineau's girlhood study of composition—"a capital way of introducing some order into the chaos of girls' thoughts" (Martineau 1983, 1:64)—leads to a rhetorical practice in which Martineau views "public discourse as 'masculine,'" resulting in her "appropriation of traditionally masculine personae and genres" (1990b, 172). Peterson links her mode of composition, which is without revision, to the masculine tradition of nonfiction prose writing, although she does not make clear why this spontaneous writing style is particularly masculine. This accounts, she argues, for Martineau's early decision to pursue nonfiction prose writing (masculine) rather than fiction writing (feminine): "by the late 1830s, she had moved *beyond* a typically feminine phase of fictionalizing to a more abstract, masculine phase of deep thinking and writing" (173). Peterson's claim that Martineau thus "lost her fictionalizing capacity" (174) does not account for the tales she continued to produce throughout her life, like *Deerbrook,* her writing for Chapman's *Liberty Bell,* the seminal "Dawn Island," and the popular *Playfellow* series; much of her nonfiction writing, in fact, illustrates that her affinity for fiction writing never left her. By assuming that Martineau's entry into the literary realm depended on her ability to reproduce masculine linguistic and rhetorical styles, Peterson elides the fact that the writer's "credibility and authority, how to make herself heard" was never a problem from the moment Martineau first put pen to paper and saw her work in print.[7]

Part of what makes Harriet Martineau such a rich subject for academic inquiry stems from her persistent challenges to boundaries of all sorts: disciplinary and linguistic, private and public, masculine and feminine, logos and pathos. A study of Martineau's work reveals it to be genuinely interdisciplinary, which in part explains the obscurity into which it fell following the strict codification of disciplines during the late nineteenth and twentieth centuries. Such a study also reveals that the resurgence of interest in this writer in the last decade coincides with the academy's growing interest in interdisciplinary studies, which challenges the limitations of dichotomized, compartmentalized thinking. Herein lies the problem: the urge to dichotomize—masculine/feminine, reason/emotion, nonfiction/fiction—even in the ostensible pursuit of recuperating her reputation for a feminist purpose, is the powerful impulse impeding Martineau studies whose analyses depend on conventional notions of gendering. Resistance to this writer continues today in the attitude that her ability to write in virtually all genres makes her a Jill of all trades, mistress of none and in the pervasive view that her success must always be attributable to masculine factors, never simply to her talent and her prodigious "need of utterance."

Fortunately, not all Martineau studies are inhibited by this thinking, and some investigate the ways that she departed from and redefined genre boundaries *as a woman writer* rather than trading her distinctive authorial identity for a masculine one. Offering a suggestive avenue for assessing Martineau's writing, Amy Schulman claims that "Genres do have identifiable characteristics in particular social, historical moments" but they "are not fixed or inherent" and require assessment and constant reassessment in shifting contexts (1993, 73). Maria Frawley's analysis of *Society in America,* for example, posits that Martineau's contribution to sociological discourse through her travel writing is distinguished by its synthesis of morality, "a feminine domain," with scientific method, which lends "to the study of morals and manners the weight of science, and by implication of public, masculine, and serious discourse" (1992, 16). Frawley argues that, far from "appropriating" masculine discourse, Martineau strikes out on her own, essentially reinventing the travel-writing genre to suit her sociological purpose: "she wanted to map out an area of inquiry for which she as a woman is uniquely qualified, and she wanted that area to have the same credentials, to be as legitimate, as those from which she would by virtue of her gender be disqualified." Resisting the gendered dichotomy, Martineau argues specifically "for the fundamental value of auxiliary work. . . . [W]omen, as both guardians of and experts in the moral, are singularly qualified to be investigative travelers." By applying scientific method and rhetoric to her study of the domestic and moral realm, "Martineau in essence validates it; the credibility of her argument derives from the status accorded by her culture to discourse considered public, rational, and male" (17). I will push the claim of "fundamental value" further by arguing that Martineau promotes women's sphere not by embracing its *auxiliary* usefulness but by presenting it as *just as essential* to the functioning and understanding of culture as political institutions and the marketplace, in the process deftly reshaping public perceptions of traditional hierarchies. As I have shown in my discussion of critical responses to *Society in America* (chapter 3), critics' objections to her innovations in the travel-writing genre were cloaked in rhetoric attempting to reify the separate spheres she had so boldly and openly challenged by substituting sociology for "picture-writing."

If ever a writer required a genuinely "woman-grounded epistemology" it is Harriet Martineau. Josephine Donovan's observation that Aristotelian standards for literary plots—the movement is progressive and unified, with a clear beginning, middle, and end—"is at odds with the traditional woman's fundamentally repetitive or cyclic existence" (1984, 102–3) accords with Jane Tompkins's (1985) and Elaine Showalter's (1986) analyses of Harriet Beecher Stowe and Sandra Holton's work on Florence Nightingale. These studies argue that the chronic "interruptibility" of women's existence, a concern of Martineau's in her own life and work and in her writing about the status of women, shapes a literary ethic that more appropriately reflects women's writing than the model employed by male writers and critics as the standard of measurement. While as a "universal" model the Aristotelian standard applied to women's writing leads at best to charges of appropriation or linguistic cross-dressing and at worst to the accusation that women simply cannot write, a woman-centered epistemology—by definition "contextual and relational" (Donovan 1984, 108) as well as process-oriented—promises more adequately to accommodate the work of Harriet Martineau, to which the epistolary genre is essential.

## Toward a Theory of Epistolary Writing

Of all genres, the novel—said to be Martineau's singular failure—offers the richest source through which to explore these issues. Studies in novel theory attribute its development to the custom of letter writing, demonstrated by the early trend in epistolary novels.[8] Some of the most representative novels in English are structured around letter formats, like Samuel

Richardson's *Pamela* (1740–1741), Fanny Burney's *Evelina* (1778), and Mary Shelley's *Frankenstein* (1818), while Austen's novels (like *Pride and Prejudice* [1813], which was originally an epistolary novel) rely heavily on the epistolary device to promote the plot. Other important textual influences on the novel include biography and autobiography, history, travel writing, and journalism, all of which Martineau produced throughout her career. Thus she employed the forms contributing to the novel without ever fully achieving (to her satisfaction, at least) a synthesis of them, in a sense writing *around* the genre without writing comfortably from *within* it. *Deerbrook*, although a perfectly respectable novel and an influential one, is stilted and stiff in its aim to conform with the accepted conventions of domestic romance novels, whereas her other, comparatively experimental writing enjoys a freedom and flexibility reflected in its superior writing quality and vibrant energy.

Yet the development of the novel as a distinct literary genre, with its association to women writers and its claims to realism, bears no small relation to Martineau's writing. Although her greatest strengths as a writer do not rest with novel writing per se, her "didactic fiction" series (which might be termed "novelettes") are credited with playing a pivotal role in the development of the modern novel. Dickens's *Hard Times* (1854) is clearly indebted to "A Manchester Strike" (1832), even to the doomed, downtrodden Stephen Blackpool, the counterpart to Martineau's William Allen; and I have already noted Martineau's literary influence on Gaskell, Brontë, Eliot, and Stowe, whose work represents the continued evolution of the genre's development. After *Deerbrook*, she concluded that the difficulties of creating and sustaining a plot from the omniscient viewpoint presented literary challenges beyond her powers and decided she was not to be a novelist. But despite the distinction she attempted to establish here, the omniscient viewpoint is also required to write histories, biographies, and autobiographies, as well as journalism, all of which she managed with great skill.[9]

Although Martineau employed the epistolary device only sparingly in her fiction writing, she proved to be an inveterate letter writer throughout her life. The literary connections are suggestive, particularly in view of her assertion that nonfiction writing, such as history and journalism, blunted her skills as a fiction writer; she claimed to be keen to return to fiction writing but questioned her ability to retrieve and cultivate the necessary skills. Some critics argue that her didacticism compromises the imaginativeness essential for good fiction writing—as in the *Illustrations of Political Economy*, for instance, whose passages of literary eloquence are punctuated by dutifully instructive precepts, suggesting either an author in conflict with herself, two distinct genres in conflict with each other, or both. But didacticism has always been part of the novel genre and continues to be so today: "Didacticism is a standard feature of the novel, early and late, and the rhetoric associated with didactic aims remains crucial to its tone, pace, and effects. . . . [I]ts aggressive attitude toward readers and its critical view of contemporary social mores—both products of didacticism—played a vital role in the emergence of the species" (J. Hunter 55). Clearly, however, as her career as a social reform writer developed, Martineau thought it more efficacious to subordinate didactic fiction to "serious" nonfiction, rather than the reverse.

By the mid-1840s, she articulated her conviction that social-problem writing more directly accomplished its goal through nonfiction rather than fiction; on the topic of game laws, she wrote: "I positively refuse to write *fiction* on a subject on which my heart is so sore. . . . Fiction is not the appropriate vehicle for what I want to utter." Similarly, to publisher Edward Moxon she expressed her unwillingness "to make fictions of harassing human miseries. . . . It goes against me, in every way, so to trade in griefs for the profit of literature."[10] Nevertheless, she did go on to write and publish *Forest and Game Law Tales* (1845–46), but the series enjoyed only a lukewarm reception, testifying to the author's struggle to reconcile fiction and realism with her narrative purpose and humanistic aim. By 1859, her commitment to realism in writing was firm, seen in her response to Nightingale's suggestion that they model their sanitary reform project after the *Illustrations of Political Economy:* "Society has outgrown illustration by fiction, it appears to me. . . . Society is now more solid, more practical, and more accustomed to political topics than 1/4 of a century ago. . . . Nothing but grave facts would suit our national mood."[11] Her words emphasize that her primary commitment was to "political topics" and to whichever genre best accomplished disseminating them in the public realm.

A pronounced quality throughout much of Martineau's writing is the autobiographical origins of many of her topics. So marked is this tendency that she seemed to regard it as her mission to transform her private experiences or, at least, the personal value system resulting from them, into instructive texts for public consumption. Such a compulsion for self-assessment and for recording and publishing one's experiences stems from a variety of influences, according to novel theorists, from religious and confessional to self-justification and the desire to instruct. Daniel Defoe's character Robinson Crusoe, notes J. Paul Hunter, once conscious of the implications of his island exile, kept a journal of his experiences; his completed narrative, consisting of a "revision, retelling, and summary from a perspective later in life," combines his immediate impressions (the journal) with the memories surfacing in retrospect, edited and polished for clarity (1990, 46). Offering an unlikely but relevant analogy to Martineau, Defoe was also a Dissenter; under that influence, "the awareness of recorded experience, habits of self-examination, and repeated readings of life experiences in quest of meaningful patterns clearly affected the way he organized things when he came to write lives, factual and fictional" (312). Hunter clarifies the links between epistolary writing, journaling or diary writing, autobiography, and the demands of periodicals writing: "The epistolary mode masks somewhat the essentially autobiographical strategy. . . . [W]riting-to-the-moment originates in the diaristic impulse." Journalism, Martineau's particular forte, best captured for public viewing this sense of "writing-to-the-moment"; therefore "it is no accident that journalism and the novel . . . got their impetus primarily from Protestantism in general and Dissent in particular" (199).

Unlike the fictional Crusoe and unlike most real writers, Martineau rejected the practices of revision, editing, or even recopying, which was at times a cause for worry when sending the only existing manuscript copy through the mail. I have argued that several activities served as substitutes for such practices, each affording her a means of rehearsing ideas and expressions prior to committing them to print. This process allowed her to clarify her positions on unfamiliar ideas, a rehearsal she sometimes found stressful: "Wrote five long letters," she recorded in 1836 in her journal. "Wrote too much, and had slight sick-headache. . . . Why do long and full letters always make my heart heavy? Is it the dislike to new and grand ideas . . . ? The amount is oppressive" (Chapman 1877, 207). Another form of rehearsal was verbal narrative, such as her Ambleside winter lecture series for the "workies" and storytelling for her visitors.[12] "Her conversation . . . was by no means monologue," wrote James Payn; "but her talk, when not engaged in argument, was, which is unusual in a woman, very anecdotal," resulting from the wide variety of acquaintances, experiences, and travels comprising Martineau's life (1884, 89). George Eliot, writing in 1877 after reading Martineau's *Autobiography*, recalls hearing some of its stories when she had visited Ambleside twenty-five years earlier: significantly, "almost in the very same words" as the written version. Eliot prefers the oral versions to the printed because "they were all the better for being told in her silvery voice. She was a charming talker" (Cross 1885, 3:249–50). Storytelling seems an unlikely gift for a deaf writer, yet Eliot's point illustrates the importance of dress rehearsals, verbal and nonverbal, to Martineau's idiosyncratic mode of composition, contrasting with the more conventional devices of drafting and revising.

The primacy of these alternative modes of composition, then, indicates that they served as a drafting stage for works intended for publication; the same is true of much of her writing, a survey of which reveals that her narrative persona was continually refining itself throughout her career. Martineau's autobiography, for example, ostensibly reconstructs her life from the harried perspective of a fifty-three-year-old woman who believed death would strike at any moment, and she aims to set the record straight before it does. That it was written at a rapid pace, then printed privately and stored for posthumous distribution, prevented the benefits and pitfalls of revision and eliminated the threat of editorial tampering with her account after her death. Yet we also know that she made several earlier attempts at autobiographical writing—in 1831 and the early 1840s, as well as through private journals and letters and in 1849's *Household Education*—all of which might be regarded as early drafts of the final *Autobiography*. Similarly, as I will discuss later in this chapter, such publications as "Letter to the Deaf," *Life in the Sickroom, Letters on Mesmerism, Letters from Ireland,* and *Letters on the Laws of Man's Nature and Development* are also in part autobiographical. Even in examples of seemingly spontaneous composition, then, Martineau's previous writings may be seen as a rehearsal, a kind of drafting, for the definitive versions offered for publication.[13]

Ruth Perry argues that the eighteenth century's preference for realism "dictated that much fiction be framed as first person writing: diaries, journals, travelogues, confessions, memoirs, autobiographies, and letters. . . . [L]etters were a very significant part of the written culture" (1980, xi–xii). Such writing reflects the ethic of self-evaluation and, far from hubristic, accords with the values of realism and social progress. Letter writing was especially amenable to "the scope and expectations of a woman's life" (68) with its chronic interruptibility, even during periods of invalidism. As a "medium for weaving the social fabric," Perry argues, "many private relationships came to be conducted in letters . . . [which were] understood as the repository for emotions usually enclosed by convention, the place to look for records of a person's secret doings" (69–70). The publication of such records, a popular trend in the nineteenth century, raised several issues, for example, privacy—which, "like virginity, invites violation"—and propriety: "It was considered indecent to have one's letters published" (70–71). Such influences and attitudes, still prominent during Martineau's early years, shaped her thinking about the destruction of her letters: not because she had anything to hide, but because she keenly felt the threat to privacy, decency, and trust posed by the potential for publication.

Similarly, Elizabeth Cook's *Epistolary Bodies* analyzes epistolary novels as "paradoxical crossroads of public print and private bodies" that are "never *not* political. . . . [I]t was perceived as a form freighted with dangerous implications" (1996, 173, 175). Applied to Martineau's epistolary writing, including correspondence as well as nonfiction prose structured as letters, "the private is thoroughly colonized by the public" (177), but the reverse is equally true, giving a double meaning to her plea, "(*entre nous,* please)." For example, the Martineau-Nightingale correspondence moved easily between private health concerns and state secrets involving the War Office: the latter, not the former, being regarded as information *entre nous* only. In contrast, Martineau's American correspondence ranged between family news and the latest political developments in the Civil War, prompting her to censor carefully, in this instance, the former in order to convey the latter to the British reading public. This "double perspective genre" constitutes "a new kind of subjectivity, a new way of being a self. . . . [T]he new private subject could now be implicated in other discourses as well, even those that appear to belong to a domain of public knowledge" like political economy, history, and sociology (178).

Valerie Sanders argues that the importance of letters in Martineau's life is linked with her early retreat, if not entirely from public life, then at least from easy accessibility:

[She] remained both inside and outside the political and literary establishment: . . . she preserved an ideological, and later, geographical, distance from party officials and institutional gatherings. She used the private letter to do business, drop hints, and perform behind-the-scenes manoeuvres. . . . In that respect, the letters throw further light on the strategies adopted by Victorian women who were debarred from active participation in running the country, but who were, nonetheless, politically influential. (1990, xiv)

Aside from the obvious political influences and machinations accomplished through her immense correspondence, two other factors require consideration here and to quite different ends: first, her concern that the trust shared between correspondents not be threatened by fear of publication on either side, and second, that the nonfiction prose writing published in letter form—so explicitly defying the public/private genre boundary—is also "never *not* political."

## "Freedom of epistolary speech"

The phrase frequently repeated throughout her personal correspondence, *entre nous,* heightens the sense of voyeurism with which we read letters never intended for public viewing. One of the first surprises confronting a Martineau scholar is the abundance of correspondence that survived her insistence that it be destroyed. Several collections are quite large, for instance that at the University of Birmingham, which houses approximately seventeen hundred pieces in its Harriet Martineau papers; the Speck Collection at the Bancroft Library holds over five hundred pieces, and the British Library, the National Library of Scotland, and the University of Keele Library hold hundreds more. Smaller collections exist in library manuscript collections and county record offices throughout the United Kingdom and America. What makes these numbers so surprising is that they represent only a portion of what she actually sent and received throughout her life. It is anyone's guess how many correspondents obeyed her edict to destroy her letters and to what extent, although the quantity of letters preserved is quite astonishing, proving that Martineau's private correspondence in itself constitutes a major portion of her productivity as a writer.

Fortunately for Martineau scholars, the failure of her appeals to individual ethics, to social morality, and even to the "sanction of the law" (Martineau 1983, 1:7) in this matter yields documents that shed important light on a figure whose life has been in most respects an open book. Leaving aside the possibility that less scrupulous correspondents might attempt to capitalize on Martineau's fame by publishing or selling her letters,[14] we are fortunate indeed that so many recipients, recognizing the loss to posterity of this valuable resource, quietly preserved them despite her edict. Her extant letters offer insights—and never to Martineau's disadvantage—not afforded by reading her autobiography alone.

Martineau's concern about the significance of letters was evident long before fame brought an added dimension to the issue. An 1827 letter to Helen Martineau illustrates an early awareness of her epistolary persona: "May I trust you to keep my letters to yourself, and to forgive all marks of weakness you may find in them?" (Sanders 1990, 11). As the characters Dora Sullivan and Anne Lebrocq demonstrate, putting pen to paper can have profound political consequences, a point also illustrated by the quality of letter writing by American women: Americans "may travel over the whole world, and find no country but their own . . . where women write miserable letters, almost universally, because it is a settled matter that it is unsafe to commit oneself on paper" (Martineau 1837, 251). Knowing, as she did, that in some southern states the death sentence awaited those publishing anti-slavery propaganda—like William Lloyd Garrison and Martineau herself—and having had to hide her journals, letters, and papers when her life was threatened with vigilante "justice," Martineau understood that the power of the printed word is more than a political and ideological issue: it can also be a matter of life and death.

Although she was always a prolific letter and journal writer, such self-histories assumed greater significance when she became ill during the late 1830s. Indicating that her condition was serious enough to consider the fate of her papers, she confided in an 1843 letter to William Fox her renewed commitment to completing her autobiography and to urging the destruction of her letters. "My secret is that I expect to leave behind me perhaps the amplest account of a life ever written," she wrote, with more ambition than might be expected from an invalid; "I have taken measures to prevent my private letters being ever printed: but I shall leave otherwise the fullest possible revelation of myself. . . . It makes me ill,—the efforts, but I feel it to be as clear a duty as any that ever lay before me" (Sanders 1990, 69). Her obligation to the reading public included not only producing an accurate account of her "somewhat remarkable" life but also preserving trust with her correspondents, with whom she shared an intimacy threatened by the period's growing trend to publish private letters. Thus for her the writing of the autobiography and the destruction of her letters were part of the same process.

Another letter from this period more clearly articulates her concern with delineating the boundaries between what she wrote for publication and what must be preserved *entre nous*. "My letters are . . . talk,—a flowing out of the moment to you and the fire," she wrote to Henry Crabbe Robinson. "I do hope you don't keep my letters. I preserve few or none . . . and my correspondents generally, knowing my feeling about letters,—that they are *talk*, and should be treated as such,—are kind enough to give me perfect freedom in writing by destroying my letters. . . . My letters are all *talk* and I could not write them if they were not to be sacred to the friend to whom they are addressed" (Sanders 1990, 71–72). The depth of Martineau's commitment to this issue was intimately connected with the writing of her memoirs: "I maintain this ground very firmly, partly for the sake of my own freedom of epistolary speech. . . . I may possibly be found to have sufficiently provided for society knowing what it likes of me, without having prostituted my private correspondence to that end." She will do her duty to posterity, in other words, but through a memoir of her own writing, not by *prostituting* her correspondence—a remarkable word choice emphasizing the tenacity of her views on this point.

Later that same year, she wrote what might conceivably have been sent to all her correspondents:

> Permit me to give notice to you . . . that I have made testamentary provision against any private letters of mine being ever printed. You know, of course, that by our law no one can print private letters except the writer,—or by the writer's consent. My [executor] has directions to see the law observed in my case; and I give notice of this to my correspondents, that they may be protected, by the expression of my desire, against all solicitation after my death.

She admits she has little real control over past letters, although she hints darkly "in regard to my future letters,—which depend on this condition being observed." She insists that her concern is not with having inadvertently exposed herself to ridicule or condemnation in her letters: "Suffice it to say that it arises from no care in regard to my own reputation,—which I never tried to gain or to keep, and shall not begin to trouble myself about now."[15] Instead, her concern is to preserve the spirit of trust and confidentiality between correspondents that would be destroyed by the threat of publication on either side. Her awareness of the potential for exploitation is keen: "My volume [autobiography] would show you my principle and practice about letters," she wrote to Bulwer-Lytton, "—that I keep none without a recognized reason,—(*knowing* the press to be in wait for my going, and being resolved to assert the true morality)" (Sanders 1990, 85). Proving the accuracy of her insights about the significance of her letters, her "interdict" generated quite a stir among friends, family, and other correspondents. Some complied with the request to burn her letters, while others refused overtly and some, as extant collections indicate, covertly; her brother James took the novel approach of destroying the letters after he secretly made a shorthand transcription of them. Given his ambivalence toward his sister and the potential this secret code affords for censorship, the credibility of James's shorthand version is questionable. Martineau herself validates my caution on this point in an 1843 letter to Fox asserting that she will write her autobiography to replace the letters she urged correspondents to destroy: "I wish to keep my mind clear from all family influences, and have therefore not told even James;—nor shall" (Sanders 1990, 69).[16] But although this first serious brush with mortality prompted her to take aggressive steps on behalf of her papers, her reprieve from ill health and recuperation of physical vigor (about 1844–1845) led her to return to active life with relish. Thoughts of death and memoirs retreated, for a time, preempted by new travels, new literary projects, and a new home.

The mid-1850s mark the second major period of invalidism serious enough to confine her to the sickroom, where she was preoccupied with managing her health and with completing and printing the autobiography. Valerie Sanders claims that Martineau's autobiography "comes closest to the open confession of her thoughts, which a modern audience's familiarity with the mode has made both desirable and more readily attainable" (1986a, 69). But I had a different response to the *Autobiography:* true, Martineau's persona in her memoirs is engaging and charming, and her narrative punctuated by anecdotal name-dropping interspersed with the unfolding of major events in her life, but there is a lack of intimacy in the autobiography. Although her design was to present a formal, retrospective account of her life, including the controversial episodes she did not shrink from articulating, she nevertheless maintains a distance in this narrative, where we least expect it.

Insofar as the *Autobiography* is more public than private in its orientation, it is significant that she offers this account, over which she exerts absolute control, specifically as a substitute for her letters. The opening pages of the *Autobiography*—the very positioning of her discussion attesting to its importance—present her views, to a public audience, about private correspondence, again asserting that her concern is not with reputation: "I have no solicitude about fame, and no fear of my reputation of any sort being injured by the publication of any thing I have ever put upon paper. My opinions and feelings have been remarkably open to the world; and my position has been such as to impose no reserves on a disposition naturally open and communicative" (1983, 1:3). Her objection to the publication of letters is based on a more subtle point than reticence about self-revelation: that of honor.

> Epistolary correspondence is written speech. . . . The most valuable conversation, and *that which best illustrates character,* is that which passes between two friends. . . . How could human beings ever open their hearts and minds to each other, if there were no privacy guaranteed by principles and feelings of honour? (1983, 1:3–4; emphasis added)

Given her insistence on her letters' destruction, Martineau's assertion that the content of private correspondence is what "best illustrates character" verifies the selectiveness I have detected in the *Autobiography*. Although in the spirit of self-assessment she presents herself as one who is "naturally open and communicative," her characteristic willingness to publish accounts of personal experiences does have certain limits after all.

"From my youth upwards I have felt that it was one of the duties of my life to write my autobiography" (1983, 1:1). So begins the two-volume work presented as the definitive account of Martineau's life, work, and relationships. Once she realized that hers is a "somewhat remarkable" life that ill health threatened to cut short, Martineau felt obliged to provide posterity with an official record of her life. To that end, "I made up my mind to interdict the publication of my private letters"; she spends most of the next eight pages defending her position: a curious introduction to an autobiography and therefore worth our attention. Martineau devoted countless hours to her written correspondence (Charlotte Brontë attested to Martineau's daily habit of writing letters until midnight), which she then regarded as a disposable aspect of her oeuvre. By considering the importance of the epistolary genre to this study of primary themes in Martineau's life and work, my guiding question is, what can we learn from this significant portion of her work that was not intended for public view and that was, to an indeterminate degree, systematically destroyed?

Knowing her tenacity on this issue, one reads her private correspondence with a sense of guilt, even 125 years after her death; but her assertion that letters reveal "that which best illustrates character" presents a temptation difficult to resist. The letters yield little to compromise her reputation and much, in fact, to recommend her. She was most concerned about the special trust assumed between correspondents who rely on each other's discretion as well as on an appreciation for the context from which one writes. Private correspondence is based on a mutual understanding of audience; clearly, trust is breached when a letter intended for a private audience is exposed, out of context, to public view or is written—or received—with a view toward publication. Condemning the "importunities of hunters of material," she notes that other contemporary public figures have taken steps to secure their private correspondence from the public domain and regrets that concerns about this issue cause some to forego letter writing altogether. It is time, she concludes, "to bear testimony against such an infringement on personal liberty" (1983, 1:5) as the threat to "epistolary freedom" posed by potential publication.

Martineau was prepared to confront the objections she anticipates being raised against her perspective. To the argument that she owes the world her story, she offers her autobiography; to suggestions that, like other writers, she maintain control by arranging for the publication of her letters herself, she returns to the analogy with conversation and authenticity in relationships: "What were the letters worth, as letters, when these arrangements became known? What would fireside conversation be worth, as confidential talk, if it was known that the speaker meant to make it a newspaper article the next day?" (1983, 1:5). She also refused to leave the issue unresolved, to be dealt with by her survivors and executors, because "it is my business to assert for myself" (6). As for the profit motive, there are plenty of "consenting" letter writers ready to answer this demand; for her part, Martineau claims the "sanction of every principle of integrity, and every feeling of honour and delicacy," and if that fails, she will resort to the law (7). On that ominous note, she abruptly shifts to a capsule history of her family tree before ending the introduction and beginning the story of her life.

Given Martineau's tenacity on this issue, her profound regard for Maria Weston Chapman was demonstrated not only in her entrusting Chapman with the writing of her official biography but in providing her with private journals, letters, and other papers to do so. Commenting on the centrality of correspondence to her friend's life and work, Chapman marveled when "the records of a lifetime—and such a lifetime!—[were] placed in my hands and at my discretion" (Chapman 1877, 270). Martineau sent her the following packets of letters, marked "For publication if you wish it":

1. Accounts and correspondence with booksellers.

2. Letters of pecuniary business.

3. Letters of moral business.

4. Letters from strangers or otherwise curious.

5. Letters from deceased persons.

6. Letters to be returned unopened.

7. Correspondence with reviews and newspapers.

8. Letters of literary business.

9. Letters of family business.

10. Letters of Testimony and American Intercourses.

The very organization and quantity of these papers indicates their importance to Martineau, seen in the scrupulous care with which she categorized them. Chapman quotes Martineau's 11 June 1855 response to her request to employ the Chapman-Martineau correspondence in the *Memorials* as well:

> You desire my permission to publish, after my death, certain letters of mine to yourself. . . . I give you my sanction with entire willingness, and I hope you will employ it as freely as you like. . . . Such use of them is perfectly consistent with the principle on which I have forbidden, in my will, the unauthorized publication of my private correspondence. That interdict is grounded on the objection that all freedom and security in epistolary correspondence are destroyed by the liability that unreserved communication may hereafter become public. No such danger is incurred when writer and receiver agree to make known what they have said to each other. . . . You

have, therefore, my full permission to make any use you please of anything I have written to you. (294–95)

Like her letters, Martineau's journals demonstrate "on every page the fullest proof that it was kept for her own use and behoof exclusively; and she would then have been startled at the thought of its being seen by other eyes or after times; and, excepting only as given by the friend to whose judgment she entrusted it, this feeling was paramount as long as she lived" (Chapman 1877, 187). Chapman relied freely on the journals and letters to compile the *Memorials,* after which the fate of these documents became a mystery; whether destroyed or preserved, they are not available to today's scholars.[17]

Whereas Chapman's intense loyalty to her friend suggests she would dispose of these materials as asked, her keen awareness of Martineau's significance to American and British history would have made her, at the very least, strongly tempted to preserve what constitutes some of the most important of Martineau's writings. Chapman cannot resist expressing her regret that she has access to material designated by Martineau as off limits:

> I regret inexpressibly that Miss Martineau's long journalising letters of this period cannot, in consistency with her introductory principle, be made public. . . . [O]ne cannot help wishing this whole collection came within the terms she has laid down. Every letter is full of charm and instruction. . . . [T]hey might all go to press as they stand, without a word of omission. They show, not the hidden springs of life, but the severely beautiful life itself. (25–26)

Although Chapman was clearly biased in favor of her friend, reading the letters that did survive validates her suggestion that Martineau is perhaps better known through her private letters, written spontaneously and without fear of disclosure, than through all the texts written expressly for publication.[18] Chapman longed to make use of this "material for a most interesting and instructive volume," but her scruples gain the upper hand: "my instructions left no doubt. . . . [I]t is a self-confidence as rare as well deserved, when one on the confines of age can thus confide to another's eye the records of youth. But she knew they were all right when they were written" (89–90).

The very structure of the *Memorials,* organized primarily around excerpts from Martineau's journals and letters, supplemented by memorials, letters, reviews, eulogies, and obituaries from correspondents and with minimal commentary from Chapman, marks this volume as of a piece with the *Autobiography:* even in Chapman's biography, Martineau continues to speak for herself. From the introduction, consisting of two letters from Martineau to Chapman, this reliance on private letters is clear. Martineau's 24 January 1855 letter announces her conviction of impending death, serving in effect as her farewell: "my beloved friend, take my blessing on yourself and your labours, and my assurance that my knowledge of you has been one of the greatest privileges and pleasures of my life. . . . My life has been a full and vivid one,—so that I . . . am abundantly satisfied with my share in the universe" (2–3). The second letter, dated 26 March 1855, expresses Martineau's concern with finishing the *Autobiography* before her death and asks Chapman "to render the last services to me" (4) in case she cannot. She justifies choosing Chapman because of her "peculiar qualifications to treat of the whole remarkable American period of her life, which had so largely modified all that remained," although she worries that Chapman might find it "injurious to the cause" of abolitionism for her to be involved with "the biography of 'such an infidel as herself.'"[19] But Chapman makes clear her suitability for this task: "there was nothing she could ask that I could refuse: I was wholly at her disposition, living or dying." Employing the imagery of needleworking so appropriate to Martineau's story, Chapman concludes: "Thus it was that it became my duty to take up the parallel thread of her exterior life,—to gather up and co-ordinate from the materials placed in my hands the illustrative facts and fragments."

By 1859, when Martineau, her health improved, was in the midst of one of the most productive literary periods of her life, the *Autobiography* had been completed and stored for posthumous distribution: as it turned out, a full twenty-one years before her death. The stand articulated in the opening pages of the autobiography receives public airing in a *Daily News* article condemning the publication of letters as an "annihilation of the highest order of conversation" (22 March 1859). She blames this trend for the general decline in the quality of letter writing, due to fear of exposure on both sides: "What had appeared to be the spontaneous utterance of heart to heart and mind to mind was in fact a *production* in the writer's eyes. From that moment . . . [letters became] so many pages of authorship—very clever and very interesting, but with no confidential character in them." Prophetically insightful, as always, she wonders whether the "institution of private epistolary correspondence" is to be preserved or permitted to deteriorate, prostituted to Mammon or fame. Judging by the virtual disappearance of the custom of letter writing in the postmodern era, the latter proves to be the case.

A survey of Martineau's letters to regular correspondents reveals her to be an astute businesswoman, a committed social reformist, and a loyal friend. Her letters to publishers (who were exclusively male) demonstrate her clarity about business and financial matters, which she dictated authoritatively, although her manner was typically diplomatic. She was as much at ease asking for outstanding royalties checks as she was negotiating publishing contracts or reprints; she sometimes dictated her work's retail price out of a concern that the "workies" be able to afford her books. Such correspondence demonstrates her sharp business sense while evidencing an awareness that she was too famous and too lucrative a commodity to be trifled with merely because she was a woman. Other correspondence, for

instance to Lord Grey (1844) and Lady Grey (1848), demonstrates a similarly diplomatic tone, but again without compromising her principles of social reform. Writing to Lady Grey to protest Lord Grey's parliamentary
speech on the game laws, Martineau argues against the "old aristocratic
privilege which so encroaches on the welfare of the public," adding pointedly: "I need not observe that the hope of our country rests on the middle
classes." To Lady Grey's reply regretting their difference of opinion, Martineau responds: "We do indeed differ widely: . . . You consider the House
of Commons the people, I see. I think it dangerously far from being any
representation of them." These letters reveal a writer working aggressively
to influence public policy makers on behalf of the unrepresented classes;
Martineau is both respectful and firm, asserting her pleas for reform with a
vigor and tenacity free of false flattery about class differences. Her inadver-
tent quip at the expense of the aristocracy just days before the 1848 French
Revolution—"My talk happened to be of revolutions. I hope she will not
think I had a hand in it"—does little to thaw Lady Grey's coolness toward
Harriet's democratic ideology.[20]

Similarly, her correspondence with Florence Nightingale (from 1858 to
1871) is also highly revelatory, featuring letters illustrating the mutual respect and professionalism of women drawn together by ideological similarities. Their correspondence traces a relationship that spanned the personal
and professional realms, indicating what women can accomplish when
they assume authority and responsibility and work together for the public
good. The Martineau-Nightingale correspondence was remarkable from its
inception, from the intensely personal discussions about philosophical
preparation for dying (both were seriously ill at the time) to debate about
how best to frame their literary collaboration on public health reform.
Nightingale pleaded for the confidentiality of politically sensitive War Office reports, statistics, and officials' names; Martineau vowed to protect her
privacy, since "a future is more important in your case,—for the world's
benefit, I mean." Nightingale's concern with anonymity stemmed from her
recognition that Martineau's style was too distinctive to conceal from public scrutiny: "I do believe there is not the smallest chance of anything you
write not being discovered," Nightingale wrote, advising: "If therefore you
will not think me wholly impertinent . . . I would say, do not write anything which, you do not wish to have known, is by you. . . . Whatever _you_
write will be _known._" Interestingly, Nightingale's letters, like Martineau's,
were often signed with some variation of "Please burn this, ever yours living or dying." Martineau regrets the necessity of doing what she herself requires of her correspondents: "In all ways your letter is precious. . . . Yet—I
am going to burn it, I ought, and I must and will: and I am not likely to
forget any of it. . . . With all sympathy, love, and reverence, yours."[21]

Martineau's long friendship with Fanny Wedgwood also incorporated
both private and professional realms, recorded in letters filled with shared
personal griefs and joys and infused with references to people and events

spanning thirty-five years (1834–1869). Editor Elisabeth Arbuckle notes that the over 120 letters from Martineau to Fanny Wedgwood constitute one of the largest collections of Martineau correspondence to a single person. Although Fanny had apparently promised to destroy Harriet's letters, she instead preserved them, perhaps unable to resist the temptation Chapman confronted. This collection offers the most extended evidence that all of Harriet Martineau's correspondence typically mixed business matters, family news, and personal health reports with *entre nous* asides, usually consisting of political critiques, making such writing her most authentic autobiography.

Near the end of her life, the ailing Martineau wrote to her niece Spring that her doctor urged her to give up writing altogether. *"That* I really cannot do; but I must try to be brief to my correspondents, and self-denying to myself; and you will all understand and excuse my short comings."[22] From age twenty-five, when young and physically vital, to age seventy-five, when old age interfered increasingly with her customary activities, Martineau wrote compelling letters yet modestly begged forgiveness for her "short comings" as a correspondent. That her affinity for the epistolary form carried over into her nonfiction prose writing intended for publication offers an alternative example of the significance of this format to her "need of utterance."

## "Letters are the thing"

Writing to Justice Story from on board the *Milwaukee* on Lake Huron, Martineau expressed her regret that their parting was not in person but through a letter. "But there is a sort of pleasure in doing it in writing," she added, "I suppose because there is, at the same time, a feeling that it is not really parting, since this means of communication remains."[23] Her words indicate an early preference for letters as a medium in some ways superior to direct communication for conveying emotion and meaning, for connecting with others despite temporal and spatial distances, and for the consolation offered by letters' promise of relational continuity. Accordingly, some of Martineau's most significant and revelatory publications are those written in epistolary format, like her 1834 "Letter to the Deaf," published in *Tait's Magazine*. Without preface or editorial explanation of any kind, the article is addressed to "My Dear Companions" and signed, "with deep respect," by "Your affectionate sister, Harriet Martineau." The aim of this piece is consistent with the deeply ingrained habits of self-reflection and analysis stemming from her Dissenting background, an impulse dictating that what one learns from this process should be shared for the public's benefit. The author's humility and frank advice for managing deafness poignantly clarify her vigorous assertion of control over her letters as intimately linked with her inability to hear. Martineau's "need of utterance," in other words, prompted her to produce an impressive amount of writing, both public and private; but her deafness presented her with social complications in which privacy (whispered confidences) and the subtle nuances of verbal conversations were inaccessible to her. Socially, her ear trumpet—an imperfect but crucial link with the auditory world—served at best to discourage confidentiality and at worst to dissuade people from talking with her altogether. In light of her assertion that epistolary correspondence is "the most valuable conversation, and that which best illustrates character" (1983, 1:3–4), Martineau's deafness heightened her concern to preserve epistolary privacy, writing letters without restraint being one of the great joys in her virtually silent existence.[24]

Martineau's motivation for writing "Letter to the Deaf" stems, she claims, from the *inadequacy* of ordinary conversation to convey her thoughts on deafness: "it never occurred to me to print what I had to say, till it was . . . urged upon me as a duty. I adopt this method as the only means of reaching you all; and *I am writing with the freedom which I should use in a private letter to each of you*" (1834c, 174; emphasis added). Though writing in a public forum, she excludes from her audience "those who do not belong to our fraternity," adding that in future she might "tell the public our secrets," but for now "I address only you." What follows is a remarkable example of what we might now term self-help literature. Martineau's conspiratorial tone—"our fraternity," "our secrets"—invites active participation in this unofficial club comprised of those typically excluded from social intercourse because of deafness. Gentle yet firm, compassionate yet insistent, she urges her readers to take responsibility for improving the quality of their lives by making the best of what resources they have. Her own experience with deafness qualifying her to speak on these issues with authority, she anticipates protests against her suggestions as excuses to be overcome assertively.

Martineau understands the social limitations as well as the psychological distress deafness engenders, but she refuses to accept either as an excuse not to participate fully in life. She acknowledges but rejects the impulse toward isolation—"The first thing which we are disposed to give up is the very last which we ought to relinquish—society" (175)—and urges readers to put aside their vanity and adapt the use of hearing devices wherever possible, since "quiet is our greatest enemy, (next to darkness, when the play of the countenance is lost to us)" (178). But she concedes that the emotional stamina required to participate in society may be too difficult for some, who are better off at home, since "Nothing is worth the sacrifice of your repose of mind." Deafness can even be an asset by providing "opportunity for meditation, one of the chief means of wisdom" (179): a "privilege" sages strive, often in vain, to attain. She concludes by urging readers to look squarely and honestly at "our lot": "The worst is, either to sink under the trial, or to be made callous by it. The best is, to be as wise as is possible under a great disability, and as happy as is possible under a great privation."

A similar piece of writing is her substantial dedication to *Life in the Sickroom: Essays by an Invalid* (1844), a work produced as a result of her illness during the Tynemouth period. As an invalid writing to other invalids, Martineau encourages readers to transcend self-pity and to assume responsibility for managing their environment. But what interests me more than the content of the essays is the book's lengthy dedication, structured as a letter to an anonymous recipient ("To ———") from an anonymous writer ("Yours, ———"). The dedication employs devices introduced in "Letter to the Deaf," including the appeal to a fraternity of shared experience, and invites readers to regard the book as a conversation among people whose circumstances permit only indirect, vicarious contact. To the generic "you" of invalids in the general public, reading her advice from the privacy of their individual sickrooms, she wrote: "the whole book is truly a conversation with you. I shall . . . trust to the most infallible force in the universe,—human sympathy,—to bring these words under your eye" (xv). Should her words prove to be a comfort, she concludes, "I may have the honour of being your nurse, though I am myself laid low,—though hundreds of miles are between us, and though we can never know one another's face or voice." The circumstances of *Life in the Sickroom*'s composition—she claims the book "wrote itself"—emphasizes a spontaneity that characterizes much of Martineau's best writing: "It was done . . . without pause, without waiting for a word,—without altering a syllable. I had the M.S. preserved, for a legacy, and some day I may show you how a book writes itself. . . . I never for one moment wavered" (Arbuckle 1983, 70).

*Life in the Sickroom* also rehearses Martineau's concern with epistolary privacy, which she regarded a more significant issue for invalids than for the rich and famous. But not even fame justifies public intrusion into one's private realm: "If the people of note in society were inquired of, they would say that the privilege—the right—of privacy of epistolary correspondence now exists only for the obscure" (91). In her transparent guise as anonymous author of this volume, she asserts: "I would keep the old and precious privacy,—the inestimable right of every one who has a friend and can write to him;—I would keep our written confidence from being made biographical material, as anxiously as I would keep our spoken conversation from being noted down for the good of society. I would keep the power of free speech under all the influences of life and fate,—and leave Biography to exist or perish" (93–94). Her concern with this issue clearly predates the writing of the *Autobiography*, although it intensified during periods when her link with life seemed most fragile. The clarity with which she dictated the standards governing publication of her memoirs illustrates her determination to leave a full account of her life while at the same time resisting the period's voyeuristic trend simply to publish one's correspondence as a substitute.

Martineau used letters for other book introductions as well. For example, her introduction to *Mind amongst the Spindles* (1845), produced by the cooperative of women sewing-factory workers in Lowell, Massachusetts, is a reprint of her 20 May 1844 letter to the book's editor. Illustrating the fine

quality of her letter writing—suitable for publication—as well as her unflagging support for this and other American experiments, her introduction begins warmly: "My dear friend— . . . in reading the 'Offering,' I saw
again in my memory the street of houses built by the earnings of the girls,
the church which is their property, and the girls themselves trooping to
the mill, with their healthy countenances, and their neat dress and quiet
manners." She recalls sitting with the women during Ralph Waldo Emerson's lecture, an opportunity she employed to study the effects of "double
work" (manual labor and intellectual pursuits) on the countenances of
these energetic young women. "There they sat, row behind row. . . . I
could not but feel my heart swell at the thought." The letter-introduction
concludes by emphasizing the importance of cultivating the mind, even
"amongst the spindles": all things are possible when workers "are so educated as to have the command of themselves and of their lot in life, which
is always and everywhere controlled by mind, far more than by outward
circumstances. I am very truly yours, H. Martineau." This letter was
printed in the same year as *Life in the Sickroom,* with its similar message to
cultivate mind over matter.

A letter to abolitionist Elizabeth Pease concerning the split within the
abolitionist movement served as an introduction to John Collins's *Right and
Wrong among the Abolitionists of the United States* (1841). The value of this
letter, which addresses the rift threatening the stability of the abolitionist
movement, is emphasized by another printing, as an article in Chapman's
abolitionist annual, the *Liberty Bell* (1845). Although written in 1841, notes
Chapman, the relevance of Martineau's letter continues to be both timely
and timeless: "As long as the warfare then begun against the American Abolitionists, by the organization of a hostile society, and carried on under the
name of a 'Liberty Party,' shall continue, so long will this Letter be as useful
to the cause of the Slave, as it is beautiful and true in general principle, and
noble and faithful in individual deed" (Chapman 1845, 248).

The Pease letter expresses "a strong and painful interest" in impressing
a "sense of the duty of every one interested in the cause of the Negro—of
human freedom at large—to read and deeply meditate this piece of history." Anticipating a similar standoff in 1861 during her confrontation
with the Republican faction of the *National Anti-Slavery Standard,* Martineau warns that political posturing has no place in the abolitionist
movement, where the focus belongs on the emancipation of slaves. "If I
had a voice which would penetrate wherever I wished, I would ask, in the
depths of every heart that feels for the Slave, . . . whether, in declining to
do justice to the true friends of the Slave, . . . we may not be guilty of
treachery as fatal as compromising with his enemies." Therefore, it is "our
duty to withdraw our sympathy and countenance from our fellow-labor-
ers, . . . when they compromise the cause. It is our duty to expose their
guilt, when, by their act of compromise, they oppress and betray those
brethren whose nobleness is a rebuke to themselves." In the division be-

tween those abolitionists advocating change through the political system, complete with political parties and candidates, and the Garrisonians urging immediate, universal emancipation, Martineau declares her support for the latter by asking: "May we dare to call ourselves workers in the Anti-Slavery cause while thus deserting the chief of its apostles [Garrison] now living in the world?"

Although known for her influence in political circles and her writing on political topics, Martineau had clear reservations about the efficacy of politics as the best path to social reform in general and emancipation in particular, as this letter demonstrates. In a letter to Lord Brougham, Martineau praises "the non-political character" of American abolitionists as superior in terms of motivation: "The American Abolitionists . . . have succeeded admirably in giving its *highest* aspect to their cause,—that of *general humanity instead of national politics*" (emphasis added).[25] That slavery as a "national institution" is in inevitable decline, she continues, is owed primarily to "agencies outside of the political [arenas] of action," an idea emphasizing the grassroots activism of abolitionists, who privilege the will of the people over political posturing. As demonstrated by her willingness to criticize politicians and their institutions, Martineau's perspective on the inferiority of politics to human rights challenges the general readiness, in our era, to accept the political realm as the primary site through which social problems are perpetuated and through which change may be realized. For Martineau, the political realm was created to serve human interests, not, as is now common practice, the reverse.

Although it might seem that she thus employed the epistolary format because it was less taxing to her strength than other prose forms, the fact is that illness never stopped Martineau's tremendous literary output: the exception being her last years, when declining health due to old age curtailed but still did not eliminate her writing.[26] These letters illustrate the pervasiveness of the epistolary form throughout Martineau's work, writing characterized by spontaneity and naturalness yet infused with an authority and strong emotion that depends on privacy. As both private and public documents, letters demonstrate Martineau's strong commitment to these issues through language fueled with persuasive rhetorical energy. Her "freedom of epistolary speech," combined with her passion for the issues, shows that she mined this genre for all the linguistic power it afforded her to "talk" through the written word. In the case of letters printed as book introductions, the unique combination of Martineau's highly recognizable name, her enthusiasm for the topic, and the expectations normally signaled by the genre—a private arena, here made public—marks yet another example of her literary innovativeness.

Consistent with Martineau's impulse to share publicly truths gleaned from private experience, the publication of *Letters on Mesmerism* in 1845[27] signaled her triumph over the illness that had curtailed her active life for six years. Martineau turned to mesmerism at the suggestion of her physician and became a student and avid practitioner of the method when her health showed signs of improvement. The dramatic shift in her condition resulting in her return to an active life with redoubled vigor so inspired her that she of course shared her experiences by publishing them. According to the *Autobiography,* Martineau felt "compelled to publish" her carefully recorded account of the process, assuring readers that so objective and thorough was her record keeping of her case history that a "professional observer" declared that mesmerism was clearly responsible for her healing.

Martineau's preface to the second edition of *Letters on Mesmerism* begins by asserting that she offers this volume without revision, preferring to preserve "A faithful narrative of first impressions. . . . I see no reason to suppress any part of it" (v). Her desire to instruct or, at least, to bear witness, is as always a primary concern, although she has no intention of converting the closed-minded: "My aim is, what it always is in publishing, to utter what I know and think, secure of its reaching those whom it may concern, and uninterested as to its reception by those whom it does not" (vi). Rightly expecting to earn notoriety yet again for her "infidel" tendencies, she concludes that, to "conjecture or calculate" on the *Letters'* reception is, to her, an "intolerable" insolence in which she refuses to engage. She does predict that increased discussion of mesmerism, to which her book contributes, will serve to eliminate the medical establishment's prejudice: a prediction never fulfilled, as physicians' pressure to debunk this popular pseudo-science intensified.

That *Letters on Mesmerism* aroused "professional bigotry, and popular prejudice" (Martineau 1983, 2:194) stemmed, she argues with her usual sharp insight, from its challenge to the medical establishment. Attesting to its author's continued public influence, *Letters on Mesmerism* generated a storm of letters to newspaper editors from angry medical men condemning her implication that, whereas six years of conventional medical treatment did nothing to alter her condition, mesmerism almost instantly provided relief. Inwardly disgusted but outwardly cool under the pressure of such public scrutiny, Martineau wrote another letter, not to the newspapers but to a scientific journal, for which she was promptly accused of "rushing into print" (195). Public outrage greeted this audacious piece of "quackery," prompting some to speculate that Harriet Martineau had literally lost her fine, intellectual mind under pressure of prolonged illness.

Martineau's condition, an enlarged uterine tumor that pressed on her other organs, did not disappear as a result of mesmeric or any other treatment. It is now believed that the tumor may have somehow shifted or altered in size or shape, allowing her nearly instant relief from debilitating pain and discomfort of many years' duration. Since her enthusiasm for the practice of mesmerism waned over time, she perhaps later believed that her "cure" was simply a coincidence, which it was. This episode earned Martineau scorn and ridicule, prompting subsequent commentators to question her lack of discernment. But the mesmerism debacle is instructive in its demonstration of her fierce loyalty to controversial ideas that to her mind shed light on human progress. In this instance, her loyalties were misplaced, and the intensity with which she had courted notoriety (albeit unintentionally) shifted to other interests. Her conclusion to *Letters on Mesmerism* emphasizes a genuine humility and earnest desire to share her good fortune rather than to shock or antagonize:

> While regarding with shame all pride of intellect, and with fear the presumption of ignorance, I deeply feel that the truest humility is evinced by those who most simply accept and use the talents placed in their hands; and that the most childlike dependence upon the Creator appears in those who fearlessly apply the knowledge he discloses to the furtherance of that great consecrated object, the welfare of the family of man. (65)[28]

But these sentiments were lost in a flurry of public backlash that began with *Letters on Mesmerism,* intensified with *Eastern Life, Present and Past* (1848)—combining travel narrative and spiritual autobiography, the book exhibits "infidel tendencies"—and continued beyond *Letters on the Laws of Man's Nature and Development,* for which she was erroneously labeled an atheist. The primary institutions governing Victorian life—medicine, politics, the nuclear family, and religion—were all scrutinized by Harriet Martineau, who did not always set out to pose a threat to the hegemony, but who nearly always managed to present herself as such, however inadvertently. "Human pride and prejudice cannot brook discoveries which innovate upon old associations, and expose human ignorance," she observed; "and, as long as any thing in the laws of the universe remains to be revealed, there is a tolerable certainty that somebody will yet be persecuted, whatever is the age of the world" (1983, 2:199).

Martineau's concern to promote "the welfare of the family of man" motivated *Letters on the Laws of Man's Nature and Development* (1851), coauthored with Henry George Atkinson. Emphasizing Martineau's chief interests during this period, Elisabeth Arbuckle characterizes this volume as an examination of "metaphysical beliefs in the light of Baconian science and according to the phrenological and mesmeric findings of Henry Atkinson" (1983, 113). Martineau's collaboration with Atkinson resulted from their correspondence debating philosophical speculations through a question and answer format: her letters posed the questions, his letters supplied the answers. This seemingly gendered division of labor prompted some critics to charge that the intellectual Martineau demeaned herself by playing the pupil to the dilettante Atkinson, her master; but Atkinson retorted, "She was herself a master mind, and sat at the feet of no one" (Chapman 1877, 488).[29] Study of the letters reveals, in fact, that her role in this dialogue was far more complex in that her skills both as a thinker and a writer prove essential for giving order and shape to a discourse that is by its nature slippery and indeterminate.

Her preface stresses the book's origins—private correspondence—now edited and transcribed for public reading: "This book is in reality what it appears to be,—a correspondence between two friends. The responsibility for its publication is mine" (1851, v). She explains that these topics had long interested her and that finding a kindred spirit in Atkinson, so liberating to her philosophically, prompted her to break one of her own taboos—publication of private letters—for the public good: "Last year, I asked him to permit me to inquire of him, in some sort of sequence, about his researches into the nature and position of the Human Being; and the replies I have received seemed to me to require of us both the discharge of that great social duty,—to impart what we believe, and what we think we have learned. I therefore suggested the publication of our letters." Her justification is purely utilitarian: "Among the few things of which we can pronounce ourselves certain, is the obligation of inquirers after truth to communicate what they obtain." She is circumspect about what she hopes the book will accomplish, acknowledging that multiple volumes in treatise format would be better suited to these complex topics. The correspondents offer only one volume, and that is "merely expository," yet "I believe that it has substance and connection enough to make it of value in its actual shape. Such as it is, we send it forth" to those who "estimate truth and freedom as we do" (vi).[30]

Ambitiously, the Martineau-Atkinson letters address such topics as epistemology, the functioning of the senses and nervous system, the brain and its organization, brain abnormalities, knowledge and ideas, and science and theology. Underpinning all is a shift from an unquestioning faith in religious dogma to a trust in the laws of "Nature" (in other words, science), which places full responsibility for one's life, including spirituality, with the individual and in the mundane realm. Such responsibility is frightening, even blasphemous, to some, yet dizzyingly liberating to Martineau:

> And what a *feeling* it is,—that which grows up and pervades us when we have fairly returned to our obedience to Nature! What a healthful glow animates the faculties! what a serenity settles down upon the temper! . . . no more raptures and agonies of selfish hope and fear,—but sober certainty of reliance on the immutability of Nature's laws; and the lofty liberty that is found in obedience to them. (283)

Although she again declined to "calculate or conjecture" about the reception of the *Letters* (vi), Martineau was aware that the controversy surrounding her recent publications would be exacerbated by this volume: "It seemed to me probable that, after the plain-speaking of the Atkinson Letters, I might never be asked, or allowed, to utter myself again. . . . I anticipated excommunication from the world of literature, if not from society" (1983, 2:343). Professionally, this was not the case, although some of her personal relationships declined. One of the most caustic responses was from James Martineau in his review entitled "Mesmeric Atheism," prompting Harriet to remark: "I need not say that this will not do. My course is plain enough . . . I do not repent having allowed James before to play fast and loose with me: but it would now be my fault if I gave him the opportunity of repeating such treatment. . . . Above all, he has forfeited my esteem irrevocably."[31] That her beloved brother became her most vitriolic critic because she followed a course that brought her spiritual contentment—a course of inquiry typical of the Unitarian background they shared—is poignantly expressed by Chapman's phrase for the siblings' rupture, "The Life Sorrow" (1877, 313).

In view of this discussion, it is most significant that what she termed "the greatest literary engagement of my life," her work for London's *Daily News*, both began and ended with a series of articles structured in letter format. Martineau's first assignment as leader writer featured twenty-seven letters entitled *Letters from Ireland*. The letters, collected and printed in volume form by John Chapman, record her 1852 Irish tour and address various aspects of Irish culture, economy, and social concerns. "The writing those Letters was a pure pleasure," she asserted, "whether they were penned in a quiet chamber at a friend's house, or amidst a host of tourists, and to the sound of the harp, in a *salon* at Killarney" (1983, 2:407). Illustrating her claim that correspondence best reveals one's character, the letters quickly betrayed the writer's identity, proving the impossibility of journalistic anonymity for Martineau. Her attempts to conceal her identity in the *Daily News* were futile; she admitted that within the first month, "All the early attempts at secrecy are over" (1852, 409). People "knew me by my style," prompting editor William Hunt to write that "all concealment was wholly out of the question, and that I need not trouble myself further about it."

Her preface to the collected edition emphasizes the relaxed, unfettered manner of the letters' composition, a mode most natural to her writing style:

> My readers will take them for what they are—a rapid account of impressions received and thoughts excited from day to day, in the course of a journey of above 1200 miles. I have thought it best not to alter them, either in form or matter. There would be no use in attempting to give anything of the character of a closet-book to letters written sometimes in a coffee-room, sometimes in the crowded single parlour of a country inn,—now to the sound of the harp, and now to the clatter of knives and forks, and scarcely ever within reach of books; therefore have I left untouched what I wrote, even to the notices of passing incidents as if they were still present, and references to a future already fulfilled. (iii)

Interestingly, both in the *Autobiography* excerpt about the Ireland tour and in this preface, Martineau mentions writing these letters while accompanied by sounds: harps, the clatter of silverware, voices in conversation. This indicates that she did not remove her ear trumpet, nor did she seek out privacy, while engaged with this assignment. In this instance, she regarded writing in the midst of activity and noise integral to the authenticity she sought to capture as a "foreign correspondent," aided by the immediacy of the epistolary format.[32] The preface concludes by acknowledging her debt to the sources that guided her observations of Ireland: the Dublin Statistical Society, the Belfast Social Inquiry Society, and Professor Hancock of Dublin, a reminder that sociologically oriented travel writing, like correspondence, was an enduring interest shaping Martineau's writing. Less intimate than *Life in the Sickroom* and less conspiratorial than "Letter to the Deaf," more substantive than the *Mesmerism* and Atkinson books, the tone of *Letters from Ireland* is relaxed and friendly even while offering serious sociological analysis. As a literal *correspondent* to the *Daily News,* Martineau deliberately recast the private/public boundaries of letters (private circulation) and newspapers (mass distribution), now redefined by raising conventional genre expectations: not to disappoint them but to herald her distinctive contributions to periodicals writing as "the first and greatest woman journalist" (Arbuckle 1994, xviii).[33]

The popularity of *Letters from Ireland* prompted her to adapt the same method for her articles to the *National Anti-Slavery Standard,* although to far different effect. As "one of the earliest abolitionists," wrote Chapman, "she knew the ground and the subject thoroughly in all its bearings" (1877, 367); when the *Standard*'s executive committee requested her services, she agreed, stipulating that her approach would be as uncompromising as the situation required. Chapman notes that, along with her official letter accepting the position with the *Standard,* Martineau enclosed a private note, urging that if her work did not suit the committee's aims, "you are simply to say 'stop'" (369). Citing the need for brevity at this time, she anticipates that soon, "I can have some real long talks with you"—epistolary talks, that is.

Writing of Martineau's tenure with the *Standard* (1859–1862), Chapman reaffirms the centrality of the epistolary form to her writing: "She always bore in mind Lord Bacon's opinion,——'letters are the things,'—and it was agreed . . . that the articles should appear in this form, as insuring greater ease and freedom of expression, and as to plainness of speech and choice of topics, the committee gave her *carte blanche*" (1877, 369). Under the by-line "Our European Correspondent," Martineau wrote sixty-two letters to the editor of the *Standard* aimed at promoting open communication between America and England on the topic of slavery. In her letter accepting this assignment, she wrote: "It has long appeared to me that a link was wanting, namely, a comparison of the doings of the two continents, as they affect the destinies of the . . . negro race in particular. I have long endeavored to make your case understood here; and I am most heartily disposed to try what I can do on the converse side." Published in New York by the American Anti-Slavery Society, the *Standard* assignment offers the only instance during her career that Martineau contracted with an American publisher to write directly to an American audience as a British authority on American current events.

Her first letter to the *Standard,* published 9 April 1859, articulates her aim to "facilitate a mutual understanding between your countrymen and mine, such as may render possible a higher and more express interaction than has ever taken place yet." This letter outlines the abolition of the slave trade among European countries, and concludes by targeting America's continued practice of slavery: "The one great comfort is that the disguised slave trade [in Europe] is given up. The real one is now at the disposal of the United States." Urged by the editor to "exercise the freedom and frankness of speech" (Chapman 1877, 370), Martineau makes clear from the outset that her friendly, informal tone also conveys sharp criticism; she conceives her mission as that of political commentator motivated not, as some thought, by animosity but by her high regard for the American democratic experiment and her impatience to see it realized. Over time, her mode of forging international understanding employed an increasingly blunt plainspokenness—at least, that is how she was perceived—that some Americans found more irritating than enlightening. Defending her approach, she argued: "I am sure it is not the way to secure peace to flatter the Americans to their faces when they are doing unendurable things. It is safer to tell them that, as a self-governing people, they are bound to be better informed, and to show more sobriety than at present" (Arbuckle 1983, 215).

Although the *Standard*'s editor encouraged Martineau's political critique—"Any views which you may be moved to express in relation to these matters would, I am sure, be well received by all concerned"—Chapman notes that "by and by, some were offended" (1877, 370). Her unpopular stands on the *Trent* affair and the Morrill Tariff signaled the end of this epistolary engagement, as Americans from Horace Greeley (a Republican and an "enemy of the anti-slavery gospel") to Lydia Maria Child contributed to the flurry of letters printed in the *Standard* calling for her resignation.[34] Martineau declined to defend herself: "My course has always been—to fight your battles on this side the water . . . and to speak the plain truth on the other side. This is not the way to gain popularity. . . . [But] it is the course most conducive to peace and a clear understanding between the two nations" (*Standard,* 15 February 1862).[35] What ultimately concerned her was not random, isolated incidents but that the Americans' "playing fast and loose" with British neutrality threatened to cost the abolitionists the momentum that had been gathering for thirty years, undermining abolition with self-indulgent political posturing. Recalling her request to "*tell me in the plainest and broadest way if I do not answer the committee's expectations*" (Chapman 1877, 369), the 1 March 1862 *Standard* marks the termination of their relationship. "Happily, the larger part of my work for the anti-slavery cause lies here [in England]," she noted in her resignation letter. "In that, I hope to labor while I live; and I am sure that

that Cause and its promoters will always have my heartfelt good wishes, as they have had my faithful service. It is in the spirit of that service that I now bid you farewell."[36]

Chapman argues that the break with the *Standard* was fortuitous, since it freed Martineau to concentrate on her *Daily News* writing, so much of which introduces American issues to a British audience. Martineau's February 1862 letter to Fanny Wedgwood about the *Standard* incident speculates on a generation gap among the abolitionists, in which the younger generation (represented by the *Standard*'s editorial board and correspondents) rejected her as a foreign meddler (see Arbuckle 1983, 218–20).[37] But the abolitionists with whom she had been associated since 1835, like Chapman and Garrison, remained loyal to their controversial friend, regularly supplying her with American newspapers and letters to assist her *Daily News* work. The packets from America themselves raised concerns about epistolary privacy: "It is a real trouble to me to have such letters as I get,—all to myself: and every one of them has some bit of private confidence in the very middle, and mixed up with the rest" (Burchell 1995, 110). In this instance, editing is required in order to make private correspondence suitable for publication while preserving a balance between personal trust and public duty.

Her series of letters protesting contagious diseases (CD) legislation, printed in December 1869, neatly bookends Martineau's career with the *Daily News*.[38] She sent the letters to editor Thomas Walker, whose wife insisted on their immediate publication; over the protests of the editorial board, he took her advice. Although willing to print the letters, Walker doubted that the issue warranted a regular article, but Martineau predicted that other newspapers' responses to the controversy would force Walker to rethink his position. Signing herself simply "An Englishwoman," she denounces CD legislation as "one of the most conspicuous disgraces of our time" and seeks to raise public awareness by explaining "what the danger is in which we find our country and everybody in it involved" (*Daily News,* 28 December 1869). She rejects this method of policing as an "utter loss of the sacredness of person . . . the outrage and heart-break . . . of personal violation under sanction of law and the agency of the police" being indefensible. Anticipating the objection that decent women should not even know of such issues, much less agitate in public on their behalf, she proclaims: "What society supposes of the ignorance of many of our countrywomen is but too true; but, under the pressure of their present danger, women are awaking, day by day, to a sense of the realities about them. *When the mind is awake all the rest follows of course*" (emphasis added). While her defiance is, she might say, "pretty well" for an old woman, it is based on the same assertion she made as a twenty-year-old girl: all hope for individual and communal social progress rests with one factor: an awakened, inquiring mind.

Martineau's perception that women need to speak for themselves, to prove themselves and claim what is rightfully theirs rather than waiting passively for men to grant them rights and privileges, found apt expression in these *Daily News* letters. "We cannot, will not, must not, surrender any of the personal liberty which is our birthright," she insisted (*Daily News,* 30 December 1869). She pleaded even more eloquently—and militantly— in her private correspondence. To Edwin Godkin she sent a copy of a volume entitled *The Constitution Violated,* a tract that aimed to warn both "eminent lawyers" and the general public that the English constitution "has recently been more grossly outraged than ever before since the days of the Stuarts" by the passage of the 1869 acts. And to a "Dear friend" she wrote: "We, opponents of such legislation, were abundantly disgusted. . . . We never acknowledged that jurisdiction . . . as long as the Commission was used as the Government reply to our remonstrances, we were either trickily used, or our complaints were not in the least understood.—Both suppositions turn out to be true." She is struck by the "wickedness" of "men who go to church on Sundays and call themselves Christians,—who set out from the supposition that men's passions must be gratified, and that, if women are ruined in that process,—it is simply necessary, and a matter of course." Martineau questions whether "the existing government has the courage to avow its mistake in proposing the Act of 1869, and sufficient political faith to change its course," and she concludes by asserting, "the controversy will never subside . . . till we have blotted out of our lawbooks the most detestable enactments that ever cursed our country and people." What she had mildly termed, in an 1864 *Daily News* leader on the topic, "awkward and difficult," she condemns, in 1871, as a "deplorable piece of misgovernment . . . the audacious sacrifice of virtue to passion, and of the defenceless to the strong and self-seeking half of society."[39]

Nearly thirty years after they were written, Josephine Butler asserts in her *Reminiscences of a Great Crusade,* Martineau's 1869 letters to the *Daily News* were still "extremely weighty, and wonderful to read" (1896, 8). But Martineau's private correspondence from this period attests to the price, in terms of health, well-being, and peace of mind, that these letters exacted from her. Having relinquished virtually all activities but needleworking and letter writing due to her increasingly fragile health, she found that the urgency of the issue required a disruption in her routine sufficient to exhaust her. Several times during this period, she wrote to Chapman apologizing for putting off her usual Wednesday letter to America because of other, more pressing, business: her published and private letters aimed at fanning the flames of public outrage against CD legislation. Once that task was accomplished, "it feels like a holiday to be able to pour out to you to-day in the free way which makes writing a relief" rather than a burden (Chapman 1877, 429). Not all letter writing required the same degree of effort, clearly; it depended on whether her impetus was social reform or socializing.

My study of the significance of the epistolary form in Martineau's life and work is predicated on exploring notions of women's authorial identity, on questioning the gendering of genres, and on challenging the assumption that our linguistic system—aside from certain arbitrary "gender markers" like pronouns—is masculine-oriented. Offering a more relevant concept about gendering, and one strikingly similar to Chapman's comparing Martineau to university educated men, is J. Paul Hunter's observation that literacy, traditionally reserved for men while actively excluding women, became associated with civilization, relegating women to the nature category, which must be controlled by the male culture: "Encouragement of literacy at whatever risk and acceptance of private time and space . . . are important marks of a culture committed to evolving" (1990, 158). Such a concept of literacy reveals that the dearth of literary grandmothers does not derive from some inherent deficiency in women but from a social construction Martineau insightfully termed the "jealousy of men." The intersections of literacy, privacy, and social evolution in Hunter's equation are analogous to the substantial roles played by needleworking, hiking, and letter writing in Martineau's intellectual development and mode of composition; her deafness and inclination for solitude provided further opportunities to cultivate the qualities necessary to become a writer.[40] The high premium placed on privacy is central to conceptualizing gender roles, since women were relegated exclusively to the private realm but forbidden any privacy for themselves; they were barred from public life yet perpetually on display to the public view. This false dichotomy clarifies the demand for women's constant availability and visibility, which sabotages the potential subversiveness of women who think and write. Martineau's affinity for the epistolary genre is of a piece with her insistence on preserving the privacy essential to cultivating a life of the mind. Because of the unique circumstances shaping her life, her example demonstrates not only the social evolution of women but also survival of the fittest as a woman writer in a man's world.

EPILOGUE

# "The One Thing Needful"

No one who inspects her portrait can wonder at her celibate pro-
clivities, or is likely to attempt the seduction of the "fair philosopher" from her doctrines on the population question. . . . Is it a
woman, or a man, or what sort of an animal is it? . . . There she
came, stride, stride, stride,—great heavy shoes, stout leather leg-
gings, and a knapsack on her back!—They say she mows her
own grass, and digs her own cabbages and taturs!
—**Daniel Maclise**

But Miss M., she *is* wonderful. Now we have other clever women
more of her style; twenty years ago I think there was not one. She
was the first; she has helped on by her example all the others.
—**Bessie Rainer Parkes**

She kept a high aim in life, an unsullied integrity, and a power
almost unequalled amongst women, and rarely equalled
amongst men.
—*Spectator*

Harriet Martineau is a sign of this country and time.
—**Thomas Carlyle**

• The mere fact that as a woman writer Harriet Martineau prevailed
throughout the Romantic and Victorian eras with both personal and professional reputations intact marks her as a particularly apt representative of the
spirit of the age: an age during which gender respectability was paramount.
Despite the period's urge toward conformity, Martineau was a genuine original, not only in her pursuit of a literary career based primarily on "masculine" topics written in "serious" genres but in her aggressive participation in
the period's social debates, into which she herself often figured as a woman
with little to recommend her by way of the class and gender privileges—like
an advanced education and professional connections—often available to

her male colleagues. The uncanny timeliness of her own development as it coincided with certain historical events illustrates compellingly the circumstances enabling a woman to write, publish, and be read, requirements outlined by Virginia Woolf in *A Room of One's Own* a generation after Martineau's death as literary ability, economic independence, and privacy. But the anomaly presented by the example of Harriet Martineau is not that she prevailed through seemingly insurmountable obstacles to enjoy a career spanning over fifty years: the real anomaly is her virtual disappearance from literary history to the extent that she is now often little more than a footnote in the biographies of Victorians who once sought her literary advice. As repeatedly demonstrated in recent Martineau scholarship, she was a literary predecessor on whose shoulders such writers as Stowe, Eliot, Brontë, Gaskell, Barrett Browning, Browning, Arnold, and Dickens stood. But her pioneering work as a social-problem writer, journalist, and social reformist has yet to receive the critical and analytical attention it deserves.

My analysis of primary themes in Martineau's life and work concludes by bringing together three seemingly unrelated topics: her appearance, her humor, and her contemporaries' eulogies. Those quick to dismiss her as a shriveled bluestocking, the Victorian equivalent of the humorless postmodern feminist, rely on a prevalent stereotype that not only avoids assessing Martineau's work on an intellectual basis but ignores a quite engaging side of her character. Similarly, what amounts to critics' obsession with her appearance, whether to ridicule its defects or to insist on its plain-but-pleasant qualities, features another way of keeping attention focused on biology and gender at the expense of the intellect. Finally, Martineau's contemporaries summarize her life and work as well as the themes and issues to which she lent her name, attesting to the influence that continued long after her death. The image that emerges out of such a patchwork reveals Martineau to be a literary grandmother par excellence whose obscurity in literary history stems from the impossibility of pigeonholing her contributions neatly and conveniently into the categories dictated by Aristotelian conventions and modern academic divisions.

Because she wrote at a time when women acquired social status through marriage and motherhood—and rarely from writing books and editorials—the idea that a woman's appearance is her fortune assumed special significance for Harriet Martineau's critics. In view of male critics' propensity to avoid assessing her work by ridiculing her appearance, her disability, and her resulting (so they assumed) singleness, Martineau's attitudes toward female beauty as presented in her writing are especially revelatory: not only did she aim to free women of the hoops, corsets, and whalebones that so aptly symbolized their intellectual and social oppression, she also shifted readers' attention away from qualities denoting youth and beauty to focus on characteristics such as social commitment, morals and ethics, and education and employment. In a revealing contrast, critics' compulsion to account for the anomaly of a professionally successful woman writer resulted in their keen interest in her appearance, an interest conspicuous from reviews of the *Illustrations of Political Economy* to the obituaries and posthumous reviews of her *Autobiography* over forty years later.

Martineau had particular reason to confront reigning standards of female beauty in her writing since, according to some contemporary accounts, she was woefully lacking in desirable feminine attributes. Although some thought her "very coarse of aspect," others more charitably deemed her "plain—very plain." She was described as of average height and weight, with brown hair and grayish, green/blue eyes—all quite ordinary characteristics. Phrenologists were amazed that Martineau's small, undistinguished head could house such a formidable intellect. The singular-looking George Eliot, interestingly, thought Martineau's appearance "vulgar," while other contemporaries referred to her as kind, cheerful, intelligent, humorous, womanly, and unaffected: terms designed to skirt the issue of her physical qualities as tactfully as possible. Perhaps here, too, she drew on personal experience in her rejection of standards of woman's worth based on appearance, instead promoting an unfashionable appreciation for women's character, intellect, and state of health.

In her own words, as a child Martineau looked "cross," "unhappy," "pale as a ghost," "frowning and repulsive-looking" (1983, 1:94–95), descriptors that reflect chronic ill-health and a pronounced lack of self-esteem. But as a young woman, her one marriage proposal convinced her that, looks notwithstanding, she was indeed marriageable, although she later pragmatically regarded her fiancé's death as deliverance from a life of servitude to husband and children. By the age of twenty, she was a confirmed spinster free to pursue the life of the mind: although well into her fifties she periodically records having to discourage potential suitors. True, this may have had more to do with fame than with attractiveness; but regardless of the motivation, Martineau was as immune to false flattery in old age as she had been in her youth.

Americans' assessment of Martineau's personal characteristics focused largely on her *virtue*, although some comments indicate more political standards. Mr. Gilman, one of her South Carolina hosts, employed Harriet's own standards—character over beauty—to describe his English guest: "We expected an elegant, talented, good woman. We did *not* expect, in addition to all this, a lively, playful, childlike, simplicity-breathing, loving creature, whose moral qualities as much outshine her intellect as these last do those of the ordinary run of mankind" (Chapman 1877, 109–10). Catharine Sedgwick's description more specifically demonstrates how even plain features and a *masculine* profession can be transformed by inner "grace." Martineau is

> a plain woman with nothing in her face indicative of her splendid talents. . . .
> [H]er forehead is low—her nose short and thick—her mouth not well
> formed—her teeth so-so—rather pale and thin faced—tall and spare with *very*

> pretty hands and feet. . . . [B]ut from hour to hour she grew upon us—so
> modest, gentle, and kind, and before she went away we began to see the
> graces of her soul in her face as in a mirror. (Kelley 1993, 144–45)

Maria Weston Chapman's comments similarly honor Martineau's resistance to physical descriptions in favor of more substantive qualities: hers is
a "presence one did not speedily tire of looking on,—attractive and impressive; yet the features were plain . . . of serene and self-sufficing dignity
. . . [and] benevolent repose, . . . a face of simple, cheerful strength" (1877,
135–36). By the same token, considering Martineau's support of the abolitionist movement, one wonders if her condemnation as "the ugliest
woman in the world" (Webb 1960, 2) by the wife of the governor of
Louisiana is less a reflection of Martineau's actual demeanor than of her
ideology, an idea with suggestive possibilities for exploring the responses
of other critics to her social politics.

In an 1837 letter to Ralph Waldo Emerson, Thomas Carlyle termed her
"One of the strangest phenomena. A genuine little Poetess, buckramed,
swathed like a mummy into Socinian and Political-Economy formulas; and
yet verily alive in the inside of that!" (Carlyle 1883, 1:126). His quaint imagery is notable for avoiding either physical or moral qualities, focusing
instead on the intellectual, which would have pleased her. However, the
combination of poetry and political economy does signal some concern
with feminizing Martineau as a *poetess*—and a diminutive one at that—as
does his surprise that she is "alive" despite the masculine intellectual
propensities assumed to "unsex" her.

Nearly a century later, modern critics continue to perpetuate the sort of
conflicted assessment put forward by Carlyle. R. K. Webb's influential *Harriet Martineau: A Radical Victorian* (1960) devotes its opening pages to rehearsing, but not critiquing, derogatory comments made about Martineau's appearance by her contemporaries. The prominent placement of
this extensive presentation, and the fact that it remains unanalyzed by
Webb or by subsequent scholars, speaks volumes about what even twentieth-century critics consider important for readers to know about Harriet
Martineau. On the contrary, what we really need to know is what she
wrote, how she wrote it, and to what end, not subjective opinions about
her appearance that have no bearing on literary ability.

On a more hopeful note, *Norwich Notables* records another popular
theme—that her appearance, if disappointing in her youth, improved over
the years:

> Her appearance was characteristic—the keen grey eyes, with an expression
> more penetrating than emotional; the decided, firmly closed lips, the lower
> one slightly projecting; the thin, bony face and mass of black hair; the very
> broad and somewhat low forehead. These traits improved in attractiveness
> in later years, when the face becoming fuller, the features looked smaller

and less marked; and there arose a suspicion of softness and gentleness about the mouth, which so many years of unselfish labour could not fail to throw over it.[1]

Here, too, the compensation offered for plainness is virtue, which serves to "soften" sharp features over time. To this portrait, writer James Payn adds in a letter to Chapman an essential feature for redeeming a plain woman—maternalism: "No more gentle, kindly, and . . . 'motherly' nature ever existed than that of Harriet Martineau. She delighted in children, and in the friendship of good wives and mothers; one of her chief virtues, indeed, was a simple domesticity, that gave her a wonderful charm with those who prefer true gentlewomen to literary lionesses" (Chapman 1877, 483). Although Martineau was neither a mother nor a literary lioness, this ostensibly positive emphasis on maternalism in contemporary assessments of her appearance attests to the eagerness to account for the anomaly presented by Harriet Martineau, even among her friends.

Chapman, an eyewitness to this alleged transformation from plain to attractive, agrees that with age Martineau acquired a physical appeal denied her earlier: "There was a remarkable change in her appearance in mature age. Every one noticed it. 'How handsome she looks!' 'One of the handsomest old ladies I have ever seen!' '*Doesn't* she look like a sovereign princess!' and such like notes of admiration were continually heard. . . . Happily a trace—necessarily a faint one—yet remains in . . . Richmond's admirable portrait" (272). The 1850 portrait by George Richmond to which Chapman refers is indeed one of the most popular images of Martineau in its depiction of a middle-aged face displaying character, compassion, and a high degree of intelligence, framed and, of course, softened by the requisite lace cap. This late-blooming beauty, asserts John Nevill, continued well into old age: "That physical beauty which had been so long with-held from her was hers in abundance towards the close of her life. She was a really exquisite old lady. Her hair had turned snow-white, her thin, angular features had become softened and rounded, and a lovely air of patience, kindliness, and serenity shone forth from her face" (1943, 121–22).

Martineau's awareness of public curiosity about her appearance, from the lofty to the low, was one she handled gracefully. During his vigorous "courtship" of Martineau for the Society for the Diffusion of Useful Knowledge, Lord Chancellor Brougham succumbed to "certain droll speculations as to whether I am handsome or not," somewhat like the anticipation of Garveloch's "laird" about the Scots fisherwoman, Ella. Writing to Mrs. Ogden about the wildly disparate accounts currently circulating about her physical characteristics, she observed: "Mr. Smith calls me a 'little stuggy woman,' . . . and W. Wells Brown calls me 'a tall and stately woman.' I measure 5 ft. 4 1/2 in." She also appreciated the irony in the portrait work of Miss Gillies, whose unauthorized portraits of Martineau after not having seen her for years caused her to appear younger, rather than older, with

each rendering: "It is a droll thing to see, now and then, somebody's disbe-
lief that I am I, after seeing one of Miss G's pictures." She did endorse,
however, Richmond's popular portrait: "The drawing is, people say, so
good that there is nothing to be said about it. It is just me."[2]

The comments of some visitors no doubt would have pleased her in their
reflection of the vigor and vitality she acquired in middle age after moving
to Ambleside. Actor Charles Macready described her as a "brown-faced looking woman," emphatically not a quality valued among society women, who
dosed themselves with arsenic to achieve the translucent pallor of invalidism. "I could not but look with wonder at the brown hue of health upon
her face," he continued, "and see her firm and almost manly strides as she
walked along" (Chapman 1877, 274). Despite the inevitable analogy with
masculinity, Macready's sense of "wonder" implies an admiration for his
old friend who, having spent years on the invalid's couch, gladly embraced
her brown hardiness despite its unfashionableness. Of all these accounts,
Nathaniel Hawthorne's is particularly refreshing in its avoidance of gender
considerations and in its honest admiration for the woman behind the
writer: "She is a large, robust, elderly woman, and plainly dressed; but
withal she has so kind, cheerful, and intelligent a face, that she is pleasanter
to look at than most beauties. Her hair is of a decided gray, and she does
not shrink from calling herself old" (Chapman 1877, 275).

The stereotype of the plain-looking spinster as dry and pinched led inevitably to the assumption that such a woman lacked a sense of humor, particularly if she had the added misfortune of being a "bluestocking." Janet
Courtney, who argues that Martineau's abolitionism hindered (rather than
shaped) her career, also expresses regret over her humorlessness: "Perhaps
she had no strong sense of humour. If she had possessed one, she would
scarcely have suggested such a title for a series of tales 'on Sanitary subjects,'
to be contributed to *Household Words*" (1920, 238).[3] Courtney concedes, at
least, that Martineau "could see the fun of the old lady who confessed that
she 'did not care to know about anybody's views or reasons which will not
confirm me in my own faith.'" That Martineau perceived the "divine comedy" in the narrow-mindedness she combated all her life in itself attests to a
rich sense of humor and a character far from shriveled or warped.

Martineau's more playful side surfaces, not surprisingly, in her private
letters and journals. True to her valuing of domestic order, the annual autumn cleaning at The Knoll was "always a merry time. . . . The odd sayings
of maids and 'help' cause many a laugh." But negative rumors about her
domestic standards was not matter for amusement, although here her tone
borders on the ludicrous: "'Objection to soup'! We are wondering what
this *can* mean. I never said a word, in public or private, against soup. On
the contrary, for thirty years . . . I have been preaching up soup on every
occasion. . . . There never was a more complete mistake." Elsewhere, it is
difficult to discern whether her drollery is intentional or not—"Richard
Martineau called with bank-notes for 1,020£ for me. . . . Hope we shall

have no burglars this week"—although her next remark suggests she is unconcerned: "Browning sent me 'Robinson Crusoe,' . . . I am going to sit down to it and be a child again" (Chapman 1877, 202). While highly protective of her privacy and of preserving the charm of Ambleside from the onslaughts of tourists, she maintained a sense of humor even when a woman tourist boldly picked a bouquet of flowers from her garden, accidentally leaving her umbrella behind: "Don't you envy her the satisfaction of sending for it?" she wrote waggishly. But Lake District culture was no less eccentric than its famous resident: "I sent you 'false news' the other day," she wrote to Mr. Pigott, "and must retract accordingly. The gentleman who stepped out of the window is doing well. But the townsfolk, hearing the bell tolling, assumed he was dead, and announced it to the world accordingly! That is the sort of thing we do in these parts."[4]

Martineau also maintained humor through the storm of controversy surrounding her agnosticism, which must have become a tedious subject to her over time. Of an adverse review of *Eastern Life, Present and Past,* she noted: "What precious stuff it is. . . . The best thing in it is the contrast of Cleopatra wafting down the Nile, and H. M. sailing up,—clear-starching. This is rather good."[5] And to her cousin Henry Reeve she wrote of receiving an apology from a clergyman who mistook a typographical error as an editorial choice, accusing her of instructing her publishers to print the word "God" with a small g: "We laughed half the day after; but I gave the preacher a sermon which he will be sure to remember" (Sanders 1990, 178). She was no more impressed with academic scholars than with irate clergy; on being invited to Professor Nichol's observatory in Glasgow, she quipped: "Only think of us in the Observatory,—among the telescopes! What do you think is his only regret! So sad!—that 'it is not a good year for the *upper* nebulae.' *Can* we be happy with only the lower? We must try. A spirit of contentment is a great blessing." The letter concludes with a reminder of the celebrity that allows her to dictate the terms of her professional writing engagements from Ambleside rather than London: "London is so very civil as to say that it can travel with less fatigue than I, (being less bulky, no doubt) and it is coming to me,—to occupy my spare room!" She accepted the added girth of late middle age with humor and grace yet was baffled by another perplexing conundrum—the logistics of willing her ears to a doctor for research into the causes of deafness after having already willed her brain to Henry Atkinson for phrenological analyses: "[I am] busy with an odd correspondence today,—about who is to have my ears after death," she wrote. "An eminent surgeon begs for them; and the question is whether his having them is compatible with my legacy of my skull and brain to another."[6] Her head was destined to remain intact, however, with neither party receiving their "legacy."

Martineau was quite close to Thomas and Jane Welsh Carlyle for a time, and some early correspondence attests to an almost girlish delight in the friendship. During her Tynemouth period, she proposed arranging adjoining accommodations for the Carlyles, her excitement—despite her illness—infectious in this engaging letter to Jane:

> We can knock thro' the wall;—we can nod out of the window,—you can run in the back door without your bonnet;—and I shall probably invite myself to tea with you. My neighbours hear us laugh now sometimes. . . . How much more when you come! The soldiers will catch it up in the castle,—and the fishermen in the haven,—and the fish in the sea,—and the grasshoppers in the hay on the down. The whole region shall laugh, if you come.[7]

Her lighthearted enthusiasm illustrates Martineau's generosity, particularly where her friends were concerned.

Far from a soured spinster, Martineau had an attitude toward romantic relationships that was alternately bemused and amused. "What I was thinking of, about the life of a literary woman, was, chiefly, the love-making by strangers," she wrote to Henry Atkinson. "Such offers are, no doubt some of them mercenary; but some are from the spirit of hero-worship. You can't think how odd the declarations look!" To such "declarations"—which her wording suggests were not infrequent—she typically sent "some sort of quiet, rebuking answer. . . . Men can be just as romantic and silly as any school girls." In 1849, in her prime and at the height of the vigorous period in between her two bouts of invalidism, she wrote to Helen Martineau of "the singular scene of my drinking tea with nine young men,—I the only lady. It was uncommonly pleasant, I assure you." On several occasions, Martineau's careful training of maidservants resulted in her losing a valued companion to marriage. After taking her servant Martha to be registered for her wedding, she remarked: "Indeed, the getting married seems such an easy affair that I have half a mind to try it myself."[8]

Her young friend and admirer James Payn offers several instances of the more quixotic side of Martineau. On her taking up smoking "for her health"—chibouque smoking was one of the more unusual habits she brought back from the Middle East—Payn assures readers that "No one who knew her would suspect her of anything 'fast' or unfeminine" (Payn 1884, 99). He acknowledges, however, that if her neighbors had known of her cigar smoking, "it would, we agreed, have really given them something to talk about."[9] Of her deafness, he wrote:

> Owing to her keen intelligence, I found it difficult to realize her extreme deafness, and used often to address her when she was not prepared for it. She never lost her sense of the absurdity of this practice, and I can see the laughter in her kind eyes now, as she snatched up her trumpet. She loved a goodnatured pleasantry, even at her own expense. (99)

Like Nathaniel Hawthorn, who compared her agility with the ear trumpet to an insect flexing its antennae, Payn asserts, "I had by that time got so well accustomed to her ear-trumpet that I began to look upon it as a part of herself," and he recounts a "ludicrous incident" resulting from this familiarity: the trumpet "was lying on the table a good distance away from her, and having some remark to make to her, I inadvertently addressed it to the instrument instead of her ear. Heavens, how we laughed! She had a very keen sense of fun, of which, however, she was quite unconscious" (Payn 1884, 85–86).

Payn relates another incident that may well be apocryphal yet is quite in accord with her characterization as a feisty old woman with a keen sense of the absurd. Martineau, protesting a member of the local gentry refusing hikers right of way on his property, reputedly marched across the land anyway as a sign of her displeasure. His mock-heroic rhetoric heightening the absurdity, Payn recounts:

> She alone, not indeed "with bended bow and quiver full of arrows," but with her ear-trumpet and umbrella, took her walk through the forbidden land as usual. Whereupon the wicked lord . . . put a young bull into the field. He . . . prepared to attack her, but the indomitable lady faced him and stood her ground. She was quite capable of it, for she had the courage of her opinions, . . . and at all events, whether from astonishment at her presumption, or terror of the ear-trumpet (to which of course he had nothing to say), the bull in the end withdrew his opposition . . . and suffered her to pursue her way in peace. . . . [W]ith no weapon but her ear-trumpet . . . this dauntless lady withstood the horrid foe. (87–88)

Even if the story is a fabrication, Payn may be forgiven—and no doubt would be by Martineau, who surely would laugh at the vision—for presenting an image that so aptly captures her uncompromising commitment to fighting for justice. Wielding a needle or pen, umbrella or trumpet, Martineau never backed down from a foe, whether resistance assumed the form of political posturing, social ignorance, or a bull in a field. It is most symbolic of Martineau's presence that, although astonished at her "presumption," the bull, as Payn points out, is the one who retreats.

The conclusion to Chapman's *Memorials*, "Waiting for Death," records that Martineau "preserved through her latest hours the infantine playfulness that was so attractive in her earlier time" (1877, 451). Prior to her professional success in the early 1830s, we know little of that playfulness, although existing accounts indicate that her childhood and youth were not the periods of carefree lightheartedness typically associated with one's early years. But once Martineau began to realize her powers as a writer and an independent woman, and to comprehend the gravity of the professional path she had chosen, she also cultivated the sense of humor necessary to sustain herself in the fray. That she laughed more in America than in the "thirty years previous" initiated a lifelong pattern in which what her adversaries termed "grim determination" was always tempered by a healthy appreciation for the absurd.

John Nevill lends dignity to James Payn's fanciful anecdote by observing that an "imitation of life was not for her. Always she had resisted easy compromises and polite evasions. Her private conception of the truth was no adversary from whom she warily edged away, but a friend she went forth to welcome with outstretched arms" (1943, 123). Equally insightful assessments were offered in obituaries that focused on her strengths as a nonconformist: "It was her good fortune to be exactly suited to the times in which she lived," reported the *Inquirer*. "The work she could do was a kind of work which her generation needed. . . . When Miss Martineau wrote things were different, and she helped to create the difference. . . . She had the merits of strong-minded women without a trace of their faults. . . . She was not the patroness, but the friend, of the lowest of her neighbours." The *National Reformer* agreed: "No woman more brave, or wise, or untiring in the public service, has lived this century. No one better understood that work is worship; none ever surpassed her in the piety of usefulness—the most wholesome of all the religions of humanity"; the writer concludes by praising her "profound sympathy with religion, society, and political progress." Thus is Martineau's scandalous agnosticism recast as the religion of social usefulness, vindicated by service to the greater public good.

Even Daniel Maclise, whose irreverent memorial to Martineau employs the usual gender insults (although offered somewhat sardonically), owns that she "earned our respect and gratitude for a long and consistent life of labour, whose sole object was the improvement and benefit of our generation" (Maclise 1883, 206). Maclise gallantly vindicates Martineau of the notoriety resulting from John Croker's 1832 review of the *Illustrations*, which he terms "coarse and ungenerous."[10] Emphasizing her ability to "see truth one generation ahead," a writer in the *Nation* wrote: "One looks in vain, indeed, for a parallel to this remarkable woman as a moulder of public opinion through the press and through printed works." Despite her condemnation as a heretic, the *Christian Union* adds, "That she will be remembered as one of the most vigorous thinkers of her generation there is not the slightest doubt" (Chapman 1877, 491).

W. R. Greg notes that "doubt seems to have been a state of mind unknown to her" (Greg 1877, 102), an impression challenged by Chapman's regret that Martineau's "genius" was impeded by "her want of general self-esteem, of which deficiency I have seen a thousand instances" (Chapman 1877, 76). The humility prompting Martineau, in her own obituary, to dub herself a popularizer demonstrates the chronic lack of confidence which, Chapman implies, she never fully overcame. "Genius never recognizes itself as such:—it is true," Chapman wrote while composing the *Memorials*, "and that is why Harriet Martineau saw nothing in herself which should justify the general estimate of herself as a genius."[11] In a letter to Chapman, Henry Atkinson offered this assessment of Martineau's intellectual capacity: "She is not an investigator, a discoverer in science, but she is, strictly speaking, a philosopher, as a lover of truth in a highly practical sense, for the sake of mankind. She is not an original philosophic genius, but her artistic power and ability to learn is extraordinary: and more extraordinary still is the power of seizing on salient points, and reproducing in a clear form what has been imperfectly stated by others" (Chapman 1877, 298). Chapman adds: "Her one great gift seemed then to be utterance; not rhetoric, not elocution, not eloquence, not wit, though her talk was full of short-corner touches" (136).

Earlier debates about masculinity and femininity in Martineau's appearance and writing shift, in some posthumous accounts, to praise of her *womanliness*. Despite her concern that political economy is a masculine pursuit, Catharine Sedgwick wrote, "her spirit and influence have been in harmony with the spirit of the age—because she has gone with the current. . . . She is *womanly*—strictly with sympathies fresh from the heart" (M. Kelley 1993, 148–49). James Payn's commentary highlights the gender anxiety Martineau was perpetually forced to negotiate at the hands of critics and the general public: "I never knew a woman whose nature was more essentially womanly than that of Harriet Martineau, or one who was more misunderstood in that respect by the world at large" (1884, 89). And Chapman quotes a visitor's impression of Martineau that aligns her truthfulness with womanliness: "I am so struck with her absolute, candid, *real* love of truth. She seems utterly destitute of prejudice. Then she is so *womanly*, in the good sense of the word" (1877, 277). In his death notice of Martineau in the *Index*, George Holyoake adds the idea of beauty to this picture, terming her "the most womanly woman of all public women I ever knew. . . . Like most women of thought, as she grew old she grew more beautiful" (1876). And in his review of the *Autobiography* in the *Secular Review* (1877), Holyoake associates Martineau's womanliness with intellect and timeliness and the courage to act on both: "Her mastery of public affairs was prodigious. Her knowledge of questions with which men usually deal was of the highest kind, and yet her sympathy with domestic life was supremely womanly. Never was intellect so strong, marking her life all through with good sense, combined with so much personal tenderness, simplicity, and affection."

Even a negative assessment of Martineau's influence had the probably unintended effect of adding to, rather than detracting from, her reputation. Attesting to her continued influence nine years after her death, the *Spectator*'s article on "Emancipated Women" (1885) effectually celebrates Martineau's accomplishments in the very process of condemning them:

> We earnestly trust that the emancipated women of the future will not set before them as "a splendid example" that great deficiency in reverence and humility which disfigure the striking character of the able and courageous woman who was the first to claim political economy, politics, and religious philosophy as women's subjects, and to leave her mark on all three, though hardly in a form for which women of the highest culture can now feel specially grateful, or of which, as women, they can be proud.

But as contemporary women's studies in all academic disciplines attest, the search for literary grandmothers with which my study began is not

limited to women poets and novelists but extends as well to our foremoth-
ers in the so-called "masculine" disciplines, such as economics, philosophy, and theology, where they are even more likely to have been marginalized or erased. Finally, twenty years after Martineau's death, a retrospective
obituary in her old nemesis, the *Times,* indicates that this "rotten old oracle" was, in the end, a magnanimous opponent: "If any lady of the 19th
century, in England or abroad, may be allowed to put in a claim for the
credit of not having lived in vain, that woman, we honestly believe, was
Harriet Martineau."

Two of the people Martineau most revered throughout her adult life,
Chapman and Garrison, demonstrate perhaps the clearest understanding
of her impact on Victorian society and culture. "What *we* did in talk *she* always did in reality," wrote Chapman. "She was, I think, the most whole-
minded, large-minded, right-minded person I ever met in any country; the
most capable of discerning the end from the beginning in human affairs;
and hence her instinctive power . . . to discern halfness, untruth, and in-
sufficiency in human character" (1877, 151). And Garrison, rejecting the
furor surrounding the publication of the *Autobiography,* pronounced that
reading the book resulted in "a higher appreciation . . . of the intellectual
strength, solid understanding, conscientious integrity, fearless independence of thought and expression, courageous 'heretical' non-conformity,
far-reaching humanity, intuitional grasp, varied knowledge, and literary
fertility of that extraordinary woman . . . privately and socially, how admirable her characteristics!" (Garrison 1969, 4:269). For Garrison, social
heresy could be no less than a way of life, and in this Harriet Martineau
was as much his coadjutor as Maria Weston Chapman.

In her "Essay on Moral Independence," Martineau wrote: "Not only
does individual peace depend on freedom from authority, but the very existence of society rests on individual rectitude" (1836, 184). Although the
Victorian era was one typically associated with social conformity, the democratic strain of individualism inherited from the Romantics was an
equally dominant influence: both factors were integral to the spirit of the
age manifesting itself in Martineau's life and work. Harriet Martineau
strove with all her intellectual vigor to reconcile her own idiosyncratic
needs—among which was an irrepressible "need of utterance" freed from
the shackles of gender constraints—with the needs of a society rushing
away from preindustrial innocence headlong into early modern experience. Of her own search for truth in the midst of the period's social up-
heavals, she concluded that "Philosophy founded upon science is the one
thing needful. The source and the vital principle of all intellectuality, all
morality, and all peace to individuals, and goodwill among men,—had become the crown of my experience, and the joy of my life" (1983, 2:335).
Her words attest to the sharp prophetic insight of a mind capable of envisioning the future through the lenses of the past and present, and of finding the perspective to be one that is cause for joy.

# TO THE
# WOMEN
## OF
# COLCHESTER.

As Englishwomen loving your Country, and proud of it, as many generations of Englishwomen have been, listen to a word from three of your Countrywomen.

The most endearing feature in our English life has been the quality of its **Homes.** Married life is with us, we have been accustomed to think, more natural and simple than in most other countries, youth and maidenhood at once more free and more pure, and womanhood more unrestrained, more honoured and safe beyond comparison in person and repute.

Are you aware that this eminent honour and security of our Sex and our Homes are at present exposed to urgent danger, and even undergoing actual violation? You Women of Colchester ought to be aware of this fact; for the violation is going on within your own Town.

The story is short.

Some fifteen months ago a Bill was carried through Parliament, by trick and under a misleading title, and without awakening the suspicions of the country, by which the personal violation of hundreds of thousands of Englishwomen is not only permitted but rendered inevitable. And it is the aim and purpose of the authors of the law and its policy to have the act extended over the whole country. It was asked for on account of our Soldiers and Sailors. It is now sought to be extended to the population of the whole kingdom. It was intended to mitigate the disease occasioned by debauchery; but it has aggravated it. It has not diminished the vice, but encouraged it by a false promise of impunity. It gives a distinct Government sanction to profligacy, and is degrading English Society wherever it operates, to the fearful condition of health and morals existing on the Continent wherever such legislation has been established long enough to show its effects.

Foremost among the promoters of this fearful system and fatal law is **Sir Henry Storks,** one of the Candidates for the Representation of Colchester.

He was a Candidate at the Newark Election, some months since, but the Newark people knew what he had been doing, and they would not hear of him as a representative. He had no chance when the facts were understood, and he withdrew from certain defeat.

Do the people of Colchester know those facts? let it be your work to take care that your husbands, fathers, and brothers, hear of them. **Sir Henry Storks's** own words are to be found in the printed evidence offered to the committee of the Lords on the Acts. At **Newark** he complained of false accusations and libels; but the following words written by his own hand in a letter produced in that evidence, are full justification for any efforts you will make to drive him from **Colchester.**

"I am of opinion that very little benefit will result from the best-devised means of prevention **until Prostitution is recognised as a necessity!**"

This is the professed "opinion" of a man who is regarded as a Christian gentleman, who cannot but be aware how Fornication is denounced in the Scriptures.

Let his evidence be further studied, in regard to the operation of the legal outrage which **Sir Henry Storks** is endeavouring to introduce wherever the sceptre of our virtuous Queen bears sway, and there can be no doubt of his rejection at **Colchester** by every Elector who values as an Englishman should, the sanctity of his home, the purity of his sons, and the honour and safety of his daughters.

You surely will not weakly sacrifice greater things to less by any indulgence of prudery. The subject is painful, even hateful, to every one of us; but that is not our fault, and our country is not to be sacrificed to our feelings as women. We are not **fine Ladies** but **true-hearted Englishwomen;** and there are thousands at this hour who have proved that in this cause, they can sacrifice whatever is necessary to save our country from the curse of these Acts.

It is your business to lift up your voices within your homes and neighbourhoods, against being ruled by lawmakers like the authors of these Acts:—in other words, against **Sir Henry Storks,** as Candidate for **Colchester.**

**HARRIET MARTINEAU.**
**URSULA BRIGHT.**
**JOSEPHINE BUTLER.**

# NOTES

## Prologue

1. "I look everywhere for Grandmothers and see none," Barrett wrote to H. F. Chorley (7 January 1845, in Kelley and Lewis 1992, 10:14).

2. "With . . . nothing approaching to genius, she could see clearly what she did see, and give a clear expression to what she had to say. In short, she could popularize, while she could neither discover nor invent" ("An Autobiographical Memoir," *Daily News*, 29 June 1876).

3. An American reviewer of *Society in America* expressed regret at her distaste for the Shaker community's ideology of celibacy: "We are sorry to hear a maiden lady be so inconsistent as to condemn these societies for living in celibacy. And it is a very natural question to ask, why has she not furnished herself with a husband?" (Boyle 1837, 38).

## Chapter 1

1. Angel-in-the-house or madonna-or-harlot ideology was a middle-class standard. However, despite lacking economic status, working-class women were also judged by this sexual standard: if not within their own class, then by other classes. Although such stereotypes, as my analysis shows, were largely fictional and did not reflect the reality of most women's lives, the standards were frequently invoked to keep all women subordinated to separate spheres ideology.

2. To Louisa Gilman, a young acquaintance from Charleston, South Carolina, Martineau wrote that, during girlhood, she rose at 5:00 in the morning to sew, read, and write; she taught herself French and Italian, translated Tacitus and Petrarch, learned Wordsworth "by heart by the bushel," read philosophy, and "puzzle[d] out metaphysical questions in my own mind, all day long" (10 November 1834, Norwich Record Office, 1834). It is her fond hope that Louisa will enjoy a similar "joy of her youth."

3. Martineau preferred to depict her entry into a literary career as passive. Early encouraged by her mother to write, she told her sister of her ambition only to be labeled conceited, whereupon she "instantly resolved 'never to tell anybody any thing again.' . . . The ambition seems to have disappeared from that time; and when I did attempt to write, it was at the suggestion of another [James] and against my own judgment and inclination" (1983, 1:117). Her literary response to her "mourning period" is reflected in the lives of other Victorian women: Elizabeth Gaskell wrote to help her through mourning the loss of a child while social purity activist Josephine Butler, who also lost a child, channeled her grief into working on behalf of prostitutes.

4. Janet Courtney notes that the title "Mrs." "was conferred in the eighteenth century alike upon married and unmarried ladies of age and standing" (1920, 232). The "Misses Martineau" refers to Martineau's nieces. George J. Holyoake (1876) adds that she resisted the "juvenile prefix, which merely indicated eligibility for marriage."

See also Martineau to "My dear friend," 12 December 1854, Harris-Manchester College Library, Oxford: "Do me the favour to direct to me henceforth as 'Mrs.' Harriet Martineau. . . . It will be a convenience as well as propriety in my case."

5. According to Martineau's nieces and nephews, Chapman notes, "the conduct of the family was 'all jealousy of her superiority.' She was, in short, the swan among ducks, geese and barn-door fowls" (Boston Public Library, ms.a.9.2.6, p. 3). Writing to her sisters Caroline and Deborah in 1845, Chapman observed that James Martineau was "biler than ever," he "appears to be jealous of her being in higher society than he . . . and scorns to enter into the exclusive realms by means of her spencer" (Boston Public Library, ms.a.9.2.4, p. 19).

6. Her publishing contract (with Fox) was predicated on the assumption that the series would not sell; it was therefore up to Martineau to generate sufficient interest among friends and relatives prior to publication by securing five hundred prepaid subscriptions. Fox vowed to discontinue the series after the second number unless a thousand copies were sold. To her, even this impossible contract was better than none at all, and she quickly found herself vindicated by a vigorous public reception that eclipsed all expectations. Louis Cazamian notes that each monthly number of the *Illustrations* sold more than ten thousand copies (1973, 58), "which Fox calculated to mean about 144,000 immediate readers" (Webb 1960, 113). Martineau averaged one tale a month over a two-year period (1832–1834).

7. Martineau wrote to an unknown recipient: "I am anxious to see all that I can lay hold of with any reliance, for the sake of my *great pupil,* the public. . . . I am very greedy of effectual help, and make few apologies for the trouble I give, as it is for a public object" (14 September 1833, University College of London Library).

8. The 1832 Reform Bill extended the franchise and officially recognized and sought to alleviate the problems and concerns of the middle and lower classes resulting from rapid industrialization and urbanization. Given the subjects she treats in the series and the audience they are aimed at, her timing was impeccable, suggesting that publishers' reluctance stemmed from reservations of another sort: including, possibly, resistance to a woman writer and to the Reform Bill itself. R. K. Webb writes that Martineau "grew up as the manufacturing class to which she belonged experienced its greatest access of confidence and power. She became famous in the year of what members of that class and most historians since have considered its legislative triumph; the Reform Act of 1832 was . . . a limited victory, but there was no denying its symbolic importance, then or now" (361).

9. Garrisonian abolitionism, dedicated to liberating slaves and women, welcomed the participation of women activists. This caused a split in the abolitionist movement when some members argued that women belonged in the home, not out in public working for social causes. Both sides regarded the abolition of slavery a "holy war," but only the Garrisonians included women: who, in their role as society's moral gatekeepers, served most appropriately as its reformists.

10. Of course, if books are out of print, it is impossible to determine whether, given the chance, they can or cannot "stand the test of time."

11. Martineau to Miss Bacon, n.d., Cambridge University Library, ms 6246, f. 45. Of her political influence, Janet Courtney notes that Lord Chancellor Brougham "climbed two pairs of stairs to pick her brains" while Sir Robert Peele "consulted her on the Corn Laws" (1933, 14). During the same period that she wrote the twenty-five numbers of the *Illustrations,* Martineau also wrote *Illustrations of Taxation* (five parts) and *Poor Laws and Paupers Illustrated* (four parts) for

Brougham and the Society for the Diffusion of Useful Knowledge.

12. When Martineau expressed interest in working with class issues, her mother objected, prompting this response: "If, as my mother says, the high quit me on that account, let them. They will not be worth the keeping. But I don't believe it. I *must* keep my mission in view, and not my worldly dignity. . . . I ought either not to communicate so much, or not to fear my mother's opinions and remarks about it" (Chapman 1877, 216).

13. Indicative of her fascination with America and its institutions was her aim to reside there permanently. But her extended illness after returning to England prompted her to settle instead for the more efficacious route of employing her writing skills to document events in America during its "martyr age."

14. Martineau was concerned about her mother's well-being; but the friction between them made their living together impossible and contributed to Martineau's ongoing struggles with her health. Even when her mother was looked after by her other children, Martineau continued to have nightmares about her. Far from condemning her mother, she is careful to "pass it over as lightly as possible" (1983, 1:249); her passivity on this point seems to be an important measure of daughterly propriety and respectability, regardless of her age and despite the literary success earned by aggressiveness, tenacity, and ambition. She remained critical, however, of the family dynamics that scarred her well into adulthood.

15. Martineau's humility may be seen in her relationships with Catharine Sedgwick and Elizabeth Barrett. She chastised both women vigorously when she sensed their admiration for her bordered on lionism, a form of flattery so excessive as to seem insincere. On Sedgwick, see Martineau 1983, 2:66. Barrett was mortified by the accusation, despite Martineau's attempt to clarify her concern: "We are *very* unlike in our powers. Each sees in the other powers of which the possessor is not half conscious. We *must* look with reverence upon each other. . . . We are ordinary women in our need and power of affection. Let us then treat each other with . . . simplicity and affectionate fidelity" (Kelley and Hudson 1991, 9:106). Her words urge a relationship based on equality, not hierarchy.

16. Publisher Lord Francis Jeffrey observed: "she must not only be rescued from all debasing anxieties about her subsistence, but placed in a station of affluence and honour; though I believe she truly cares for none of these things" (Chapman 1877, 234). He was right: Martineau refused a government pension, arguing that, since it was funded by taxes, she would not be supported by the poor classes who—like Martineau herself—had no say in how their tax money was spent. Some condemned her as priggish and ungrateful, yet her attitude evidences her own alignment of practice with principles.

17. For children's fiction, see *The Playfellow* series, for example. Gillian Thomas notes: "Although the vast majority of Martineau's fiction is of interest to the modern reader because of the light it sheds on the history of the period rather than because of its literary merit, her novels and tales are chequered with episodes and passages which suggest that she narrowly missed becoming a Victorian novelist of some significance" (1985, 110).

18. Martineau to Dr. Combe, 19 July 1842, National Library of Scotland, Edinburgh, ms 7265, f. 44.

19. Chapman wryly notes that Martineau's publications during this "passive period" include *Deerbrook, The Hour and the Man, Settlers at Home, The Peasant and the Prince, Feats on the Fiord, The Crofton Boys, The Guide to Service, Life in the*

*Sickroom,* and *Letters on Mesmerism:* a total of sixteen volumes (1877, 249).

20. The mature Martineau regarded solitude as necessary for one's general well-being: "How much less I think of illness than I used to do! I used to make the most of it, from vanity and want of objects; now I make the least of it, for fear of being hindered in my business. I suffer much less for this. But I am not near so happy as I was. I want inner life" (Chapman 1877, 220). Her writing throughout the 1840s attests to her quest for a rich, deliberately cultivated "inner life."

21. Martineau lived a full, busy life, with many professional and personal gratifications. She stated repeatedly that she had no wish to live beyond her allotted time; because she did not believe in an afterlife, she promoted living this life to the fullest: "I never dream of wishing that any thing were otherwise than as it is, I am frankly satisfied to have done with life. I have had a noble share of it, and I desire no more. I neither wish to live longer here, nor to find life again elsewhere" (1983, 2:438).

22. Martineau to Catherine Macready, 29 December 184[?], National Library of Scotland, ms 3713, f. 112. Her trumpet, a hearing-aid device, required extra effort of both speaker and listener that she was glad to avoid during times of poor health.

23. Martineau anticipated a reordering of Britain's class system as a result of industrialization. The upper class must acknowledge the growing economic and social power of the middle classes and adjust its attitudes and behaviors accordingly, while the lower classes could potentially improve their economic standing as greater means of self-sufficiency became available through industrialization. The "Golden Mean" of society thus represents a new social order whose power is earned rather than inherited, whose achievements result from merit rather than privilege. Despite this idealization of the "Golden Mean," she was correct in foreseeing that the middle classes would comprise the hegemony of the modern era.

24. Webb characterizes Atkinson as an independently wealthy man who could afford to be a dilettante, a dabbler in such social trends as mesmerism and phrenology. "This insignificant man," he argues, was "unquestionably attractive" and probably homosexual (1960, 19), the latter based on his bachelorhood and on the sort of fashionable resorts he was known to frequent. Webb posits that Martineau had an inflated notion of Atkinson's intellect; their friendship (according to Webb, Martineau sent him over a thousand letters) puzzled many observers and friends.

25. Martineau to E. Moxon, 6 November 185[?], Fitzwilliam Museum, Cambridge; Martineau to Miss Winkworth, 13 June 1857, National Library of Scotland, ms 6044, f. 186. She is again too modest: her fidelity to truth is highly courageous, hardly, as she states, cowardly.

26. Illustrating yet again Martineau's timeliness, R. K. Webb observes: "The great burst of interest in Comte in the forties and fifties is an important symptom in Victorian intellectual life, and Miss Martineau's particular brand of enthusiasm has implications which are more than biographical" (1960, 305). Gillian Thomas adds that Comte's positivist philosophy stressed *social* evolution, an idea central to Martineau's social reform writing (1985, 73).

27. Martineau to Mrs. Combe, 14 May 1846, National Library of Scotland, ms 7281, f. 7.

28. An early tale, "Solitude and Society," depicts a bookish man unjustly imprisoned and forbidden books or companions. His adjustment to this state is painful but he eventually concedes "that the discipline to which he was now subjected was intended to rectify his estimate of human duty" (1836b, 49). Once released, he values nature and relationships over books; his former life "would not

now be my choice. I should fear to banish the influences of nature, and to reject the purest elements of knowledge and enjoyment which can be afforded" (54). This tale anticipates Martineau's extended illnesses and her resulting intensified attunement with nature.

29. Martineau to Emerson, 2 July 1845, Houghton Library, Harvard University, Cambridge, ms am 1280 (2076). Martineau to Emerson, 5 November [n.y.], Houghton Library, ms am 1280 (2078). Martineau to Lidian (Mrs. Ralph Waldo) Emerson, 25 September 1848, Houghton Library, ms am 1280 (2082).

30. Martineau to Mrs. Barkworth, n.d., Fitzwilliam Museum, Ashcombe II, 23. Earlier, Martineau had rented out her house during the summers to allow her to escape the tourists. Martineau to Garrison, 25 June 1867, Rheinhard Speck Collection of Harriet Martineau Papers [hereafter referred to as the Rheinhard Speck Collection], Bancroft Library, University of California, Berkeley, 3:2 (box 3, f. 2).

31. Martineau to Nightingale, 2 November 1861, British Library, shelfmark 45788, f.123.

32. Martineau wrote her obituary in the third person. Like the autobiography, it was composed in 1855 and published in 1876.

## Chapter 2

1. For the purposes of this discussion, the term "needleworking" includes plain sewing (straight sewing used for most garments and household items), fancywork (embroidery, lace making and related ornamental crafts), and wool work (knitting and crocheting).

2. Laurie Lieb notes that virtually all women characters in the novels of Austen and Dickens perform needlework, with some telling exceptions: the adulterous Maria in *Mansfield Park* and Edith Dombey of *Dombey and Son,* and the "once unchaste" Lady Dedlock of *Bleak House* (1986, 29). Symbolizing the pointless ineffectuality of women's lives are Mrs. Gradgrind *(Hard Times)* and Lady Bertram *(Mansfield Park),* whose lives are marked by producing endless lengths of useless needlework. By the same token, notes Rohan Maitzen, "the needle confirms the gender and class fitness" of women—for example, writing women, like Martineau— potentially "seen as outside their proper sphere" (1998, 77).

3. Writing of Fanny Burney's ambivalence toward needleworking, Kristina Straub notes that the writer retains "both her femininity and her self-respect" by establishing "the female subject within the conventional territory of feminine employments and pastimes while disassociating the subject's worth from that territory" (1986, 63). Similarly, Burney's character Evelina "complicates and breaks down a too-simple binary opposition" of female propriety as defined by society (66). Like her creator, Evelina "achieves value as one whose ambivalence places her both morally outside and socially within the ideology that defines women as what they do." The parallel with Martineau, a generation or so later, is striking.

4. Laurie Lieb notes, "women are characterized by the type of needlework they do," therefore "you are what you sew" (1986, 33). But in her view, the class distinctions delineating the types of needlework women perform is "less significant than the fact that they all do it" (29).

5. See Laurie Lieb's analysis of one of the Oxford English Dictionary's definitions of "work": as a verb, "to work" means to perform needlework; as a noun, it is cited as "a distinctly feminine occupation" (1986, 29).

6. An example is Eliot's Hetty Sorrel *(Adam Bede)*, a dairymaid seeking vicariously to experience the life of a lady by learning fancywork. On the way to her lessons, she meets young Squire Donnithorne, by whom she is seduced and abandoned; now a fallen woman rejected by her family, she is convicted of infanticide and transported. Her fate is, apparently, a fitting retribution for one seeking upward mobility—through types of needlework and sexual liaisons that are inappropriate to her station—from the class into which she was born.

7. Ambivalence toward sewing was also directed at the craft itself. Carol Wilson discusses Jane Taylor, who preferred writing to needlework; as a result, her brother was anxious to defend her reputation against posthumous charges of impropriety (1994, 179). See also Elaine Hedges, "The Needle or the Pen: The Literary Rediscovery of Women's Textile Work," in *Tradition and the Talents of Women,* ed. Florence Howe (Urbana: University of Illinois Press, 1991), 338–68. Hedges's analysis of American women writers argues that their relationship with the needle was "adversarial."

8. Janet Courtney claims that Mrs. Martineau "stuck firmly to the ancient ways of a Spartan frugality and objected to her famous daughter's even engaging a maid or a work-woman to mend her clothes. So she was sitting up at nights repairing her wardrobe when she ought to have been sleeping and resting her brain" (1933, 195). Courtney offers no source to verify this point, which is inconsistent with Martineau's claim in the *Autobiography* that she resisted her mother's pressure to adapt a materially loftier lifestyle in accordance with her fame: hiring a maid, for instance (see Martineau 1983, 1:249).

9. Typically, the top cover of a quilt features designs made out of patchwork and could include panels with ornaments like buttons, embroidery, smocking, cross-stitch: in other words, virtually all other forms of needlework could be incorporated into a quilt cover. Batting is placed between the top and bottom covers, the latter usually being a plain, solid color. The stitching that joins all three layers is the actual quilting and has its own design or logic that can be even more elaborate in its skilled simplicity than the showier top cover. Although the quilting stitch could be termed "plain sewing," its elaborate pattern prevents terming it "straight sewing." The process is far more complex than hemming a straight edge.

10. Susan Glaspell's *Trifles* (and her short story "A Jury of Her Peers," from which the play derives) depends on the idea that women share a needleworking "language" dismissed by men as irrelevant. The women characters' ability to read their neighbor's stitches solves the murder case that the men continue to investigate with blustering authority. Evidence that is obvious to the women is ridiculed by the men as inconsequential.

11. See also Ice 1993. Ice emphasizes that expert quilters assessing quilt quality are less interested in the pattern on the top layer than in the skilled execution of the less ostentatious pattern of stitching on the reverse side. Recalling Daly's criticism (1978), Ice notes that the increasing tendency to quilt by machine transforms quilting from a skilled, manual, communal activity to a mechanized, solitary process, thus altering the dynamics or *process* of the craft and the essence of the finished product.

12. The idea of invisibility is employed by Martineau in *Society in America,* which features a section discussing American women's lack of status, aptly entitled "The Political Invisibility of Women."

13. For a contemporary example of political activism through needleworking,

see Pershing 1993. The AIDS Quilt is another famous example. Stanton's drolly phallic imagery in effect ridicules cultural anxieties linking sewing with sexuality. Whereas hand sewing denoted sexual decorum, some feared that the rhythmic movement of the sewing machine's foot pedal might be sexually stimulating. According to the *Lancet* (1869, 1:23), "the motion of the limbs in working the machines occasions a sexual excitement, and may bring on great feebleness and enervation in women." Later in the century, the same objection was raised against women's bicycle riding. I thank Professor Beverly Taylor for providing me with this reference.

14. See also Janice Radway's *Reading the Romance: Women, Patriarchy, and Popular Literature* (Chapel Hill: University of North Carolina Press, 1991), a study that investigates women who read romance novels: their motivation, what they "get out of" this activity, what role it serves in their lives, and what oppositions to the activity they must contend with. Radway concludes that what is meaningful to these readers about this activity is the *process* of reading, not literary devices or other concerns. The act of reading is not a means to an end, but an end in itself.

15. Merely on suspicion of illicit behavior, Maggie Tulliver (in Eliot's *The Mill on the Floss*) is hounded by the "world's wife": the collective term for small-minded, mean-spirited moral hypocrites whose own inadequacies find expression through persecuting a communal scapegoat, especially a female suspected of sexual deviance.

16. Laurie Lieb's study of eighteenth-century sewing culture is pertinent to Martineau's example in its claim that the sewing circle permits socializing and learning through reading aloud, making it "a classic image of female community" (1986, 40). Lieb qualifies the derogatory implications of the term "gossip" (so-called by men wishing to trivialize women's activities and concerns) in this context by presenting "socializing" in the sewing circle as a means for women to exchange information about politics, health, and other practical matters.

17. Martineau wrote "The Dress-maker and the Milliner" (1840) for a related series, *The Guide to Trade* (also published by Knight). In 1839, she wrote to Fanny Wedgwood that she was working on it a few pages at a time but it was "tiresome" in her invalid state (Arbuckle 1983, 19); her journal records that it was completed: "Great satisfaction in a finished thing. This one much approved" (Chapman 1877, 227). According to Rivlin 1946, the British Museum holds a copy of "The Dress-maker," although he adds that this is by report only and that he had not actually seen it. But the complete series' listing on the dust jacket of the set held by the British Library features no such title, and the library has no other record of "The Dress-maker."

18. Carol Wilson notes the importance in early-nineteenth-century culture of the moral legacy of needleworking passed from mother to daughter (or from Martineau to her maids): "she will perpetuate a stable culture by teaching her daughters to sew and ensure order by supervising her servants' needlework. Her sewing stitches together family and nation, making possible a strong, prosperous, harmonious . . . society" (1994, 174). Martineau further develops that theme through the idea of "double work": to wield moral influence in the public realm, sewing women—including servants—must educate their minds while occupying their hands.

19. Like Martineau, Gaskell did not allow her literary ambitions to interfere with her domestic responsibilities. In her advice to an inept needlewoman, she recommends constant access to the workbasket, "so that you can take it up at any odd minute and do a few stitches. . . . But *try*, my dear, to conquer your 'clumsiness' in sewing; there are a thousand little bits of work, which no sempstress ever does so well as the wife or mother who knows how the comfort of those she loves depends

on little peculiarities which no one but she cares enough for the wearers to attend to" (Hellerstein et al. 1981, 337).

20. The "creaking door" at the Austen House in Chawton was never repaired, according to popular legend, by Jane's particular request. The door, which creaked when opened, conveniently announced visitors or callers from whom she was bound to conceal her writing. While this natural alarm system served Austen well, it illustrates the superficiality of the social obstacles confronting literary women. Laurie Lieb notes that Austen resisted the offer of a spinning wheel, wryly protesting, "I would spin nothing with it but a rope to hang myself" (1986, 31). Rohan Maitzen's discussion of Margaret Oliphant reveals a similar imperative to keep needlework at the ready so as not to be caught in the act of writing (1998, 68–69).

21. See Myers 1980b for a psychoanalytic perspective on the complex relationship between Harriet and her mother. See also Postlethwaite 1989.

22. Carol Wilson notes, "the powerful icon of the Good Mother . . . [is] often depicted as sewing or knitting for her family. . . . [T]he Good Mother was diligent, frugal, moral, selfless, and devout. . . . Reinforcing the identification of women, sewing, and domesticity, the very sewing case that a woman carried was known as a 'housewife'" (1997, 80).

23. James Martineau, for one, refuted this negative portrayal of Mrs. Martineau. Yet James, who was notoriously critical of his sister, had as great a commitment to maintaining his perspective as Chapman and Harriet did theirs. Given the fact that we are hard-pressed to get beyond the "he said, she said" conundrum, I suggest that Mrs. Martineau's approach to child-rearing was typical of the time and may not necessarily have stemmed from malice. However, Harriet's nature was of the type that is weakened, rather than toughened, by the "taking-down" system of child-rearing. The fact remains that, as a child, Harriet was emotionally compromised by her large family, who were collectively less interested in cultivating individuality—particularly in a mousy, sickly child unable to smell, taste, hear, or digest her food easily—than in maintaining the greatest good for the greatest number.

24. Martineau to Frances Place, 12 May 1832, British Library.

25. Rohan Maitzen draws a direct analogy between women's writing and respectability: "Historically, writing has demanded a level of education unusual, unsuitable, or often simply impossible for a woman; further, if intended for public consumption it bespeaks an unladylike degree of self-assertion, even self-aggrandizement" (1998, 62). Martineau's legitimation of domesticity helped her negotiate the false dichotomy that compromised women writers' respectability.

26. Valerie Pichanick notes that, had Martineau accepted Saunders and Otley's proposal that she be the editor of their new political economy journal, "she would have been the first Englishwoman to be afforded such a journalistic distinction" (1980, 136).

27. "Frame-breakers," or Luddites, were workers unemployed because of machinery. The Luddites smashed machinery as it was en route to factories or attacked the factories themselves to protest their loss of income. Martineau argues that ultimately machinery would create more jobs, although jobs for machine operators rather than for skilled craftspeople.

28. Quoting a mock-heroic poem by William Cowper, "The Task" (1788), Carol Wilson notes his use of the term "female industry" as a metaphor for the sewing woman (1994, 168). Martineau makes apt use of the idea in her article of the same name.

29. For further reading on the treatment of needleworkers in women's writ-

ing, see Joseph Kestner, *Protest and Reform: The British Social Narrative by Women, 1827–1867* (Madison: University of Wisconsin Press, 1985).

30. Martineau offers these statistics of female workers, based on the 1851 census: 385,000 in textile industries and 500,000 in dressmaking. Adding to these figures the Irish weavers and needlewomen, she estimates there are approximately one and one-quarter million of her countrywomen "earning an independent subsistence by manufacturing industry" (Martineau 1859b, 320). Neff 1967 offers a slightly higher number, 388,302: up from 159,101 in the 1841 census.

31. Aside from the extremes of valorizing and denigrating needlework, argues Rohan Maitzen, is its alternative presentation "as part of a distinct women's culture, marginal perhaps, but nonetheless important, interesting, and sometimes even empowering" (1998, 71). This is the position from which Martineau writes on the topic.

32. In no sense is this the case for Martineau, whose stint as a seamstress occurred while living at home with her family, which avoided her having to pay for lodging and food out of her earnings. She was never an unchaperoned, single woman working full-time in a sewing factory or as a dressmaker's apprentice. Her sewing-for-pay was conducted as her sewing-for-propriety was earlier: in the protection of the family circle, while studying poetry. This is not the case for most women made homeless and self-dependent by sudden poverty. See Walkowitz 1980 for a discussion of the threat—an economic, rather than a moral, one—posed by prostitutes whose profession enabled them to participate as free agents in the marketplace. This economic threat is what the "jealousy of men" responds to, despite the moralistic rhetoric employed to denigrate these and other working women.

33. See Elizabeth Gaskell's *Mary Barton*. Mary's working-class father refuses to allow her to do factory work because he considers it demeaning. Instead, he arranges for a sewing apprenticeship which, because of the late hours and unchaperoned walks home, nearly results in Mary's sexual downfall with, ironically, a factory owner's son. The orphaned title character in Gaskell's *Ruth* suffers the very fate Mary avoided when she is seduced by an aristocrat's son. See also Maggie Tulliver (in Eliot's *The Mill on the Floss*), the dark-haired heroine whose poverty—symbolized by her plain sewing—contrasts with the fancywork performed by privileged, blond Lucy Deane. Lucy's suitor is attracted to Maggie, resulting in her "fall": a fall based not on actual sexual impropriety but entirely on innuendo and gossip. Class distinctions dictated that upper-class men sought sex, not marriage, from lower-class women, as these literary examples illustrate. That Maggie had been middle class and would have been a suitable partner for Stephen Guest before she lost economic caste complicates society's determination to discredit her respectability.

34. See also *Daily News*, 2 April 1856, on female culpability for prejudice against working women: "Will these ladies bear with us if we speak to them as unceremoniously as if they were men? We have to tell them, or some of them, that they are not blameless in this matter."

35. In a letter to Mrs. Horner, Martineau notes a forthcoming series in *Knight's Weekly Volume:* "Our second issue, not advertized, nor spoken of yet, but, *entre nous,* called 'Mind amongst the Spindles,' will interest Mr. Horner extremely, I know; and we expect a great sensation from it" (n.d., National Library of Scotland, ms 2213, f. 254). See also *Daily News*, 16 February 1856 on female labor.

36. To Barrett, Martineau wrote: "you will perceive that *mind* is the spring under which twelve hours of toil become tolerable, and not fatal to health of mind or body" (Kelley and Hudson 1991, 9:46).

37. The sewing machine was patented in England in 1849 and shown at the Great Exhibition in 1851. By the time of the Paris Exhibition just a few years later, more than fourteen types of sewing machines were on display.

38. In the sewing trades where women worked for hire, "slopwork" refers to plain sewing, often done as piecework by the poorest women, who worked long hours for a pittance. Out of this they were to pay for their own sewing supplies as well as candles for light to sew by. Because they were forced to economize on the latter in particular, blindness was a common occupational hazard. Slopworkers were the most exploited of needleworkers. Of the advent of the sewing machine, Martineau observes, "No machinery can supersede sewing altogether, though it may, and ought to, extinguish slopmaking at fourpence a day" (1859b, 328). See also Henry Mayhew's discussion of needlewomen in *London Labour and the London Poor;* Neff 1967 on slopworkers reduced to prostitution to feed their children (134); T. J. Edlestein's "They Sang 'The Song of the Shirt': The Visual Iconology of the Seamstress" on women forced to pawn their sewing for food, the inspiration for Thomas Hood's "The Song of the Shirt"; and *The Ghost in the Looking Glass: The Victorian Seamstress* by Christina Walkley.

39. Roszika Parker notes that "The Factory Act of 1833 required employers to provide two hours' schooling a day for child workers. In girls' schools an hour and three quarters were devoted to needlework" (1984, 173). This "curriculum" rendered girls' education "safely feminine" rather than "dangerously masculine," ensuring opponents of girls' education that it "would not undermine marriage." The gender and class dyad is evident well into the twentieth century, when all girls in secondary education studied needlework, though to different ends: working-class girls were steered toward domestication as housewives or servants (plain sewing) while middle-class girls learned the decorative arts (fancywork).

40. See Deirdre David's *Rule Britannia* for a discussion of the role women played in maintaining the fiction of empire and domestic ideology on which Victorian Britain's self-concept rested.

41. Educator Frances Mary Buss, questioned by the School Inquiry Commission on the topic of needleworking in girls' curriculums, responded: "[E]very girl in the school learns plain needlework but no other kind of needlework, and a large quantity of plain clothing is made every year, which is always given away amongst the poor of the neighbourhood. I think it is most desirable that every girl should know how to use her needle." Asked whether, "besides any indirect advantage there may be, it trains the eye and the hand a good deal?" Buss commented "Yes; I think it does" (Hellerstein et al. 1981, 78). "Indirect advantage," we may assume, includes training in proper morality and in knowing one's social place.

42. Martineau probably refers to "Report on the Condition of our Dressmakers," published in 1843 as a result of parliamentary investigations resulting in Blue Books (collected reports and statistics) on the topic. See also her 26 June 1863 *Daily News* leader on milliners.

43. Martineau to Frederick Knight Hunt (editor of the *Daily News* until his death in 1854), 1 April [n.y.], University of Birmingham Library, hm 473. Her postscript to this letter recalls Martineau's own connection with the needleworking profession: "I have been 'a poor needlewoman' myself. When we lost our money . . . I maintained myself by fancywork for some time. I know well the strain."

44. She alludes to recent reform legislation that gave married women "the disposal of the fruits of their own industry, and of their inherited property." This

probably refers to the Matrimonial Causes Act (1857) resulting from the Lady Caroline Norton case, which argued that women's earnings and property should be retained by them rather than automatically appropriated by their spouses. Subsequent related legislation includes the Married Women's Property Acts (1870 and 1882). These decisions mark dramatic turning points in the history of women's rights in Britain.

45. Neff notes that there were two London "seasons," April to July or August and October to Christmas (1967, 118). During such times, according to testimonies gathered by government inspector R. D. Grainger, many apprentices worked from 5:00 in the morning through 2:00 or 3:00 the next morning, others worked 4:00 in the morning through midnight, and others had only two hours' sleep a night for the duration of the season.

46. In a letter to Edward Walford, Martineau notes that her friend Miss Napier, who "left off crinoline" as a result of reading one of Martineau's articles, told her of other ladies who, along with their female servants, also took a stand against the custom. Especially flammable, crinolines were notorious for causing the burning deaths of many women whose skirts brushed against the fireplace (14 October 1864, Rheinhard Speck Collection, 5:5). Miss Napier requested Martineau to send extra copies of her article, to be distributed among her friends.

47. Wanda Neff (1967) points out that the employers of dressmakers were all women, both shop supervisors and customers, and charges that the exploitation of women factory workers by male overseers paled in comparison to that perpetrated by women. Apprentices who gave evidence to labor commissioners, to inspectors like R. D. Grainger or journalists like Henry Mayhew, lost their positions and were blacklisted among other shops in the profession. To counter such oppression, customers were urged to patronize shops with humane employment practices, while needlewomen received free medical and other assistance in return for their testimonies.

48. See also *Daily News,* 18 February 1864.

49. See also Martineau's 4 August 1864 article in the *Daily News,* which reports on various women's colleges, their successes and remaining challenges.

50. Martineau also wrote many *Daily News* articles on the situations of sewing factory workers unemployed due to the American Civil War, when the cotton supply became scarce. She wrote "on behalf of the sewing-schools of Lancashire and Cheshire . . . [that] furnish at once a safe refuge for the unemployed factory-girls, a good training in domestic needlework, and the means of buying clothing exceedingly cheap" (Chapman 1877, 388). Martineau appealed for donations of fabric and used clothing to keep the enterprise going, specifying that donations should be clean and sent "in readiness for the needle": this "will add a grace to the gift if every thing that can be wanted is put into the parcel,—linings, tape, buttons, hooks and eyes, thread, and even needles and pins. The very completeness will be a lesson to the girls, and will give pleasure in places where pleasures are very rare at present" (389). Clare Midgley notes, "Women abolitionists supported the giving of practical aid to these distressed cotton workers as a part of the anti-slavery cause" (1992, 183), citing this as one instance in which Martineau felt that charity (not a sound principle of political economy) was justified.

51. David Turley notes, "From the 1830s onwards British female abolitionists sent consignments of fancy work across the Atlantic, the sale of which was to raise funds for American antislavery bodies. Goods for the Boston Bazaar of the American Anti-Slavery Society each year became a focus for the work of British Garrisonians

in the 1840s and 1850s, at one time engaging the efforts of 300 people in Bristol" (1991, 198). Needleworked contributions must have been considerable, since, at one point, Maria Weston Chapman requested cash rather than sewing, which caused great disappointment among the ladies. The enthusiasm for this activity demonstrates how, once endorsed as a moral imperative with a substantive social purpose, needleworking and the women who performed it assumed social status and contributed directly to political change.

52. Martineau to Catherine Macready, 29 December 184[?], National Library of Scotland, ms 3713, f. 112. To Chapman she implies otherwise: "I have a long piece of woolwork in hand which I destine for your . . . fair. I am fond of the work, and it beguiles many an hour: but only in the intervals of other things" (25 August 1843, Houghton Library, Autograph File). Among the beneficiaries of her "charity purse" is an army barracks, which acquired a new library.

53. On 2 January 1845, Eliza Follen wrote: "To the friends who have presented to me Harriet Martineau's beautiful work for the Eleventh Massachusetts Anti-Slavery Fair. . . . I do indeed feel humble . . . when I find myself associated in your minds with Harriet Martineau and the Cause of human Freedom. . . . It will be a legacy to my son, which I hope may help to move him to noble deeds, so that whenever he looks at it, and thinks of the life and of the honor of her who, through long hours of pain wrought with her feeble hands these undying flowers and fruits so beautifully and remembers the names of the noble souls who contributed towards giving it to his mother, he shall dedicate himself anew to the glorious work to which they devoted their lives and all they possessed" (Boston Public Library, ms.a.9.2.20, p. 136).

54. In *The Daughters of England* (1845), Sarah Ellis wrote that woman's "highest duty is so often to suffer and be still" (Vicinus 1972, x). Laurie Lieb notes several literary precedents in which women were ordered off to spin, leaving men unencumbered for more serious pursuits: Homer's *Iliad*, Defoe's *Roxana*, and Fielding's *Amelia* (1986, 33).

55. Martineau to Mrs. Combe, 5 December 1857, National Library of Scotland, ms 7366, f. 56; Martineau to "Dear friend," 9 October 1858, Rheinhard Speck Collection, 4:55.

56. Martineau to Nightingale, 2 September 1863; and Nightingale to Martineau, 9 September 1863, British Library; Martineau to Spring [Brown], 22 October 1857, National Library of Scotland, ms 1889, f. 192.

57. On a related but no doubt unintentionally droll note, Martineau wrote, "It is sometimes said that the needle is to a woman what the cigar is to a man" (1860d, 597).

58. The Contagious Diseases Acts aimed to curb the epidemic of venereal diseases, particularly among the military, by allowing for the arrest, incarceration (in hospitals), and enforced treatment and examination for up to nine months of any woman suspected of prostitution (men, presumably, were not carriers of venereal diseases). The acts' obvious potential for gender-biased abuse outraged women of all classes and occupations.

59. Josephine Butler to Martineau, March 1872, University of Birmingham Library, hm 120. See also letter from Josephine and George Butler to Mrs. T——— acknowledging receipt of "Mrs. Martineau's . . . very beautiful fine wool work," the box ottoman in which Butler intended to store her papers, employing it as a sort of desk; "I am touched to think how much trouble you must have taken to get this

kind idea carried out" (n.d., Boston Public Library, ms.a.9.2.6, p. 1). The pattern in which Martineau's needlework, intended to be sold for public causes, was purchased for presentation to her good friends—Chapman, Eliza Follen, and Butler—offers a compelling illustration of women's networking through political activism and sewing.

60. Martineau to William Fox, 8 July 1832, Rheinhard Speck Collection, 2:37.

## Chapter 3

1. Martineau to unknown recipient, National Library of Scotland, ms 7261, f. 58.

2. For a discussion of Martineau's treatment of the slavery issue in *Society in America* (1837) and *Retrospect of Western Travel* (1838), see Deborah Logan, *Fallenness in Victorian Women's Writing* (Columbia: University of Missouri Press, 1998), chap. 6, "Harem Life, West and East." See also Harriet Martineau, *Writings on Slavery and the American Civil War,* ed. Deborah Anna Logan (DeKalb: Northern Illinois University Press, 2002). Although *Retrospect* was intended to be the more conventional book, it is as consistently outspoken about slavery as is *Society in America.*

3. Commenting on the political influence of this unknown, informally educated writer following publication of the *Illustrations,* Lord Chancellor Brougham, of the Society for the Diffusion of Useful Knowledge, referred thus (affectionately, if patronizingly) to Martineau.

4. Webb records New York governor W. L. Marcy's 1835 letter to historian George Bancroft: "I regard Miss M. as an exceedingly clever writer *whose opinions of us will go far in Europe to give us a character."* Webb adds, "I know of no better indication of the seriousness with which her visit was regarded" (1960, 148).

5. While it is true that Martineau was sympathetic to abolitionism prior to arriving in America, it was not until her pronouncement at the Boston Female Anti-Slavery Society meeting that she actively began to align her private principles with her public activities. This episode dramatized the idea that abolitionist practice required more than just words on a page.

6. Martineau's compulsion for adventure during this period is evidenced in her assertion that, during a storm while crossing the Atlantic, she persuaded the captain to secure her to a binnacle on deck so she could more fully experience the excitement. The ocean certainly seems to bring out her playful side: "The sea! the sea! I have been looking at and listening to it all the day light most of last week," she wrote to W. Fox. "The luxury is to lie on the land side of a ridge of shingles, one's chin resting on the top, with a *rough* sea *coming up* and splashing one's face. It has much the effect of a storm,—waves mountains high" (31 May 1832, Rheinhard Speck Collection, 2:36). A few years later, the storm during her transatlantic crossing enabled her to experience the genuine article, much to her delight, while her less intrepid companions cowered under the bunks in their cabins.

7. Henley's certainty that Americans "have got at" essential humanistic principles was quickly disproved to Martineau and other foreign visitors curious about how the "peculiar institution" of slavery aligned with American principles. More to the point, America's official confrontation with the slavery issue—the Civil War—only initiated "getting at" the racial issues continuing to plague its social fabric to this day.

8. Martineau to William Tait, 29 August 1833, University College of London Library. Captain Basil Hall wrote *Travels in North America in the Years 1827 and 1828* (1829); Frances Trollope wrote *Domestic Manners of the Americans* (1832).

9. An obvious parallel to Martineau's American travel books is Alexis de Tocqueville's *Democracy in America* (1835). Although she admired this writer immensely (see her article "Representative Men" in *Once a Week* [7 September 1861]), she argued that his perception of American democracy was seriously flawed in two ways: first, he never traveled further south than Washington, D.C., and therefore did not witness slavery, the most direct affront to democracy; and second, he did not account for domestic institutions and the status of the women whose work in the private realm makes possible men's work in the public realm. Martineau's own access to people and institutions during her tour far surpassed that of de Tocqueville. Similarly, of Dickens's *American Notes* she observes that the author did little socializing with ordinary people, a class representing to Martineau a more genuine test of principles and practice than the privileged classes.

10. *How to Observe Morals and Manners* (also 1838) is not technically a travel journal, but it is one of the three books published as a result of the American tour. It provides the analytical framework for cultural assessment, the theory Martineau puts into practice in the other two titles.

11. Clearly, there is no way around this paradox: she is a writer, therefore she perceives the world through "author spectacles"; as for the Americans, they are interested in using her professional influence to promote their various political agendas. In Martineau's defense, avoiding any publishing agreements until after her return to England attests to her concern with ethics and credibility as a social observer.

12. In December 1834, Martineau wrote to her family: "All Philadelphia has called upon me,—people of many ranks and all opinions, religious and political. . . . [They] have made much of me for my Political Economy, and the best of the Quakers on account of 'Demerara.' So that I do believe that I have been in the best circumstances for accomplishing my object" (Chapman 1877, 121).

13. Martineau's progress through America was reported in the 21 December 1834 *Observer:* "The arrival of this lady in the United States has, according to the American papers, produced a very lively sensation. They state that she will pass a part of the winter at Washington, where she will be 'the lion' of the season. She will also visit New Orleans, and thence return by the Mississippi to New York, so as to be in Boston next summer" (University of Birmingham Library).

14. Chapman has been criticized for her effusiveness, although the device was commonly employed by Victorian writers to dramatize their points and does not necessarily connote either insincerity or lack of veracity. However one responds to her style, the fact remains that Martineau chose Chapman as her biographer, providing her with private letters and journals that are not available anywhere else but in the *Memorials.* Martineau's choice should not be surprising, given that it was Chapman who gave shape and force to her friend's abolitionist tendencies in 1835, with lifelong repercussions. See Martineau 1983, 2:22–32 for Martineau's discussion of Chapman's influence.

15. Martineau responded with spirit: "I cannot honestly let you suppose that I agree with you in thinking that there has been any attempt or wish to blind me as to the real state of things at the South. I have been freely shown the notoriously bad plantations *because* they were bad, and have been spontaneously told a great number of dreadful facts which might have just as well been kept from me, if there had been any wish to deceive me" (Martineau to E. G. Loring, 27 May 1835, in Chapman 1877, 131).

16. On 4 July 1834, protests against abolitionist meetings erupted into eight days of violent rioting in New York City; in October, anti-abolitionist rioters in Philadelphia destroyed property belonging to blacks. Martineau landed in New York on 19 September 1834.

17. Colonization, an early form of organized abolition, promoted the establishment of Liberia, an all-black settlement in Africa. The scheme aimed to eliminate slavery from American soil while providing displaced blacks with transportation and resources to establish self-reliant communities. Martineau initially supported the Liberian scheme but changed her mind after learning that colonization merely perpetuated racism and increased slavery when opportunists recaptured and sold the settlers into slavery again. See Martineau 1983, 2:13.

18. See Martineau 1983, 2:1–92, and the introduction to *Society in America* for detailed itineraries.

19. The writer probably refers to "Sowers Not Reapers" and "Weal and Woe in Garveloch," the *Illustrations* tales notorious for promoting sexual abstinence as the most logical solution to overpopulation.

20. Martineau to Ticknor and Fields Publishers, 19 March 1861, University of Birmingham, Martineau Papers, 892 [hereafter referred to as the Martineau Papers].

21. Transcendental philosophy, originating in Boston and Cambridge (Harvard University) intellectual circles, is based on the idea that truth or reality resides in cultivation of the mind, intuition, and spirit and in transcending mundane concerns like social activism. Abolitionists, in contrast, sought to articulate in graphic detail the horrors of slavery in order to generate support through compassion. As a transcendentalist, Emerson did not sympathize with abolitionism until much later in the conflict, while the precocious Margaret Fuller evaded involvement in the great civil cause of her own country (to Martineau's disappointment), although she later championed Italian independence. Martineau viewed such examples as wasted potential during a crisis when all who could help should help, particularly those in intellectually prominent or socially privileged positions. While Fuller's initially warm attitude toward Martineau became antagonistic, Emerson remained a lifelong friend.

22. Martineau was an agnostic, not an atheist, as some have claimed. She rejected the dogma of organized religions (although she vigorously defended individual choice and freedom of worship), but she was unwilling to posit that there is no First Cause. She concluded that First Cause is unknowable and unprovable but plausible: "I am not an atheist according to the settled meaning of the term. An atheist is 'one who rests in second causes,' who supposes things that he knows to be made or occasioned by other things that he knows. This seems to me complete nonsense; and this Bacon condemns as the stupidity of atheism. I cannot conceive the absence of a First Cause" (Chapman 1877, 291). Challenged by the Reverend Patrick Brontë's accusation that she was an atheist, she retorted: "I have never said 'there is no God'" ([1857?], Martineau Papers, 89). Not surprisingly, and unlike many of her contemporaries, Martineau praised Darwin's theories *because* they do not "require the notion of a creation" (Martineau to Holyoake, 26 [?] 1859, British Library).

23. Martineau to Reverend Robert Graves, n.d., Martineau Papers, 2. "Mean whites" refers to poor whites, especially in the South, whose low economic status placed them on a level with black slaves. This class was reviled for its unwitting yet inescapable reminder that white skin was no guarantee of superiority, economic or otherwise.

24. Martineau to William Fox, 13 May 1837, Rheinhard Speck Collection, 2:63.

25. Her refusal to censor certain commentary (on women and slaves, for instance) is vindicated by a review of her American travel books in the *Edinburgh Review*, which she terms "Poor and stupid, except a good passage or two,—such as a clever woman getting at the minds of foreigners better than men" (Chapman 1877, 220). Indeed, what she critiques of American society *as a woman* proves to be central to her value today as a prominent voice of Victorian social reform.

26. Martineau's contentious relationship with the *Times* predates their feud over Civil War reporting during her tenure with the *Daily News*. She notes that, during the writing of the *Illustrations*, "my mother was distressed at finding in the *Times* a ribald song addressed to me" (1983, 1:307–8). This was followed by the *Times*'s disparaging review of *Society in America*. For late-twentieth-century assessments of her impact as a sociologist, see Seymour Lipset's introduction to *Society in America* and Michael Hill's introduction to *How to Observe Morals and Manners* (both reprints).

27. This "fragmentary" quality is accounted for in two ways: first, scientific method (which Martineau applies sociologically) works by breaking the whole into increments to be studied and analyzed, the results being brought back to bear on the whole. Second, as my discussion of needleworking illustrates, the fragmentation of women's daily domestic lives is reflected in the forms and styles they employ as writers. As a result, their work has been denigrated for failing to conform with Aristotelian notions of textual unity, long held by male critics to be the primary standard of literary excellence.

28. Martineau to Dr. Combe, n.d., National Library of Scotland, ms 7265, f. 42.

29. Originally published in the *Southern Literary Messenger, Slavery in America* was later reissued as a pamphlet. Martineau may not have read this review, but she was aware that such tracts, aimed at promoting particular agendas by attacking her credibility, existed in the North and in the South. I am grateful to the staff at Special Collections, Duke University Libraries, for providing me with access to this pamphlet.

30. Martineau's appeal to maternalism does not rely on the dubious concept of "maternal instinct": understandably, children conceived under such conditions might well inspire rejection or revulsion in the mother. Slave motherhood challenged the period's promotion of maternal ideology, further complicated by "natural" or wanted children, who were born into a life of slavery with all the hopelessness that entailed.

31. In her American journal, Martineau wrote: "Sight-seeing,—infirmary,—medical school. *Subjects* almost exclusively supplied from the coloured people, because they can't resist. . . . So these dusky bodies are not contemptible when they are dead[?]" (Chapman 1877, 125). Her comment highlights the irony of racism in medical science, in which anatomy studies on black corpses and the more unthinkable practice of vivisection were justified as necessary to the advancement of scientific understanding. That medical knowledge based on an assumed inferior race was then applied to the presumed superior race constructs a curious paradox, not to say scientific model, indeed.

32. See Martineau's "The Negro Race in America" (1864) for a discussion of this issue. On "quadroon connexions" see the sections on New Orleans in *Society in America* and *Retrospect of Western Travel*.

33. The South Carolinian's example bears a striking resemblance to that of her own brother, James Martineau. James criticized his sister in print in various covert ways, but his most blatant attack was an anonymous, forty-page condemnation, in the guise of a review, of her *Letters on the Laws of Man's Nature and Develop-*

*ment* (which she coauthored with Henry Atkinson), entitled "Mesmeric Atheism." James was as religiously conservative, anti-abolition, and anti-Garrisonian as Harriet was the reverse. The very title of James's article contributed to the erroneous idea that Harriet was an atheist.

34. A popular genre during the eighteenth and nineteenth centuries, conduct books were written by men and women but aimed primarily at an audience of young middle-class females (see, for example, Sarah Ellis's *The Women of England* [1841]). Offering detailed instructions on deportment, appearance, and behavior, conduct books taught middle-class women how to perpetuate the separate spheres dichotomy that kept them chained to the domestic hearth, excluded from the academic studies enjoyed by the men in their class. In some circles, apparently, Martineau's bold textual observations prompted a resurgence of conduct book ideology so as to counteract the "pernicious" effects of this strong-minded woman.

35. Chapman's point is relevant throughout Martineau's life. Whether traveling, attending social functions in England, or at home with her nieces, Martineau was rarely without a companion to assist her with communication problems or advise her in matters of voice projection or articulation during talks or presentations. Of her traveling companion for the American tour, "Miss J." (Louisa Jeffrey), Martineau writes she "was for ever on the watch to supply my want of ears,—and, I may add, my defects of memory" (1983, 2:5). Chapman counters, "her memory . . . was wellnigh unexampled. Those who knew her best say she outrivalled [the historian] Macaulay. 'She never forgot anything'" (1877, 258).

36. For all of the clamor surrounding the publication of Martineau's American travel journals, she never received any royalties for their sale in America. International copyright reform was a cause she later championed, along with Dickens and others.

37. Martineau to Catherine Macready, 29 December 184[?], National Library of Scotland, ms 3713, f. 112.

38. Ibid.

39. Martineau to William Fox, 21 January 1843. Dickens does not present himself as a sociologist, although he was one of the foremost social-problem writers of the period and was extremely influential on both sides of the Atlantic. In preparation for his 1842 tour, Dickens "familiarized himself" with Martineau's American travel books, which he pronounced "the best . . . that had been written on America" (1974, 3:viii–ix). Martineau regarded Dickens as a "man of genius who cannot but mark the time, and accelerate or retard its tendencies." Because of his "genius" and his popularity, she regretted his lack of a "sounder social philosophy" (*A History of England during the Thirty Years' Peace* 2:704–5).

40. Not, however, to the younger generation of abolitionists. Many of her *Standard* letters were signed H. M., prompting "the youth of the cause . . . to call Harriet Martineau 'Her Majesty,' as an expression of their satisfaction" (Chapman 1877, 370). Judging by the outcome of this literary relationship, however, the term might just as easily have had derogatory implications as well.

41. Martineau, who was ill at this time, was unable to attend the 1840 London conference as an honorary delegate representing Massachusetts. Although Turley's book (1991) claims in its very title to record "the culture of English antislavery, 1780–1860," women abolitionists are all but absent from his account. Stowe is mentioned only once in the index, while Martineau and Chapman—there are no index listings at all for them—are mentioned only in passing in the text. This omission

indicates that, of the ideological split within abolitionism for which he accounts, Turley espouses the Evangelical viewpoint for the purposes of history and not the Garrisonian one. To exclude Martineau from a discussion of this era in American history and Anglo-American relations is curious indeed.

42. Printed in 1839 in volume form, *The Martyr Age of the United States* was originally published in the *London and Westminster Review* in December 1838 as a review of the annual reports of the Boston Female Anti-Slavery Society for 1835, 1836, and 1837, compiled by Maria Weston Chapman.

43. Martineau to George Combe, [circa 1840s], National Library of Scotland, ms 7265, f. 42.

44. See Hassett 1996 for a discussion of the striking parallels in the relationships between abolitionist Harriet and her clergyman brother, James, and between abolitionist Chapman and her conservative pastor-mentor, William Ellery Channing. Both women were as determined to persist in their anti-slavery activities as the clergymen were to silence their public activism. Writing to Chapman of her visit to Martineau, activist Lucretia Mott relays Harriet's hope that "much good will result from your labors against clerical assumptions and priestly power" (Boston Public Library, ms.a.9.2, v. 13, p. 24).

45. Martineau refers to the gender iconography popular at the time, in which men were imaged as virile supporters (like an elm tree) of weak women, providing a framework (trellis) for women's vinelike dependence on men.

46. Despite its name, the *National Anti-Slavery Standard,* for which Martineau wrote many articles, was published by the American—not the National—Anti-Slavery Society.

47. The trend established by the nineteenth century's alliance between feminism and abolitionism resurfaces in the twentieth century in the association between second-wave feminism and the American civil rights movement during the 1960s. However, the debate concerning the efficacy of joining these two forces continues, as each contingent strives for adequate representation, a goal that some believe is diminished, rather than enhanced, by joining forces.

48. Specifically, freedom of speech. Most of Adams's congressional career was spent trying to overturn the "gag" bill, which forbade any discussion of slavery and related issues in Congress. The bill was eventually rescinded in 1844. In her 31 March 1776 letter to her husband, John Adams, during the framing of the Constitution, Abigail urged: "I desire you would Remember the Ladies, and be more generous and favourable to them than your ancestors" (Rossi 1988, 10).

49. Although capitalizing on woman's "moral superiority" proves ultimately to be of limited value to feminist aims in that it is an argument notorious for suppressing (rather than liberating) women, Adams employs it effectively at this stage in feminist history, as do others seeking to bring women's concerns to the political forefront.

50. "Unanticipated" in the sense that Martineau's two major periods of invalidism, during the 1840s and again in the 1850s, seemed so positively to herald her demise that she was prompted to wind up her business and personal affairs in anticipation of death. Yet she continued to write during both periods, building steadily and gradually toward the career as a journalist that was to distinguish her mature years.

51. Martineau's 1,642 *Daily News* leaders have been catalogued by R. K. Webb in "Handlist of Contributions to the *Daily News* by Harriet Martineau" (Martineau Papers at the University of Birmingham Library) and by Elisabeth Arbuckle (1994). Martineau also contributed eighteen articles to the *Spectator* in 1858, most of them

addressing American slavery, as well as about seventy letters to the *National Anti-Slavery Standard* between 1859 and 1861. My selections for this discussion aim to illustrate her regular work for the *Daily News* as well as representative articles from other periodicals.

52. Martineau to Nightingale, 29 October 1861 and 2 November 1861, British Library. Chapman identifies one of those sources of a "high political judgment" as the Rt. Hon. W. E. Forster, who asserted that "Harriet Martineau alone was keeping this country straight in regard to America" (1877, 405–6). Martineau's loyalty to the *Daily News* is also seen in this 25 June 1867 letter to Garrison: "I am aware that passionate Americans . . . hate and revile me for not worshipping their country and its political course as faultless. This does not matter in the least . . . but it is quite another matter to try to discredit a newspaper of the very highest character, and of proportionate influence" (Burchell 1995, 18).

53. By 1861, her confidence in America's capacity for redemption had peaked: "I am anything but unhappy about America. It is the resurrection of conscience among them,—the renewal of the soul of the genuine nation. . . . It has come exactly when and as all expected who had a right to an opinion" (Martineau to Nightingale, 8 May 1861, British Library).

54. Martineau to "Dear friend," 7 July 1856; 19 September 1856; and 29 September 1856, Harris-Manchester College Library. Believing she was dying, Martineau wrote to Chapman in January 1855: "I hope to work to the last in the *Daily News,* which is easy work, and the most important possible; and now the more so because the present editor is more up to American subjects than any Englishman I have met with. It is really a substantial comfort to find how sound and enlightened and heartily conscientious he is about the vices of Yankeedom and the merits of your true patriots" (Chapman 1877, 3).

55. Martineau to Sarah Martineau, 4 November 1858, Cumbria Record Office, Kendal.

56. Martineau to unknown recipient, 29 December 1860, Cumbria Record Office, hm 19.

57. Although Garrison often relied on British monetary contributions to the abolitionist cause, the cotton crisis prompted the American abolitionists to raise funds, forwarded through Martineau, to aid in relieving Britain's mill workers.

58. Martineau to Sarah M., 27 May 1865 (hm 44) and 23 February 1866 (hm 50), Cumbria Record Office.

59. This 1848 poem was first published in Chapman's abolitionist periodical, the *Liberty Bell.* The poem's extreme radicalism caused its publication to be delayed. Lynching, rape, and infanticide are posed against such ideals as freedom and equality and Christian compassion. Among the poem's many disturbing qualities is the black slave narrator's persistent appeals to the white, Christian God she has been taught to worship but who never responds to her pleas for justice or, at least, deliverance.

60. These men were all deceased by 1862. See Martineau 1983, 2:90 for the letter of introduction for Martineau and "Miss J." written by the "majestic old judge," Chief Justice Marshall. On her relationship with Judge Story, see Culver 1984. For her links with Henry Clay, see John S. Gatton, "'Mr. Clay and I Got Stung': Harriet Martineau in Lexington," *Kentucky Review* 1:1 (autumn 1979): 49–57.

61. South Carolinian John Calhoun, a planter-politician, served as secretary of war under President Monroe for eight years and as vice president to two presidents: John Quincy Adams and Andrew Jackson. Charismatic orator Daniel Webster

was a Massachusetts senator, nicknamed "dean of states' rights"; politician Henry Clay is best known for his work on the Missouri Compromise. On Sedgwick, see Kelley 1993 and Martineau 1983 2:64–67.

62. William Lloyd Garrison to Martineau, 4 December 1855, Martineau Papers, 349. Demonstrating the strong affinity among himself, Chapman, and Martineau, Garrison adds: "My appreciation of her [Chapman's] genius, intuition, far-sightedness, moral heroism, and uncompromising philanthropy . . . is equalled only by my profound regard for your own exalted intellectual and moral endowments."

63. Garrison to Martineau, n.d., Martineau Papers, II/iv/10/2 (uncatalogued).

64. Garrison to Martineau, 12 June 1867, Martineau Papers (uncatalogued).

65. *New York Independent,* 26 August 1876, 568.

66. *Boston Inquirer,* 12 January 1884.

## Chapter 4

1. See also Ruth Y. Jenkins, *Reclaiming Myths of Power: Women Writers and the Victorian Spiritual Crisis* (Lewisburg: Bucknell University Press, 1995). Jenkins's chapter on "Florence Nightingale's Revisionist Theology" addresses Nightingale's views on religion and social reform.

2. For the purposes of this discussion, religion and philosophy are interchangeable concepts in their shared aim to explain the human condition, to establish a framework through which to comprehend human life. Where Nightingale employs the term "religion," Martineau employs the term "philosophy," although both have the same purpose in mind. Similarly, in Martineau's usage of the terms, nature and science share the same conceptual foundation, in which the laws of science reflect the laws of nature. This reflection contrasts with the aim of twentieth-century science to conquer, rather than harmonize with, nature.

3. For example, *Letters on the Laws of Man's Nature and Development* and "Two Letters on Cow-keeping."

4. *Essentialism* is a contemporary term for the Victorians' separate spheres dichotomy in which gender roles are regarded as biologically determined. In order to improve their status, women must leave the domestic circle to participate in the dominant (public, professional, economic) culture, thus challenging accepted notions about gender roles. Feminists like Martineau worked toward improving the status of women from within that framework (no other viable options being available), claiming that women's "special" qualities should be put to work in the public realm to benefit society. Subsequent feminists claimed that gender roles are not inherent but rather a convenient social custom benefiting men at women's expense. Both perspectives are valid in the context of their respective times; harnessing domesticity and moral values as the means to get women out of the house and into the public realm was the necessary precursor to getting women into positions from which to claim that gender roles are learned social constructs, not inherent value systems.

5. Martineau was a member of the General Committee promoting the medical education of women. An 1871 document listing 973 supporters outlines the committee's goals: "To arrive at a thorough understanding of the real difficulties of the case, distinguishing clearly between those hindrances which are interposed by prejudice or self-interest, and the real obstacles (if any) which are inherent in the question." See Martineau Papers, which include a copy of the official summons dated 23 March 1872 from Sophia Louisa Jex-Blake suing Edinburgh University for

excluding women from medical studies (Martineau 1378). In 1873, Martineau also contributed money "to secure complete medical education for women, after the persecution to which the lady students had been subjected there" (Chapman 1877, 449). Martineau writes: "The question is so important, and the lady students have manifested so fine a spirit and temper under their harassing trials, that a large proportion of their countrymen will, I trust, feel the obligation of sustaining them during their conflict with jealousies and prejudices which will scarcely be credited by a future generation." Women were barred from medical studies by men who argued that familiarity with the bodies and bodily functions of strangers (even cadavers) compromised their moral purity. On the contrary, argues Martineau, the real issue is the professional and economic "jealousy of men."

6. Martineau to W. Fox, 31 December 1849: "If you think, at any time, that I can do anything for Womanhood Suffrage, I am ready to try" (Rheinhard Speck Collection, 2:93). But women must first prepare themselves to assume full citizenship: "I hope by the time that universal suffrage will suit us to help to choose our representatives, every woman will understand German full as well as French is understood now. We shall not be so fit as we might be to exercise our franchise else" (Martineau to Ellen and Margaret Wansey, 6 May 1831, Dorset County Record Office, Dorset, packet 2, C58). She thought it ludicrous that women did not have the vote but believed the time was not yet right for successful franchise agitation; she was correct (Englishwomen did not get the vote until 1918). Of Victorian feminist activism Judith Walkowitz writes: "At this early stage suffrage was an important feminist goal, but not the overriding concern it would become for subsequent generations of feminists" (1980, 125).

7. Mary Wollstonecraft wrote: "When I treat of the peculiar duties of women . . . it will be found that I do not mean to insinuate that they should be taken out of their families. . . . I may be allowed to infer that reason is absolutely necessary to enable a woman to perform any duty properly, and I must again repeat that sensibility is not reason" (1975, 63–64). Wollstonecraft's republican motherhood compares favorably with Martineau's perspective in *Household Education.*

8. See David 1987, which claims that Martineau's "career is defined by her auxiliary usefulness to a male-dominated culture" (31). Early anticipating this charge, Webb notes that, in the *Illustrations,* Martineau's radicalism "outweighs the conservative"; her reformist aims went against the accepted social grain. If her "usefulness" had been merely "auxiliary," "something more on the hygienic order of Mrs. Marcet's fairy tales would have resulted" (1960, 118). Martineau loosely modeled her *Illustrations* after Marcet's political economy series for children published earlier in the century.

9. See, for example, Gaskell's "Lizzie Leigh," "The Well of Pen-Morfa," *Ruth,* and *Mary Barton,* which confront the idea that the inherent innocence of girls who are kept ignorant of sexual snares will protect them from "falls" into worldly sexual experience. This pattern challenges the assumption that a "good" girl will know instinctually the difference between right and wrong without having her ears contaminated by hearing the actual details.

10. In Victorian society, women's philanthropy finds acceptance (grudgingly) because it is work untainted by remuneration, recalling Aurora Leigh's lament that women, in being paid nothing, are paid the worth of their work. See F. K. Prochaska, *Women and Philanthropy.* Significantly, that women should be paid for what they do is central to Nightingale's nursing reforms: "She believed the

paid employment of ladies would be an important aspect of raising the moral tone and social standing of nursing" (Holton 1984, 62).

11. Despite its name, the workhouse forbade inmates to work while living there. Inmates' time was primarily unstructured, although some were kept occupied with crushing bones, breaking rocks, and picking oakum (hemp). Such meaningless busywork ill prepared them to return to society as productive, self-sufficient citizens.

12. Aunt Bell represents the type of undeserving poor that invents fictional relatives to increase their dole or stipend. A related issue is infanticide, in some cases committed in order to collect money from burial clubs sooner rather than later or to claim a larger dole without having the extra mouth to feed.

13. Although workhouse inmates were not officially criminals, they were criminalized by analogy. Some workhouses forced inmates to wear stigmatizing uniforms and cut off their hair to prevent them from mixing freely in public; inmates were arrested if they attempted to leave the system without permission. As a former workhouse inmate, Jane is not free to make decisions about her life independent of the poorhouse board. Hence, although offered sanctuary by Cousin Marshall to prevent being sent back to the workhouse, she is arrested, like a fugitive, once her hiding place is revealed.

14. Martineau returns to this theme of women's "political invisibility" under the law (introduced in 1837's *Society in America*) in her *Daily News* leaders on the legal status of women, discussed later in this chapter.

15. Martineau applauds the professional and economic successes of famous women of the day—actresses Fanny Kemble and Rachel, novelist Harriet Beecher Stowe, singer Jenny Lind, physician Dr. Elizabeth Blackwell, and women artists— throughout her *Daily News* writing on women.

16. Unions between conquerors and conquered were urged by officials to discourage Polish resistance and to complicate their hopes for regaining their homeland.

17. Nightingale to Martineau, 21 December 1858: "The most effecting thing I think I ever read . . . was your tale of the death of a drinking woman [Margaret Kay] in one of your Political Economy stories. . . . I have seen this in real life frequently and in its most terrible aspects—But I have never forgotten the lesson you taught—to look upon it with even friendly interest" (British Library). See also Chapman 1877, 480.

18. See Martineau's *Dawn Island* (1845) and *Forest and Game Law Tales* (1845–1846), both written to benefit the Anti-Corn Law League.

19. This practice was common among factory workers, who dosed their children with "Godfrey's Cordial," putting them to sleep for ten or more hours at a stretch and allowing the mothers to go to work without hiring a baby-sitter. Many children failed to survive either the years of dosing or the "seasoning" (withdrawal); if they did, the long-term physical and psychological effects were tragic and irreversible. See Hellerstein et al. 1981, 235–38.

20. When Angus overhears the fishermen gossiping about Ella—"jesting on the fishwoman who carried herself as high as a princess"—he is relieved because it tells him "she had lost none of her dignity under the pressure of her cares" (81–82).

21. Despite the family's thrift, too many mouths to feed burden society as well, causing problems not limited to the nuclear family. An unforeseen occurrence like widowhood would cause Ella's massive family to burden the community directly. See also "Private Economy" (*Once a Week* [10 January 1863], 79–82) on the moral imperatives of managing one's economic affairs responsibly, for individual, familial, and communal welfare.

22. See the following *Daily News* articles by Martineau on infanticide, foundling hospitals, and brutality toward children: 13 February 1863; 30 September 1863; 28 July 1864; 8 August 1865; 8 September 1865; 19, 20, and 28 October 1865. These problems existed in Victorian England no less than in China and India. Nor was infanticide limited to the lower classes: middle- and upper-class women wishing to limit family size for convenience could afford to purchase the services of a birth attendant who would ensure them a "stillbirth."

23. I omit Martineau's only full-length novel, *Deerbrook* (1839), from this discussion because, although it was popular and influential, its women characters are uniformly conventional (in Valerie Pichanick's sense of the term) without demonstrating feminist qualities or issues, as do many of her other characters. In my view, *Deerbrook* is Martineau's nod to novel writing of the domestic-romance school, and as such it avoids the gender critiques enlivening her other work. *Deerbrook* was a necessary experiment, after which Martineau returned to the genres and topics that were clearly better suited to her literary and reformist inclinations.

24. Part of this difference depends on the quality of life specific to one's class: living in working-class squalor hardly prepares one for maintaining upper-class standards of hygiene; on the other hand, it is equally likely that upper-class women employers of domestics would be at a loss in the kitchen. Another factor is the increasing trend for women to work outside the home, leaving them no time to care for their own homes, much less to teach their daughters. The decline in domestic standards Martineau bemoans reflects a major shift created by industrialization, which threw into relief many existing social anomalies while creating some new ones of its own.

25. See also Martineau's *Daily News* articles on domestic labor: 11 December 1856; 12 February 1857; 24 October 1863; and 29 June 1865.

26. See *Daily News*, 5 December 1860 on the training of girls in "Common Things" or the rudiments of practical housekeeping.

27. Like needleworking, domestic labor was also associated with prostitution. Judith Walkowitz writes, "the previous work experience of registered women [prostitutes] had been as maids of all work—the bottom rung of the ladder of domestic service—although their moves into prostitution had usually been occasioned by a period of unemployment" (1980, 194). Working women found that prostitution earned them more money for less labor; thus, the charge that working women were sure to end up prostitutes has some validity. The solution is not, Martineau argues, to prevent them from working in order to curb prostitution but to provide them with education, respectable occupations, and a living wage in the first place.

28. Cy Frost observes: "While specifying the exclusion from economic opportunity as the instrument of a general subjugation of women, Martineau persuasively makes a further connection between the relegation to menial work and the poorer morals and health of the relegated" (1991, 266). While she heralds the rise of pauper girls to the ranks of domestic service as progressive, she also welcomes the advent of machines wherever possible to free them from unnecessary drudgery. The "further connection" Martineau makes is to present domestic skills as an essential key to improved morals and health.

29. Bessie Rainer Parkes was one of the "ladies of Langham Place," a group of women who established the *Englishwoman's Journal*, the Society for the Promotion of Employment for Women, Victoria Press, and various training opportunities and employment bureaux for women workers.

30. See the following Martineau *Daily News* articles on women and work: 16 February, 2 April, 21 October, and 2 December 1856; 18 March 1857; 27 and 29 November 1858; 17, 23, and 25 November 1859; 9 January and 2 November 1860; 9 July 1863; 18 February and 5 May 1864; and 20 May 1865. See also her entries in Knight's *Guide to Service* (1838–1839) and *Guide to Trade* (1838–1844) as well as "Nurses Wanted" (1865), which compares the degraded occupation of governessing with the newly elevated field of nursing. Another reason to welcome the extinction of governessing is that the practice allows middle-class parents to "skimp" on their daughters' education, something they did not do with their sons'. Governesses were not, typically, formally educated themselves, raising well-founded doubts about the quality of their teaching.

31. In *Household Education* she argues: "Men do not attend the less to their professional business, their counting-house or their shop, for having their minds enlarged and enriched, and their faculties strengthened by sound and various knowledge; nor do women on that account neglect the work-basket, the market, the dairy and the kitchen" (1849, 155–56).

32. Martineau wrote this article, significantly, to assuage the sting of having to remain at home with her needlework while brother James was off at university. Fortunately for literary history, she was a natural scholar who taught herself when formal education was denied her.

33. On female education, see *Daily News,* 26 November 1855; 4 December 1856; 25 November 1859; 5 December 1860; 27 January 1863; 4 August 1864; 30 September 1865; and 24 November 1865.

34. Martineau's 8 June 1844 letter to Lord Howrick (later third Earl Grey) offers an example of her promoting women's cause in her private correspondence. Of the trend toward delayed marriages among the middle classes due to economic constraints, she writes: "there is one [benefit], to me, of very great consolation,—the rapid improvement in the cultivation and standing of Women. It is a trying time for them now,—in the transition between the old understanding that every woman is provided for by her husband or father, and that which is coming—that every lady must work, the unmarried for themselves, as the married for their children. Multitudes are under the necessity now, before the requisite variety of employments is opened. But the gain is worth the suffering. These middle class women are, by hundreds of thousands, the conservators of purity of morals, while they are finding themselves possessed of new powers, and are opening up a new and higher destiny to those who follow them. . . . [N]o subject can be more worth a statesman's deep consideration" (Lord Grey Papers, Durham University Special Collections). This letter demonstrates Martineau's respectful but firm tone when appealing to the peerage on behalf of social causes and related parliamentary bills.

35. Admittedly, while Martineau's egalitarian notion of "good taste" is laudable, there are those who are heavily invested in preventing such a sharing of expanded sensibilities. Throughout history, groups in power fought vigorously to suppress the intellectual impulse in the masses; literacy was forbidden to slaves, peasants, and women since it reveals that oppression is a social construct, not "natural" or divinely ordained. Despite the example of the Lowell factory women, factory workers are just as likely to be less, rather than more, contented with their situation as a result of intellectual enlightenment.

36. Lorna Duffin notes an obvious reason for denying Sophia Jex-Blake's bid to admit women to Edinburgh University medical school: "a body of female doctors attending women would displace an equivalent number of male doctors or dimin-

ish their incomes" (1978, 49). Further, assuming that married women are perpetually pregnant, they could not be doctors because "they would be 'inactive for some months annually.' . . . If to be a doctor a woman needs to remain celibate then medicine for women is unnatural" (50).

37. See Barbara Ehrenreich and Deirdre English, *For Her Own Good: 150 Years of the Experts' Advice to Women* (Garden City, N.Y.: Anchor Books, 1978), for a discussion of the development of domestic science. See also *Daily News,* 4 August 1864 on the achievements and remaining challenges of working women's colleges.

38. An 1848 letter to Mrs. Bensusan indicates that her interest in nursing as a profession for women predates her affiliation with Nightingale. She suggests that a solution for "forlorn" (orphaned) young women is to emigrate as nurses: "I think the most honourable (because most needed) vocation at present is that of sick nurse" (Rheinhard Speck Collection, 1:11).

39. Nightingale's brand of nursing combines "feminine" nurturance with "masculine" administrative skills. On Nightingale and related articles on nursing, see also *Daily News,* 2 June, 4 September, and 22 November 1855; 22 January 1856; and 25 June 1860, 23 February 1865 and 31 January 1866.

40. Both Martineau and Nightingale urged nurses' obedience to the attending physician as necessary for regulating the nursing profession. They sought to eliminate the problems created by nursing's links with prostitution and, at the other extreme, with religious orders (sisters' first loyalty was to their order, priest, and God). The standardization and secularization of nursing, with its attendant emphasis on higher education, were to both women the paramount issues of nursing reform.

41. Rejecting the links between nursing and promiscuity, Martineau turns this argument against men (see *Daily News,* 21 October 1856 on female health practitioners, and 25 March 1859 on Dr. Elizabeth Blackwell). Taken to its logical extreme, female modesty, decency, and decorum, so vigorously promoted as central to Woman's Mission, depend on women being attended by female doctors. Martineau further argues that "bachelor doctors" cannot presume to know better than women how to treat children. Nightingale's variation on this theme is to resist the idea of female doctors patterned after the male standard, arguing "There is a better thing than making women into medical men, and that is making them into medical women" (Holton 1984, 65). Rather than women entering male-driven medical schools, she urged the creation of a completely separate curriculum designed to train women to care for the health needs of women and children; male doctors should attend male patients only. This proposal reifies the separate spheres dichotomy, but in a way that clearly strengthens the position of women as professional (rather than domestic, volunteer, unpaid) caregivers.

42. Although the language of decorum and morality was used to condemn prostitution, the real objection stemmed from the spectacle of women working in the public realm *for remuneration.* The most significant factor in Victorian women's status is their crippling economic dependence which, in a capitalist culture, renders them powerless to compete with men on any level. Examples of the equation between respectability and work include governessing, in which penurious middle-class women lose caste permanently by working for a living, and philanthropy or volunteer work, in which women were permitted to work outside the home for social causes, provided no money was exchanged. The message, of course, is that women's work is worthless, which is why they either work for free or degrade themselves as real or metaphorical prostitutes.

43. Both Martineau and Nightingale promote a brand of nursing centered around the home, through the visiting nurse. Sandra Holton (1984) notes that Nightingale was relatively uninterested in hospital or institutional nursing, preferring to promote the idea of a grassroots health movement linking cleanliness with morality and good health. Like Martineau, Nightingale regarded "medicine" as merely a temporary solution to acute health problems; in contrast, attending to the daily minutiae of domestic hygiene offers a permanent self-generated path to maintaining good health through preventive measures, a perspective that flatly challenges the medical establishment's authority. Martineau's *Household Education* comes to mind here.

44. Nightingale was so concerned to eliminate any association between nurses and immorality that she desired male rather than female attendants to nurse male patients who had venereal diseases or who were convalescing. She further insisted that nurses be directly answerable to matrons only, never to male staff members, even in military hospitals. Obedience to doctors in medical matters was expected; otherwise, "no male was to have a disciplinary jurisdiction over them. A quite autonomous women's sphere of authority was to be created, with its own hierarchical structure" (Holton 1984, 66).

45. Both Martineau and Nightingale knew from direct experience that the "jealousy of men" infects the healing professions as it does every other avenue of women's employment: seen, for instance, in the exclusion of women from medical schools. They hoped that women nurses would be more palatable to a resistant male medical establishment than women doctors, thus serving to open doors in medical careers for women.

46. As George Eliot observed: "On one side we hear that woman's position can never be improved until women themselves are better; and, on the other, that women can never become better until their position is improved—until the laws are made more just, and a wider field opened to feminine activity" (1998, 234). Although Martineau denounced feminist "declaimers," her increasing impatience with the extreme slowness of social and political reforms led her to border on this behavior in her own activism, on several occasions, particularly later in life.

47. Socialite and writer Caroline Norton earned notoriety when her husband took her children away from her and refused to disclose their location. Stunned to learn that he had the legal right to do so and that she had no rights at all, Norton wrote to earn money for her legal expenses, which her husband promptly seized—again, legally—as his own property. He accused her of adultery to further discredit her cases. Norton devoted her life to the reform of custody laws, married women's property laws, and divorce laws and lived to see considerable progress in all three areas. That her elevated social status was no protection against such blatant human rights abuses speaks eloquently for those women who had no class standing or social contacts to assist them in securing justice.

48. Over ten years later, little had changed for women in this respect. Martineau writes of brutality against women who are unprotected by the law, citing coroners' reports of women who were starved or beaten to death by drunken, abusive husbands and the alarming propensity of juries to acquit them: "On marrying he becomes possessed of his wife's property, and of whatever she may earn, and he may destroy her by hunger afterwards. By her surrender of her property, and of her future earnings, she does not become entitled to a maintenance from him, if he thinks proper to evade the obligation" (*Daily News*, 30 August 1865).

49. In her journal, Martineau writes: "Read 'Katherine and Petruchio' [*The*

*Taming of the Shrew]*, with the same effect that that play ever has; with wonder at its fun and cleverness, and much enjoyment thereof, but intolerable pain at the treatment of Katherine. Such a monstrous infringement of all rights, leading to such an abominable submission, makes one's blood boil as much as if it were not a light comedy, but a piece of history. I have always found myself more sad at that comedy than at any tragedy" (Chapman 1877, 207).

50. For Martineau's *Daily News* articles on women's issues and the law, see 25 March and 8 September 1853; 28 June 1854; 29 February, 26 March, 2 April, and 15 December 1856; 4 March 1857; 28 May 1858; 2 July 1864; and 30 August 1865 and the CD letters, 28, 29, and 30 December 1869.

51. Nightingale observes, "The dress of women is more and more unfitting for any 'mission,' or any usefulness at all. . . . Compelled by her dress, every woman now either shuffles or waddles" (Holton 1984, 62). Lorna Duffin draws a compelling analogy between fashion and the cult of invalidism: "The image of the perfect lady . . . became the image of the disabled lady, the female invalid. The agent of conspicuous consumption became the conspicuous consumptive" (1978, 26).

52. As Martineau recognized, fashion was more than just a superficial pastime: it was a powerful indicator of women's degraded status. For her articles on dress, see *Daily News,* 17 June 1856; 17 July 1856; 13 January 1857; 15 October 1861; and 19 January 1865. Also see *Once a Week,* 5 November 1859; 24 November 1860; and 5 November 1863.

53. This is only one of many examples in which Martineau's earlier promotion of laissez-faire government has shifted over the years to her promotion of government intervention in order to secure social reforms.

54. Nightingale to Martineau, 9 March 1863 and 14 March 1864 (British Library). Their correspondence rehearses the two women's concern with Nightingale's difficulties in having her work taken seriously by the War Office and medical establishment. On the difficulties Nightingale faced, Rev. Elwin wrote: "The physicians I understand denounce Miss Nightingale's sanitary precepts. The faculty can never endure unprofessional interlopers. The part of her work which relates to Nursing—and which is indeed the main part—they pass by altogether. I have had some strong testimonies to its immense value" (Elwin to Martineau, 26 April 1860, Martineau Papers, 288).

55. Chapman outlines the petition for "The Ladies National Association for the Repeal of the Contagious Diseases Acts," signed by Martineau and others: "Unlike all other laws for the repression of contagious diseases, to which both men and women are liable, these two apply to women only, men being wholly exempt from their penalties. The law is ostensibly framed for a certain class of women, but in order to reach these, all the women residing within the districts where it is in force are brought under the provisions of the Acts. . . . [I]t is unjust to punish the sex who are the victims of a vice, and leave unpunished the sex who are the main cause both of the vice and its dreaded consequences" (1877, 430–32).

56. With the challenges to class assumptions posed by working women dressing above their station, appearance was no longer a reliable indicator of either promiscuity or purity. Thus, any woman walking down any street became fair game for suspicious policemen. "Any honest girl might be locked up all night by mistake by it," notes Nightingale (letter to Martineau, 31 May 1864, British Library).

57. Of the women's movement, Janet Courtney writes: "Harriet Martineau upheld it in principle, though indifferent to its propaganda" (1933, 13). As the examples outlined in this chapter prove, "she found [other] ways of 'putting women forward'" (202).

58. See Leila Ahmed, "Western Ethnocentrism and Perceptions of the Harem" and *A Border Passage*. See also Martineau's chapter "The Hareem," in *Eastern Life, Present and Past* (1848), which details her visits to harems in Cairo and Damascus.

## Chapter 5

1. Martineau to Dr. Combe, 23 November 1857, National Library of Scotland, ms 7366, f. 52; Martineau to Mrs. Combe, 5 December 1857, National Library of Scotland, ms 7366, f. 56. For women, Martineau envisions a curriculum that incorporates humanities (to elevate the mind and spirit), "common things" (domestic skills and household management), and health sciences like sanitation reform and anatomy classes (to curb preventable illness and death through responsible, informed lifestyles). That "proper" women regarded the former as unnecessary and the latter as scandalous indicates the narrowness of the period's gendered thinking on female education. It was not until over a century after her death that women began aggressively to take responsibility for their own health, encouraged by feminist groups and women's studies classes.

2. With the exception of Maria Martineau, my discussion focuses on Martineau's relationships with famous or public women who are today considered feminist models, and for this reason I do not address her friendship with Fanny Wedgwood. The relationship is not featured in the *Autobiography* nor is it mentioned in Martineau's extant correspondence with other people; theirs is a strictly private relationship, although the letters are enriched by discussions of contemporary people and events. See Arbuckle 1983 for a thorough record of this extraordinary friendship, which links Martineau with Charles and especially Erasmus Darwin. I focus instead on women who contribute to an understanding of Martineau's feminism as it is articulated throughout her private and public writings.

3. Wollstonecraft writes: "To rise in the world, and have the liberty of running from pleasure to pleasure, they must marry advantageously, and to this object their time is sacrificed, and their persons often legally prostituted" (1975, 60).

4. Martineau confronts this issue several times in her life, through the extramarital relationships between William Fox and Eliza Flowers, George Eliot and G. H. Lewes, and John Stuart Mill and Harriet Taylor, leading some to label her a prudish, bluestocking spinster. On the contrary, her writings demonstrate that her attitude is prompted by her concern with promoting Woman's Cause. Writing to Milnes on her falling out with longtime friend and mentor William Fox over his unconventional relationship with Eliza Flowers, she wrote: "Because I think Love, like other passions, guidable by duty, he pities me as an unfeeling person" (21 April 1844, in Sanders 1990, 87). Her focus on the distinction between *sense* and *sensibility,* and her emphasis on self-discipline, are evident in this early letter (12 May 1825) to Helen Martineau on controlling one's feelings: "Try to turn your attention from your feelings altogether. They will obtrude themselves sometimes I know but drive them out by instantly fixing your thoughts upon some object unconnected with yourself. Feelings are given us to be directed and controlled, not to be thought about: much less talked about. . . . Beware of it, as you value your own happiness" (Sanders 1990, 5).

5. Although compelled to warn Catharine on several occasions to cease her excessive flattery, Martineau praised her combination of literature and domesticity: "I had a great admiration of much in Miss Sedgwick's character, though we were too opposite . . . to be very congenial companions. . . . The insuperable difficulty be-

tween us,—that which closed our correspondence, . . . was her habit of flattery" (1983, 2:65–66). See also *Westminster Review* (October 1837) for Martineau's review of Sedgwick's writings, which, Martineau observed, "had better be passed over with the least possible notice" (1983, 2:67). Two years later she wrote in her journal: "my having hurt C. Sedgwick is more pain to me than all the rest can compensate. I really thought I was right, and am not sure now but I was; but I will look into it. I must be brave about the consequences of my own mistakes as well as about undeserved blame" (Chapman 1877, 188).

6. Martineau's success with *Illustrations* and her trip to America comprise her own declaration of independence from family strictures. But Chapman's concern that Martineau was being "beguiled" was probably justified, since at the time her letter arrived, the charismatic Henry Clay had been vigorously attempting to persuade Martineau to endorse his colonization schemes. See also Martineau to E. G. Loring, 27 May 1835, in Chapman 1877, 131, in which Martineau seems defensive about her southern experiences or, perhaps, about her ability to maintain objectivity on these issues.

7. Martineau to Harriet Grote, 6 February 1867; Martineau to Nightingale, 7 April 1860 (both at British Library).

8. See, for example, Theodora Bosanquet's *Harriet Martineau: An Essay in Comprehension* (London: Frederick Etchells, 1927). The appendix reprints a 30 December 1884 letter from James to the *Daily News*, taking issue with certain points made by Mrs. Fenwick Miller in her biography of Harriet (1884). Chapman devotes an entire chapter to the break between Harriet and James, entitled "The Life Sorrow," which she justifies thus: "One undertaking to throw light upon the life of Harriet Martineau cannot with truth or justice or common-sense ignore the act by which her 'own brother' placed himself in the same category with the defamers of old times whom she must never again meet. . . . I am not surprised to find, in her Autobiography, so few words given to this great calamity of her life. But what in her is magnanimity in me would be unfaithfulness" (1877, 321–22). See also Arbuckle 1983, 141 n. 4.

9. Chapman to Martineau, 23 August 1869, Martineau Papers, 136.

10. According to Helsinger, Sheets, and Veeder, eds., *The Women Question*, "For the first time, in 1843 and 1844, she [Fuller] wrote with admiration of abolitionism, a subject she had once barred from her Boston 'Conversations'" (1:43), but she never became a champion of this cause. On a related point, Fuller's journalism career began with Horace Greeley and the *New York Tribune*. In a heated 1861 exchange involving Greeley in the pages of the *National Anti-Slavery Standard*, Martineau again confronted a major ideological obstacle: Greeley's brand of expansionist, protectionist, republican Unionism (compare with Sedgwick) stood in direct opposition to Martineau's insistence on immediate, universal emancipation. Martineau's ideological clash with Fuller anticipates that with Greeley.

11. Martineau to Emerson, 25 February 1852, Houghton Library, ms am 1280 (2083). Despite her criticisms of Fuller (for which she was condemned by William Clark (see Boston Public Library, ms am 1450 [204], 18 April 1877), Martineau deeply felt the "needless waste" of Fuller's untimely death. Responding to reviews of the work in the *Athenaeum*, she adds that Fuller's *Memoirs* unfortunately "confirms existing prejudices" against her. Recalling the ideological discord between the two women, Martineau concludes that her own "free and wholesome" Ambleside life—"It is curious that one so solemn in youth should be growing merry in her fiftieth year," she wrote of herself—would doubtless arouse Fuller's disgust at her common "vulgarity."

12. Martineau to Mrs. Peabody, 3 May 1870, Martineau Papers, 610. According to Helsinger, Sheets, and Veeder, eds., there is some doubt as to whether Fuller actually married Ossoli (1:44); if Fuller was mistress rather than wife, and her child illegitimate, Martineau would surely have regarded her last days as disgraced rather than crowned.

13. Martineau's 22 April 1853 *Daily News* leader uses the Stowes' visit to broach the topic of the cotton supply. In this and many subsequent articles over the next ten years, she urges the exploration of alternative markets that could supply the product without implicating England in the perpetuation of American slavery.

14. See also Pichanick's discussion of Martineau's observation in *Society in America* that, whereas British women occupy themselves with fashionable follies, American women develop a morbid preoccupation with religion as a "substitute for boredom" (1980, 95).

15. Stowe to Martineau, October 1856, Martineau Papers, II/iv/21 (uncatalogued).

16. Stowe to Chapman, 10 October 1869, Martineau Papers, 152. Stowe wrote *Lady Byron Vindicated* (Boston, 1870), a biographical sketch of Lady Noel Byron that was critically ravaged in the British press. See also Martineau Papers, 134 and 140 and Martineau to Mrs. Shepherd, Boston Public Library, mss acc. 358, n.d. on this episode.

17. Stowe records the "lionizing" she enjoyed while visiting England in *Sunny Memories of Foreign Lands* (1854). Chapman, according to Martineau's letter to Fanny Wedgwood (6 February 1862), inspired a rather different response, at least among some of Martineau's friends and acquaintances: "My friendship with Mrs. Chapman is a real misery to her [Mrs. Reid]—as it is a vexation to another intimate of mine,—Mr. Atkinson" (Arbuckle 1983, 218). Atkinson did, however, gratify Chapman's request that he contribute remarks on Martineau to her *Memorials* volume (see 1877, 486–88). Elizabeth J. Reid, a close friend of Martineau's, founded Bedford College for Women in 1849 (with Martineau and Fanny Wedgwood serving on its board) and was active in the transatlantic anti-slavery campaign. The source of Reid's animosity toward Chapman is curious since, according to Clare Midgley, Reid "aligned herself with the Garrisonians" and often hosted visiting American abolitionists in her home (1992, 163).

18. Martineau refutes the apocryphal story concerning Lord Rolle's "disaster" as the rumor of a "wag" (1983, 2:126–27). According to popular legend, Lord Rolle tripped and literally rolled off the dais at the moment of his presentation to the new queen. Visiting foreign dignitaries, told this was a uniquely British custom honoring the monarch, were supposedly urged to do the same, but they wisely declined.

19. On the strength of Victoria's enthusiasm for her *Illustrations* and other series, Martineau wrote to R. M. Milnes of her proposal to Victoria concerning the plights of factory children: "In order to secure perfect freedom of speech, I pledged myself that *she* should not be committed in any way,—that her name should not be used at all; and I particularly requested that no sort of acknowledgment,—no notice of my letters whatever should be thought of. . . . I have a gracious answer, and her commands to forward my letters to her through Sir J. Graham" (22 July 1843, in Sanders 1990, 79–80). She requested that Milnes intercede for her with Graham so that her letters would be taken seriously, but the project, apparently, never came to fruition.

20. Martineau to Mrs. Horner, National Library of Scotland, ms 2213, f. 254. Along with the issue of "distressed needlewomen," Martineau objected to cousin-marriages. To Nightingale she wrote: "I am so glad you touch upon cousin-marriages.

The Queen has sadly increased our difficulties about that: but I have written as freely on the subject . . . and especially when her husband laid the foundation stone of the Asylum for Idiots" (15 July 1860, British Library). Victoria and Albert, who were cousins, married at a time when cousin-marriages were increasingly under scrutiny as genetically undesirable.

21. Letter to the editor signed "A" and attributed in Arbuckle 1994 to Martineau.

22. Martineau to Mr. Pigott, 1 September 1865, Rheinhard Speck Collection, 4:48.

23. For further discussion of Victoria, see Martineau's *History of England during the Thirty Years' Peace*, 4:80–162, passim.

24. Weston Family Papers, Boston Public Library, ms.a.9.2.5, p. 108.

25. Elizabeth Barrett was neither the author (as some speculated) nor the dedicatee of *Life in the Sickroom*. Valerie Sanders writes that if there was a particular dedicatee, Martineau "offers no clue to her identity"; instead, the *Autobiography* "implies a vague and general dedication" (1979, 11). Martineau's own words— "There could not be a stronger proof of how I *felt* that book than my inability to speak of it except to my unknown comrades in suffering" (1983, 2:171–72)—attest to an audience of invalids in the general public, her message personalized through the epistolary format and through an appeal to the implied privacy of the sickroom environment she shares with them.

26. On the other hand, *Life in the Sickroom* also serves as a self-help manual offering guidance for chronic invalids, based on the idea that life can be as fully appreciated in the microcosm of the sickroom as in the macrocosm of the active outside world. Invalidism in fact forces people into a more direct confrontation with a realism that the healthy can and do avoid.

27. Intending to raise her as her own child and provide her with everything from immunizations to education, Martineau had made elaborate preparations for Ailsie's arrival, but the child's former owner reclaimed her before she could sail to England. See Martineau 1838c, 1:269–70 and 1983, 2:143–44.

28. While Martineau praised "Paracelsus," she was disappointed in "Sordello." When Browning asked her advice on the latter, she told him to "choose between being historian or poet. [He] cannot split the interest. I advised him to let the poem tell its own tale" (Chapman 1877, 207). Browning raged, "all that conceit—and such conceit!" (Sanders 1979, 12) against the criticism he himself had pressed her for. To a "dear friend," she wrote: "I knew him only in his hoity-toity days, twenty years ago; and it would be hard to judge him by that. His insolence, quarrelsomeness and conceit were then only equalled by Robertson's; but there was a fine independence, frankness and kindliness about him which made me hope much from his manhood" (28 August 1856, Boston Public Library, ms.eng.289).

29. Barrett was intrigued by Martineau's mesmeric cure, which was credited with the latter's release from the Tynemouth sickroom, but she preferred spiritualism, which Browning condemned and Martineau shunned as unscientific. During her most intense interest in mesmerism, Martineau diagnosed Barrett—"a woman who does not know what science is, and who has been in one long reverie about 'spirits' all her life" (28 August 1856, Boston Public Library, ms.eng.289)—as unsuited to this sort of treatment.

30. See Martineau to Mr. Graves (27 November 1857): "I have long ceased to consider C. Brontë truthful. . . . E.g. her stimulating and encouraging me to the utmost to bring out the Atkinson Letters, while, at that very time, and from my house, she was writing to a stranger, prepossessing him against the unpublished

book" (*Brontë Society Transactions* 16 [1973]: 200). This assertion indicates that the dissension between the two women was hardly one-sided, with "poor delicate Currer" critically savaged by what this *Brontë Society Transactions* article terms "that 'acid feminist'," Harriet Martineau.

31. Martineau to Leigh Hunt, 24 January [n.y.], British Library.

32. Martineau to Mrs. Ogden, 1 December 1850, Armitt Library, Ambleside, no. 12. "Coarseness" in this context relates to Brontë's candid (though hardly graphic) presentations of female sexuality through her passionate, though studiously chaste, heroines.

33. Although no champion of organized religion, Martineau resisted religious prejudice and defended religious freedom. Charles Dickens' anti-Catholic attitude contributed to the break in his literary relationship with Martineau. Martineau's second novel, *Oliver Weld,* was submitted to publisher George Smith personally by Charlotte Brontë but rejected, apparently, because of its favorable portrayal of Catholicism. In what seems to me a highly uncharacteristic act, Martineau burned it soon after to avoid issues (to publish or destroy) likely to arise posthumously (Martineau 1983, 2:381–83). A writer of Martineau's stature could surely have found another publisher rather than resort to destroying the manuscript. Brontë's role in promoting this work is also curious, given her anti-Catholic bias.

34. Although accused of acrimoniousness, Martineau was not alone in her critiques of *Villette.* See "New Novels by Lady G. Fullerton and Currer Bell," *Christian Remembrancer* 25 (1853). See also Barker 1994, which notes other reviews that are similar to Martineau's in that they both praise the novel's craft and complain about its gloomy atmosphere and anxious female characters. See the *Spectator,* 12 February 1853, 155–56 on the "bitter complaint" of women who must work for a living and the *Guardian,* 23 February 1853, 128–29 on the author's "somewhat cynical and bitter spirit." For a general overview of reigning attitudes toward the "coarseness" of women writers, see W. R. Greg, "The False Morality of Lady Novelists," *National Review* 8 (1859). See also G. H. Lewes's review of *Jane Eyre* in *Fraser's* 36 (1847) and of *Shirley* in *Edinburgh Review* 91 (1850).

35. When Martineau read of Brontë's regard for Constantin Heger in Elizabeth Gaskell's biography, she expressed sympathy for the Hegers, who "received C. B. into their home and daily life. . . . [H]ow foul a treachery Mme H, even more than her husband, has to endure" as a result of adulterous passion, both real (Charlotte) and now fictional (Lucy Snowe) (Arbuckle 1983, 152). That Brontë's attachment to Heger was unrequited matters not at all to those ready to point to such scandals as proof of women's inferiority.

36. Literary history and Martineau's reputation have been poorly served by accounts of the Martineau-Brontë relationship in which Harriet is portrayed as a malevolent aggressor and Charlotte the unwitting victim. See, for example, the following articles in *Brontë Society Transactions:* C. H. L. 1973; Sir Tresham Lever, "Harriet Martineau and Her Novel *Oliver Weld*" 16 (1974): 4–84, 270–73; and Margaret Smith, "'A Warlike Correspondence': More Letters from Harriet Martineau" 18 (1985): 5–95, 392–97. Any discussion that begins by terming Martineau "that acid feminist" (as in the first-named article) constitutes bias, not balanced scholarship.

37. See Martineau Papers, 89–109. This furious exchange is characterized by Nicholls's pomposity, Patrick Brontë's accusations that Martineau suffers from atheistical delusions, and Martineau's rigorous insistence on strict adherence to facts and, especially, on the return of her letters to Brontë: "Not a line of any letters will be

published without my express authorisation; and I entirely disapprove of the publication of private letters" (Martineau to Nicholls, 15 November 1857, Martineau Papers, 101). See chapter 6 for a discussion of the seriousness of this issue to Martineau.

38. Martineau to Moxon, 22 July 1857, Bodleian Library, Oxford University, d.2, ff. 198–235; Martineau to Miss Winkworth, 13 June 1857, National Library of Scotland, ms 6044, f. 186. See also Martineau to Snow Wedgwood, in Arbuckle 1983, 149–54.

39. Elizabeth Gaskell to Martineau, [circa November] 1857 (102) and 9 November 1857 (92), Martineau Papers.

40. Martineau to Mrs. Ogden, 11 February [n.y.], Armitt Library, no. 26.

41. Haight's version of their first meeting differs strikingly from that of Eliot's husband, J. W. Cross: "Harriet Martineau called on Monday morning with Mr. Atkinson. Very kind and cordial. I honour her for her powers and industry, and should be glad to think highly of her. I have no doubt that she is fascinating when there is time for talk" (Cross 1885, 202). The disparity between the two quotations is certainly curious.

42. Martineau to John Chapman, 29 October 1852, in Haight 1954); Martineau to "My dear friend," 29 August 1873, British Library.

43. See also Sanders 1986b, 123 and David 1987, 63.

44. George Eliot to the Brays and Sara Hennell, 2 June 1852, in Haight 1954, 2:32.

45. According to Valerie Pichanick, Harriet "had privately told George Eliot that 'from the beginning of her success [James had been] continually moved by jealousy and envy towards her'" (1980, 136). Eliot was relieved to learn that Martineau's breach with her brother James was not exposed to public view, overtly at least, in the *Autobiography*.

46. Martineau to Charles Bracebridge, 21 November 1859, Martineau Papers, 83.

47. Though scandalous, Eliot's alliance with Lewes—like those of William Fox and Eliza Flowers, and of John Stuart Mill and Harriet Taylor—did at least validate the heterosexual values of the dominant ideology. Martineau's singleness placed her outside of this gender system, making her—theoretically at least—a sort of loose cannon and therefore more threatening to the sex/gender framework, perhaps, than an adulterous woman.

48. William Clark to M. Higginson, 18 April 1877, Boston Public Library, ms 1450 (204). James Payn offers a plausible explanation: "Miss Martineau revelled in argument," he wrote (1884,85), attributing his long, successful friendship with her to his "prudence to abstain from argument with ladies of whatever rank or age or genius."

49. Martineau to Mrs. Combe, 5 December 1857, National Library of Scotland, ms 7366, f. 56.

50. Martineau to Mrs. Beeton, 4 March 1862, Additional Letters, University of Birmingham Library, hm 175. Martineau suffered all her life from digestive problems and perpetually experimented with foods and cooking methods that would minimize the condition. She was a great believer in the power of food to create, to aggravate, and to heal physical conditions; carrot tea, a nightly glass of champagne, and chibouque smoking were some of her more unusual remedies. Mesmerism is not hypnosis but a mode of working with energy fields to clear obstructed energy paths (believed to be the cause of illness). Denounced by some as quackery, mesmerism claimed many famous Victorian adherents. Its theory is strikingly similar to that underpinning acupuncture, acupressure, polarity and Reiki therapies, and other ancient and so-called "New Age" alternative healing practices.

51. Martineau to Bessie Rainer Parkes, 17 May 1863, Girton College, Cambridge, BRPIX, 37. Martineau to Sarah Martineau, February 8, 1860, Cumbria Record Office, 15.

52. Martineau to Nightingale, 7 January 1860, British Library; Martineau to Nightingale, 17 May 1863, British Library.

53. Martineau to Mr. Chambers, 19 January 1853, National Library of Scotland, ms 341/87, f. 39; Martineau to "Dear Madam," 22 February 1862, Rheinhard Speck Collection, 5:59; Martineau to Nightingale, 7 January 1860, British Library.

54. Martineau to H. Grote, n.d., Armitt Library, no. 4.

55. Maria Martineau to B. R. Parkes, 21 February 1860, Girton Library, BRP ix 38.

56. Martineau to Spring [Brown], 2 February 1864, National Library of Scotland, ms 1890, f. 25.

57. J[ane] Arnold to Martineau, 1[?] March 1864, University of Birmingham Library, hm 13. Jane (or "K") was Matthew Arnold's favorite sister. Russell Martineau to Martineau, 3 March 1864, ibid.

58. Nightingale to Martineau, 12 February 1864, British Library.

59. Martineau's attempts to grapple with philosophical issues in the face of her own mortality did not, clearly, prepare her for the inexplicable loss of someone younger and healthier than herself, someone for whom she had great ambitions and hopes, someone who embodied, to her mind, the best qualities for promoting Woman's Cause.

60. Nightingale to Martineau, 28 February 1864 and 7 March 1864, British Library. George Eliot, in her letter to Sara Hennell (7 March 1864), wrote: "I was more sorry than it is usually possible to be about the death of a person utterly unknown to me, when I read of Maria Martineau's death. . . . For an invalid like Harriet Martineau to be deprived of a beloved nurse and companion, is a sorrow that makes one ashamed of one's small grumblings" (Cross 1885, 375).

61. *Cassandra* was written in 1852 and privately printed seven years later. That Martineau read it is uncertain, as is the range of the pamphlet's circulation, although the relationship between Martineau and Nightingale did coincide with its printing.

62. Nightingale to Maria Martineau, 27 October 1863, Martineau Papers, 703.

63. A survey of their correspondence indicates that their initial relationship was professional, being based on Nightingale's desire to promote hygiene reform through Martineau's literary influence. Judging by the former's frequent expressions of concern over confidentiality—much of the documentation she provides Martineau with concerns high-ranking officials in government and the military—the issues were controversial and potentially explosive. Martineau was as anxious to ensure Nightingale's anonymity and privacy as she was to protect her own. See also Martineau to Nightingale, 17 May 1863, British Library on the concern of the *Daily News'* lawyer about the potential for a libel suit by the War Office due to Martineau's leaders promoting Nightingale's reform measures and critiquing the army's resistance to implementing them.

64. Nightingale to Martineau, 30 November 1858; Martineau to Nightingale, 3 December 1858, British Library.

65. To Nightingale she wrote: "*Our* book *[England and Her Soldiers]* is at present quoted largely and incessantly in American medical journals, as a guide [for] military management in the northern states." Of her American articles she adds: "I thought it [the war] a good opportunity to interest their public in saving their citizen-soldiers' health. It is more to the purpose that the medical journals are learning from us" (20 September 1861, British Library).

66. Nightingale wrote: "Your book ['Sowers Not Reapers'], though it must be some 18 years since I read it—stays by my memory, as everything you write does. And I believe I could repeat it pretty nearly all, as I could nearly all your 'Deerbrook' and much of your 'Political Economy' Tales" (Nightingale to Martineau, 8 February 1860, British Library).

67. Martineau to Nightingale, 13 May 1867, British Library.

68. See Martineau's "Miss Nightingale's *Notes on Nursing*" (1860). The article compares *Notes,* which is about healing, with Martineau's own *Life in the Sickroom,* which is about how to be an invalid, asserting that "each is the counterpart of the other" (394). Both agree on the importance of solitude and privacy for healing and that illness is a great instructor.

69. Martineau to Nightingale, 7 January 1860, British Library.

70. Martineau to Sarah M[artineau], 23 April 1865, Cumbria Record Office, 43; see also letter of 16 March 1865.

71. Pilkington Jackson to Martineau, 19 January 1863, Martineau Papers. Jackson exaggerates: Martineau does not, like Nightingale, come from the "ranks of luxury."

72. Chapman apparently refers to a series of *Daily News* articles on army hygiene in 1859, which were written at the height of Martineau's collaboration with Nightingale, followed by her *Atlantic Monthly* articles in 1861. The letters specifically addressing the CD Acts were published in the *Daily News* in December 1869.

73. Martineau to Mary Martineau, 25 November 1869, Martineau Papers, Additional Letters, no. 85. F. or Frances ("Fan") Arnold was one of Matthew Arnold's sisters.

74. Martineau to Mary Martineau, 29 March 1871, Martineau Papers, Additional Letters, no. 89; Josephine Butler to Martineau, 22 December 1872, Martineau Papers, 119.

75. Butler's capsule history of the CD Acts' beginnings highlights a wonderfully Victorian political intrigue: Parliament could not bring itself to put this issue before Victoria, the "young virgin Queen." With the advent of Albert, the cause was reintroduced but foundered when he dismissed it in disgust. But during Victoria's extended mourning, the bill was slyly passed, without Albert's political influence or, seemingly, Victoria's awareness of its import. As their work demonstrates, Nightingale, Butler, and Martineau served as political watchdogs during a period when Victoria's unavailability directly threatened Englishwomen of all ranks.

76. Martineau to Nightingale, 7 April 1860, British Library. Martineau associates Chapman—at the forefront of America's second revolution, the abolition of slavery—with George Washington, a primary figure of the first.

## Chapter 6

1. There are a few exceptions to this, notably her early work for the *Monthly Repository* and some of her writing for *Once a Week* (signed "From the Mountain").

2. See Anne D. Wallace, "'Nor in Fading Silks Compose': Sewing, Walking, and Poetic Labor in *Aurora Leigh,*" *ELH* 64 (1997): 223–56 for a discussion of this theme in Barrett Browning's poem.

3. Unknown writer to Maria Weston Chapman about Martineau, n.d., Boston Public Library, ms.a.9.2.5, p.36.

4. Webb notes that Howitt's notice of Martineau was "not exactly to her taste" (1960, 266).

5. Webb argues that Martineau's spinsterhood and warm admiration for her

female friends signal her latent lesbianism (1960, 51); I am not sure where that leaves her warm admiration for her many male friends, for children, or for the "workies" or working classes. As justification for his claim, he terms Martineau's disapproval of extramarital relationships as "hysterical self-righteousness," a term he also applies to her reaction to certain American Civil War policies. Such reliance on sexist stereotypes trivializes her intellectual judgment while dismissing those attitudes with which Webb disagrees: attitudes that were, to Martineau's mind, politically legitimate and socially significant. Valerie Pichanick responds: "Webb's allegations are without foundation; the existence or non-existence of lesbian tendencies in Harriet Martineau can simply not be proved; and his attempt to do so was perhaps motivated by the desire to try and explain Martineau's literary prolificity, and her unfeminine prominence in the highly masculine society of Victorian England" (1977, 29). See also Pichanick 1980, 109–10.

6. See Martineau 1983, 2:409 for an account of Martineau's inability to conceal her identity in print, either through anonymity or masculine "gender markers." See also Nightingale to Martineau, 8 February 1860, British Library.

7. Peterson argues: "Martineau's rhetorical style in *Household Education,* as in virtually all of her writing, is masculine. . . . Her feminism in this book is . . . a demonstration of a woman's achievements in a male literary style" (1990b, 189). She concludes that "Martineau avoids the professionalization of domestic responsibilities" (192), a claim disproved by an analysis of Martineau's writings on women and work and its relation to the public realm, to women's education, and to their occupational and economic progress.

8. Margaret Anne Doody, in *The True Story of the Novel* (New Brunswick, N.J.: Rutgers University Press, 1996), bases her study of this point on the argument that the novel's origins can be traced in cultures throughout the world: in Western civilization, back to ancient Greece and especially Egypt. This confronts the idea that the genre is essentially an eighteenth-century English invention, marginally influenced, perhaps, by *Don Quixote,* but essentially "created" by Defoe and Richardson. Doody's study reveals that letter writing played a central role in the development of the genre in cultures throughout the world.

9. In his introduction to an American reprint of Martineau's *History of the American Compromises* (1856), the editor praised her ability to see the significance of contemporary events within the "big picture" of social history, contrasting with most journalists, who only "write to the moment." To E. Moxon, Martineau wrote: "Few know what very high and *peculiar* ability is required for newspaper writing" (Bodleian Library, n.d.): for example, an omniscient perspective such as that associated with fiction writing. Martineau had a remarkable facility for interpreting the present through the lenses of history.

10. Martineau to John Bright, 7 August 1845, British Library; Martineau to Moxon, 16 August 1845, Rheinhard Speck Collection, 4:8. To H. Bright, Maria Martineau wrote that her aunt is "profoundly indifferent to fictions" (1 April [n.y.], Rheinhard Speck Collection, 1:27).

11. Martineau to Nightingale, 9 January 1859, Martineau Papers, II/i/20 (uncatalogued).

12. Even after she had become an invalid, Martineau was not reclusive but, as in Tynemouth, a force for the public good. She established a lecture series in Ambleside to instruct the "workies" on the evils of alcohol and the benefits of sanitation reform. She convinced them to avoid the pubs and invest their earnings by sub-

scribing to the Ambleside Building Society, which aimed to provide affordable housing for the poorer classes. She posited that moral standards in this class would improve once their living conditions improved. She also records lecturing on American slavery to prepare the locals for the arrival of William and Emily Craft, escaped American slaves on the abolitionist lecture circuit.

13. Of *Household Education,* Gillian Thomas writes: "the book clearly served as something of a dress rehearsal for the more systematic personal reminiscence of the *Autobiography.* Many incidents from her own childhood are presented in the first person; others"—those depicting painful events—are thinly "disguised by third-person narration" (1985, 65).

14. Correspondence with Frederick Hunt (*Daily News* editor) demonstrates that her fears on this point were well founded: she learned that Hunt's son, to pay off his debts, sold some of the letters she had written to his father (Martineau Papers, 490).

15. Martineau to "Dear Sir," 2 July 1843, National Library of Scotland, ms 7269, f. 110.

16. Porter 1998 has this to say about James Martineau's shorthand transcriptions: "Abstracts by James in Rich's shorthand of Martineau's letters to him, 1819–43, together with a typed transcript made in the U.S. by W. S. Coloe in 1958 for Prof. R. K. Webb. It should be noted that the transcript is not very accurate as far as names (in longhand in the original) are concerned and should be treated with a degree of caution." I am indebted to Mr. Alan Middleton, secretary of the Martineau Society, for providing me with this citation.

17. I found the following fragment in the Weston Family Papers, written by Maria Weston Chapman: "Mem. to copy that Document before I pack up the papers for —— Martineau c/o solicitor, 26 Coethorpe Rd, B'ham. Colshorpe" (n.d., Boston Public Library, ms.a.9.2.6, p. 2). This tantalizingly suggests that Chapman shipped the letters, papers, and journals used for the *Memorials* to a Birmingham solicitor; my attempts to trace these materials further have yielded no leads.

18. James Payn also regretted having to speak on Martineau's behalf when her letters are so articulate, but he too complied with her wishes: "It is a great pity, for she discussed people and things that have an interest for everybody with a personal knowledge of them that is most unusual. I regret this veto the more, since but for it I could cull many an extract illustrative of a side of her character the least understood and appreciated—namely, its tenderness and domesticity" (1884, 95). Payn's concern to establish Martineau's feminine qualities aimed to counteract critics' urge to masculinize her for her challenges to separate spheres ideology. His twenty-year friendship with her gives him greater authority to comment on her qualities, he claims, than those critics who do not know her personally.

19. Martineau employs similar language when refusing one of several government pensions: "the queen and her premier would be, though they perhaps do not know it, exposed to insult for showing friendliness to an infidel like me. I could not think of exposing the queen to such anonymous abuse as has come to me" (Chapman 1877, 447).

20. Martineau to Lady Grey, 8 April 1848 and 13 April 1848, Special Collections, Durham University. For publishing correspondence see, for example, the following Martineau letters: Truebner and Company, Ticknor and Fields, John Chapman, George Smith (Smith and Elder), F. Hunt (*Daily News*), and Charles Knight (all at University of Birmingham Library and indexed). See also Martineau's letters to Lord Chancellor Brougham, University College of London Library, 1832.

21. Martineau to Nightingale, 7 December 1858; Nightingale to Martineau, 8 February 1860 and 22 May 1866; Martineau to Nightingale, 6 September 1867 (all at British Library).

22. Martineau to Spring [Brown], 20 October 1874, National Library of Scotland, ms 1890, f. 52.

23. Martineau to Justice Story, 7 July 1836, Rheinhard Speck Collection, 4:69.

24. Although Martineau regarded her deafness as a "peculiar disadvantage," she also claimed that her "trumpet of remarkable fidelity" allowed her to "gain more in tete-a-tetes than is given to people who hear general conversation. Probably its charm consists in the new feeling which it imparts of ease and privacy in conversing with a deaf person" (1837, xv).

25. Martineau to Lord Brougham, 21 November 1858, Martineau Papers, Additional Letters, no. 18.

26. Martineau's correspondence was at times burdensome, for example at the height of her *Illustrations* fame. "The correspondence threatened to become infinite," she notes. As for the "operatives, young persons, and others" whose circumstances she addressed in her writing and who wrote to her, "I could not find [it] in my heart to resist such clients" (1983, 1:195).

27. Originally published as a series of letters by the *Athenaeum* in November and December 1844.

28. Some of the most aggressive resistance to Martineau's experiments with mesmerism came from her own family. For a time, she resisted the urge to try the practice, out of respect for them; but when she heard with increasing frequency accounts of others' success with the process when her own case was pronounced "hopeless," she gave the method a try. Even when it apparently cured her, some family members never forgave her. See Martineau 1983, 2:191–204.

29. Atkinson alludes to J. S. Bushnan's 1851 review of *Letters on the Laws of Man's Nature and Development* entitled "Miss Martineau and Her Master" (London: John Churchill).

30. Illustrating the quality of spontaneity intrinsic to epistolary writing, Martineau claims that her role as editor was minimal, since she found it unnecessary to "alter a single sentence" of Atkinson's prose (1983, 2:336). She discusses this topic at length in the *Autobiography* (see 2:329–70), detailing the range of public responses but persistent in her loyal defense of the work, which afforded her profound spiritual and philosophical liberation.

31. Martineau to Mrs. Ogden, n.d., Armitt Library, no. 23.

32. The exact details of Martineau's deafness are unclear. She seems to have been able to hear only when someone spoke directly into the trumpet tube, but her *Ireland* preface suggests that she could hear peripheral sounds as well. James Payn claims her ability to hear varied with the general state of her health, so that in periods of strong health (1852, for instance) her hearing ability was amplified somewhat more than usual.

33. Aware of her impact on society through the *Daily News,* Martineau delights in the genre-bending interplays between epistolary correspondence and leader writing. To Sir John Walsham she sent fair warning about her use of this "double perspective genre": "*Entre nous,* I was nearly the first person the editor applied to for contributions; and I have gone deeper and deeper into it, till now I supply 4 or 5 leaders a week, besides other matter. I tell you this simply to show you that any information you may be kindly disposed to send me will not be thrown away" (17 May 1854, Rheinhard Speck Collection, 5:7).

34. The British ship *Trent* was boarded first by Confederate emissaries to Europe and then by gun-shooting Union soldiers in pursuit of them; Britain was outraged, and the two countries narrowly avoided an international incident by President Lincoln's apology. Martineau's disgust with the Union's actions stems from its affront to British neutrality, and its placing British abolitionists like herself in the awkward position of having, in effect, to defend southern interests: regardless of conflicting ideologies, she maintained, the Confederates had every right to board a neutral ship. The Morrill Tariff was a protectionist tax levied to finance the war; Martineau, who was adamantly antiprotectionist (seen in her anti–corn law activism), denounced the tariff as a regression into Old World ways unworthy of the New World's promise. Together, these events highlighted the fact that the Civil War was not simply a North-South polarity; instead, northern concerns were further split between the abolition of slavery and the preservation of the Union, two related but separate issues.

35. Martineau's wording provides an illustration of how she "rehearsed" ideas in private correspondence. She used nearly identical phrases in a letter to Fanny Wedgwood a month earlier (20 January 1860, in Arbuckle 1983, 214–15).

36. To Chapman, she wrote: "If I stop, it must be publicly and clearly made known that the arrest of the correspondence is by the committee's desire, and not mine" (Chapman 1877, 374). Martineau declined to publish the letters in volume form, saying only, "It would defeat my plan to grant such requests" (380). This is curious and unaccountable, given her other volumes of published letters; such a collection of the *Standard* letters would have been efficacious in promoting the abolitionist cause by widening this paper's admittedly narrow audience, particularly once her relationship with it terminated.

37. Martineau wrote to Henry Reeve on her being criticized for her politics: "it is a very small fine to pay for the privilege of making the Americans and their country better understood in England than they might otherwise be. . . . If I were 20 years younger, and able to go I should probably find my second unpopularity [the *Standard* affair] got over as wonderfully as my first [the Boston Female Anti-Slavery Society meeting]" (Sanders 1990, 206).

38. More precisely, although Martineau implies in the *Autobiography* that her *Daily News* assignments began with the Ireland letters, Arbuckle's list (1994) indicates that she wrote leaders several months prior to her Irish journey. Similarly, although regular contributions ceased in 1866, she continued to write occasional pieces as late as 1874.

39. Martineau to Edwin L. Godkin, 27 February 1871, Houghton Library, ms am 1083 (577); Martineau to "Dear friend," 16 July 1871, National Library of Scotland, ms 1890, f. 30.

40. James Payn posits that deafness directly shaped her inclinations for certain kinds of intellectual pursuits, which, if more "abstruse" (some would say "masculine") than typical of most women, "certainly never 'hardened' her" (1884, 93). In other words, deafness fostered her preference for philosophy and political and social science over fiction.

## Epilogue

1. No page number available; this little book, held at the Norwich Record Office, seems to be a local production.

2. Martineau to W. Fox, 11 October 1832, Rheinhard Speck Collection, 2:44; Martineau to Mrs. Ogden, 1 December 1850, Armitt Library, no. 12; Martineau to

Leigh Hunt, 24 January 1851, Martineau Papers, Additional Letters, no. 110.

3. Illustrating a disturbing lack of comprehension about Martineau's relationship with America, Courtney wrote, "If only she could have kept off abolitionism, she might have been quite popular in American society" (1933, 155). As editor of *Household Words,* Charles Dickens was critical of Martineau's "grim determination" to redeem and reform Victorian society (Lohrli 1973, 358).

4. Martineau to Spring [Brown], 20 October 1874, National Library of Scotland, ms 1890, f. 52; Martineau to Edward Smythe Pigott, n.d., British Library; Martineau to Mrs. Ogden, 19 July [n.y.], Armitt Library, no. 2; Martineau to Pigott, n.d., British Library.

5. Martineau to E. Moxon, 15 September 1848, Rheinhard Speck Collection, 4:13. Martineau's cultural observations and theological analyses in *Eastern Life* are punctuated with practical advice on how to dress appropriately for the climate and on how to keep fabrics free from vermin by proper laundering and ironing methods. Martineau, wielding her iron against the backdrop of the pyramids, must have presented an astonishing image to the locals.

6. Martineau to Mrs. Ogden, 1 July [n.y.], Armitt Library, no. 8 and 21 December [n.y.], Armitt Library, no. 11.

7. Martineau to Jane Carlyle, 184[?], National Library of Scotland, ms 2883, f. 104. One of the reasons the relationship deteriorated is indicated in a journal excerpt: "On Monday Crabb Robinson told me he did not care if he never saw Carlyle again, he talked so against anti-slavery and philanthropic exertions. Very withering to any young persons who might have heard him" (Chapman 1877, 201). Known today as one of the seminal minds of the period, Carlyle, in his writing on the Negro race, demonstrates a racism as offensive to present-day readers as it surely was to Martineau.

8. Martineau to Henry Atkinson, 5 May 1850, Rheinhard Speck Collection, 1:3; Martineau to Helen Martineau, 29 December 1849 and Martineau to Mr. Carpenter, 24 November 1852 (both Harris-Manchester College Library). That Martineau expresses these sentiments to Atkinson so pragmatically refutes the idea that it was the plain older woman's "crush" on the young charismatic Atkinson that led her to nearly "ruin" her career over the *Letters.* Offering yet another example of the "jealousy of men," women who explore spiritual and philosophical realms challenge the dominant Christian hegemony as surely as women whose professional success, against all odds, must be accounted for as a sexual aberration or social anomaly.

9. Payn's daughter was named after Martineau. So was the type of cigar she smoked following her return from the Middle East, a racehorse, and a heifer (Weston Family Papers, ms.a.9.2.5., p. 111).

10. Claudia Orazem notes that the review was co-authored by George Scrope, John Lockhard, and John Croker (128).

11. Weston Family Papers, ms.a.9.2.6., p.5.

# WORKS CITED

Arbuckle, Elisabeth S., ed. 1983. *Harriet Martineau's Letters to Fanny Wedgwood*. Stanford: Stanford University Press.

———. 1994. *Harriet Martineau in London's "Daily News."* New York: Garland Publishing.

Barker, Juliet. 1994. *The Brontës*. New York: St. Martin's Press.

Barrett Browning, Elizabeth. 1993. *Aurora Leigh*. Ed. Kerry McSweeney. Oxford: Oxford University Press.

[Boyle.] 1837. *A Review of Miss Martineau's Work on "Society in America."* Boston: Marsh, Capen & Lyon.

Brontë, Charlotte. 1966. *Shirley*. New York: Penguin Books.

Burchell, R. A., ed. 1995. *Harriet Martineau in America: Selected Letters from the Reinhard S. Speck Collection*. Berkeley: Friends of the Bancroft Library.

Butler, Josephine. 1896. *Personal Reminiscences of a Great Crusade*. London: Horace Marshall & Son.

Carlyle, Thomas. 1883. *Correspondence of Thomas Carlyle and Ralph Waldo Emerson*. Boston: James Osgood.

Cazamian, Louis. 1973. *The Social Novel in England, 1830–1850*. London: Routledge & Kegan Paul.

Chapman, Maria Weston. 1845. *Liberty Bell*. Boston: Privately printed.

———. 1877. *Memorials*. Boston: J. R. Osgood, 1877.

C. H. L. 1973. "Severe to the Point of Injustice." *Brontë Society Transactions* 16 (3–83): 199–202.

Collins, John. 1841. *Right and Wrong among the Abolitionists of the United States. With an introductory letter by Miss Martineau*. Glasgow: G. Gallie.

Cone, Helen and Jeannette Gilder, eds. 1887. *Pen Portraits of Literary Women by Themselves and Others*. Vol 2. Boston: Educational Publishing.

Cook, Elizabeth. 1996. *Epistolary Bodies*. Stanford: Stanford University Press.

Courtney, Janet E. 1920. *Freethinkers of the XIXth Century*. London: Chapman and Hall.

———. 1933. *The Adventurous Thirties: A Chapter in the Women's Movement*. London: Oxford University Press.

[Croker, John Wilson.] 1833. Review of *Illustrations of Political Economy*, by Harriet Martineau. *Quarterly Review* 49 (April): 136–52.

———. 1839. Review of *How to Observe Morals and Manners*, by Harriet Martineau. *Quarterly Review* 63 (January–March): 61–72.

Cross, J. W., ed. 1885. *George Eliot's Life*. New York: AMS Press, 1965.

Culver, Michael. 1984. "A Harriet Martineau Letter." *Notes and Queries* (December): 475–78.

Daly, Mary. 1978. *Gyn/Ecology*. Boston: Beacon Press.

David, Deirdre. 1987. *Intellectual Women and Victorian Patriarchy*. Ithaca: Cornell University Press.

Dentith, Simon. 1983. "Political Economy, Fiction, and the Language of Practical Ideology in Nineteenth-Century England." *Social History* 8: 183–99.

Dickens, Charles. 1974. *Letters of Charles Dickens.* Vol. 3. Ed. Madeline House and Graham Storey. Oxford: Clarendon Press.

Donovan, Josephine. 1984. "Toward a Women's Poetics." *Tulsa Studies in Women's Literature* 3, nos. 1–2: 99–110.

Duffin, Lorna. 1978. "The Conspicuous Consumptive: Woman as an Invalid." In *The Nineteenth-Century Woman. Her Cultural and Physical World,* ed. Sara Delamont and Lorna Duffin, 26–56. London: Croom Helm.

Easley, Alexis. 1997. "Victorian Women Writers and the Periodical Press: The Case of Harriet Martineau." *Nineteenth-Century Prose* 24, no. 1 (spring): 9–20.

Eliot, George. 1998. "Margaret Fuller and Mary Wollstonecraft." In *Woman in the Nineteenth Century,* ed. Larry J. Reynolds, 232–34. New York: Norton.

"Emancipated Women." *Spectator,* 3 January 1885, 14.

*Eminent Women.* 1856. London: n.p.

Fraser, Rebecca. 1988. *The Brontës: Charlotte Brontë and Her Family.* New York: Fawcett Columbine.

Frawley, Maria H. 1992. "Harriet Martineau in America: Gender and the Discourse of Sociology." *Victorian Newsletter* (spring): 13–20.

Frost, Cy. 1991. "Autocracy and the Matrix of Power: Issues of Propriety and Economics in the Work of Mary Wollstonecraft, Jane Austen, and Harriet Martineau." *Tulsa Studies in Women's Literature* 10, no. 2 (fall): 253–71.

Fryckstedt, Monica Correa. "The Early Industrial Novel: *Mary Barton* and Its Predecessors." *John Rylands University Library Bulletin* (n.d.): 11–30.

Fuller, Margaret. 1983. *The Letters of Margaret Fuller.* 2 vols. Ed. Robert N. Hudspeth. Ithaca: Cornell University Press.

Garrison, Wendell Phillips. 1969. *William Lloyd Garrison: The Story of His Life.* 4 vols. New York: Negro Universities Press.

Greg, W. R. 1877. "Harriet Martineau," *Nineteenth Century* (August): 97–112.

Haight, Gordon S. 1985. *George Eliot: A Biography.* New York: Penguin.

———, ed. 1954. *The George Eliot Letters.* New Haven: Yale University Press.

"Harriet Martineau: On This Day June 29, 1876." *London Times,* 29 June 1896.

Hassett, Constance. 1996. "Siblings and Antislavery: The Literary and Political Relations of Harriet Martineau, James Martineau, and Maria Weston Chapman." *Signs: Journal of Women in Culture and Society* 21, no. 2 (winter): 374–409.

Hellerstein, Erna, et. al. 1981. *Victorian Women: A Documentary Account of Women's Lives.* Stanford: Stanford University Press.

Helsinger, Elizabeth K., Robin Lauterbach Sheets, and William Veeder, eds. 1983. *The Woman Question: Society and Literature in Britain and America, 1837–1883.* 3 vols. Chicago: University of Chicago Press.

Hoecker-Drysdale, Susan. 1992. *Harriet Martineau: First Woman Sociologist.* Oxford: Berg.

Hollis, Susan, ed. 1993. *Feminist Theory and the Study of Folklore.* Urbana: University of Illinois Press.

Holton, Sandra. 1984. "Feminine Authority and Social Order: Florence Nightingale's Conception of Nursing and Health Care." *Social Analysis* 15 (August): 59–72.

[Holyoake, George J.] 1876. Death notice of Harriet Martineau. *Index,* December 28.

———. 1876. Obituary of Harriet Martineau. *National Reformer: Secular Advocate and Freethought Journal* (9 July).

———. 1877. Review of *Harriet Martineau's Autobiography. Secular Review* (18 March).

Howitt, William. 1846. "The People's Portrait Gallery: Harriet Martineau." *The People's Journal* 11 (14 March): 141–42.

Hunter, J. Paul. 1990. *Before Novels: The Cultural Contexts of Eighteenth Century English Fiction.* New York: W. W. Norton.

Hunter, Shelagh. 1995. *Harriet Martineau: The Poetics of Moralism.* Leicester: Ashgate Publishing.

Ice, Joyce. 1993. "Women's Aesthetics and the Quilting Process." In *Feminist Theory and the Study of Folklore,* ed. Susan Hollis, 166–77. Urbana: University of Illinois Press.

Kelley, Mary, ed. 1993. *The Power of Her Sympathy: The Autobiography and Journal of Catharine Maria Sedgwick.* Boston: Northeastern University Press.

Kelley, Philip, and Ronald Hudson, eds. 1990–1991. *The Brownings' Correspondence.* Vols. 8–9. Winfield, Kans.: Wedgestone Press.

Kelley, Philip, and Scott Lewis, eds. 1992–1994. *The Brownings' Correspondence.* Vols. 10, 12. Winfield, Kans.: Wedgestone Press.

Kenyon, Frederic G., ed. 1899. *Letters of Elizabeth Barrett Browning.* New York: Macmillan Co.

Lieb, Laurie Yager. 1986. "'The Works of Women Are Symbolical': Needlework in the Eighteenth Century." *Eighteenth Century Life* 10, no. 2 (May): 28–44.

Lohrli, Anne. 1973. *Household Words.* Toronto: University of Toronto Press.

Macheski, Cecilia. 1986. "Penelope's Daughters: Images of Needlework in Eighteenth-Century Literature." In *Fetter'd or Free? British Women Novelists, 1670–1815,* ed. Mary Anne Schofield and Cecilia Macheski, 85–100. Athens: Ohio University Press.

Maclise, Daniel. 1883. "Miss Harriet Martineau." In *Daniel Maclise, 1806–1870: A Gallery of Illustrious Literary Characters.* New York: Scribner and Welford.

Maitzen, Rohan Amanda. 1998. *Gender, Genre, and Victorian Historical Writing.* New York: Garland Publishing.

Martineau, Harriet. 1822. "On Female Education." *Monthly Repository* (November): 77–81.

———. 1827. *The Rioters; or, A Tale of Bad Times.* Wellington: Houlston.

———. 1831. *Five Years of Youth; or, Sense and Sentiment.* London: Harvey and Darton.

———. 1832–1834. "Berkeley the Banker," part 2. In *Illustrations of Political Economy.* London: Fox.

———. 1832–1834. "Briery Creek." In *Illustrations of Political Economy.* London: Fox.

———. 1832–1834. "The Charmed Sea." In *Illustrations of Political Economy.* London: Fox.

———. 1832–1834. "Cousin Marshall." In *Illustrations of Political Economy.* London: Fox.

———. 1832–1834. "Demerara." In *Illustrations of Political Economy.* London: Fox.

———. 1832–1834. "Ella of Garveloch." In *Illustrations of Political Economy.* London: Fox.

———. 1832–1834. "The Farrers of Budge Row." In *Illustrations of Political Economy.* London: Fox.

———. 1832–1834. "For Each and for All." In *Illustrations of Political Economy.* London: Fox.

———. 1832–1834. "Ireland." In *Illustrations of Political Economy.* London: Fox.

———. 1832–1834. "Sowers Not Reapers." In *Illustrations of Political Economy.* London: Fox.

———. 1832–1834. "Weal and Woe in Garveloch." In *Illustrations of Political Economy.* London: Fox.

———. 1833. *Poor Laws and Paupers Illustrated.* London: Fox.

———. 1834a. "Jerseymen Meeting." In *Illustrations of Taxation.* London: Fox.

———. 1834b. "Jerseymen Parting." In *Illustrations of Taxation.* London: Fox.

———. 1834c. "Letter to the Deaf." *Tait's Magazine:* 174–79.

———. 1836a. "Essay on Moral Independence." *Miscellanies.* Boston: Hilliard, Gray.

———. 1836b. "Solitude and Society." In *Miscellanies,* vol. 1. Boston: Hilliard, Gray.

———. 1837. *Society in America.* 3 vols. London: Saunders and Otley.

———. 1838a. *How to Observe Morals and Manners.* London: Knight.

———. 1838b. "The Ladies Maid." In *Guide To Service.* London: Knight.

———. 1838c. *Retrospect of Western Travel.* 3 vols. London: Saunders and Otley.

———. 1839. *The Martyr Age of the United States.* Boston: Weeks, Jordan & Co.

———. 1841. Introduction to *Right and Wrong among the Abolitionists of the United States,* by John Collins, 4–5. Glasgow: G. Gallie.

———. 1844. *Life in the Sickroom: Essays by an Invalid.* London: Edward Moxon.

———. 1845a. *Letters on Mesmerism.* London: Edward Moxon.

———. 1845b. *Mind amongst the Spindles,* in *The Lowell Offering.* Boston: Jordan, Swift, and Wiley.

———. 1849. *Household Education.* London: Moxon.

———. 1849–1850. *A History of England during the Thirty Years' Peace, 1816–1846.* 2 vols. London: Charles Knight.

———. 1852. *Letters from Ireland.* London: John Chapman.

———. 1857. "Female Dress in 1857." *Westminster Review* 134 (October): 173–87.

———. 1858. "The Slave-Trade in 1858." *Edinburgh Review* (October): 541–86.

———. 1859a. "Dress and Its Victims." *Once a Week* (5 November): 387–91. London: Fox.

———. 1859b. "Female Industry." *Edinburgh Review* 222 (April): 293–336.

———. 1859c. "Woman's Battlefield." *Once a Week* (3 December): 474–79.

———. 1860a. "The Governess: Her Health." *Once a Week* (1 September): 267–73.

———. 1860b. "The Maid of all Work: Her Health." *Once a Week* (19 May): 464–67.

———. 1860c. "Miss Nightingale's *Notes on Nursing.*" *Quarterly Review* 107: 392–422.

———. 1860d. "The Needlewoman: Her Health." *Once a Week* (24 November): 595–99.

———. 1860e. "The Training of Nurses." *Once a Week* (30 June): 7–9.

———. 1861a. *Health, Husbandry, and Handicraft.* London: Bradbury and Evans.

———. 1861b. "What Women Are Educated For." *Once a Week* (10 August): 175–79.

———. 1862a. "The Brewing of the American Storm." *Macmillan's Magazine* 6 (June): 97–107.

———. 1862b. "Modern Domestic Service." *Edinburgh Review* 115 (April): 409–39.

———. 1864. "The Negro Race in America." *Edinburgh Review* 119 (January): 203–42.

———. 1865. "Nurses Wanted." *Cornhill Magazine* 11: 409–25.

———. 1868. *Biographical Sketches.* London: Macmillan.

———. 1876. "Harriet Martineau: An Autobiographical Memoir." *Daily News,* 29 June.

———. 1906. *My Farm of Two Acres.* London: A. C. Fifield.

———. 1983. *Autobiography.* 2 vols. Ed. Gaby Weiner. London: Virago.

Martineau, Harriet, and Henry Atkinson. 1851. *Letters on the Laws of Man's Nature and Development.* London: John Chapman.

Mesick, Jane. 1922. *The English Traveller in America, 1785–1835.* New York: Columbia University Press.

Midgley, Clare. 1992. *Women against Slavery: The British Campaigns, 1780–1870.* London: Routledge.

Miller, Florence Fenwick. 1884. *Harriet Martineau.* London: W. H. Allen.

Mitchell, Rosemary. 1996. "A Stitch in Time? Women, Needlework, and the Making of History in Victorian Britain." *Journal of Victorian Culture* 1, no. 2 (autumn): 185–202.

Myers, Mitzi. 1980a. "Harriet Martineau's Autobiography: The Making of a Female Philosopher." In *Women's Autobiography: Essays in Criticism,* ed. Estelle Jelinek. Bloomington: Indiana University Press.

———. 1980b. "Unmothered Daughter and Radical Reformer: Harriet Martineau." In *The Lost Tradition: Mothers and Daughters in Literature,* ed. Cathy Davidson and E. Broner, 70–80. New York: Frederick Ungar.

Neff, Wanda. 1967. *Victorian Working Women: An Historical and Literary Study of Women in British Industries and Professions, 1832–1850.* New York: Humanities Press.

Nevill, John Cranstoun. 1943. *Harriet Martineau.* London: Frederick Muller.

Nightingale, Florence. 1979. *Cassandra.* New York: Feminist Press at CUNY.

Obituary of Harriet Martineau. 1876. *Inquirer,* 8 July, 455.

Olson, Tillie. 1978. *Silences.* New York: Delacorte.

Orazem, Claudia. 1999. *Political Economy and Fiction in the Early Works of Harriet Martineau.* Frankfort: Peter Lang.

Ossoli, Margaret Fuller. 1852. *Memoirs.* 2 vols. Boston: Phillips, Sampson.

Parker, Roszika. 1984. *The Subversive Stitch: Embroidery and the Making of the Feminine.* London: Women's Press.

Payn, James. 1884. *Some Literary Recollections.* New York: Harper & Brothers.

Perry, Ruth. 1980. *Women, Letters, and the Novel.* New York: AMS Press.

Pershing, Linda. 1993. "Peace Work out of Piecework: Feminist Needlework Metaphors and the Ribbon around the Pentagon." In *Feminist Theory and the Study of Folklore,* ed. Susan Hollis, 327–57. Urbana: University of Illinois Press.

Peterson, Linda. 1990a. "Harriet Martineau: Masculine Discourse, Female Sage." In *Victorian Sages,* ed. Thais Morgan, 171–86. New Brunswick, N.J.: Rutgers University Press.

———. 1990b. "Harriet Martineau's *Household Education:* Revising the Feminine Tradition." *Bucknell Review* 34, no. 2: 183–94.

Pichanick, Valerie. 1977. "An Abominable Submission: Harriet Martineau's Views on the Role and Place of Women." *Women's Studies* 5:13–32.

———. 1980. *Harriet Martineau: The Woman and Her Work, 1802–76.* Ann Arbor: University of Michigan Press.

Porter, Denis. 1998. *Catalogue of Manuscripts in Harris-Manchester College.* Oxford: Harris-Manchester College.

Postlethwaite, Diana. 1989. "Mothering and Mesmerism in the Life of Harriet Martineau." *Signs: Journal of Women in Culture and Society* 14, no. 3: 583–609.

Radner, Joan N., and Susan S. Lanser. 1987. "The Feminist Voice: Strategies of Coding in Folklore and Literature." *Journal of American Folklore* 100: 412–25.

Richardson, Betty. 1984. "The Wedgwood-Martineau Correspondence." *Papers on Language and Literature* 20, no. 4 (fall): 453–57.

Rivlin, Joseph. 1946. *Harriet Martineau: A Bibliography of Her Separately Printed Works.* Bulletin of the New York Public Library (May).

Rosenberg, Charles. 1979. "Florence Nightingale on Contagion: The Hospital as Moral Universe." In *Healing and History,* ed. Charles E. Rosenberg, 116–36. New York: Science History Publications.

Rossi, Alice. 1988. *The Feminist Papers: From Adams to de Beauvoir.* Boston: Northeastern University Press.

Sanders, Valerie. 1979. "'The Most Manlike Woman in the Three Kingdoms': Harriet Martineau and the Brownings." *Browning Society Notes* 9, no. 3 (December): 9–13.

———. 1986a. "'Absolutely an Act of Duty': Choice of Profession in Autobiographies by Victorian Women." *Prose Studies* 9, no. 3 (December): 54–70.

———. 1986b. *Reason over Passion: Harriet Martineau and the Victorian Novel.* New York: St. Martin's Press.

———. 1990. *Harriet Martineau: Selected Letters.* London: Clarendon Press.

Schulman, Amy. 1993. "Gender and Genre." In *Feminist Theory and the Study of Folklore,* ed. Susan Hollis, 71–88. Urbana: University of Illinois Press.

Shorter, Clement. 1896. *Charlotte Brontë and Her Circle.* London: Hodder and Stoughton.

Showalter, Elaine. 1986. "Piecing and Writing." In *The Poetics of Gender,* ed. Nancy K. Miller, 222–47. New York: Columbia University Press.

[Sims, William Gilmore.] 1838. "Slavery in America, Being a Brief Review of Miss Martineau on That Subject, by a South Carolinian." Richmond, Va.: Thomas W. White.

Stowe, Charles Edward. 1889. *Life of Harriet Beecher Stowe: Compiled from her Letters and Journals.* Boston: Houghton, Mifflin.

Strachey, Ray. 1978. *The Cause: A Short History of the Women's Movement in Great Britain.* London: Virago.

Straub, Kristina. 1986. "Women's Pastimes and the Ambiguity of Female Self-Identification in Fanny Burney's *Evelina.*" *Eighteenth Century Life* 10, no. 2 (May): 58–72.

Taylor, Clare. 1995. *Women of the Anti-Slavery Movement: The Weston Sisters.* New York: St. Martin's.

Thomas, Gillian. 1985. *Harriet Martineau.* Boston: Twayne Publishers.

Tobin, Jacqueline, and Raymond G. Dobard. 1999. *Hidden in Plain View: The Secret Story of Quilts and the Underground Railroad.* New York: Doubleday.

Tompkins, Jane. 1985. *Sensational Designs: The Cultural Work of American Fiction, 1790–1860.* New York: Oxford University Press.

Turley, David. 1991. *The Culture of English Antislavery, 1780–1860.* London: Routledge.

Uglow, Jenny. 1993. *Elizabeth Gaskell: A Habit of Stories.* New York: Farrar Straus Giroux.

Vicinus, Martha, ed. 1972. *Suffer and Be Still: Women in the Victorian Age.* Bloomington: Indiana University Press.

Walkowitz, Judith. 1980. *Prostitution and Victorian Society: Women, Class, and the State.* Cambridge: Cambridge University Press.

Webb, R. K. 1960. *Harriet Martineau: A Radical Victorian.* New York: Columbia University Press.

Weiner, Gaby. 1983. Introduction to *Autobiography,* by Harriet Martineau. London: Virago.

Wheatley, Vera. 1957. *The Life and Work of Harriet Martineau.* Fair Lawn, N.J.: Essential Books.

Wilson, Carol Shiner. 1994. "Lost Needles, Tangled Threads: Stitchery, Domesticity, and the Artistic Enterprise in Barbauld, Edgeworth, Taylor, and Lamb." In *Re-Visioning Romanticism: British Women Writers, 1776–1837,* ed. Carol Shiner Wilson and Joel Haefner., 167–90. Philadelphia: University of Pennsylvania Press.

———. 1997. "Understanding Cultural Contexts: The Politics of Needlework in Taylor, Barbauld, Lamb, and Wordsworth." In *Approaches to Teaching British Women Poets of the Romantic Period,* ed. Stephen C. Behrendt and Harriet Kramer Linkin, 80–84. New York: Modern Language Association of America.

Wollstonecraft, Mary. 1975. *A Vindication of the Rights of Woman.* New York: W.W. Norton.

Yates, Gayle Graham, ed. 1985. *Harriet Martineau on Women.* New Brunswick, N.J.: Rutgers University Press.

# INDEX

224–25; and history and needlework,
46–47; and political economy,
224–25; and Stowe and Martineau,
225

Disraeli, Benjamin, 18

Dissenting (religious) ideologies, 12, 30,
98, 185, 245; and the evolution of
the novel, 233–34

"distressed needlewomen," 69

divisions of labor, gendered. *See* separate
spheres ideology

divorce, as class and economic issue,
155

Divorce and Matrimonial Causes Acts,
155

domestic ideology: decline in quality,
142; and domestic economy, 141;
domestic science, 150; nursing as
professionalization of, 152; and slavery, 102; as woman-centered epistemology, 118–19

domestic trades, 142–45, 150; lack of education and training in, 144; revolution in, 143

domestic workers, elderly, 159

domesticity, and respectability, 48–51,
64; domestic drudgery, 69

"double work," 47, 49, 55, 73, 191, 194,
279; and Brontë, 197; and Lowell
women, 61–63; and Maria Martineau, 206

"Dress and Its Victims," 157

dress reform, 156–58; and Bloomerism
movement, 158; and crinolines, 158,
187, 283; and exploitation of "distressed needlewomen," 156; fashion
"despotism" and nationalism, 157;
and health, 157–58. *See also* fashion;
invalidism

"Eastern Journal," 27

*Eastern Life, Present and Past,* 27, 118,
163, 265, 300, 312; as spiritual autobiography, 251

Edgeworth, Maria, 13

*Edinburgh Review,* 104, 109, 111, 288,
304

education, female, 166; and curriculum
reform, 150; and nursing profession,

151–53; and status of women,
146–47; as solution to women's
poverty, 146; as threatening to men,
149

Eliot, George, 3, 6, 18, 23, 165, 170,
218, 232, 234, 260, 298, 305, 306; on
Fuller, 180; Martineau's critique of,
200–04; on Martineau's appearance,
200, 261. Works: *Adam Bede,* 201–02;
*Felix Holt, the Radical,* 201; *Middlemarch,* 201; *The Mill on the Floss,* 200;
*Silas Marner,* 201

"Ella of Garveloch," 24, 135–40, 263,
294; character and appearance, 135;
female head-of-household, 134–37

"Emancipated Women," 269

Emerson, Lidian, 277

Emerson, Ralph Waldo, 32, 86, 179,
248, 262, 277, 287, 301

*Eminent Women,* 226, 228

Engels, Karl, *Condition of the Working
Classes in England,* 109

*England and Her Soldiers* (with Nightingale), 213, 306

epistolary relationships, 213, 215. *See
also* Barrett Browning; Butler;
Nightingale; Stowe

epistolary writing, 7, 221–58; as drafting, 235; as introductions to books,
247–49; and Martineau's mode of
composition, 225, 234; nonfiction,
245–58; as private conversation,
237–40, 243, 247

epistemology, woman-centered, 118–20,
224, 231. *See also* process-oriented
analysis

"Essay on Moral Independence," 270

essentialism, 10, 118–20, 152, 195, 292.
*See also* Brontë

Evangelicalism, 98. *See also* Stowe

Evans, Marian. *See* Eliot, George

Factory Act of 1833, 282

factory women, 144; education of,
148–49

fancywork, 13, 37, 52, 54, 73, 277, 282;
as art, 71; and class, 41–42, 43, 59,
277–78; as consolation during illness,
71; as social-problem sewing, 71–77

of, 164–220; middle-class, and respectability, 11; oppression of, by women, 61, 66–67, 156–58; and philanthropy, 64, 149, 293 (*see also* London Dressmaking Company); as physicians, 151; as "playthings" for men, 147, 158, 163; political invisibility of, 153, 294; political activism and networking of, 216, 285 (*see also* Contagious Diseases; Ladies' National Association; Langham Place; Storks, Sir Henry); and privacy, 258; "quadroon connexions," 5, 94; redundant, and emigration, 148, 156; and self-discipline, 165, 195; single women, economic problems of, 156, 158; and slaves, 100; as slaves, 118, 158, 163; 165, 218; working-class, 6 (*see also* prostitution)

women "of the heroic order," 167, 204–20, 223; and Butler, 215–18; and Chapman, 173–77; and Ella, 139; and Maria Martineau, 204–11; and Nightingale, 211–15

women, status of, 117–22, 141–63, 169; and reform: —, academic and practical ("common things") curriculum, 143; —, curriculum, 69; —, dress, 156–58; —, education, 5, 49, 118, 141–63 passim; —, in the franchise, 5, 154, 293; —, legal—marriage, divorce, and property acts, 118, 153–56, 158; —, occupation, 118, 211

women writers: antipathy toward, 4; and biological reductionism, 7, 121–22; domesticity and genre, 44; and the formation of literary identities, 3, 4, 9–11; prejudice against, 4; and social reform, 3; and social respectability, 9, 280; and time, "interruptibility" of, 231; women's writing, as encoded language, 46. *See also* literary apprenticeships; literary grandmothers

Women's Suffrage Committee, 119

Woolf, Virginia, *A Room of One's Own*, 260

work and women, 169, 197, 222; attitudes toward, 59; devaluation of, 59–61; prejudice against, 149; and prostitution, 196; remuneration for, 60–61, 297; as unpaid labor, 59. *See also* domestic trades; factory women; *Female Industry;* governesses; needlewomen; nurses

"workies" (working-class), 14, 234, 243, 308

Working Women's Colleges, 69, 283, 297

Wordsworth, Mary, 183–84

Wordsworth, William, 25, 26, 179, 223, 273; and family, 32

workhouse, 123–25, 156, 294; and poor, elderly women, 146, 159

workhouse girls, 145

Worthington, John, 12–13, 51